SUBLIME TOBACCO

By Compton Mackenzie

Novels and Romances:

SINISTER STREET
SYLVIA SCARLETT
GUY AND PAULINE
CARNIVAL
FIGURE OF EIGHT
CORAL
THE VANITY GIRL
ROGUES AND VAGABONDS
THE ALTAR STEPS
THE PARSON'S PROGRESS
THE HEAVENLY LADDER
HUNTING THE FAIRIES
WHISKY GALORE
KEEP THE HOME GUARD TURNING
THE MONARCH OF THE GLEN
BEN NEVIS GOES EAST
THE RIVAL MONSTER
THE RED TAPEWORM
POOR RELATIONS
APRIL FOOLS
RICH RELATIVES
BUTTERCUPS AND DAISIES
WATER ON THE BRAIN
VESTAL FIRE
EXTRAORDINARY WOMEN
EXTREMES MEET
THE THREE COURIERS
OUR STREET
THE DARKENING GREEN
THE PASSIONATE ELOPEMENT
FAIRY GOLD
THE SEVEN AGES OF WOMAN
THE OLD MEN OF THE SEA
THE FOUR WINDS OF LOVE:
   THE EAST WIND
   THE SOUTH WIND
   THE WEST WIND
   THE NORTH WIND
THIN ICE

Verse:

POEMS 1907
KENSINGTON RHYMES

History and Biography:

EASTERN EPIC, VOL. I
ALL OVER THE PLACE
GALLIPOLI MEMORIES
ATHENIAN MEMORIES
GREEK MEMORIES
AEGEAN MEMORIES
WIND OF FREEDOM
MR ROOSEVELT
DR BENEŠ
PRINCE CHARLIE
PRINCE CHARLIE AND HIS LADIES
CATHOLICISM AND SCOTLAND
MARATHON AND SALAMIS
PERICLES
THE WINDSOR TAPESTRY
THE VITAL FLAME
I TOOK A JOURNEY
COALPORT
REALMS OF SILVER
THE QUEEN'S HOUSE
THE SAVOY: LONDON
MY RECORD OF MUSIC

Essays, Criticism and a Play:

ECHOES
A MUSICAL CHAIR
UNCONSIDERED TRIFLES
REAPED AND BOUND
LITERATURE IN MY TIME
THE LOST CAUSE

Children's Stories:

SANTA CLAUS IN SUMMER
TOLD
MABEL IN QUEER STREET
THE UNPLEASANT VISITORS
THE CONCEITED DOLL
THE ENCHANTED BLANKET
THE DINING-ROOM BATTLE
THE ADVENTURES OF TWO CHAIRS
THE ENCHANTED ISLAND
THE NAUGHTYMOBILE
THE FAIRY IN THE WINDOW-BOX
THE STAIRS THAT KEPT ON GOING DOWN

An American Indian Village, 1590. The communal tobacco
plots are marked E. The other crops are corn in various
stages of growth (F, G and H): and pumpkins (I). The man
sitting in the hut (F) is there to prevent birds or animals
attacking the crops. (A) is the mausoleum where the tribal
kings and queens were buried

[*Frontispiece*

SUBLIME TOBACCO

Compton Mackenzie

1957

CHATTO AND WINDUS

LONDON

Published by
Chatto and Windus Ltd
42 William IV Street
London, W.C.2
★
Clarke, Irwin & Co Ltd
Toronto

Printed in Great Britain
by Hazell Watson & Viney Ltd
Aylesbury and London

TO MY WIFE

This story of a golden leaf
to commemorate a golden wedding
November 30, 1905—*November* 30, 1955

Contents

Prologue: My Smoking Life   1
Chapter

1	63
2	76
3	88
4	99
5	109
6	121
7	129
8	148
9	163
10	176
11	193
12	206
13	225
14	240
15	249
16	264
17	275
18	290
19	299
Epilogue	323
Bibliography	345
Index	347

Illustrations

1 An American Indian Village, 1590   *Frontispiece*

2 A quayside scene in old Virginia showing
  tobacco being shipped for England   84

3 Earliest known picture of an English tobacco
  shop, 1617   100

4 18th century tobacco labels   180

5 More 18th century tobacco labels   196

6 Tom Cribb's Parlour   260

7 Time Off for a Smoke   276

8 General Montgomery distributing cigarettes   332

Note on Illustrations

The Frontispiece and the plates facing pages 84, 100 and 260 are reproduced by permission of the Trustees of the British Museum from the following sources: the English edition (1590) of de Bry's *America*; a map of the most inhabited part of Virginia, etc., drawn by Joshua Fry and Peter Jefferson in 1775; Richard Brathwait's *The Smoaking Age* (1617); and Pierce Egan's *Life in London* (1821). The photographs facing page 276 and page 332 are reproduced by permission of the Imperial War Museum. The tobacco labels reproduced facing pages 180 and 196 are from the Ingham Foster collection in the possession of The Imperial Tobacco Company (of Great Britain and Ireland), Limited.

Author's Note

I have to thank many people in the tobacco world for the trouble they have taken to provide me with valuable information, but I wish to set on record my particular gratitude to Mr. A. Balfour Scott, Mr. A. D. McCormick, the Hon. A. B. Money-Coutts, Mr. A. G. G. Cunningham and Mrs. D. E. Tovey, for the immense help they have given me over what was an enjoyable but fairly severe task. Will all the other tobacco experts and librarians who have contributed to my knowledge let me thank them as a body? If I attempted to mention every name, I should inevitably leave one or two out and be mortified in consequence.

To the five folio volumes of the descriptive catalogue of the mighty collection of George Arents Jr. my obligation is heartfelt and deep. The work is a triumph of American scholarship, and has been edited and annotated with superlative skill and accuracy by Mr. Jerome Brooks. These volumes were my constant companion for a year and they never once let me down. I have taken the liberty of modernizing the text of the sixteenth century works from which I have quoted, knowing how much inclined people are to skip when they see archaic spelling.

Much information that I should have liked to include has had to be omitted in order to keep this book within the bounds of practical publishing to-day. I have tried to preserve a mean between the exhaustive and the exhausting.

Prologue

MY SMOKING LIFE

I F a grave-eyed doctor after feeling my pulse and tapping my chest and testing my blood pressure should declare at the end of his examination that I must either give up smoking or give up drinking alcohol in any form for the rest of my life, I should reply without a moment's hesitation and with the austerity of a stoic:

"Then I renounce wine and spirits and will drink nothing but water for the rest of my life; but I will never renounce my pipe, and whenever anybody offers me a cigar I shall accept that cigar with gratitude and smoke it with pleasure. My yearly resolution on New Year's Eve shall be not to give up smoking in the New Year."

I might have become a confirmed smoker even earlier than I did if my father had been more at home when I was very young. As it was, during the 'eighties of the last century I had few opportunities to test the virtue of tobacco in action. When I could elude the vigilance of a tiresome old nurse, I would sometimes enjoy the pleasure of pretending to smoke by sucking one of my father's empty pipes and expelling from my pursed lips imaginary fumes. That experiment must have been made first over seventy years ago when I was three years old; but the seductive aroma of those empty pipes is still a pleasant memory, and one of the emotions I associate most vividly with childhood's yearning for the wonderful *au delà* of being grown-up is the thought that one day I should be a real smoker.

Meanwhile, I had to be content with chocolate cigarettes, and I can avow that the chocolate inside the paper tasted better than chocolate in any other form. One made it a point of honour to 'smoke' those chocolate cigarettes; one did not greedily strip them of their paper and devour the inside. No, no, one allowed the chocolate to seep through the paper into one's mouth, and when the end had melted away one 'smoked' on until the whole cigarette had been lusciously devoured; there was no fag-end to throw away. Chocolate cigars, too, were an occasional luxury, the top being made of fondant to suggest ash and stained with cochineal at the very end to simulate the glow of a lighted cigar.

It was at Cromer in July 1887 that I smoked my first cigarette. An American cousin was staying with us, a tall, fair-haired young man with a Southern drawl who rolled his own cigarettes with an air of what seemed almost magical insouciance. We had taken for the summer a red-brick house known as Prospect Villa, which looked out across a large meadow full of ox-eye daisies. There was a lawn in front with a circular flower-bed round which I was wont to stalk the sparrows with a funnel-shaped packet of salt in the hope of catching one of them by putting some of that salt on its tail. Worn out at last by my lack of success under the hot sun of that Golden Jubilee summer, I sat down on the grass beside my cousin who was lolling in a deck-chair and as usual rolling a cigarette.

"Would you like to try one?" he drawled.

I accepted his offer eagerly, and put the cigarette between my lips. Then he struck a wax vesta which, as he applied the flame to the end of the cigarette, seemed in its majesty to dim the very sun.

"Suck it in slowly and puff it out again."

The first attempt was not slow enough, and the smoke tickled the back of my throat, making me splutter.

"Not so fast. Gently. Watch me."

I watched him; after a couple more attempts I was able to smoke like this much-admired American cousin.

It was meet that I, with a long American ancestry on my mother's side back to the time of the first colonization of Maryland, should be allowed by an American cousin my first experience of the richest gift that the New World gave to the Old. I like to imagine that my immunity from any of the ill-effects which in moral tales always accompany childhood's first experiments with tobacco may have been an inheritance from some Red Indian ancestress of three centuries ago.

Anyway, I smoked that first cigarette with enjoyment and without a qualm.

"Now, don't go bragging about being able to smoke," my cousin warned me. "Your mother might be angry. I hear them coming back from their walk, though why people want to walk about in this heat I can't guess."

I wonder whether when I kissed my mother good night she

noticed the unfamiliar childish breath and exacted a promise from my cousin never again to give me a cigarette. Anyway, he never did, and my first cigarette remained a unique experience of that summer when I was four and a half years old.

The next three years passed without any smoking adventures that I can recall. In the spring of 1891 I overbalanced while hanging up a quoit-board and nearly tore my right hand in half on one of the hooks. The adventures of Sherlock Holmes started in the *Strand* magazine, and under their spell pain seemed to vanish. However, not even Sherlock Holmes, puffing away at his pipe in rapt contemplation, could assuage the pain that was to be mine during that summer when, twice a day for six weeks, my father had to bend my fingers back in order to prevent their closing over the palm and making my right hand for ever useless. We were spending half of June and July that year in Cromer for the second time, and it was rather a dull holiday for me because I was forbidden to take part in boyish romps on the beach on account of that confounded hand. So one day I was sitting on the sand making honey-pots with my left hand, my right arm being in a sling, when a slim and beautiful lady sitting on the beach put down on her knee the notebook in which she was writing and asked me if I wasn't finding it rather difficult to make honey-pots with one hand. I explained how I had hurt my other hand, and told her about the painful operation I had to undergo twice a day. She spoke some words of sympathy and then went back to her writing, from time to time looking up from the page and gazing pensively out to sea, while I continued to empty out my honey-pots.

The clock in Cromer church struck one. The slim and beautiful lady looked round at the tower in obvious surprise at the time. Then she said, "Good-bye, little boy. I hope your hand will soon be well," and rose to her feet. She seemed very tall and she was wearing a beige coat of some light silky material with full leg-of-mutton sleeves. As she walked slowly across towards the ramp that ran up from the beach into the town, everybody turned round to stare at her. I noticed a faint frown of annoyance as she quickly opened a very small parasol of fawn-coloured lace, which she held over her right shoulder to screen her countenance from curious eyes as she walked up the ramp.

I was gathering up my spade and bucket to go back to dinner

when my nurse bade me look at the Empress of Austria! She usually told me not to stare at people.

"The Empress of Austria?" I repeated in amazement. I had not imagined an Empress looking like this.

"And she smokes!" somebody commented with a snigger of disapproval.

I have read much about that lovely and ill-starred Empress since that encounter with her sixty-five years ago, and I have come to the conclusion that she must have been writing one of her poems in that notebook while I was busy with my honey-pots. I have also discovered that the Empress did smoke; the knowledge for me adds the last touch to my reverence for that figure of high romance.

In September of that year, 1891, I entered Colet Court, the preparatory school for St Paul's: we called it Bewsher's in those days, it having been started by Samuel Bewsher, the bursar of St Paul's, with his brother James Bewsher as headmaster. Among ourselves they were Sammy and Jimmy. Colet Court was very large for a private school. There were over 400 boys, and it was a tough place in those days because there was a Modern Class which housed young louts up to sixteen who were finishing their education at Colet Court. The bullying was ferocious until a year later fourteen was made the age limit for boys and those fifteen- and sixteen-year-old savages vanished. I need not say that smoking was prevalent. There was an old stable in the corner of the playground which had a small cellar reached by a trap-door. Into this about thirty small boys would be packed by their captors, who used to blow cigarette smoke down into what was a sort of black hole of Calcutta. It may have been the spectacle of those swaggering young smokers which made me determined to start smoking as soon as possible.

In that autumn my father produced Henry James's play *The American* at the Opéra Comique Theatre in the Strand, which meant that he was at home and that therefore in his library my younger brother and myself could always find the stubs of the cigars he had smoked before leaving every evening for the theatre. I can smell now in fancy the fragrance of those cigar fumes in the empty room. My father always used a long amber holder, and therefore the stubs were exiguous. However, they were dry, and we used to smoke them in one of his curved Petersen pipes.

One morning I received the exciting news that I was to go to the play that evening because the Prince of Wales was to be there. I sat in a box on the O.P. side; the Prince of Wales with his party was in a box on the prompt side. Naturally, at school next day I spoke of my experience. One small boy, unwilling to allow me as much glory as I thought I deserved, asked if I knew that the Prince of Wales paid half a crown for every cigar he smoked. I expressed disbelief, but his statement was supported by others, and I was left under the impression that, in spite of having sat in a box opposite another box in which the Prince of Wales was sitting, I was nevertheless fundamentally ignorant of royal behaviour. I asked my father how much he paid for his cigars.

"It depends on the cigar. I have some good cigars for which I paid fourpence; I have some cigars for which I have paid as much as a shilling. But I haven't many of those," he added hastily, for extravagance was to him one of the deadly sins, and he was obviously afraid that such an admission might set a bad example to his eldest son.

"The Prince of Wales pays half a crown for his cigars," I announced.

"Yes, well, but the Prince of Wales is the Prince of Wales."

The retort was a feeble enough truism, but I was not surprised by it; I had realized for some time that grown-ups when cornered took refuge in truisms however feeble in order to block further exploration or inquisition by the young.

It was some time early in the New Year that my father discovered—I do not remember how—that my brother and myself were smoking the stubs of his cigars in a Petersen pipe.

"And so you boys enjoy smoking?" he enquired.

I assured him that we thought it was ripping, or perhaps 'spiffing' was the adjective chosen.

"Well, since you enjoy smoking so much I will give you two of my cigars to smoke."

With this he went to the corner cupboard of Dutch marquetry in which he kept his cigars, and selected the two largest he had. They must have been two of those shilling ones; I imagine it cost him a pang to administer the lesson he believed he was about to administer.

"Light them properly," he commanded.

He passed us a big Bryant and May's box of safety-matches,

one of which would light a cigar properly whereas it takes three of the matches in the shrunken boxes of to-day to light a cigar as it should be lit before it is put between the lips. When he saw that we were puffing away, my father lit a cigar for himself from the same box. I wish I could remember what the brand was, but I know it took a full hour to smoke that cigar. Soon I noticed a questioning look in my father's eyes, and this in turn was gradually succeeded by a puzzled and finally by a baffled expression. At that date my father was just thirty-eight years old, and I was conscious of the emotion of triumphing over his venerability. I realized that he was searching our complexions for that greenish pallor which in the *Boys' Own Paper* always appeared on the cheeks of young readers who defied the threat of early blindness and stunted growth; this the editor continually insisted was the inevitable result of smoking in early youth. Alas for my poor father's self-abnegation in parting with two of his best and biggest cigars to give a lesson to his offspring, our cheeks remained rosy, our foreheads unclammy.

"Are you feeling all right?" he asked when the cigars had been smoked.

We beamed at him gratefully: filial good manners forebade us to crow over a parent whose morale was for the moment a wreck.

After my father went on tour again we discovered a key that would unlock the marquetry cupboard, and from time to time at rare intervals we helped ourselves to cigars. On his return in June he evidently suspected that somebody (and he may reasonably have concluded that it was one or both of his sons) had been helping himself to his cigars, for when we came back for the autumn term of 1892 and opened the cupboard we found written on the flap of every box the number of cigars he had left in it. We recognized those figures as the writing on the wall, and after that we regretfully left his cigars alone.

I think my father may never have really got over his early attempt to cure us of premature smoking by parting with two of his best cigars to no good purpose. At any rate, he never offered me another until I was over twenty. It was his habit after he came back from the theatre to smoke at least three cigars before he went to bed; but he never smoked out of doors or in the theatre, and if he had seen one of the members of his company smoking anywhere except outside the stage-door there would have been a solemn rebuke. As for the ladies of the company, he affected to disbelieve that any of them could smoke, and he preserved this deliberate incredulity until as late as 1915, when women had been smoking openly as a matter of course for some time and when he had often seen them smoking.

I have mentioned my father's Petersen pipes. I have a couple of them still, and they are the pipes of a man who seldom smoked them; I never smoke curved pipes myself. It was his custom after the last cigar to fill his pipe from a packet of Hignett's Pioneer—a mild but excellent gold flake. Unfortunately he had never learnt to fill a pipe, and so a pipe of his never drew properly because he always packed it too tightly. He would try to light it, his indrawn breaths sounding like a squeaky hinge, and then lay it down in exasperation.

"How you can prefer a pipe to a cigar, I don't know," he used to say to me when as an undergraduate I stayed with him on tour. But he never used to offer me a cigar. He always assumed I preferred a pipe; I am sure the memory of those two wasted cigars still rankled.

My mother disliked equally the fumes of pipe or cigarette, but much liked those of a cigar. Her father, Hezekiah Linthicum Bateman of Baltimore—I should hesitate to give an American character such a name in one of my novels for fear of disturbing Anglo-American relations—had always smoked cigars. At least, so I was told, but the smoking habits of my American grandfather raise now a question in my mind.

In 1863 he was lessee of a theatre in St Louis, which he had occasion to visit. It was in the middle of the Civil War and he was suffering a good deal mentally from having to be in New York, where his other theatre was, when all his sympathies were with the Confederacy. At the St Louis railway depôt he watched gloomily the presentation of boxes of chocolate or candy to the Federal troops by enthusiastic Northern ladies. On the box was a coloured reproduction of two little girls intended to remind the soldiers of home. My grandfather came near enough to see that these two little girls were his own youngest daughters. A young Frenchman had arrived in New York with a new colour process, and the photograph he had taken of my mother and her younger sister, aged ten and eight respectively, had been given to the chocolate makers. My grandfather was seized with such rage that he got rid of his theatrical commitments in the States and sailed to England with his wife and his two youngest daughters, where the latter were sent to school. I still have a copy of the first edition of Kingsley's *Water Babies* which was presented to them "as a reminiscence of Berth No. 195 on board R.M.S. *Scotia* and what was enacted there from their audience.

Frank A. Mathers
January 6th, 1864."

I suppose that my mother and her younger sister planned to emulate their two elder sisters who, when only two years younger than themselves, had filled the St James's Theatre for one hundred nights, playing scenes from Shakespeare, in the year of the Great Exhibition.

My mother recalled her first sight of the wintry orange sun over Green Park from their room in Clarges Street, and being reminded by it of the orange-paper seal on her father's tobacco.

But my grandfather did not smoke a pipe. Therefore this must have been plug tobacco for chewing. We are apt to forget that much more tobacco was chewed than smoked in the United States until the cigarette triumphed. I used to have to check myself from chewing the end of a cigar. Sir Winston Churchill's American origins are apparent when he smokes a cigar. He used to carry a pair of scissors with him to cut off the soggy end.

I am glad to say that my mother, after maintaining an aversion from cigarettes for most of her life, took to smoking them when she was just over eighty, and continued to smoke them until she died in her eighty-eighth year. My great-grand-father, who called himself Joseph Cowell and whose autobiography was published by Harpers in 1844, relates that on the first night he landed in New York in 1821 he was given, in a Wall Street dive, a cigar called a 'long-nine' which made him very sick, and adds that it was the first time he had ever smoked. This surprised me, because he had been a midshipman in the Royal Navy before he gave up the sea for the stage. However, in his own words: "The long-nine knocked me over as flat as a nine-pounder."

My grandfather on the paternal side took snuff, and I have a silver snuff-box presented to him on November 1st, 1836, by seventy-eight "frequenters of the Theatre Royal, Leeds, in testimony of their admiration of his Professional Excellence as a Comedian."

It is an exquisite piece of workmanship and comfortably large enough to hold the cigarettes for which I now use it.

But it is time to return to my boyhood. In the week after Christmas, 1892, my father produced a dramatized version of *A Tale of Two Cities* as one of the plays with which every winter he was accustomed to supplement his repertory of old English comedy. My brother, my eldest sister and myself were touring with him during the Christmas holidays; and it was decided that the part of the little St Evremonde in the prologue should be taken for a few weeks by my sister Viola, a decision which caused the gravest anxiety to her brothers who, having devoted much attention to curing her of all affectation and self-esteem, dreaded the intoxicating effect of this public appearance on her character. It was not a long part. Indeed the solitary line was, "Yes, I will, Mother," spoken as a promise to the Marquise that he would remember something when he grew up—perhaps to be good. The author, T. Edgar Pemberton, was staying in Norwich for the production, and my father suggested—or perhaps it was Pemberton himself, for he was the kindliest of men—that my brother and myself should accompany him to the first performance and enjoy it in his company. My father, who for an actor had a most unusual respect for authors, impressed upon us the solemnity of the occasion, for which I regret to say we prepared ourselves by taking advantage of our governess's early departure to the theatre to smoke rapidly through a packet of cigarettes that we had discovered in an empty drawer, the property doubtless of the landlady's husband or son. I was on the verge of ten, my brother seven, my sister just six.

It had been snowing all day, and it was still snowing when the time came to set out with the author. Exhilarated by that treasure trove of cigarettes, we were inclined to dally on the way in order to throw snowballs at any enthusiastic playgoers who had ventured forth on this bitter night; but at last Pemberton persuaded us to enter the theatre and sit one on either side of him in the front row of the circle. Our sister was not long in making her entrance dressed in sky-blue velvet. We stirred uneasily and glanced at one another across the author, who no doubt in the manner of authors was counting the conjunctions altered or omitted by the players. At last came the speech of the Marquise, "And you, little Charles, will you, when you are," etc., etc. There was a moment's silence at the end of it, and then through the theatre rang out the most prodigious voice from a six-year-old child ever likely to be heard by a Norwich audience: "Yes, I will, Mother." It was altogether too much for the little girl's brothers, who scandalized the house by breaking into peal upon peal of laughter. Oh, how we laughed! We prodded each other across the author. We thumped his knees. We clung to him in a helpless ecstasy of mirth. We slid from our seats to the floor, and there gasped and rolled in convulsions of delight. Members of the audience stood up and said "Hush," glaring indignantly at poor dear Pemberton, who implored us to pull ourselves together, to which entreaty we responded with more vociferous laughter.

Finally an attendant came down the gangway and insisted that Pemberton should take us out into the lobby, out of the theatre entirely indeed unless he could guarantee our better behaviour. The author blushing with embarrassment led us, or rather dragged us, up the gangway, still laughing, and then for the rest of the prologue he walked us up and down the lobby still laughing: but by this time he was laughing himself as unrestrainedly as we were, oblivious of the attendants who kept coming on tiptoe through the swing-doors to shake warning fingers at our antics. And still we laughed, until Pemberton had to take us outside the theatre altogether. Snow was lying fairly thick, and up and down we walked, still laughing. The curtain had risen on Dr Manette's garden in Soho before we were in a fit condition to take our seats in the circle again.

When I went to St Paul's in the summer term of 1894, my pocket-money was raised from sixpence to a shilling a week. This strengthening of my financial resources enabled me to turn from Wild Woodbines at five a penny to Duke's Cameo cigarettes at ten for fivepence, for the flavour of Cameo cigarettes much appealed to my taste. So did Allen and Ginter's Richmond Gem, which cost the same as Duke's Cameos and were wrapped in what looked like rice-paper.

In those days there were about three or four acres of wasteland on the east side of the St Paul's playing-fields. This was turned into a recreation ground to which various residents in West Kensington subscribed half a guinea annually for a key.

Nobody bothered what we did in the recreation-ground, which was a piece of the original country-side not built over when West Kensington was planned in the 'eighties as a select suburb, being in those days more like a large village than a suburb. The fence round the wasteland was kept intact against invaders who had not subscribed for a key; that was all.

In the middle of the recreation-ground was an abandoned gravel-pit into which we burrowed, and within a year it contained half a dozen cave dwellings owned by groups of boys and treated as sacrosanct by those who did not own them. The cave dwelling I shared with three friends was a perfect cache for cigarettes, and I am inclined to say that the smoke of the finest Havana has never tasted quite so good as the smoke of those forbidden cigarettes of boyhood puffed without fear of interruption in those small gravel caves. I was the only boy who insisted on Duke's Cameo. One of my friends provided Wills's Gold Flake, then as now in orange packets, costing threepence for ten, and another Ogden's Guinea Gold at the same price. There were times of stringency, due to a craving for ices, when we had to fall back on Woodbines. I remember a couple of weeks when we were acutely embarrassed financially by subscribing our shillings to the shilling testimonial got up by the *Daily Telegraph* for W. G. Grace to celebrate his feat in scoring a thousand runs in May 1895. Rather than fail in our duty to that great man, we went without ices and without even Woodbines. There were 100,000 subscribers.

Then somebody, probably myself, suggested that it might be more economical to smoke pipes. So we invested in clay pipes, and smoked Wills's Bird's-eye in them. We found that this burnt our tongues, and I advocated shag as a cooler and cheaper substitute. Shag was threepence an ounce at that date. Several of the weaker vessels succumbed to the effects of shag, and one of them, no doubt anxious to recover his lost face, proclaimed one day that smoking a clay pipe gave you cancer; he had heard his father say so.

"Not if you put sealing-wax round the end in your mouth," said another sage of twelve or thirteen. "I always put sealing-wax round my pipe."

We denounced him as a cad, pointing out that we might all have caught cancer just because he hadn't let us into the secret of the prophylactic. After that we put sealing-wax round the mouth-pieces of our clay pipes; but the threat of cancer cast a gloom over our pipe-smoking, and one or two of the boys who had lost face after being made sick by shag delighted in telling us what they had found out about cancer in medical books hidden away on top shelves. A reaction set in against pipe-smoking and we began to examine ourselves anxiously every morning for signs of cancer caught from smoking clay pipes. Why did we not acquire briers? Because the outlay required for a brier pipe would have deprived us of the tobacco to put in it.

Then I discovered the corncob pipe, which cost only two-pence and against the hygienic reputation of which there was not a whisper. Our valetudinarian cares vanished. Soon after this I produced a blend of Bird's-eye and shag which was voted 'jolly d.' or 'j. decent' according to one's verbal fancy. If the editor of the *Boys' Own Paper* was to be believed, a race of dwarfs was being reared in that abandoned gravel-pit, a race of dwarfs, moreover, who were doomed to early blindness and might just as well stay underground for the rest of their lives.

The whirligig of time brings its revenges. The *Boys' Own Paper* has shrunk to less than a quarter of what it was sixty years ago, and I who at twelve was smoking about ten cigarettes a week and at least an ounce of shag and Bird's-eye am much taller than I was then. What do boys of twelve do to-day? I suppose they get more pocket-money than we had, but do they get enough to buy all the cigarettes they want when ten cigarettes cost almost a florin?

I do not recall any outstanding incident connected with smoking during 1896, but there was a serious crisis in the following year. We now had a bungalow near Alton in Hampshire, in a fantastic place that was originally known as the Beech Farm Estate but to-day is called Beech. I enjoyed the advantage for my future career of consorting here with the most remarkable collection of eccentrics imaginable outside the collected works of Charles Dickens. One of the less admirable of these eccentrics sent an anonymous letter to my father, denouncing the way my brother and I had been accustomed to smoke every week-end through the spring and summer when we were visiting that collection of eccentric characters in turn. The result of this was that all pocket-money was cut off for the summer holidays of 1897, and our governess, to whose inflexible orders we had to submit, carried out the parental edict with austere enthusiasm. Thanks to our wide circle of strange friends, we were not completely deprived of an occasional cigarette, but we disliked the notion that we might be suspected of cadging and we attempted to discover substitutes for tobacco. Unfortunately, we did not know that among many other substitutes the leaves of colt's-foot, yarrow, rhubarb, sage, willow and beet had all been smoked in various parts of the world instead of tobacco, for all these were easily available. We experimented instead with the petals of cabbage-roses and with the leaves of the vine, the cherry and the Spanish chestnut, without success, and found that, on the whole, tea was the least unsuccessful substitute. Brown paper and bamboo canes we had rejected long ago.

Finally I decided that drastic steps must be taken to obtain the tobacco for which we longed. At that time new paths were being laid in our garden, and I suggested to our governess that if she would provide us with stone-breakers' glasses and hammers my brother and I would undertake to break a certain amount of flints every day for the foundation of these new paths. I recall a fleeting look of suspicion in her shrewd eyes; she knew we were always inclined to regard any domestic task imposed upon us as an attempt to rob us of our holiday leisure. However, she procured the glasses and the hammers, and we duly set to work for an hour every morning before breakfast. Luckily I had just been emancipated from the intolerable boredom of piano practice before breakfast. My brother, who was still condemned to practise, grumbled about the stone-breaking until I revealed my plan.

At that date tramps passing through Alton on their way south could obtain a night's lodging at the workhouse on condition that they did a day's work at stone-breaking, for which they were paid half a crown. One could see those heaps of unbroken flints at intervals along the roads waiting for the casual labour to make them serviceable for road mending. The tramps found this work extremely uncongenial in the hot August sun, and there was a lot of August sunshine in 1897.

"If we offer to break flints for tramps when it's most stinkingly hot," I confided to my brother, "we can be paid with baccy."

One of the characteristics of a younger brother in the closing years of the nineteenth century was a suspicous attitude towards any proposal put forward by an elder brother. "You're not going to bag all the baccy," my own young brother declared truculently.

"Keep your hair on. Of course I'm not going to bag all the baccy."

The pact was made, and we sallied forth along the Hampshire lanes in search of a tramp anxious to be relieved for a couple of hours of stone-breaking in the sun. It was a delightful experience because not only were our wages paid, sometimes with shag, sometimes with twist, but we could enjoy many anecdotes of life on the road, which were as absorbing as the yarns spun by seafarers. I should add that twist was a novelty for us, and it took a good deal of practice before we were able to fill a pipe with the snippets cut off with a Norwegian knife and rubbed expansively between two palms.

From long long ago I conjure the vision of a tramp lying on his back in the cool grass beneath the shade of a wayside tree, and the ring of our hammers on the rugose flints from which flew blue and golden sparks and, thanks to our protective glasses, innocuous fragments of stone, and with that vision I recall the sights and sounds and scents of those country roads of once upon a time. Later on the smell and taste of twist were to become associated in my mind with sailing from one small island to another on long azure days and brief moth-grey glimmering nights among the Hebrides, but I never smoke a pipe of shag without evoking again the flinty lanes of north Hampshire and hearing the creak of a waggon's wheels or the clip-clop of horses' hooves approaching. *O mihi præteritos!*

Frederick William Walker was probably the greatest headmaster of the second half of the nineteenth century. I only insert the qualifying adverb out of courtesy to other schools than Manchester Grammar School and St Paul's, for I do not really believe that its use is justified. I cannot find in the records of any other headmaster a comparable achievement.

I recognize that every boy is likely to be overawed by his headmaster as he remembers him, but I must insist that Walker's staff were all just as much in awe of him as we were,

and not only his staff but such bodies as the Charity Commissioners with whom he waged a battle for nearly ten years.
He was sixty-four years old when I first encountered that former
scholar of Corpus Christi College, who had been a double first
in Classics and a double first in Mathematics at Oxford, not to
mention being Vinerian and Tancred Law Scholar and Boden
Sanskrit Scholar into the bargain; his scholarship was matched
only by his administrative skill and his infallible judgment of
every boy's mental capacity. I quote from a description of him
I once wrote through the eyes of one of his pupils:

"He was the personification of majesty, dominion, ferocity
and awe. He was large of build, with a long grey beard to
which adhered the acrid scent of strong cigars. . . . His ordinary
clothes were stained with soup and rank with tobacco smoke,
but over them he wore a full and swishing gown of silk. When
he spoke his voice rumbled in the titanic deeps of his body, or if
he were angry it burst forth in an appalling roar."

It is clear to me now that Walker would never have become
the great headmaster he was if he had been a non-smoker. He
did not resign as High Master of St Paul's until 1905 when he
was seventy-five years old, and he lived on for another five
years in retirement, consoled, I like to hope, by being able to
smoke cigars all day long instead of only out of school.

He had one son, Richard Johnson Walker, known to us as
'Dicky' Walker, who had inherited a large fortune from his
mother. The younger Walker was as brilliant a classical scholar
as his father, to whom he acted as personal assistant for some
years. He became an Anglican clergyman in 1902, and while he
was still a parson was Mayor of Hammersmith. In 1912 he was
received into the Roman Catholic Church as a layman. By his
marriage in 1915 he became stepfather of Sir David Kelly, who
has written vividly of that most remarkable man.

In the year 1898 among my friends at school was one of the
sons in the large family of a Low Church clergyman, to whom I
presented a copy of a devotional book called *Catholic Prayers for
Church of England People*, compiled by the Reverend A. H. Stanton, of St Alban's, Holborn. My friend's father, who was on the
point of departing for Australia for some missionary society,
discovered this book, flogged his son severely, and informed
him that to save his soul from the diabolic temptations that
surrounded it he should take him to Australia.

On hearing of this I urged upon the boy the duty of escaping from such tyranny, and with another friend of mine, who is now a country parson in England, and after consulting another slightly older boy who is now an Anglican archbishop, we sent a telegram to a loveable eccentric called Sandys Wason, who invented the word 'spikes' for Anglo-Catholics and was then a curate at Ilkley, asking him if he would give shelter to a 'persecuted Catholic boy'. Wason agreed. I then arranged the escape of the martyr, who was to let himself out of the window by knotted sheets. The martyr himself told me he could always get out by the front door, but I insisted on the knotted sheets. We had a four-wheeler waiting at the corner of the road, in which we drove him to St Pancras and despatched him to Ilkley. His father informed the police, and a few days later he was back at home.

When this Low Church clergyman and his errant son had left for Australia, a two-column letter from Lord Kinnaird, the President of the Church Association, appeared in *The Times*, and horrified people with a fantastic account of the methods used by the Jesuits in corrupting the youth of England. The effect was startling. Old ladies looked under their beds nightly for Guy Fawkes; old gentlemen sat in nervous expectancy of a visit from the familiars of the Inquisition. Finally, questions were to be asked in both Houses of Parliament. The explanation of the true facts was entrusted to H. C. Richards, Q.C., the Conservative member for Finsbury.

It was my job to put Richards in possession of the facts, and after dinner in his Temple chambers we sat on either side of the fire with a carved wooden box of over 300 Russian cigarettes on the hearth-rug between us, to which I was invited to help myself. I must have smoked at least a dozen of them while I was providing Richards with material to contradict any false statements made in the House of Commons. Those Russian cigarettes, with their *café au lait* paper and cardboard mouthpieces, captivated me, and whenever I could afford to buy them after that I did so. Richards said that Lord Halifax was going to give an explanation in the House of Lords and that he proposed to take me along to see that saintly man, of whom when I met him I was to my surprise not in the least shy.

It might be supposed, with all the fuss in Parliament and the Press, that Frederick Walker would have been furious with me for bringing such unwanted publicity on the school. However, 'Dicky' presented the business to his father in its true light, and I was spared the ordeal of an interview with the Old Man, as we always spoke of him.

'Dicky' Walker lived with his father in the High Master's house, and to my amazement when I went to see him about this ecclesiastical storm he offered me a cigar. I cannot believe that many people have been offered a cigar by the thirty-year-old son of a headmaster in a room next to the headmaster's own sanctum. How did 'Dicky' Walker divine that at fifteen and a half I should be able to tackle a colorado cigar with perfect confidence? I feel that the Governors of St Paul's made a bad mistake when they failed to offer the High Mastership to R. J. Walker on his father's retirement in 1905. He applied for it and was rejected.

My next experience with a schoolmaster over smoking was less civilized. In 1899 I was in the History Eighth, a form which tradition said had been invented some years earlier to give G. K. Chesterton Eighth Form status and remove his bulk from languishing among small boys in some classical form far down in the school. The master of the History Eighth was the late R. F. Cholmeley, who at this date was the Games Master and had one of the four houses for boarders. Some years later he became the headmaster of Owen's School, Islington, and was one of the best broadcasting talkers I ever heard. By this time I was sixteen and was smoking over my homework without let or hindrance. One evening at a performance of Pinero's play *The Gay Lord Quex* I had gone out to smoke a cigarette in the interval, dressed in tails and white waistcoat as everybody in the stalls or dress circle used to be in those days, and in this nefarious activity I was observed by Cholmeley. The next morning in class he tackled me.

"You were smoking in the theatre last night."

"Yes, sir."

"You know the school rules?"

"I didn't suppose they applied to a West End theatre."

"Why not?"

"Who would know that I was at St Paul's, sir?"

"That has nothing to do with it. You deliberately broke a school rule."

I suppose he expected me to apologize, and say it should not occur again in evening dress at a play or anywhere else.

"A rule that doesn't allow for reasonable exceptions, sir, seems to me a bad rule," was what I did say.

Cholmeley's moustache twitched with irritation at what I thought was logic but which he believed to be insolence.

"Then you'd better learn the fallibility of private judgment. Perhaps you will like tobacco less when you have written out for me the *Bacchae* of Euripides—in Greek, with every accent. I shall want it on Monday morning."

The *Bacchae* is 1,392 lines long, and to write it out in Greek was a pretty severe imposition to complete in five evenings already sadly interrupted by homework.

"Very well, sir," I said contemptuously. "But I don't think that *Bacchae* is a very good pun for baccy."

And from that moment a cold war started between Cholmeley and myself.

The cigarette I was smoking during that interval between two acts of *The Gay Lord Quex* was probably a Pick Me Up. Those Turkish cigarettes were in a tin on the wrapper of which was a girl in a short striped skirt wearing a cap of liberty; they were flat, fat cigarettes of the shape associated with Egyptians, and ten of them cost sixpence.

There was a legend current at this date that Egyptian cigarettes derived their potent fumes by blending the tobacco with camel's dung. That legend can never have reached the United States, for if it had, surely the most popular of all American cigarettes with which a small amount of Turkish tobacco was blended would never have been called Camel. At this date Camel cigarettes had not been invented.

I still consider that was a preposterous imposition to set for a breach of school rules incapable of being detected except by a hawk-eyed master who should have ignored it. However, that Pick Me Up became a cigarette of destiny, for I resolved that the cap of liberty worn by the merry damsel on the wrapper should be worn by me. In other words, I made up my mind that somehow or other within the next few months I must devise a way of putting an end to the ineffable boredom of school.

If I had been observed smoking at the Earl's Court Exhibition, which I did as a matter of course every evening in that summer of 1899, I should not have resented Cholmeley's action, though I should still have thought the setting of the

Bacchae as an imposition was a poor piece of pedagogic face-
tiousness. I should have recognized that Earl's Court was too
near the school itself not to seem to be defying the school rules
too blatantly. One evening in the company of some people I
knew I met Lord Alfred Douglas at the Exhibition. He was in
his usual condition of feverish excitement at this period, and
suddenly announced that everybody must dine with him at
Scott's. I remember being staggered by his ordering a dozen
Murias cigars for about half a dozen people at eighteenpence a
piece—long slim cigars which we smoked in a box at the
Pavilion music-hall. Alfred Douglas was amusing company in
those days before he became obsessed by persecution mania. It
is significant of the important part that tobacco played in my
life that I can remember those Murias cigars but have forgotten
who performed that night at the Pavilion and all the people
who were in the party except 'Bosie' Douglas himself.

That autumn came the outbreak of the South African War,
and my younger brother, as much bored by school as I was,
managed to enlist in the Imperial Yeomanry, being still four
months away from fifteen. He was dragged out again almost at
once and sent back to school, but I was deeply impressed by his
resolution, even though it had included pawning a silver watch
of mine for current expenses. My own decision was taken on a
dreary January morning in 1900 just after my seventeenth birthday as I was walking along Hammersmith Road on the first
day of the new term. I dismissed the notion of enlisting in the
Imperial Yeomanry as impracticable; the likelihood of being
ignominiously hauled out of it as under age did not appeal to
me. Instead I made up my mind to stay awake for a fortnight,
by the end of which time I reckoned that I should be looking
pretty ill. My mother was alarmed by my appearance after
two weeks without more than an hour's sleep on any night,
and I was sent off to consult Dr Sidney Ringer, a distinguished
physician in Cavendish Place. I told him what I had been doing,
and he had the imaginative common sense to advise my re-
moval from school and my being sent somewhere to recuperate.
Thus a few days before Ladysmith was relieved I was relieved
of the boredom of school, and went down to stay at the West
Cliff Hydropathic Hotel in Bournemouth.

The only part that Bournemouth played in my smoking life
was my introduction to Brazilian cigarettes; I have forgotten

who it was that introduced me. In those days they cost six-pence for a packet of twenty; there were two kinds—one with open ends like an ordinary cigarette and the other in which the maize wrapping that took the place of paper was turned over at each end. The tobacco was dark with a rich flavour, and the maize blended with this to give it an added individuality. Thirty-four years later, when I visited Brazil and tried to acquire a good supply to bring back with me to Scotland, I failed to find the cigarettes I wanted and had much difficulty in persuading the tobacconists of Rio de Janeiro, São Paulo and Bahia that I did not want the English cigarettes of which I could get as many as I wanted at home.

Those Brazilian cigarettes at Bournemouth compensated for my inability to afford Havana cigars, though I occasionally treated myself to one of Bewlay's Flor de Dindigul Indian cigars, which cost threepence each. The pipe tobacco I smoked was Smith's Glasgow Mixture which, as I remember, cost fourpence-halfpenny an ounce.

In the summer of 1900 I went to stay in France with the mother of that American cousin who gave me my first cigarette. My aunt was married to a Frenchman who had become an American citizen, but still kept the family house at Charnay in the Lyonnais, to which they came over every summer from the States. That year their eldest son, who was a New York stock-broker, visited France after many years, and there was a reunion of the friends of his youth at one of those French family meals which last for hours. At six o'clock we went out into the garden, and about sunset I found myself talking to a captain in the Zouaves who had been one of the intimates of my cousin as a boy. He was then a man of thirty-four, with pince-nez and a grave, precise manner. I offered the captain a Caporal ciga-rette, which he accepted. Pleased with my ability to be on such good terms with a French officer, I decided to impress him with my freedom from an insular outlook, and told him how much I resented the attitude the whole of the British Press was taking about the Dreyfus affair.

"*Vous savez, monsieur le capitaine, moi, je ne suis pas du tout dreyfusard.*"

He turned round, looked at me severely through his pince-nez and said sharply:

"*Alors, vous-êtes imbécile.*"

And then he went on to say that the Dreyfus affair would be a mortal blow to the French Army.

"Look at me," he declared passionately. "Because I am known to sympathize with the Dreyfusards and to respect truth and honour, I am ruined. Next week I am ordered to Cochin-China, which means an end of my military career."

I can see him now puffing at that Caporal cigarette and, despair in his eyes, gazing eastwards to where the snowy summits of the Alps a hundred miles away were rose-dyed by the setting sun. That Zouave captain was too pessimistic. So far from his military career being finished, he was one day to become a general, command the Army of the Rhine from 1919 to 1924, and remain on the active list until he died in 1936. Whenever I smoke a Caporal cigarette—and whenever I can get hold of one I smoke it with pleasure—I am in France again, and that picture of Captain Jean-Marie-Josephe Degoute on the eve of departing for much farther east than Syria is one of my vividest memories. When the United States came into the First World War he asked for that cousin of mine to be on his Staff; by that time they were both of them men of over fifty.

I had hoped to go up to Oxford in the Michaelmas term of 1900, but there was no room in college, and the authorities at Magdalen decided that at seventeen I was too young to go into digs. I pleaded to be allowed to travel about Europe by myself for a year, but unfortunately I had gambled away all my money at the Casino in Geneva before I went to France that summer, and had had to telegraph home for funds to pay my bill at the Hôtel Bristol and my railway fare to Lyons. Therefore it was decided that I should spend the year before I went to Oxford with the Reverend F. A. Overton at High Cross Vicarage, some three miles from Ware. He used to coach young men for Responsions, but as I had already passed Responsions there was nothing for me to be coached in. So apart from reading a little German with him my time was my own, and a very agreeable time it was because I was given a commission in the 1st Volunteer Battalion (Herts) of what was then The Bedfordshire Regiment. The late Lord Croft commanded the right half-company of the Ware Company and I commanded the left half-company. Henry Croft was still up at Cambridge, so for most of the time I was the only subaltern. To-day I may be the youngest man alive with Queen Victoria's commission.

The etiquette about smoking in uniform was strict in those days. No officer would have been seen with a pipe in his mouth in the public view; even in a first-class smoker on the railway he might have hesitated to light up a pipe if there was anybody else in it.

I recall from the summer of 1901 a field day in which the Ware company, supported by the Welwyn or Hitchin company, fought a battle with the two Hertford companies supported by the Haileybury Cadet Corps. As I was going round the corner of a winding lane to see if I could ascertain anything about the enemy's whereabouts, four very young members of the Cadet Corps rushed at me with rifles levelled and in high, excited voices announced that I was their prisoner. This I undoubtedly was. The sun was blazing, and I suggested that I should retire under strict guard to the shade of a barn, where I lit a Brazilian cigarette.

"I say, what extraordinary cigarettes, sir!" one of my captors squeaked. "Can I try one?"

I was in a quandary—with the accent on the second syllable. I make this observation because as I write these words I have just been listening to three Oxford dons on the Third Programme quacking 'quándary' at one another a dozen times with the accent on the first syllable. I was in a quandáry, I repeat, because I wondered if these thirteen-year-old redcoats would be able to smoke Brazilian cigarettes without an undignified aftermath. At the same time, if I dared to suggest that such cigarettes were too strong for them I might wound their martial pride.

"I doubt if you'll like them," I said tactfully. "They're rather an acquired taste. However, try them. But throw them away at once if you don't like them. I shan't be in the least offended."

So the cigarettes were handed round, and the warriors, resting from the heat of battle, puffed away at them. Presently one of the warriors asked if it was the straw round them that made them taste so funny.

"I like Gold Flakes better," he declared. "They're jolly good."

"Throw it away," I advised, and he took my advice. So did my other three captors. An hour later a youth of about my own age with the stripes of a sergeant looked in at the barn-door.

"What the blazes are you kids playing at?" he demanded.

I wish I could record that they replied,
"We're guarding a prisoner, Attlee."

But although Lord Attlee was then in his last summer term at
Haileybury and was in the Cadet Corps, I cannot with honesty
identify him with that sergeant.

"I was taken prisoner about an hour ago, sergeant," I told
him.

"I'm sorry, sir, I didn't see you," said the sergeant, coming
to the salute in dashing style.

I was thankful that the cigarettes had been thrown away in
time. It would have been a bad moment if what was probably
a prefect had found four junior fags suffering from the effects
of Brazilian cigarettes given to them by an enemy subaltern.

"What the deuce happened to you, Mackenzie?" my company commander asked a few minutes later when the fortunes
of the day were being discussed.

"I was taken prisoner, sir."

"Humph! I shan't be sorry to have a smoke myself," he
chuckled.

I spent all my leisure, and I had plenty of leisure that spring
and summer of 1901, in writing poetry. By now I had discovered
Craven Mixture and I was willing to endorse everything that
J. M. Barrie had said about it in *My Lady Nicotine* as an inspiration. Craven Mixture cost—I cannot remember exactly how
much, but I know it was at least twopence an ounce more
expensive than Smith's Glasgow Mixture.

The first thing I did after I had looked at my rooms in St
Swithun's Quadrangle at Magdalen College on that October
day in 1901 was to visit the London and County Bank, the
Westminster Bank of to-day, and ascertain if the allowance
for my first term had been duly paid into my account. I
received the gratifying information that it had, and after sign-
ing my name in one or two books I was presented with a book
of pink cheques. I was now faced with the problem of writing
my first cheque. I knew from seeing my father write cheques
that the magic word was 'self'. So I invited the London and
County Bank to pay self five pounds.

"You've forgotten to endorse it on the back," said the clerk
when I handed it to him.

"Oh yes, how silly of me," I muttered.

"Your name as you've written it there," said the clerk tactfully.

I wrote '*E. M. C. Mackenzie*', and five golden sovereigns came tinkling from a small shovel.

With those five sovereigns in my pocket, I went to Colin Lunn's shop in the High and bought an obese tobacco-jar intended to hold a pound of tobacco but capable of holding nearly two pounds if pressed down with enough determination. That tobacco-jar of glazed brown earthenware inscribed 'Colin Lunn, Cigar Merchant, 23, High Street, Oxford', stands beside me as I write about it fifty-five years later. The rubber has nearly but not quite perished from the rim; one day perhaps I shall have new rubber put on. Yet I am reluctant to change that tobacco-jar in any way. It has waited at hand to fill at least a couple of dozen pouches which one by one have vanished through the years. All but three or four of the eighty books I have written were written to the accompaniment of the fumes for which it has stored the fuel. What that tobacco has provided in the way of mental and moral support! I estimate that I have smoked about half a ton of tobacco in my pipes since October 1901, of which all but at most a hundredweight has spent its last days out of a pipe in that tobacco-jar. It is the bottle in which the genie has been kept shut up until summoned to my service. The bottom is covered with a fine dust in which particles of latakia and perique, tobaccos I have long ceased to smoke, probably linger, because I have made a habit for many years of never emptying the jar completely, and that dust is now two inches deep. No other possession of mine has been in such continuously intimate relation with my sole self. There are a few books upon my shelves which are the seniors of the tobacco-jar and which I still occasionally consult, but they do not live at my elbow.

I have worn out two *Concise Oxford Dictionaries*, the frail pages of which occupy a place of honour on a shelf where they rest undisturbed. I hope that I shall succeed in wearing out the *Concise Oxford Dictionary* I am now using before I screw on the lid of my tobacco-jar for the last time. It is difficult not to feel sometimes that a material object with which one has been closely associated for a very long time is not a sentient creature, and at this moment, contemplating that obese jar of glazed earthenware, I cannot resist the fancy that it is aware I am engaged upon the history of tobacco and that it approves of the task I have set myself.

In 1901 every freshman at Oxford felt it to be his incumbent duty to secure at least one brier pipe the straightness of whose grain was able to vie with the straightest grain any other freshman could produce. I cannot remember what we were prepared to pay for a pipe that to-day if procurable would be priceless. Even with a silver band and an amber mouthpiece, the straightest grain would not have cost more than a guinea. I concentrated on straight-grain briers, but many of my contemporaries felt bound to colour a meerschaum. This was a solemn undertaking. The owner of a meerschaum when sitting down to bridge would never risk smoking it when he was playing even a hand of spades worth two a trick lest in his excitement he should smoke it too fast or worse still put it down carelessly beside him and crack the precious receptacle. Owners of meerschaums in the process of being coloured used to lay them down upon the table more gently than the most anxious young mother would deposit her first-born in its cradle. Then they would cast a vigilant eye from time to time upon their pipes to be sure that they were not sweating, and if the slightest moisture was apparent they would wipe it off tenderly with the silk handkerchief they carried for this purpose. At the end of the evening the meerschaum would be wrapped in a cover of chamois leather and placed in a pocket containing nothing except the silk handkerchief used when it was sweating, and of course this was never done until the pipe was as cool as the seafoam which gave it its name.

I recall one tragic moment in the life of a man and his meerschaum. The late Charles Maude, a cousin of Cyril Maude, was playing Duke Orsino in a pastoral of *Twelfth Night* with which members of the O.U.D.S. were touring during the Long Vacation on behalf of local charities. I cannot remember in the garden of which country-house we were performing, but it was a damp evening after a day of rain and we were thankful when the last scene began without more rain. Charles Maude was waiting behind a shrubbery to make his final entrance, and I, who as Sir Toby Belch had to make my final entrance a minute or two later, was waiting beside him. Maude was smoking a well-coloured meerschaum of which he was proud. His cue came and with the pipe still in his mouth he strode forward.

"Charles, Charles," I warned him, "your pipe."

What could he do? He was wearing Elizabethan costume and he had no pocket into which he could put the pipe. A look of agony passed across his face as he took the meerschaum from his mouth and flung it into a wet nettle-bed beside the path.

"Why didn't you give me the pipe?" I asked him in the dressing-room after the play was over.

"You had to come on almost at once."

"Yes, but I should have had time to find something more suitable for a meerschaum than a rain-soaked bed of nettles."

Charles Maude, whose grandmother was the famous Jenny Lind, went on the stage after he left Oxford, and married Miss Nancy Price. He had a distinguished career in the First World War, and remained in the Army without returning to the stage. There was a promise of military devotion in the way he sacrificed that meerschaum pipe when playing Orsino, Duke of Illyria.

When I first went up to Oxford, Craven Mixture was the blend most in vogue, but I was presently introduced to John Cotton's No. 2 Medium Mixture, which a few people were beginning to smoke. Within less than a year John Cotton had practically displaced Craven as an undergraduate's favourite. The only thing I had against John Cotton, which I continued to smoke for the next fifteen years and returned to again after the First World War was over for another five, was the way it was packed. It is useless to wrap up a quarter of a pound of tobacco in tin-foil and think that such a wrapping will keep it reasonably moist. Every time I put half a pound in my jar, I had to restore its moisture with a sliver or two of potato or apple, but when one was travelling around without a tobacco-jar the dryness of John Cotton became a problem. However, I must not say a word against a mixture with the aid of which I wrote my first eight or nine novels. The first John Cotton was a sergeant in the Army, and when he finished his service towards the end of the eighteenth century, he set up in Edinburgh as a tobacconist.

The bulldog was the shape I favoured first for a pipe, and it is still my second choice after a Lovat, which by 1902 was gaining adherents everywhere. The original Lovat designed by

Colonel Henry Fraser and marketed by an Aberdeen tobacconist had a white mouthpiece made of horn or bone. I suppose
the design was never patented because B.B.B., which we sur-
mised stood for Best Bloody Briers, were very soon putting out
Lovats of their own with vulcanite mouthpieces, and to-day
I doubt if any pipe manufacturers would fail to include the
Lovat among their designs. That old horn or bone mouthpiece
had one fatal weakness, which was that a smoker with a firm
grip very soon bit through it. Moreover, it was rumoured that a
bone mouthpiece for a pipe was an encouragement to cancer,
though I never heard of any medical expert who committed
himself to such a wild speculation.

For over fifty years the Lovat has remained my favourite
shape for a pipe. When I had to succumb to the false teeth of
age, I found that they made no difference. Pipe makers have
tried to put out pipes which they claim are specially designed
to suit false teeth; in my opinion, if the dentist has done his job
properly any straight pipe is as good as another. A curved
pipe can be clumsy, but a curved pipe is just as clumsy for a
perfect set of natural teeth above and below. A churchwarden
is valuable for holding forth with one's back to the fire, but
nobody would give himself the trouble of smoking a churchwarden when reading or writing. In the days when the churchwarden clay was almost the only shape available, one or two
inveterate smokers used to support them by sticking the stem
through the brims of their hats; this must have been an awkward operation when cocked hats came in.

I am under the impression that hardly anybody at Oxford
smoked Virginia cigarettes in those years when I was at the
University, but I hesitate to make too confident a generaliza-
tion. Turkish Régie cigarettes were popular, and the stately
Sullivans were sometimes to be found in the silver cigarette-
boxes of well-to-do young men who had read the tribute paid
to them by the immortal Raffles. However, the Turkish cigarettes accepted as the best were Batemans. These were plumper
than Régie and, like them, round. A miniature cedar-wood
cigar-box containing a hundred cost 12s. 6d. This will not seem
expensive to those who to-day have to fork out 19s. 2d. for a
hundred Virginia cigarettes which at that date would have
cost half a crown, but to pay 12s. 6d. a hundred for cigarettes
in the year 1901 was regarded as a sign of expensive tastes.

One always kept a box of Batemans to hand round after lunch or after a wine, but few people smoked cigarettes all the time. The pipe was the stand-by of the undergraduate smoker, and when he was wearing his normal every-day dress of tweed jacket and grey flannel trousers, he did not hesitate to smoke a pipe in the streets. On Sundays, however, we walked about in dark suits, wearing bowler hats and carrying a pair of shiny brown-leather gloves, and it would not have been considered the thing to smoke a pipe when thus attired. Only House men carried walking-sticks in 1901; by the following year people at other colleges were following their sensible example.

In summer, straw-hats were worn; they were never known as boaters. Indeed, I never heard of boaters until Noël Coward used the word in a mistaken effort to achieve atmosphere for the period of the Boer War. Homburg or Trilby hats, as they were called, were never worn. The late Sir Charles Prescott caused a sensation at Magdalen by appearing in one in 1902, but we agreed that, having been invalided out of the 10th Hussars and being at least two years older than any other undergraduate, he was entitled to sport such extravagant head-gear.

The year 1903 was a year of destiny for the cap; one morning in the Michaelmas term Adamson's in the High filled their window with what they called 'the new motoring cap'. The first person at Magdalen to venture to wear one was the late Henry Lygon, who walked down the High sporting a 'new motoring cap' of Lovat tweed to the open condemnation but secret admiration of his fellow undergraduates. Before the year was out the 'new motoring cap' had conquered, and to-day it remains almost the same shape as it was when it was first invented.

Smoking in cap and gown was prohibited, but we thought this an anachronism after dark and paid little attention to it. If one ran into the proctor, one was invited to call upon him next morning at nine o'clock to be fined five shillings. We were supposed to wear cap and gown at the theatre; but this rule was ignored, and when a new and zealous Junior Proctor tried to enforce it we continued to ignore it; after a tiring week he gave up his crusade. We used to hear with amused contempt that in Tabland, as we called Cambridge, the Tab undergraduates all wore gowns to the theatre.

I have mentioned those tours we took with *Twelfth Night*. In August 1903 we were entertained at Hams in Warwickshire, a house which is now the headquarters of Midland Electricity. The first Lord Norton, then in his ninetieth year, was still alive. A visit to Hams was to go back beyond the Victorian era, for Lord Norton had been up at Oxford in the year of the Reform Bill, having been born in 1814. He wore the same kind of collars as Mr Gladstone wore, although Gladstone himself was anathema to him. From 1874 to 1878 he had been President of the Board of Trade, and he was a Conservative of Conservatives. I wondered what he thought about his son, the Reverend James Adderley, who was a well-known High Church parson with Socialist leanings.

Tobacco was prohibited absolutely in Hams. If a guest had been discovered smoking in the most remote bedroom, he would have been ordered out of the house. We sat down to dinner at seven, which was the utmost concession the old gentleman would make to newfangled notions about the time to dine. He presided at the head of the table, and when the ladies had retired, not to be seen again, the port circulated, and when I say circulated I am thinking of the circulation of the blood, for it never stopped. On the whole Lord Norton's young guests stood up to it well and, with the tactful help of footmen, we reached our bedrooms in safety without disgracing ourselves. But how we longed to smoke!

I think it was in July 1904 that I was again the guest of a man who did not allow smoking in his house. This was Sir Clifford Allbutt, the Regius Professor of Physics at Cambridge. The late A. Forbes Sieveking had discovered in the library of Trinity Hall an unknown play by Thomas Heywood called *Worke for Cutlers*, and this was to be performed in the garden of Trinity Hall with Sieveking as Sword, myself as Rapier and as Dagger Alec Ross, the elder brother of Robert Ross, who was such a devoted friend to Oscar Wilde. Ross and I were the guests of Professor Allbutt whose house stood in a garden, and I recall that when we retired we both leaned out of our bedroom windows and smoked into the moonshine, the fragrance of the tobacco mingling with the fragrance of *Nicotiana Affinis* in the flower-bed below. Allbutt was not quite seventy then, and he lived for another twenty years. I do not grudge longevity to non-smokers, but I am not prepared to admit any cause and effect. People with long-lived constitutions live long whether they drink or smoke.

My godfather, John Bolton of Scarborough, was a fanatical enemy of smoking. He had a smoking-room like a Temple of Vesta in his garden to which guests who desired to smoke had to remove themselves, and what is more don the smoking-jackets and smoking-caps he provided for them to avoid bringing the odious fumes into the house, which always had a faint scent of hot roast beef owing to the absence of tobacco smoke to banish the smells of innumerable meals. John Bolton was a rich man, but towards the end of his life he suffered from the delusion that he might lose his money. So he used to turn inside out the envelopes of letters he received, and use the envelopes for his replies, sticking up the ends with stamp-paper, and when he had no stamp-paper with the stamp itself, which must have irritated the post office. He had at least six bedrooms all with four-posters hung with beautiful tapestries and brocades, but having decided he could not afford to sleep in any of them he slept for the last five years of his life on a wooden grating covered with a thin mattress which was put over the bath in his bath-room, the windows of which were pasted with ferns.

I shall not claim that if my godfather had taken to smoking the end of his life would not have been spoilt by these anxious eccentricities, but it would be as justifiable to do so as to claim that Lord Norton or Sir Clifford Allbut owed their years to abstention from tobacco.

I sat with that splendid veteran Sir Ian Hamilton on the terrace of 1, Hyde Park Gardens on a summer afternoon three months before he died in his ninety-fifth year, and I recall that we were both smoking cigars. I never knew anybody except Cunninghame Graham in whom the flame of life burnt so brightly and so steadily in old age as it did in Ian Hamilton. Both were smokers, and both old in years died young.

A word now about tobacco-pouches. The half-moon, which for so long was the only shape for a pouch, now seems to have been displaced by the rectangular roll-over pouch, though zip-fastened pouches for some reason I am unable to fathom are still in evidence. Nothing lends itself to zip-fastening less suitably than a pouch, because fragments of tobacco inevitably invade the zips, which are at the mercy of foreign bodies, so that a zip-fastened pouch is an almost continuous exasperation to what should be the tranquil nerves of the smoker.

I shall hazard a guess that the first pouch most of us owned was one of brown rubber made to look like crocodile or lizard skin. That kind of pouch is still a permanent feature of the tobacconist's glass-topped counter, as permanent as the snaky buckle with which the belts of small boys have been fastened for the last seventy or eighty years. One never seemed to lose one of those pouches. I wager that at the back of hundreds of drawers throughout the country that type of pouch, discarded long since by its owner, awaits hopefully a moment of emergency when it will be again filled with tobacco.

Nowhere shall I find any of those pouches I lost long ago while I was an undergraduate. They were all of the half-moon type. The one I regret most was a monkey-skin pouch dyed to the colour of spinach and possessing a curiously attractive softness and flexibility combined with toughness. I lost it in the course of a boar-hunt in the forest of Compiègne in the Easter vacation of 1903. Then I had an antelope-skin pouch of a delicate greyish-green from which it was a luxury to fill a pipe with John Cotton's Medium Mixture. I have forgotten where I lost that pouch. The third was a largish pouch of kangaroo-skin which held four ounces comfortably and six ounces at a bulge. This, too, was green, but a brighter green than the monkey or the antelope and with a rougher texture. I left it in a Great Western second-class railway carriage when I alighted at Frome in the summer of 1904; it was full of tobacco.

I did not discover the perfect ash-tray for a pipe-smoker until long after I had gone down from the University. That was in Rattray's famous shop in Perth. Mr Rattray had always devoted his attention to the needs of the pipe-smoker, whom he regarded with the respect to which the passionate pipe-smoker is entitled. One of the problems of the pipe-smoker is knocking out the ashes. The makers of motor-cars apparently assume that anybody driving in a car will be a cigarette-smoker and they will provide for him a usually inadequate tray, but no tray of any kind for the pipe-smoker. Once upon a time Mr Rattray saw a pipe-smoking guest at a dinner take a champagne cork, put it in the middle of a plate and knock out his pipe on it. So he devised a deep circular wooden tray in the middle of which is a squat wooden pillar topped with cork. Those ash-trays of his have been my constant companions ever since the lucky day I discovered their existence, and they bear the scars with which innumerable dottles have burnt them. They are more than ever necessary to the pipe-smoker's comfort to-day, when in fewer and fewer houses can he knock his pipe out into an open fire.

We all went in for pipe-racks at Oxford, usually in the shape of five-barred gates. But as I keep about forty pipes in use, a rack is no good to me, and mine cover the chimney-piece of my library; those, that is, which do not lie about on tables all over the house or hide in the pockets of jackets in my wardrobe, for whenever I go out I carry with me at least three pipes.

In our first Christmas vacation, Harry Pirie-Gordon, an undergraduate contemporary, and myself went to Spain and Morocco. On the eve of the Epiphany in Seville, it was (and probably still is in conservative Spain) the custom of the waiter to give the guests on whom he was attending a present. Our waiter at the Roma Hotel presented Pirie-Gordon and myself with eight Cabana cigars of a crop before the Spanish-American war. Pirie-Gordon did not smoke cigars, and therefore I smoked them all. Although even at eighteen I could recognize a Havana cigar of real quality, I should be surrendering to a romantic notion if I were to pretend that I discovered in those cigars made in the traditional and, by foolish modern standards, unhygienic methods a flavour that the world would never taste again. Nevertheless, it gives me the same kind of pleasure as the connoisseur of wine used to get from boasting of his memories of pre-phylloxera claret to boast here that, at an age when I was able to appreciate the experience, I have smoked the cigars of a Cuba that was still in the Empire of Spain. Much as I had enjoyed those cigars purloined from my father's cupboard, I doubt if I was yet old enough to appreciate what good cigars they were.

A sadder loss than the Havanas of once upon a time was the disappearance of the old Manilla cheroot after the Philippine Islands were taken away from Spain by the United States. The old Manilla cheroot was almost twice as large as the skimpy product of to-day, and the flavour was at least three times as good. I remember my doctor at Oxford telling me that Manilla cheroots contained a very small amount of opium; I have never been able to verify this, and it was probably a fairy-tale. Those wonderful Manilla cheroots cost twopence apiece, and a box of a hundred looked like a small packing-case. Another assertion one heard about cheroots was that people who knew how to smoke them always put the wide end between their lips and lighted the narrow end. I have never seen any hardened cheroot-smoker, whose complexion had been burnt to a yellowish-brown by the Asian sun, put the large end in his mouth, and I think any attempt I made to display an intimate acquaintance with cheroots by lighting the narrow end was as silly as sucking the end of a walking-stick, a habit to which fashionable but vapid young men were addicted in early Edwardian days.

I have mentioned the etiquette of smoking at Oxford; by the beginning of the century it was clear that the hostile attitude of the previous century was fast vanishing. However, we were still far from being able to smoke anywhere and at any time. For instance, it would not have been manners when walking with a woman young or old, whether in a public street or in the garden of a private house, to light up even a cigarette without asking her permission to do so. This was a relic of the feminine attitude towards tobacco in mid-Victorian days. I have never believed in the sincerity of that feminine disapproval. Women always play up to masculine superstitions. Men had got it into their heads that women objected to tobacco, and women felt bound to justify this belief. Throughout Rhoda Broughton's novels young women smoke. True, they were considered 'fast' for doing so, but obviously a great many young women in Great Britain during the 'sixties and 'seventies of the nineteenth century were smoking not to be 'fast' but because they liked it. As I have mentioned, my father to the end of his life claimed to be shocked by the sight of a woman smoking, and he was one of thousands. In 1903 I went with Arthur Asquith and Guy Bonham-Carter to Compiègne, and I well remember the latter's saying to me what a terrible thing it was for 'Oc' and his brothers that their stepmother smoked. One felt from the tone in which Guy Bonham-Carter spoke that Mrs Asquith's tobacco-smoke had hung like a dark cloud over their Winchester careers.

It was permissible to smoke a cigarette in any London street, but it was not considered good form to smoke a pipe in the West End. Indeed, it was not considered quite the thing to walk about the West End unless one was dressed for the promenade, either in morning-coat and top-hat or at least in a dark suit and a bowler. Frock-coats were no longer being made for young men, though older men still wore them habitually. I remember on one occasion having agreed to accompany Raymond Wavell, an intimate friend, to Piccadilly, arriving at his mother's house in South Kensington dressed in a light grey suit and wearing a straw hat. I could see that Wavell was disturbed at the notion of walking down Piccadilly with me in such unsuitable attire, but he decided to put up with it as he had had so often to put up with such Bohemian idiosyncrasies on my part. However, when as we turned into Bond Street I started to fill a pipe he looked at me in horrified incredulity.

"You're not going to smoke a pipe in Bond Street?" he gasped.

"Why not?"

"Look here, if I buy you a cigar will you smoke that instead?"

I agreed with alacrity, and we turned into Morris's shop for me to acquire a more becoming smoke for Bond Street than a pipe.

While I thought that it was absurd not to smoke a pipe anywhere if one was wearing tweeds, I should have been as much shocked as Wavell would have been to see a man smoking a pipe in formal costume. I am still capable of a faint tremor when I recall coming out of 6, North Street, Westminster, where I was then living, to behold the Home Secretary, Mr Reginald McKenna, in top-hat and frock-coat on his way to the House and smoking a large curved pipe to which the final touch of social bizarrerie was added by the fact that he was holding this large curved pipe between his front teeth. That was in the early summer of 1912 and the Home Secretary was in his fiftieth year. There was, I felt, no excuse for such *sans culottes* behaviour on the part of a Cabinet Minister.

I have passed beyond Oxford, but return there to recall the fragrance of a Bateman cigarette smoked outside the Schools to obtain a few minutes' blessed relief from 'the weariness, the fever and the fret' of that atmosphere within where men sat and heard each other groan. In those days women were not members of the University, but they were allowed to sit for the examinations and awarded an honorary class in the Schools. The sight of those earnest young women scratching away at their answers to the questions set in the finals of the School of

Modern History was exhausting and my place happened to be adjacent to them. There was one young woman wearing a dark purple blouse of velvet most inappropriate to the month of June, and in the fever and fret of displaying her knowledge a strand of hair was lying over one shoulder. I could stand no more. I applied to leave the room, and was led by a gowned vigilante to the lavatory.

"No, no, I want to smoke a cigarette outside and get a little air."

The vigilante waited while I stood on the steps and smoked my Bateman. To-day the traffic in the High would make a tranquil cigarette like that unattainable; even the spectacle of young women undergoing the ordeal of their final Schools would be a more restful sight.

One of the reproaches levelled against tobacco by its enemies was that it made people spit. The genteel use of expectoration for spitting is much less genteel really, because expectoration means getting rid of phlegm on the chest or in the bronchial tubes, whereas spitting merely means getting rid of superfluous saliva. Americans used to be credited with more spitting than other nations at one time, and the spittoons provided in the United States in hotels and bars and railway-carriages were certainly more numerous than elsewhere in the world. The earliest form of spittoon was found in West Africa and was called a 'cuspadore', which is Spanish for a spitter; the reference dates back to 1779. However, it was 'cuspidor', the Portuguese word for a spitter, which won the day in the United States as a genteel substitute for spittoon, in the same way as casket has displaced coffin.

There must have been a contest for a time between 'cuspadore' and 'cuspidor', because the cleaners of spittoons were known as cuspadorians. In 1884 the Century Magazine recorded: "The official register contains the names of nearly fifteen thousand persons, beginning with President and ending with cuspadorians, who serve the United States in the City of Washington."

> The cuspadorians at their priestlike task
> Of pure ablution round the U.S.A.

Neither Keats nor Milton would have disdained that

sonorous word—with the accent on the second syllable, as in 'decōrous' and 'acūmen'. British Broadcasting Corporation, *please* note.

Cuspidors were indispensable as long as chewing a quid or cud of plug was the most popular way of taking tobacco, which it remained in the United States until well into the twentieth century.

Spitting in England was less well served. The floor of a third-class smoking compartment on the Underground Railway was at one time the most disgusting sight in Europe. This was not due to chewing, but to smoking shag or twist in foul cutty clay pipes. Spitting was nominally an offence; but the regulation against it was disregarded, and it was not until the cigarette displaced the pipe for popular smoking that the floors of rail-way-carriages became tolerable.

The most accomplished spitter I ever saw was an exalted prelate who, while preaching in Seville Cathedral, was able to spit over the heads of a couple of dozen pious women squatting round the foot of the pulpit and hit the same flagstone every time with consummate accuracy. It may sound unpleasant, but the artistry of the performance gave one the same kind of æsthetic pleasure as watching the juggling of Paul Cinquevalli.

When I was in the United States from September 1912 to March 1913, the cigarette had already gained a spectacular popularity, though I do not remember seeing the Camel; I doubt if it was yet on the market. I always bought Richmond Gems when I wanted cigarettes. The problem was pipe tobacco. Good pipe tobacco like Edgeworth was obtainable but one had to demand it. The average tobacco store always assumed that their customer who asked for pipe tobacco wanted Prince Albert Mixture. I find it difficult to write with restraint about that black and red tin with a picture on the outside of the Prince Consort in a frock-coat. I do not suppose for a moment that anybody ever ventured to show Queen Victoria a tin of Prince Albert Mixture; my grandfather's wrath at seeing the pictures of his two youngest daughters on candy-boxes for the Federal troops would have been mild in comparison with hers. Why it was called a mixture I do not know; it consisted of what seemed to be small chips of cork, and looked much more like one of those horrible cereal foods that disfigure the contemporary breakfast-table. I shall refrain from saying what Prince

Albert Mixture tasted like, because the last thing I want to do in a book like this is to impair Anglo-American relations.

At the date of which I am writing one was not allowed to smoke a pipe in most of the New York clubs, but I used to be told that the pipe was making headway with 'college boys'. It was a custom of the Players' Club, which was the New York equivalent of the Garrick, to indulge in a monthly outburst of faintly self-conscious Bohemianism by holding what was called a Pipe Night; I do not recall that an overwhelming majority of the members smoked pipes on these occasions. This is not to be wondered at if Prince Albert Mixture was the staple tobacco smoked.

Women were not allowed to smoke in public, except between 5 p.m. and 7 p.m. at a *thé dansant* held daily in the Plaza Hotel on Central Park and at Rector's Restaurant down-town.

There was a strong anti-tobacco party all over the United States. They were alarmed by the growing popularity of the cigarette, which they had succeeded in prohibiting in several States. As we crossed the frontier of Indiana in a train, the conductors came along to warn passengers that until the train had passed out of the Hoosier State no cigarettes must be smoked.

What astonished me in New York was that, although New Yorkers accepted without a murmur the prohibition of smoking on the subway, on the elevated railway and in cinemas, they were unable to get through a meal at a restaurant like Sherry's or Delmonico's without lighting a cigarette between the courses. To be sure, the waiting was so dilatory that they usually had to wait a quarter of an hour or twenty minutes before the next course reached the table; perhaps it was the dilatory waiting of forty years ago that started the habit of smoking during meals, which now makes it impossible for many Americans not to light a cigarette between the soup and the fish. In England it was the custom to serve an iced sorbet in the middle of a long dinner and for the diners to smoke a cigarette before they settled down to the second part of the dinner.

We have a relic of the Victorian attitude towards tobacco in waiting to light a cigar or cigarette until the Loyal Toast has been drunk. Nowadays when taking the chair at a dinner I am sometimes asked by an agitated secretary to give the Loyal Toast almost before the cheese is cleared away, as anxiety to smoke is fretting many of the diners. There is a growing tendency to pass round cigarettes about five minutes before the cigars arrive. The true cigar-smoker does not want a cigarette as a preliminary to a Punch or Partaga or Henry Clay, and there is no reason why he should wait one moment after sipping his port before he lights up his cigar. I do not regard port with the veneration that some still accord it. Nevertheless, when the house committee of the Savile Club abolished the rule that no member should smoke at the dinner table, I felt a faint regret, and also a faint apprehension that within a few years members might be lighting up cigarettes in the middle of dinner. *Procul, O procul este profani.*

In March 1913 I left the United States to visit Italy and for the first time enjoy the pleasures of smoking in Italy. That statement may provoke a contemptuous snort from some readers. Let them be patient with me.

I will admit at once that if an Italian were asked to choose between a packet of Macedonia cigarettes and a packet of Three Castles or any other Inglese product in the way of cigarettes, he would without hesitation choose the Inglese cigarette. I do not inhale, and therefore the confirmed cigarette-smoker is inclined to resent it when I tell him that all Virginia cigarettes to-day taste alike to me. I am assured that if I inhaled I should recognize at once the merits of this or that brand over another. I reply that when one was offered a cigarette during and immediately after the First World War, it was sometimes offered with an apology!

"I'm afraid it's only a gasper."

That guilt complex has long been resolved now. To-day we may hear from a friend:

"I'm afraid I've only Turkish cigarettes." Possibly in explanation of his eccentricity quickly adding, "My wife likes Turkish."

My mind goes back to round about 1904 when I heard a barmaid at the Empire say to a young man who asked her for a packet of cigarettes, "Do you want Turks or Virgins?" That barmaid did not take her customer's preference for granted. And that reminds me that in the 'nineties of the last century we called all Virginia cigarettes 'Straight Cuts'. This, I believe I am right in saying, was an American term for them originally with a variety put on the market by Allen and Ginter called 'Straight Cut No. 1'.

When I went to Italy in 1913, Macedonia cigarettes were

known as 'venti-cinque', costing as they did twopence-half-penny for a packet of ten in those days. A year later they went up to threepence-halfpenny and remained 'trenta-cinque' for a long time. I shudder to think how many liras they may cost to-day.

When I spoke of the pleasures of smoking in Italy, it was not of Macedonia cigarettes but of the Napolitano cigar that I was thinking. The most pretentious Italian cigar was the Minghetti, which followed the conventional shape of a small Havana and cost thirty centesimi; it was not worth smoking. Then there was the Virginia or Veneziano, with a straw in the middle to keep its emaciated shape from collapsing. Why the Queen of the Adriatic—rich in the voluptuous glories of Titian and Tintoretto should have given her name to this El Greco of a cigar is hard to guess. The Toscano is probably the Italian cigar with which most Britons are familiar, not very plump in the middle and tapering at either end. It is usual to cut a Toscano in half, though if one does find a Toscano that draws easily it is better smoked whole. However, the trouble taken in pinching about fifty Toscani in order to find half a dozen that will draw is not as well rewarded as the pinching of fifty Napolitani. I should never have ventured to pinch them if I had not been warned by Norman Douglas to do so.

But there was more in it than pinching. One had to find if possible the Napolitano of a lighter colour than the majority. They may have cost only twenty centesimi apiece, but the tight brunettes were not worth a penny and the tender blondes were worth sixpence.

"*Dei napolitani, prego.*"

A large drawer with four or five hundred Napolitani would be pulled out.

"*Prego, signore.*"

And then laboriously one searched among that multitude for the tender blondes. I have often spent half an hour choosing half a dozen cigars.

When we had chosen well, what a delicious smoke it was!

> *Here with a Loaf of Bread beneath the bough,*
> *A Flask of Wine, a Book of Verse—and Thou*
> *Beside me singing in the Wilderness—*
> *And Wilderness is Paradise enow!*

More dear to me than the paradise Omar Khayyám conjured for himself is the memory of sitting on a terrace, in the shade of an overhanging carob tree, above the silver-blue Salernian Gulf, beside me what is left of a loaf of bread rubbed with garlic, a jug of Capri wine, a fresh cacciacavallo cheese and a bowl of anchovies in olive-oil, and also beside me Norman Douglas talking in the noontide hush as we smoke two Napolitani chosen with solicitude for our contentment. What well-loved wraiths of the happy past float in the fumes of that great psychagogue, tobacco!

Before reaching the war of 1914–1918, I may recall two ludicrous incidents. The first was when I threw the end of a cigarette off an omnibus in a high wind which carried the lighted end to land in the middle of the flowery hat of a woman who was just stepping off the pavement to cross the road behind the omnibus. If it had been a Virginian cigarette of a few years earlier, I should not have been perturbed, because in the earlier days of the hand-made cigarette a Virginian went out immediately one ceased to puff at it. On the other hand, a Turkish had to be stubbed out as we stub out, or *should* stub out, all cigarettes to-day. This cigarette I had tossed from the omnibus was a Virginian, and I decided that it was my duty to get off the omnibus and warn the recipient of its arrival on her hat. I was glad I had done so when upon overtaking her I perceived that from the flower-bed upon her coiffure a wisp of smoke was blowing in the wind.

"Madam," I called out, "your hat is on fire."

She swung round and faced me with what Cockneys call a perishing look.

"Do you want me to give you in charge?" she asked sternly.

"If you take off your hat you'll see that it's on fire," I urged.

In those days a woman could not snatch her hat off her head. She had to pull out at least a couple of hat-pins first.

"You may think it very funny to try and make an April fool of a lady, but if you molest me any more I'll call a policeman to you."

It seemed to me that the wisp was perceptibly thicker, and I became so anxious that I hurried across to a policeman on the other side of the road and told him I thought the woman's hat was on fire. She had continued on her way by this time, but from where we stood the smoke was clearly visible.

In those days, before the policemen of London all looked

like Boy Scouts, a London bobby ran with considerable difficulty.

"You'd better run after her and tell her again," he advised. "And I'll follow you."

I hurried off after the lady and assured her that her hat really was on fire. She swung round again, prepared to complain to the police of my behaviour when she saw the bobby advancing.

"Take off your hat, mum. It's alight," he told her.

"How can my hat be alight?" she asked indignantly.

"Take it off, mum, and you'll find out."

When she did, several of the flowers were smouldering, but the fag end of the cigarette had burnt itself out.

"This is a perfect mystery," she declared. I did not feel that the laws of chivalry demanded I should solve the mystery; instead I proffered my help to extinguish the glowing petals.

"I'm sorry I spoke so sharp to you, young man," she said. "But being April Fools' Day, I thought you was having a game with me."

We parted with mutual cordiality.

A similar incident occurred after my American publisher had given Martin Secker and myself a capital lunch at Romano's.

"Don't look round," he said to me as we emerged into the Strand. "I think the end of that cigar I threw away has gone into a man's pocket."

Of course I did look round, and I was in time to see a man thrust a hand into his pocket and disembarrass it of that cigar-butt, simultaneously glaring back with fury at a portly middle-aged gentleman who had just passed him.

A moment later he had tapped the middle-aged gentleman on the shoulder.

"Who the hell do you think you are, putting lighted cigars into people's pockets?"

A group of passers-by, attracted by the angry tones, stopped to gape.

"We'd better get out of this quick," said my American publisher, and we crossed the road to make for the seclusion of the Adelphi. I looked round to see that the group of passers-by had become a small crowd by now, and I wished I could hear the argument that was obviously going on between the portly middle-aged gentleman and the enraged recipient of my American publisher's discarded cigar-butt.

"It's always wiser to slip away quickly on these occasions," he said.

"Do you make a habit of putting lighted cigars into the pockets of passers-by?" I asked.

"Why no, I don't believe I ever did such a thing before," he replied with a smile.

I reached Gallipoli from Capri in the second week of May 1915, and here as a Marine of the Royal Naval Division I was able to draw four ounces of naval tobacco each week. It was a really good smoke in a pipe, and it may have been that naval tobacco which prompted the first inclination to turn away from mixtures containing latakia. However, I was to remain faithful for some years yet to John Cotton as the main ammunition for my pipe.

When after being invalided out of the Mediterranean Expeditionary Force in October I started a counter-espionage organization in Athens, I was still able to obtain naval tobacco through the British Naval Mission, and John Cotton reached me through the Legation bag.

In October Sir John Ward (he was then Major the Hon. John Ward) on his way to London as a War Office Messenger came through Athens. Of him fifteen years later I would write in the second volume of my war memories:

> The mind clings to the memory of such talks as those I had with John Ward, whose name expresses so completely his personality that I feel it superfluous to add a word of professional description. They seem in retrospect to have put one's conscience right like a good confession. There was a moment one reminds oneself, when all that we could say was said and when all that we said was proved by later events to have been a completely accurate forecast of what would happen. It was at that date a level-headed judgment, given before I was become like everybody else in Greece the prey of faction, prejudice, impatience, and suspicion, before the nerves had begun to sear the brain with their lightning, before that dazzling sun and that intoxicating air of Athens had turned life into a spinning-top in one's endeavour to act and think and write fast enough for such a scene.

Before John Ward went on to London, he asked me if there

was anything he could send me from England. I told him that
I had lost most of my pipes on the Gallipoli peninsula, and that
I should be most grateful for a Lovat pipe. I quote again:

A fortnight later I received from John Ward a present of
twelve Lovat pipes, some of which I am still gratefully
smoking, and much more coolly than I smoked them during
those feverish months ahead of me fifteen years ago.

Forty years have now passed since that generous gift, and
probably the last of those Lovats that John Ward sent me has
been lost or smoked to pieces. *Athenian Memories* was finished on
the anniversary of our silver wedding and dedicated to my wife.
The opening chapter of my history of tobacco will be finished
by the anniversary of our golden wedding, and the whole book
when it is finished will be dedicated to her.

In November 1916, after the proclamation at Salonica by
Venizelos, Admiral Coundouriotis and General Danglis of the
Provisional Government, the pro-German, or more accurately
the anti-Venizelist, party in Athens tricked the French
Admiral into delivering a demand that the Greek Government
should hand over their mountain-batteries to the Allied Command in Salonica. This ultimatum was resisted by arms. Many
French sailors and British marines were killed and Athens was
at the mercy of the mob, which took vengeance on the Venize-
lists in the city. The British Legation and the house next door,
known as the Annexe, in which the British and French Intelligence Services worked in harmony, were in a state of siege.
Two or three of my men had been wounded and one was dying.
The result of this was something like a panic when the French
were ordered to withdraw under escort to the Admiral's flagship at Salamis.

My French opposite number was much upset at what seemed
like desertion, but I assured him I realized it was not his fault.

He grasped my hand and said:

"It will perhaps be a pleasure for you in this *mauvais quart
d'heure* to know that the *Légion d'Honneur* has been granted to
you."

I quote from my third book of war memories, the publication
of which in 1932 led to my being prosecuted under the Official
Secrets Act. The book was suppressed, but it was reissued in
1939 when it seemed less dangerous to the authorities:

We felt a little quiet and lonely after the French drove off; but at a quarter to eleven a loud fusillade broke out close to the Legation. The bullets were whistling continually over the back garden. From one of the houses just behind the Annexe the shooting was so furious that somebody cried out that a machine-gun had been turned on us, which set up another panic and people began pulling out pistols and revolvers. I said I was tired of these panics, and that everybody must give up his arms. I was never free from the fear that one of our fellows would start firing from the Annexe and provoke an attack. Nevertheless, when I ordered the arms to be brought into my room I was met by an excited refusal. They did not mind fighting, but they were not going to be butchered like sheep. If the Annexe was attacked, they wanted to put up a show.

I promised that if the Annexe was attacked I would let them have their pistols, but insisted that meanwhile they must hand them over to me to be locked up in my room until I gave the word to use them. Still they refused to obey me, and I realized that I must do something to stimulate their obedience. News had come that my house had been shot up and sacked early that morning, and I availed myself of that to point out that the only person in the Annexe of importance to the other side was myself.

"And now," I said, "I'll prove to you how unlikely they are to attack the Annexe by proving to you that they daren't even attack me."

With this I walked downstairs and out through the gate into the side-street that led to Stadium Street up and down which, the main street of Athens, the mob was surging. I doubt if I should have mustered the courage to walk along those hundred yards without a cigarette. A pipe or a cigar can give one the confidence for fearless speech, but neither helps one to carry off a gesture. The fact that I was smoking a cigarette enabled me to stroll slowly along to the pavement in Stadium Street and stand there smoking with a simulation of insouciance while the mob swayed now this way now that along the roadway empty of traffic. One wretched Venizelist, a fat man, was being dragged along by half a dozen of the Reservists whom the Government had brought to Athens to stir up trouble. Every time he stopped to protest he was hit on the face, which was streaming with blood, and prodded in the back with bayonets to make him move on.

I knew that I must remain standing where I was for at least five minutes if I was to prove my contention, and as I was in the blue uniform of a captain in the Marines I was a conspicuous figure on that pavement. Looking back to that scene after many years, I have come to the conclusion that my not being attacked must have been due to that cigarette, because it enabled me to stare back into the eyes of those that stared at me as they surged past without seeming to be making a conscious effort to look indifferent. Once or twice I heard my name called, and soon the mob was obviously beginning to pay attention to me. I decided it was time to depart. When I was standing on the pavement my heart was beating fast, but I did not feel really frightened; when I turned round to walk back along the hundred yards to the Annexe my knees suddenly became cotton-wool. I began to reflect that in the words of Coriolanus a mob was a 'common cry of curs' to which the fright of its victim was as the scent of blood. I knew that to move the least little bit faster (if I *could* move faster with those woolly knees) might be fatal. So by an effort of will I stopped and without looking back over my shoulder I tossed away the cigarette I was smoking, took another from my case and lighted it. Then slowly I walked on, the noise of the mob very gradually growing fainter and the likelihood of a bullet in my back less probable.

When I reached my room again the floor was covered with revolvers, daggers and cartridge-belts, and the rifles were stacked away in a corner. Some of those ex-brigands and smugglers who had refused to obey my orders were in tears. Such is the power of a cigarette at the right moment.

Three years later I was travelling from London to Naples at a time when the French were inclined to think that we were being too solicitous about the Germans. Before the war, when a traveller was passing through Paris on the way to Rome, nobody ever bothered about his luggage. So when I told the young *douanier* at the railway-station I was *en route* for Rome, I expected he would chalk my dressing-case and despatch-case and wave me on. Instead, when he saw my dressing-case on the counter, he said brusquely, "*Ouvrez ça*".

"*Mais, monsieur,*" I protested. "*Je suis en route pour Rome.*"

"*Ouvrez ça,*" he repeated with the insolence that only a Parigot can command.

When I had unlocked and opened the dressing-case he began to rummage about in the contents, from which a moment later he picked out a small red case.

"*Qu'est-ce que c'est que ça? Des cigarettes, hein?*" he demanded with a triumphant curl of his disagreeable lips.

"*Non, monsieur,*" I replied gravely, "*c'est la Légion d'Honneur.*"

I never saw any man, let alone any official, look so utterly mortified as he closed the lid of that dressing-case and chalked the top of it.

"*Ignoble! Ignoble!*" gasped an elderly Frenchman behind me in the queue who had the rosette of the Legion in his own buttonhole.

I shrugged my shoulders with a sad smile for the gaffes of which officialdom is capable.

In September 1894 a Customs officer at Southampton had made me unfasten in the rain seven or eight cigar-boxes in which were pinned the butterflies I had caught that summer in Brittany, by which surly and stupid display of self-importance he ruined the collection. From 1894 until 1919 animosity had marked my attitude to Customs officials. Since the mortification of that young French *douanier* I have regarded them almost with affection.

That story above is the pendant to the Legion of Honour of the award of which I was notified on that first of December 1916. Now comes the pendant to the cigarette.

In November 1932 there was the first hearing of the ridiculous case launched against me by some of the people at M.I.5, who were afraid that if I was not checked I should laugh them out of their jobs. When the court at the Guildhall emptied, the usher in his rich uniform put on his top-hat and diving into the tails of the blue frock-coat pulled out a packet of Capstan cigarettes and offered it to me.

"But can one smoke here?" I asked, looking round at the lion and unicorn and the figure of Justice over the seat where Alderman Sir George Truscott had been listening to the arguments of the Crown.

The usher gave a contemptuous little laugh.

"When they're all gone out this court is just the same as anywhere else," he said, and one felt that the eyes of the female figure of Justice were twinkling behind their bandage.

When I descended from the dock in the Old Bailey some

weeks later to wait for the payment of the fine before being allowed to leave, I was shown into a small whitewashed kitchen. Here a young policeman offered me a chair and a cigarette.

"If anybody comes along, throw the fag into the fire," he warned me.

When we were young we believed that a policeman could arrest on sight a boy under fourteen whom he saw smoking. This legend was kept alive, no doubt by interested parties.

If I had been told then that one day I should be smoking while a young policeman kept a vigilant watch on the approaches to a kitchen in the Old Bailey, I should have asked if anybody could see any green in my eye. When I look back to the policemen of my youth, they all pass across the screen of memory as middle-aged men, tall and bulky, with moustaches like that of Jimmy Edwards and a hint of bunions. I cannot believe that they appeared as young to septuagenarians at the end of the nineteenth century as the blue-collared stripling police of to-day appear to the septuagenarians of the mid-twentieth century.

In 1920 I obtained a lease of the isles of Herm and Jethou in the Channel Islands, and among the many advantages of living there was that the price of tobacco was normal again. It may seem absurd now to be commemorating with satisfaction the shilling an ounce one saved by living in the Channel Islands, now when we are paying the fantastic duty levied upon tobacco during the Second World War and raised since.

In Guernsey I discovered a mixture which displaced the John Cotton No. 2 to which I had been faithful for twenty years. It was a blend of dark Virginia flakes with some lighter flake and a small amount of perique but no latakia, and it had an individual flavour which I had never tasted before and have never tasted since. This mixture saw me through a time when I was smoking literally all night, for in 1923, finding the financial burden of Herm too heavy, I parted with the lease and settled down on Jethou, the fifty acres of which comprise within the circumference of a mile a richer variety of attractions than any island of its size in the British Isles. To pay off the debts incurred by my tenancy of Herm, I had to work even harder than I had ever worked, and throughout the spring and summer of 1924 I used to write sometimes from dusk until seven or eight in the morning, sustained by my pipe and gramophone until two or three in the morning and for the rest of the time only by my pipe. I doubt if many readers will know what it means to smoke a pipe for hours at a stretch like that, but let me say that few tobaccos will stand such a test because they affect the tongue of such a persistent smoker. This mixture was blended by an old retainer of the firm, and he refused to part with the secret. After smoking it for nearly five years I suggested that it should be put on the market as Mackenzie Mixture, and the head of the firm thought the idea a good one. The only snag was the secrecy which the old retainer insisted upon preserving. I said that I would come over and try to persuade him to initiate one of the younger men in the firm so that the secret did not die with him.

About a fortnight later my usual weekly consignment of tobacco arrived; at the first pipe of it I smoked I exclaimed:

"What on earth has happened to my tobacco this week?"

It looked exactly the same as usual, but the 'nuttiness'. That is the only word I can find for the flavour peculiar to it, inadequate though it is as a description, because it can be applied to other mixtures with a 'nuttiness' quite different from the elusive 'nuttiness' of this particular mixture was gone. A day or two later I went over to see the head of the firm in Guernsey, and asked him what had changed the flavour of the mixture. His face fell.

"I was afraid of this," he said. "Old X—— died last week. We knew the tobaccos that went into the blend and we could estimate the proportions. So we made up a mixture and sent it over to you as a trial. If you had said nothing, we should have assumed that there was no difference. But the old boy always used to maintain that there was more to it than just blending. What that something was we never knew, and now we shall never know."

I shall not try to speculate about that secret; it may have been some process of baking. The old boy used to shut himself up like a medieval wizard to produce his mixture, and nobody was allowed to enter the room while he was at work.

It would not be fair to mention the various mixtures and non-mixtures with which I experimented for the next year or two. All I will say is that latakia in any of them ruled it out at once;

I have noticed, as a sign of oncoming middle-age, that the pipe-smoker loses his taste for latakia which is a tobacco for youth. Inasmuch as most mixtures contain latakia, one finds the middle-aged smoker turning to pure Virginia flake which the pipe-filler without years of practice is apt to find a problem for his fingers.

In 1929 I discovered in Scotland the virtues of Lambert and Butler's Warlock, and I have smoked it ever since. Apparently it is too strong for the less hardy Londoner in whose city it is produced. The Scots are the people who appreciate this noble dark flake, of which I smoke about an ounce and a quarter a day. I had a suspicion that for a time the Warlock of to-day, which has to rely on Empire-grown leaf for some of its make-up, had not quite the quality of the Warlock produced before dollars became such a headache, but I have been able to satisfy myself that the Warlock of the present day is, in fact, now indistinguishable from the original Warlock made from Kentucky tobacco. I used to hear it said that the secret of Warlock was that it had been soaked in rum! I need hardly add that this was just a fairy-tale, but that such a fairy-tale could win any credence may indicate the satisfaction that the smoker of Warlock derived from his favourite tobacco. I may add that I have several times been asked in railway-carriages what tobacco I was smoking, so agreeable to the nose was the smell of it.

And that reminds me of a story. Round about 1937 I was dining in Simpson's with my friend Wilfred Macartney, the other guests being Harry Pollitt and Willie Gallacher. Macartney likes to entertain lavishly, and his exuberant spirits were depressed when Willie Gallacher, after looking carefully through the bill of fare with a frown on his benevolent face, put his finger on one item and said to the waiter, "I'll have some of that."

That was shepherd's pie, the cost of which was eighteenpence, cheaper than anything in the whole bill of fare. Pollitt and I revived our host's spirits by ordering lobster to start with and some other expensive dish to follow.

"You'd like champagne?" asked Macartney hopefully.

Pollitt and I at once fell in with such an admirable suggestion; Willie Gallacher frowned again.

"I'll take a cup of tea," he said.

When we had eaten and drunk, Macartney called for the biggest and best cigars the restaurant could provide.

"You'll smoke cigars, of course?" he enquired of his guests.

I was just going to utter an enthusiastic affirmative when I saw a cloud pass across Willie Gallacher's countenance.

"No, no, you and Pollitt have cigars," I said. "I'd rather smoke a pipe."

Willie Gallacher's brow cleared.

"Ay," he agreed with evident satisfaction, "that's more like it."

With this he plunged a hand into his pocket and drew it out full of black twist already cut up.

"Will you try some of mine?" he asked me.

I put out my hand and both of us rubbed the twist between our palms before we filled our pipes and lit up.

Two days later there was a letter in *The Times* or the *Daily Telegraph* from a distinguished actor complaining of having been gassed in a well-known restaurant in the Strand by the stench of two pipes. There can be little doubt that those pipes belonged to Willie Gallacher and myself.

I suppose that black twist might be a trial for tender noses, but I do enter a protest against the habit of some London restaurants of forbidding pipes. The fumes of cigarettes to-day can be just as unpleasant to pipe-smokers as the fumes of a pipe can be to cigarette-smokers, and as either can be to non-smokers. That superstition about the smell of a pipe has affected the aircraft lines, which forbid any smoking except that of cigarettes. Surely passengers by air who dislike tobacco dislike it as much in the form of a cigarette as in any other form. If smoking were forbidden altogether in an aircraft, I should recognize it as a reasonable prohibition; to penalize the pipe-smoker is a remnant of Victorian snobbery. Campoli the violinist has solved the problem by smoking very thin little Brazilian cigars which he insists are cigarettes.

It is said that King Edward VII as Prince of Wales founded the Marlborough Club as a protest against the conservatism of clubs which banished smokers to dingy and uncomfortable smoking-rooms. The Reform was still forbidding members to smoke in the atrium in the early 'twenties. Robert Ross once told me an amusing story about this in connexion with Arnold Bennett. Ross and H. G. Wells had put up Bennett for the Club, and he had been duly elected. Thereupon the newly elected member wrote to ask his sponsors to meet him for lunch because he always felt shy when he made his first appearance as the member of a club. Wells could not manage the lunch, but Ross agreed to meet Bennett. He had been unexpectedly detained, and therefore was ten minutes late on reaching the Reform. He asked the hall-porter if Mr Arnold Bennett had arrived and, Ross continued,

"When the porter said coldly that he had, there was something in the tone of his voice and the disapproval of his eyes which presaged disaster. With a sinking feeling inside, I hurried up the steps into the atrium through which every now and then a very senior member will pass quickly, concealing a half-smoked cigar under his coat, but where no member of whatever age or eminence would venture to put a cigar in his mouth. When I entered the atrium my apprehensions were justified. Arnold Bennett was standing in the very middle of it, looking up at the marble columns and the gallery that runs round above the hall. He was wearing an orange and red waistcoat into which he had stuck both thumbs, and in his mouth was a very large lighted cigar. Members who passed back and forth gazed with horrified amazement at the unhallowed spectacle, and I could feel that when Arnold Bennett exclaimed, "There you are at last. You're late, Robbie," those members all shook their heads and murmured, 'Ah, of course, a friend of Ross.'"

In the fatal year of 1939 the Princess Hermine, the second wife of the Kaiser, let a German friend of mine know that His Imperial Majesty had read my book, *The Windsor Tapestry*, and that he had expressed a desire to meet me with the possibility of entrusting me with the task of presenting a just portrait of himself to the world. I was given to understand that if his impression of myself was favourable, he might place in my hands various papers of the existence of which nobody except his intimate entourage was aware. Then suddenly the Kaiser asked the Empress and Queen, for as such he always expected her to be addressed, although since his abdication it was merely a courtesy title, whether I was any relation to Morell Mackenzie. It was Morell Mackenzie who was called in by the Crown

Princess over the heads of the German doctors for consultation about the Crown Prince's throat, and who had opposed the operation for cancer. The Kaiser had always resented his father's living long enough to ascend the Throne, because he did not want his mother to be Dowager Empress and Queen. In the end the Crown Prince did succeed his father and lived for six months as Emperor of Germany and King of Prussia.

When the Kaiser heard that what he regarded as his enemy Morell Mackenzie was a first cousin of my father, he was inclined to call off the proposed meeting. Nevertheless, the Princess suggested we should go to Amsterdam in the hope that the Kaiser would change his mind. So that beautiful Whitsuntide of 1939 found us in Amsterdam, where we received a telephone message from the Princess inviting us to tea with her at Doorn next day but warning us that there was no likelihood of our being received by His Imperial Majesty. It was a long drive from Amsterdam to Doorn, and exact punctuality being essential my friend and I hung about, drinking coffee at a small inn until we could arrive on the stroke of five. We drove through the entrance gates of the castellated lodge, and as we came in sight of the house my companion exclaimed, "There he is! And he's wearing Harris tweed. He has made up his mind to receive you."

The Kaiser reached the end of the broad paved walk from the front of the house just as we pulled up by the gate before it. We had brought with us a lot of gardening catalogues from the Chelsea show which the Kaiser told his equerry to look after, and he then started at once to talk to me about trees. I was surprised to find that he was at least half a head shorter than myself. He had been telling me about the losses he had suffered with his evergreens from the hard winter, particularly, as I remember, with the Thuyas, when I asked him if he had tried our Scots fir, *Pinus Sylvestris*.

"No, no, but of course I remember them so well at Balmoral long ago."

And as he said this there was a moisture in those vivid blue eyes of his; perhaps feeling that he was displaying too much emotion for royal dignity he asked quickly,

"Do you believe in the Loch Ness Monster?"

"No, Sir. I am not convinced by the evidence so far."

"Ah, I'm glad to hear that. I think it is a joke played by the

——" he hesitated for an instant until a word came back to him which he probably hadn't used since those days at Balmoral long ago. "Played by the gillies," he said with a boisterous laugh. After that for the next minute or two he lost no opportunity of bringing gillies into the conversation.

Suddenly he turned on his heels.

"You are expected for tea, I believe," he looked back over his shoulder to say, and then set off on his walk with the equerry who was finding it rather difficult to hold that slippery pile of gardening catalogues with the decorum expected of an equerry.

The Princess had never been in England, but she spoke English with hardly a trace of accent. It was a typical royal boudoir of the 'nineties, crammed with photographs mounted on crimson plush in silver frames. Beyond the grand piano above what I thought was the door of an inset cupboard was the picture of the Kaiser in his glory, in white uniform with gleaming breast-plate and helmet, familiar from many a chromolithograph. After tea the Princess offered us those cigarettes smoked by royal ladies, half of which consist of a cardboard mouthpiece. The Princess had been a widow when she married the Kaiser, and she said in the course of conversation,

"My boy has been in trouble with Goebbels over a lady. There was to be a duel, but he has been put in prison for two or three months. Thank God, it is not a concentration camp!"

As she uttered this passionate exclamation the door of the room opened and a servant in a white jacket came gliding in. The Princess turned pale.

"It is terrible how you exaggerate in England about our concentration camps," she hastily exclaimed, with an eye on the white-jacketed servant who glided out again almost immediately.

"We have to be a little careful what we say," our hostess explained; when she lighted another cigarette her fingers were trembling. The thought of that exiled court at the mercy of Nazi spies was disagreeable; the Jacobite Court in Rome was similarly infested by servants in the pay of the Hanoverian secret service.

The conversation had passed to talking about the prospect of my writing that book, about which the Princess was optimistic, when suddenly there was a rumbling noise from what I had thought was a cupboard beyond the grand piano. The Princess jumped up, and stubbed out her cigarette; I instinctively followed her example. A moment later the Kaiser was standing in the door of what was, in fact, a private lift immediately under the picture of himself in his glory, an old man now on the edge of eighty. He stepped forward into the room, and after kissing his wife formally said to me:

"The chestnuts in Bushey Park must be looking very beautiful now. I remember how beautiful they were when I was in England for King Edward's funeral."

Then he went on talking in rather an excited way about trees. At last he said:

"I wish you to look at my rosarium here. Baron D——, a gentleman of Mecklenburg, will show you round. The roses are not yet in bloom, but you will be interested." And before I could reach the door to open it for him the Kaiser had shot out of the Princess's boudoir.

"Did you see how moved he was?" she asked in obvious astonishment.

I felt that a courtier's reply was demanded.

"Indeed, Ma'am, I was too much moved myself to notice what His Imperial Majesty was feeling."

I wanted to ask the Princess whether she had stubbed out her cigarette because the Kaiser disapproved of women's smoking or because it would not have been etiquette to greet him formally with a lighted cigarette in her hand, but I doubted if such inquisitiveness would be becoming.

The rest of the story has nothing to do with smoking, but it shall be told briefly.

Downstairs on the way out with Baron D—— we passed through the spacious hall full of tables on which were pinned large maps. The Kaiser was studying one of these.

"Why are you behaving so stupidly over Palestine?" he demanded of me. And after giving me a little lecture on what we ought to do, I was dismissed to look at his rosarium.

I recall on the only mound in the rose-garden a summer-house in which, on a marble bench, there were two cushions covered with purple velvet and stamped in gold with the Imperial Crown. The summer-house was reached by two paths, across the entrance to both of which was a chain about eighteen inches from the ground beside which *Verboten* was painted in white letters on a black notice-board. It would have been simpler to step over the chain but Baron D—— bent down and unhitched it ceremoniously for us to pass up the little path.

"Their Imperial Majesties sometimes sit here to watch the playground His Imperial Majesty has presented to the children of Doorn."

The playground was a sandy triangle beyond the rose-garden in which children were digging pits for themselves or swinging. Beyond was the main road along which innumerable bicyclists were passing in either direction, representatives of the new world from which that Imperial residence was as remote as a castle in a fairy-tale by the brothers Grimm.

Baron D—— escorted us to our car in the stable-yard, and as he clicked his heels in a farewell salute the clock in the tower began to strike seven. He looked at his watch with an expression of incredulous dismay, and the last we saw of him was almost running back to the house in a suit cut in pre-1914 style. He was evidently going to be late for dinner, and he looked as fussed as the White Rabbit hurrying to the garden-party in *Alice in Wonderland*.

I visited Doorn again a week before the outbreak of war. The Kaiser was laid up in bed with an attack of gout. I sat on the balcony of the Princess's boudoir looking down at the orange and scarlet dahlias and zinnias and salvias in the hot August sunlight. A daughter of the Princess was with us; she and her mother were both smoking.

"I am afraid we can do nothing about the book at present," said my hostess. "If this horrible war comes, I hope we shall still be friends."

As she was speaking a half-company of Dutch soldiers arrived to take possession of the orangery, where they had been stationed to preserve neutrality. A Scottish priest had accompanied me on this second journey to Holland, and we spent a night at Utrecht on the way to Rotterdam. I smoked a lot of Dutch cigars, but I did not derive a great deal of pleasure from them. However, it is not fair to judge cigars when the mind is preoccupied with the certainty of impending war. At The Hague, touts offering for sale picture-postcards of the Palace of Peace clustered round the car, but souvenirs of peace seemed out of place now, and I was anxious to get one more glimpse of the Rembrandts in the Mauritshuis. It was closed and over the door hung a cardboard notice all askew on which was written in rough inky capital letters: "Closed until further notice".

The crossing to Gravesend from Rotterdam was breathless; Mars, large and red and low in the sky, was reflected in an orange streak across the duckpond sea.

At Victoria our luggage had to be examined in case we were I.R.A. emissaries with bombs.

"What we want in this country is a Hitler," our porter observed.

As we emerged from the station and saw the tattered scare posters of war's approach blowing about the Sunday street, I was back again in August 1914 with this difference. Then I had been in despair because I was afraid we might keep out of war and leave France in the lurch: now I was in despair because we seemed to be plunging inevitably into war.

I shall not comment at this stage on the ferocious duty imposed on tobacco during that war beyond saying that it made no difference to the amount I smoked. Remembering the contribution made by smokers to national defence I could say, "They also serve who only sit and smoke."

When the task I have set myself is accomplished I hope to make some reflections on the boon that tobacco has been to mankind, and in making those reflections I shall doubtless be driven to declare that the present duty upon tobacco is an unjust method of raising paper money to balance a paper budget and that such budgets savour too much of the methods of financiers who at intervals have paid the penalty for indulging in the confidence trick on a grand scale.

I recall a Brains Trust at Broadcasting House about five years ago at which Mr Leonard Brockington, the distinguished Canadian lawyer who gave those outstanding broadcasts during the last war, was a guest. He offered me a cigar with these words:

"Tell me, why do you assume in this country that only rich men like cigars?"

I am glad to note that during the last few years the great Tobacco Houses have been paying much attention to the whiff, that is, the very small cigar or cheroot. This enables those who find a cigarette a meaningless subscript to a good meal but who cannot afford the preposterous price that governmental extravagance compels the Chancellor of the Exchequer to place upon them to enjoy for at least ten minutes the grateful influence of a cigar.

I wish that women would cultivate the whiff habit. Nobody appreciates a cigar more than a woman when she has learnt how to smoke it. Lord Lonsdale, of sporting renown, used to hand round to his lady guests after dinner miniature Havana cigars from a miniature box. I have one of those boxes, the cigars in which are just over an inch long. The brand is not marked, but *Flor Fina* and *Claro* are stamped on two sides. Every box held fifty in bundles of twenty-five tied up with yellow silk ribbon. The box in my possession has one complete bundle left.

The first woman I ever saw smoking a cigar was the late Mrs Bernard Berenson, a sister of Logan Pearsall Smith, the gifted author of *Trivia*, and a Quakeress. That was fifty years ago.

The mention of that relic of Lord Lonsdale reminds me of another relic I once possessed. This was a silver churchwarden pipe which unscrewed into three pieces to be packed away in its case. This pipe was reputed to have belonged to Dr Johnson and its pedigree seemed authentic. It was acquired by my father after he had produced a one-act play by Frankfort Moore called *The Jessamy Bride*, in which Oliver Goldsmith and Dr Johnson both appeared upon the stage. When I was Rector of Glasgow University I presented this pipe to the Ossianic Society because I have always felt that Dr Johnson's attitude towards the Highlands has been misjudged. I am convinced that he set out in 1745 to join the Prince, but failed to reach the Jacobite Army. This for me has always been the explanation of that journey to the Hebrides with Boswell.

In October 1946 I set out on a 50,000-mile journey by sea, air, road and rail in three continents to follow through ten fascinating months in the steps of the old Indian Army during the Second World War. At the end of that tour came nearly six months at Simla, and then the long journey home by way of the Seychelles Islands and Kenya.

During those first ten months it was difficult to maintain my supplies of Warlock. Luckily I found that in the tropics and in the sizzling heat of the North-West Frontier I did not want to smoke a pipe: the cheroots of Trichinopoly and Burma became my staple smoking.

The most surprising tobacco incident I recall was at Keren in Eritrea. Towards the end of lunch a large but slim and elegant chocolate-coloured ram came into the dining-room to beg for cigarettes to eat. Everybody in turn gave him a cigarette which he chewed up with evident relish. When Edgar, for that was the name of this engaging animal, came round to me I offered him a cigar, and this he chewed up with obviously an even keener relish than he had shown for the cigarettes. I had not hitherto had much respect for sheep, but since meeting Edgar I have had a much higher opinion of their intelligence. I hope that when Eritrea was so incomprehensibly given back to the Abyssinians, the smoking prohibition imposed by the Negus Menelek because a pipe once made him sick had lapsed. I do not like to think that Edgar died as the result of being deprived of his cigarettes like the chimpanzee in Indianapolis who died when the cigarettes he had been accustomed to smoking were prohibited in the Hoosier State.

I have always considered one of the marks of the cat's superiority to the dog to be the cat's comparative toleration of tobacco. Offer a pipe to a dog's nose and it will leap back as if it had been stung by a bee. Not so the cat. It always amuses me to hear some sentimental cynophile maunder on about his two best friends being his dog and his pipe, when neither of them is on speaking terms with the other. Nobody, so far as I have been able to discover, has made any attempt to establish the reactions of various animals to tobacco, or for that matter of birds and reptiles. It would be at least as profitable as the investigations made by American professors into the reactions of various human beings.

The Muslims of what used to be north-west India smoke, but they do not drink wine, spirits or beer; the Sikhs, on the other hand, drink but they do not smoke. One may suspect that this was a deliberate display of contrariety by the Sikhs. What can we deduce from the respective effects of these two prohibitions? Both the Punjabi Muslims and the Sikhs are magnificent warriors, and both are strictly religious. Perhaps deliberate abstention either from alcohol or nicotine endows the abstainers with a kind of puritan strength. However, neither of them, like so many puritans,

Compound for sins they are inclined to
By damning those they have no mind to.

I have left to the last that country which is the spiritual home of all good smokers. In the course of this history I may be able to learn who brought tobacco to Burma and salute his memory with a pious epitaph, but known or unknown I give thanks to his spirit for the pleasure that smoking in Burma gave me.

I had occasionally smoked Burmese cheroots at home because they were strong and once upon a time cheap, but either because, like some of the world's best wines, the Burmese cheroot will not bear exportation or because the Burmese cheroots exported to this country have been badly chosen, there is no doubt that we do not know here what a Burmese cheroot can be. When they cost threepence apiece the strength of them compensated for their comparatively inferior aroma, but to-day when they cost two shillings apiece I have to admit that the Burmese cheroots which I have been able to find in Great Britain are not worth bothering about.

If I could only find here a brand called Moonriders, fifty of which were presented to me in Kalewa by L. Kwan Lone, the District Supply Officer, a Chinese of exceptional charm even for a Chinese. Moonriders were large and they were strong but they had a wonderful flavour, and each of them lasted for an hour when smoked in a jeep travelling along those magical roads through the jungle; indoors they lasted for an hour and a quarter. I used to smoke ten a day, and had almost finished that box of Moonriders when we reached Mandalay. Here I visited a cheroot-maker's shop and ordered another fifty cheroots which were promised for the next morning. Four rupees was the price asked by the bright-eyed woman who ran the shop with her daughters. I was shown a great bowl of ripened tobacco leaf from which my cheroots were to be rolled of the size I wanted. I showed them one of the last Moonriders I had, and next day the fifty cheroots were ready, too damp for immediate smoking; but as we were going up to Maymyo I went back to a pipe for a day or two.

Each of these cheroots, which proved to be even better than the Moonriders, cost me three-halfpence. If I smoked twelve a day every day for a year my tobacco bill would be about £27 10s. Let us say £30 a year to include plenty to offer those of my friends capable of enjoying this noble smoke. In Great Britain that amount of smoking and smoking hospitality would cost me £480 a year.

The simple people smoke what look like Roman candles, but are in fact tobacco wrapped in what appears to be maize. I have read in some old book that this wrapping is made of the leaves of the Then-net tree, but what the Then-net tree is I have not been able to ascertain. I tried one of these giant cheroots; I cannot say that I enjoyed the experience. However, you can see children of two years' old being offered puffs by their mothers, and it may well be that there is an art in smoking these cheroots which I did not master. My old friend Eric Linklater told me that he won kudos when he was in the United States by showing a gathering of young people, girls and boys, how to smoke a cigarette like an Indian coolie, that is by holding it between his cupped hands and swallowing a deep draught of smoke before passing it on to his neighbour to do likewise. According to Linklater, most of the young women were put out of action by this method.

A scene to warm the heart of a devoted smoker is of a Burmese family watching a play that goes on all night, and to observe how first father and then mother hands his or her cheroot round to the family of children who are enjoying the play with them.

The Burmans have a keen wit, and their attitude towards life has some of the quality of the Irish approach to it. The world was made for man not man for the world they rightly feel. There was a strike for higher wages by railway workers in Rangoon; when the Burmese workers won the day they used the extra money to pay Indian coolies to do some of the work while they sat round smoking and talking and laughing. I regret the decision of Burma to leave the Commonwealth but I understand it perfectly, and it may well be in the future that only in Burma will man avoid the insect state the idea of which threatens to captivate the whole of Asia, and indeed for that matter the whole of that world which politicians with their tongues in their cheeks have the impudence to call 'free'.

That tobacco has played a vital part in preserving Burmese freedom I am convinced, but I begin to trespass on the fanciful aspect of smoking . . .

On the way home from India I spent nearly four months in

the Seychelles, where a certain amount of tobacco is grown. The local cigarettes are good, and I found the pipe-tobacco, which one clips off from a solid wedge called a *carotte*, a pleasant enough smoke. One of these *carottes* was presented to me by a hospitable planter, and I brought it back to England as a souvenir of these enchanted islands. At Tilbury I was informed that the duty payable on my *carotte* would be nearly £23. I pointed out that the tobacco was a present, and that I did not intend to smoke it or to let anybody else smoke it. I pointed out that the Revenue would be losing not a doit of the exorbitant duty they would be charging me on the Warlock I should now be smoking again. It was no use. That Customs officer had in his eyes the same expression of determined petty officialdom I saw first in the year 1894 in the eyes of that Customs officer at Southampton who ruined my butterfly collection by insisting on my opening cigar-boxes in which there were obviously no cigars, or of that young French *douanier* who thought that the red case of the Legion of Honour was a packet of cigarettes. No doubt the Tilbury guardian of the Revenue was completely within his rights over the *carotte* of Seychelles tobacco, but when he wanted to charge duty on a bamboo pipe which had been given to me as a present on my sixty-fourth birthday after I had spent a night in the Kabaw Valley not far from the Chindwin, then I knew that he had a paper soul. Presently he found an ash-tray for which my secretary had paid half a rupee to a Tibetan pedlar in Simla, and he wanted to charge her duty on that. What a privilege it is to live in the free world at the mercy of officials with paper souls. "*Monsieur*," said a taxidriver in Nice to me after the officials at the airport there had wasted two hours of travellers' time over some petty hold up, "*aujourd'hui nous sommes la proie des fonctionnaires parasitiques.*"

I wonder what happened to that *carotte* of tobacco I surrendered to the Customs at Tilbury rather than pay the duty. I am sure it was not smoked by that paper-souled Customs officer. He himself was obviously a non-smoker, and probably a total abstainer as well.

I do not like to end this factual account of my smoking life with hard thoughts about a non-smoking official who deprived me of a *carotte* of tobacco. I who have smoked half a ton of tobacco during this century can afford to be charitable. Yet how little that seems when I read that in the year 1871 the smokers of Rotterdam scattered tobacco-ash in mourning on the grave of Mynheer van Klaes who had died at the age of eighty-one, having smoked four tons of tobacco during his lifetime. But can that be true? It would have involved smoking about half a pound a day for sixty years, and I find such an amount hard to accept as possible even if that puffing Dutchman smoked Boer tobacco in a calabash pipe, which burns as fast as any tobacco I have smoked.

I prefer an authentic obituary in the newspapers of February 12th, 1954:

"Mrs Mercy Coffee, who had smoked shag tobacco in a clay pipe since she was fifteen, died in a Maidenhead, Berkshire, Hospital yesterday aged 101. At one time she got through 8 oz. a week, but cut it down to 2 oz. in recent years. She had a pipe a few hours before she died."

That enough asphodels may have been cleared away from a patch in the Elysian fields to grow tobacco for Mrs Coffee in eternity is my pious hope.

As for myself, could I be granted a perfect end to this transitory life I would choose to leave it like the father of George Blake the novelist. When he was in his hundredth year he was sitting at sunset by a window that looked over the Clyde. He lit his pipe, and as he blew out the first fragrant puff of smoke his spirit followed it.

Chapter 1

AT ten o'clock on the night of October 11th, 1492, Christopher Columbus from the deck of the *Santa Maria* saw a light ahead, the record of which in the log every smoker to-day should contemplate with reverence as that of an auspicious guiding star. At two o'clock in the morning of Friday, October 12th, a sailor on the look-out in the *Niña*, a forty-ton caravel accompanying the Admiral's ship, sighted the land of the New World, a small island in the Bahamas which was named San Salvador by Columbus, and is believed to be the island that to-day is called Watling Island. Later on that morning Columbus, who was supposing this to be off the coast of Asia, dressed himself in his richest attire and landed with the Royal banner of Spain to take possession of the island in the name of their Catholic Majesties of Castile and Leon. The Arawak natives offered the impressive stranger some dry leaves as a token of friendship. Three days later the Admiral recorded in his log that between the islands of Santa Maria de la Concepcion (now Rum Quay) and Fernandina (Long Island) he had found a man in a canoe with some of these same dry leaves which were held in much esteem by the natives and had a pleasant scent.

By November 2nd, Columbus was off Cuba (or some say Haiti), and he despatched ashore the two of his crew he considered most suitable to establish relations with any official they might meet from the court of the Grand Khan of Cathay, for Columbus still believed that he was near Asia, and to-day the memory of that belief of his is preserved by the name 'West Indies'. One of these men was Luis de Torres, a well-graced Jew with a knowledge of Oriental languages; the other was Rodrigo de Jerez of Ayamonte. Their names deserve commemoration, because they were the first Europeans to witness the phenomenon of smoking. They went inland with an Arawak guide, and returned to the ship on the night of November 5th with the news that they had met many natives who carried a burning firebrand with which to kindle some dry leaves and scent themselves. Whether or not Luis de Torres had read the account of this Scythian habit in Herodotus as a substitute for bathing, it was a mistake easy enough to make.

The incident was recorded by Columbus in his log.

Bishop Las Casas, whose *History of the Indies* written some time after 1527 remained at Madrid in manuscript until it was printed at long last in 1876, amplifies that brief entry in the log. He says that de Torres and de Jerez met many people with firebrands and herbs 'to take their smokes'. These herbs were dry and wrapped in a dry leaf, like the paper 'muskets' boys smoked at Pentecost, and after being lighted at one end the smoke was sucked in. These 'muskets' were called *tabacos*.

It was a pity that the history written by Las Casas remained in manuscript, when the history of the Indies written by Gonzalo Fernandez de Oviedo y Valdés was printed and published at Seville in 1535. Oviedo, as he was generally known, for two years in 1513 and 1514 had been captain of the fortress of San Domingo in Hispaniola. Las Casas, perhaps resentful over the publication of Oviedo's history when his own was still in manuscript, had no use at all for Oviedo, whose book, he says, should have been prefaced by the admission that he was a robber and murderer of the Indians, many of whom he had sent to perish in the mines.

Whatever value Oviedo's history may have had in other respects, he managed to obscure the origin of the word *tabaco* by reporting that the method of smoking was through a Y-shaped tube, the shape of a boy's catapult. The forked end of this was inserted in the nostrils and the smoke from the wrapped-up burning leaves was inhaled until the smoker was unconscious. This forked instrument, he says, was called a *tabaco*, when in fact it was called a *taboca*. It seems more than probable that Oviedo was confusing the operation of snuffing the powder of a narcotic leguminous tree (*Piptadenia peregrina*) with the smoking of tobacco, of which process called *cohoba* more anon. Furthermore, he was responsible for the belief in the healing qualities so long attributed to tobacco by describing a herb called *perebecenuc*, used by the Indians as a vulnerary, which the credulous leeches of Europe identified with tobacco.

Much ink has been used in etymological argument about the origin of the word tobacco. Some have identified it with Tobago. the island that Daniel Defoe used as the setting for *Robinson Crusoe*; he was never there himself, but no doubt he was able to get a first-hand account of it, which he would have been puzzled to get from Alexander Selkirk's Juan Fernández.

Others have found its origin in the Mexican province of Tabasco. The most ingenious piece of etymology was put forward by Dr Ernst in *The American Anthropologist* in 1889. The learned doctor suggested that when those first two Spaniards saw the natives smoking their 'firebrands' or 'muskets', they asked one of them what he was doing and that he replied 'I am smoking'. In modern Arawak this would be *dattukúpa*. Transpose the last two syllables (and we all know how easily the ear can transpose the syllables of unfamiliar languages) and the reply would sound like *dattupaku*, or remembered by the Spanish strangers as *tupaku*. Later on, the forked instrument called *taboca* was noted; it is not difficult to understand the confusion.

And now before discussing further the problems created by the voyagers, historians, botanists and physicians of four centuries ago, it will be as well to be clear what the tobacco plant is.

The genus Nicotiana is one of about eighty-five genera belonging to the great family of the Solanaceæ which numbers about 1,800 species of trees, shrubs, climbing plants and herbaceous plants, most of which are tropical in origin and most of which were discovered in the New World. Some of the Solanaceæ introduced as food to the Old World often had a mixed reception. MacDonald of Clanranald was pelted by his people with the potatoes he brought to South Uist, and well guided missiles they were. Within living memory the tomato was regarded as a barbarous American vegetable, and the guest was asked by an anxious hostess if he minded the taste of them in a salad. The egg-plant was more favourably received. The chilli and the Cape gooseberry are Solanaceæ. All of that great family, however, are not esculent. Indeed, the potato itself can be poisonous in certain conditions. We have two solanaceous plants, natives of Great Britain, which are highly poisonous. One is *Atropa belladonna*, the Deadly Nightshade; the other is *Hyoscyamus niger*, the Henbane. Nor are the red berries of the Bittersweet or Enchanter's Nightshade which festoons our hedges the best of rural delicacies for children. Among the flowers of the Solanaceæ the petunia, the salpiglossis and the schizanthus are near relations of the tobacco plant.

The genus Nicotiana was established by the great Linnaeus

in 1753 with the two species *Nicotiana tabacum* and *N. rustica*, from which all tobacco originally came and still comes. To-day more than fifty species are listed, and though the leaves of some of these were smoked as a *pis aller* by Indians in the western parts of North America, they were abandoned when they were able to obtain *N. tabacum* and *N. rustica*. The only Nicotiana indigenous outside America is a small group in Australasia of which *N. suaveolens* is the best known, the leaves being chewed by the aborigines. Everybody is familiar with *N. alata* (*affinis* of once upon a time), the white flowers of which perfume our gardens after sunset. There is also the more robust *N. sylvestris*, and a garden hybrid, between *N. alata* and *N. Forgettiana*, called *Sanderae* which has rosy and carmine flowers.

Nicotiana tabacum, the tobacco plant *par excellence*, has never been discovered in a wild state, and it would be as difficult to find the prototype of it as to find the prototype of the grape-vine. To-day under the influence of diverse soils and climates and methods of cultivation, it assumes like the vine different characteristics all over the world. For a long time botanists recognized the Shiraz tobacco of Persia as a separate species under the name *N. persica* native to that country, but *N. persica* has turned out to be *N. tabacum* in a smaller form and with white flowers instead of the rosy-pink ones characteristic of almost all varieties of *N. tabacum*, the seeds of which reached Persia possibly before the sixteenth century came to a close. *N. tabacum* var. *persica* grows not much more than two feet high: the average height of *N. tabacum* is six feet and it grows in certain parts as high as nine feet. Its leafage is very large; a single plant with eighteen leaves can produce over twenty-five square feet. The minute seeds are of extreme vitality, and have been calculated at 400,000 to the ounce. It is treated for agriculture as an annual and the growth is rapid. Its chief of many enemies in America is the hornworm, which is the caterpillar of a large greyish-brown hawk-moth with a wing-spread of five inches. The green caterpillar with oblique white stripes is three and a half inches long and has the usual hawk-moth horn over its posterior. No lepidopterist within my knowledge has discovered what purpose this horn serves. It may be a warning to birds, for the only birds prepared to tackle the hornworm are the turkey and the omnivorous and uncritical domestic-fowl. The laborious task of handpicking is the

accepted operation against the voracious hornworm. Fortunately for potato-growers, the Death's Head hawk-moth has
trouble with our winters, and its solanaceous appetite is represented by a few caterpillars every year to rejoice the hearts
of schoolboys.[1]

The other species used for making tobacco is *Nicotiana
rustica*. This is a smaller plant than *N. tabacum*, and it does not
grow much taller than three feet. The leaves are broad, heavy
and thick, with rounded instead of pointed tips. The flowers of
N. rustica are smaller and of a pale greenish-yellow colour. For a
long time botanists supposed *N. rustica* to be a Hyoscyamus or
Henbane. The original habitat is vaguely attributed to
Mexico, whence it may have spread under cultivation as far
north as Canada. It has been stated that the Cuban tobacco
smoked by the natives at the time of the arrival of Columbus
was *N. rustica*, and that *N. tabacum* was introduced about 1535
from Yucatan, where it had been cultivated for centuries.
To-day *N. rustica* has been virtually superseded by *N. tabacum*
as a commercial smoking product, but it is still grown in parts of
Asia for local consumption and in the Soviet Union, where it is
smoked as 'makhorka'. It is also grown to a small extent in
some other countries including Syria, but the famous latakia
of Syria is *N. tabacum*.

There have been several attempts by scholars to maintain
that *Nicotiana tabacum* and *N. rustica* were indigenous to Europe,
Africa and Asia; but every one of their arguments has been
refuted, and there does not seem much point in knocking down
such easy Aunt Sallies. We know from Herodotus and others
that smoke played a part in religious rites: we know that the
smoke of herbs was inhaled for maladies of the chest in medieval
England. We still inhale the steam from a basin of friar's
balsam in boiling water under a towel to relieve a cold on the
chest. In the middle of the nineteenth century the imaginary
antiquity of smoking was used to support the most preposterous
arguments against tobacco. Misguided preachers would proclaim from the pulpit that the Forbidden Fruit that led to the
Fall was in fact tobacco. No doubt if women had smoked as
freely as they do to-day, the preachers would have been more
certain than ever about Eve's part in the unfortunate business.

[1] Reports of the perfect moth all over the west of Scotland and even in the
Hebrides are numerous in this year, 1956.

If either *N. tabacum* or *rustica* had grown in Eden, they would have provided much more adequate wearing material than the fig-tree.

The accepted judgment of scholars is that Amerigo Vespucci's claim to have discovered the mainland of South America in the month of June 1497 is not justified, and that John Cabot's discovery of the mainland of North America, a week later in the same year, entitles him to the honour. Whether that be so or not, Amerigo Vespucci managed to get the New World called after him. However, the Bristol of to-day may take pride in the fact that Cabot's enterprise was largely financed by Bristol merchants and that the *Mathew* sailed from Bristol to give Europeans their first sight of the continent which would one day be the greatest producer of tobacco in the world. If that sinister skinflint Henry VII had had the enterprise to back Columbus, which he missed doing, England might have had the whole of the New World.

An account of the four voyages of Amerigo Vespucci was published in 1507 by Waldseemüller, a professor in the college of St Dié in Lorraine; it was he who suggested that the New World should be called America. His book was a success, and when he realized that the honour of discovery belonged to Columbus it was too late to get the name changed to Columbia. Vespucci is of importance in the history of tobacco, because on the voyage which he undoubtedly did make to the New World in the summer of 1499 he visited an island off Venezuela where he saw tobacco being chewed.

"We found therein," he would relate in 1504, "the most brutish and uncivilized people and yet the most gracious and kind . . . each had his cheeks bulging with a certain green herb which they chewed like cattle. . . . And hanging from his neck each carried two dried gourds one of which was full of the herb he kept in his mouth, the other full of a certain white flour like powdered chalk. Frequently each put a small stick (which had been moistened and chewed in his mouth) into the gourd filled with flour, each then drew it forth and put it in both sides of his cheeks, thus mixing the flour with the herb which their mouths contained."

It is fairly safe to presume that this herb was tobacco and that the flour was powdered shells, providing the lime that would help to release the mild narcotic qualities of the leaf.

Now we come to the process of what seems to be snuffing. Oviedo's Y-shaped *taboca* was not used for smoking; it was used for *cohoba* or snuffing. As mentioned previously, *cohoba* was not tobacco. However, Oviedo's mistake, obtained currency, and *cohoba* came to be accepted for a while in Europe as a native word for tobacco. The snuffing of the powdered seeds of *Piptadenia peregrina* may have led to the snuffing of the powdered leaves of tobacco, but the phrenzy induced by *cohoba* had nothing in common with the soothing qualities of tobacco.[1]

We find in Oviedo what may be considered the first reference to the cigarette. A Spanish captain, Juan de Grijalva, made an expedition to Mexico in 1518, and in Yucatan he and his men were received in friendly fashion by an old cacique, who caused a bower to be built in the shade of which they sat and were each offered a small tube alight at one end. Oviedo goes on to relate that these tubes slowly consumed themselves without giving forth a flame, the smoke being fragrant like an incense stick of Valencia. The strangers were advised by signs to inhale this smoke. From Mexico some years later would come reports of the Aztecs smoking reed tubes filled with tobacco and the fragrant resin of liquidambar, the sunset hues of whose leaves in autumn may be seen in many of our own gardens.

There remains to record what some smokers, including the present writer, will regard as the most important smoking news given to the Old World by those ancient mariners that ventured into the mysterious West: this was the first mention of the pipe.

In 1545 was published in Paris the *Brief Recit* of the Breton seafarer, Jacques Cartier, who between 1534 and 1536 made two voyages to Canada. In 1580 this was 'turned into English' by John Florio, whose version of Montaigne's Essays is one of the glories of translation. It was at Hochelaga (Montreal) that Cartier saw the Iroquois Indians smoking pipes, and it could be wished that adventurers in the Spanish Main had given the earlier chroniclers as clear an account of their first experience

---

[1] This snuff is called *yopo* by the Indians of Colombia and Venezuela. There is another snuff called *yakee* made from the bark of the Virola, a tree closely related to the nutmeg. In the *Illustrated London News* (September 29th, 1956) Dr R. E. Schultes of Harvard describes the way this *yakee* snuff is taken by the Indians of Colombia: "using the characteristic V-shaped birdbone by means of which the natives blow the powder into the nostrils."

of men smoking as Cartier gave. Here it is in the words of Florio's translation:

> There groweth also a certain kind of Herb, whereof in Summer they make great provision for all the year, making great account of it, and only men use of it, and first, they cause it to be dried in the Sun, then wear it about their neck wrapped in a little beast's skin made like a little bag, with a hollow piece of stone or wood like a pipe: then when they please they make powder of it, and then put it in one of the ends of the said cornet or pipe, and laying a coal of fire upon it, at the other end suck so long that they fill their bodies full of smoke, till that it cometh out of their mouth and nostrils, even as out of the tunnel of a chimney. They say that this doth keep them warm and in health; they never go without some of it about them. We ourselves have tried the same smoke, and having put it in our mouths, it seemed that they had filled it with Pepper dust it is so hot.

In one paragraph we have for the first time the mention of tobacco-growing, tobacco-curing, the tobacco-pouch and the pipe itself; we have also the first intelligible presentation of the smoker's point of view. The word 'pipe' for a musical instrument goes back all but a thousand years in English, but the word 'pipe' for a tobacco-pipe was used for the first time in English by John Florio in the year 1580 when 'he turned into English' that "short and brief narrative of the two Navigations and Discoveries to the Northwest parts called New France" as "worthy the reading of all Venturers, Travellers, and Discoverers". The first authority for 'tobacco-pipe' quoted by the *Oxford English Dictionary* is from an anonymous play in 1594, and with profound respect to the editors and compilers of that mighty work it may be suggested that the next supplementary volume issued of the great Oxford dictionary should attribute the first use of pipe as an instrument for smoking to John Florio, who was himself an Oxford man from Magdalen College.

Now we approach the vexed questions who first brought tobacco to Europe and who first smoked it there. The *Jewish Encyclopædia* says that the scholarly Luis de Torres settled in Cuba, learned there the use of tobacco and introduced it into Europe. Corti [1] says that his companion on that November day in 1492, Rodrigo de Jerez, returned to Europe and gave a

[1] Count Corti, *A History of Smoking* (Harrap, 1931).

demonstration of smoking in his native town of Ayamonte, which persuaded his neighbours that the Devil had taken possession of him. The parish priest denounced de Jerez to the Inquisition and he was committed to prison for several years, on emerging from which he found that his countrymen were smoking without interference. Alas, it is impossible to find any evidence to justify either statement. The two members of Columbus's crew who saw the first cigars being smoked near Havana vanished forthwith from recorded history.

Eighty years were to pass before smoking became so general in Europe that tobacco assumed importance as an article of commerce. This was accepted by historians until Thacher in his life of Christopher Columbus quoted a clause in the second will of Christopher's son Diego executed in 1523, which began "*A Antonio, tobaco mercador*", translated by Thacher as "To Antonio, tobacco merchant, a Genoese who was accustomed to live in Lisbon, 2,500 reals of Portugal". Henri Harrisse, however, in his life of Christopher Columbus published at Paris in 1884 before Thacher's biography appeared, had already queried the clause, pointing out that *tabaco* not *tobaco* would have been good Spanish and further that Antonio should have been described as *mercador de tobaco* not *tobaco mercador*. However, the matter was not finally cleared up until 1893, when the publication in Rome of the *Raccolta di documenti* revealed that the clause began "*A Antonioto Baço, mercador*", and in fact that Baço was the name of the beneficiary and had nothing to do with tobacco. Yet the mistake is still repeated from time to time, and I am reminded of Dr Routh's advice to an undergraduate predecessor of mine at Magdalen College always to verify his references, though I hasten to admit humbly that I do not expect to fulfil the task I have set myself without being convicted of erroneous statements, try I never so hard to verify my own references.

Columbus brought back after his first voyage some unfortunate Indians and the novel *hamaca* which became 'hammock' in English, but there is not a tittle of evidence that he brought back any of those dry tobacco leaves he had seen for the first time on that October day in 1492. What seems to be the earliest reference to the cultivation of tobacco in Europe occurs in a herbal by Rembert Dodoens printed at Antwerp in 1554. In this appears the first illustration of *Nicotiana rustica*, under the name *Hyoscyamus luteus*, yellow henbane, but the Mechlin physician does not say anything about its novelty and identifies it with the henbane mentioned by Pliny and Galen. Twenty years later, in another work on purging roots, he reprinted the illustration of *H. luteus* and added another which he called *H. peruvianus*, henbane of Peru.

In 1558 Frère André Thevet, a Franciscan of Angoulême who had been in Brazil three years earlier, published a book called *Les Singularitez de la France Antarctique*, which at that moment was the French name for America. This was translated into English by Thomas Hacket, and published in London under the title of *The New Found Worlde* in 1568. It contains the first account in English of tobacco:

There is another secret herb which they name in their language *Petun*, the which most commonly they bear about them, for that they esteem it marvellous profitable for many things. . . . They gather this herb very charily, and dry it within their little cabanes or houses. Their manner to use it is this; they wrap a quantity of this herb being dry in a leaf of a Palm tree which is very great, and so they make rolls of the length of a candle, and then they fire the one end, and receive the smoke thereof by their nose and by their mouth. They say it is very wholesome to cleanse and consume the superfluous humours of the brain. Moreover being taken after this sort, it keepeth the parties from hunger and thirst for a time, therefore they use it ordinarily. Also when they have any secret talk or counsel among themselves, they draw this smoke, and then they speak. The which they do customably one after another in the councils of war. . . . The women use it by no means. If that they take too much of this perfume, it will make them light in the head, as the smell or taste of strong wine. The Christians that do now inhabit there are become very desirous of this herb and perfume, although that the first use thereof is not without danger, before that one is accustomed thereto, for this smoke causeth sweats and weakness, even to fall into a syncope, the which I have tried myself.

Brother André Thevet has been accused of romancing about his travels, but he seems without doubt to have accompanied that abortive French expedition to prospect for a colony in Brazil, and he gave a much more accurate account of the use and effect of tobacco than several others. The last sentence from that excerpt might serve any schoolboy as a description of the result of a rash adventure with a cigar. The word *petun* will be noticed. Either as *petun* or *petum*, the word of the Guarani Indians of Brazil for tobacco competed in Europe for a while with tobacco itself. Tobacco won, but *petun* was awarded the petunia as a godchild, that popular cousin of Nicotiana from the Argentine, whose flowers are the joy of the professional gardener.

But the most important claim of Thevet is that he was the first man to bring the seeds of that *petun* or *petum* from Brazil to Europe, and that he was growing it in his garden in Angoulême some years before Nicot was given the credit for sending seeds to France from Lisbon.

Jean Nicot was Ambassador to the King of Portugal from 1559 to 1561, and according to one story when visiting the Lisbon prisons he was presented by the keeper with a strange herb given to him by a mariner from Florida. Nicot planted the herb in his garden, where it flourished and multiplied. A relative of one of Nicot's pages suffering from an ulcer was cured by a poultice made of the crushed leaves. Soon afterwards the Ambassador's cook nearly cut off his thumb, and he too was cured by the new plant. Nicot, impressed by various tales about the healing powers of the herb, sent seeds to Catherine de Medici the Queen Mother and to others at the Court. He wrote to the Cardinal of Lorraine in 1560 that he had acquired a marvellous Indian herb of proved efficacy against ulcers and fistulas given up by the physicians. He added that he would send the Cardinal's gardener some seed and a specimen of the plant itself packed in a barrel with instructions for replanting and cultivating it. This he did when the Cardinal's brother, Francis, the famed Prior of France, arrived at Lisbon with a fleet of galleons. The seeds sent by Nicot were duly sown and in the enthusiasm roused by the cures effected it was proposed to call this panacea of a herb *Nicotiane*, though some were for calling it *Herbe de la Reine* in honour of the Queen Mother. On the suggestion of the Duke of Guise it was called *Nicotiane*, to become *Nicotiana* in Latin, and finally, when the alkaloid in tobacco leaves was obtained by the experiments of Posselt and Reimann in 1828, it was designated nicotine.

Poor old Thevet, who by now was sixty and was to live for another thirty years, felt bitter about Jean Nicot's name being used. He declared that he had brought the seeds of *petun* from Brazil to France several years before his rival. It has been suggested that Thevet did not make any claims for his garden in Angoulême until the new plant became famous as a panacea. This can hardly be true because Thevet, in his work *La Cosmographie Universelle*, published in 1575, protests in obvious exasperation against the curative virtues that were being proclaimed for the new herb, and declares that the account he gave of its use by Indians was authentic.

An opinionated Geneva minister, Jean de Léry, who had been in Brazil soon after Thevet, when the Protestants of France were considering an early *Mayflower* project, declared that Thevet could not have grown the tropical *petun* in a French garden. By 1570, when de Léry's *Histoire d'un Voyage* was published at La Rochelle, the gardens of France were full of *Nicotiana rustica; N. tabacum* was still a rarity. On the whole, we can accord to Thevet the justice of his claim to have brought the first seeds of *petun* or *N. tabacum* to France; as he pointed out, it was unknown in Florida whence Nicot's seeds had come. Yet *N. tabacum* must very soon have reached Portugal, because one or two writers about this time speak of the beauty of the new Indian herb as a garden plant. That would be true of *N. tabacum*, but nobody could claim floral beauty for *N. rustica*.

In conclusion, we can decide that Nicotiana is a more euphonious name than Thevetiana would have been.

Seeds sent by Nicot to Duke Charles, of Lorraine, flourished in his garden; the Duke, who may have read about *cohoba*, experimented with the powdered leaves of tobacco, and was the first Frenchman to make snuff, of which he became so fond that he was said to take three ounces a day of it. The Queen Mother took medicated snuff for headaches, and medicated or not, snuff gained increasing popularity at the French court, to become the rage in the early years of the reign of Louis XIII.

In 1570, a new edition of *L'Agriculture et Maison Rustique* of Charles Estienne by his son-in-law Jean Liébault, put the name *Nicotiane* into print for the first time, and claimed that he had received information about the new herb, which "deserveth Palm and Price among all other Medicinable herbs", from Jean Nicot himself.

Dr Nicolas Monardes, a Seville physician, who had not mentioned tobacco in the first part of his book *Las Indias*

Occidentales, now published a second part in 1571 in which he put forward the claim of Spain, where it had been growing in the gardens for some years, to have introduced the new panacea to Europe. Francisco Hernández, physician to Philip II of Spain, had been despatched by his royal master to study the flora of Mexico, and in 1558 had brought back numerous specimens to Spain, among them both *N. tabacum* and *N. rustica*. Hernández may have been the first with *N. tabacum*, but we know from Dodoens that probably as early as 1554 *N. rustica* was growing in Belgium.

The work of Monardes gained immediate favour, and to him must be attached the chief responsibility for that renown of tobacco as a panacea which was to last for another two hundred years and make us wonder to-day how physicians managed to remain so credulous.

Castore Durante, writing in Italian, was as uncritically enthusiastic about the new panacea as Monardes. He proposed to call the new plant *Erba Santa Croce* in honour of Cardinal Prospero di Santa Croce who in 1571 had brought seeds to Rome from Lisbon where he had been a papal nuncio, thereby, Durante adds, providing as great a boon for the people of Rome as his ancestors did when they brought back the wood of the Holy Cross for the consolation of all Christendom. The seeds that the Cardinal brought to Italy from Portugal must have been *N. rustica*, but *N. tabacum* arrived there by 1574 from France, having been sent to Italy by Nicolò Tornabuoni, the Tuscan Ambassador to France, as a cure for an episcopal relative of his in Florence.

It is to be noted that none of these mid-sixteenth-century writers says anything about smoking in Europe, and yet mariners in various parts must surely have indulged in it. If the Spaniards in Cuba bothered to import the seeds of *N. tabacum* from Mexico in 1535 it suggests a taste for cultivated tobacco, and it does seem extraordinary that there is no record of smoking in Spain beyond a few apocryphal tales published much later.

Cardinal Crescenzio was credited with the introduction of smoking into Italy, and of snuffing too. He was said to have learnt to smoke from Virginio Orsino, who himself had learnt how in England, where by the beginning of the seventeenth century the habit was general. What one would be glad to discover with certainty was the man who introduced smoking to England.

Chapter 2

I N January 1571 there was published in London a botanical work written in Latin by Pierre Pena and Matthias de l'Obel, but the work was in manuscript at least by 1569 and probably earlier. Pena and de l'Obel speak of tobacco as a familiar plant in English gardens, and connect it with the cultivation of *N. rustica* in Portugal. De l'Obel's services to botany are commemorated by the lobelia. William Harrison, writing of 1573 in his *Great Chronologie* some of which is even to-day still in manuscript, stated:

> In these days the taking-in of the smoke of the Indian herb called 'Tabaco' by an instrument formed like a little ladell [an early clay pipe?], whereby it passeth from the mouth into the head and stomach, is greatly taken-up and used in England against Rheums and some other diseases engendered in the lungs and inward parts, and not without effect. This herb is not so common but that for want thereof divers do practise for the like purposes with the Nicetian [i.e. *N. rustica*]; otherwise called in Latin, Hyoscyamus luteus or the yellow henbane, albeit not without great error; for, although that herb be a sovereign healer of old ulcers and sores reputed incurable outwardly, yet is not the smoke or vapour thereof so profitable to be received inwardly.

Harrison was no doubt considering the two species of Nicotiana from the point of view of medicine rather than aroma, but how right he was in according the superiority to *N. tabacum*, of which he goes on to give the first original description in English:

> The herb is commonly of the height of a man, garnished with great long leaves . . . bearing seed, coloured and of quantity like unto, or rather less than, the fine marjoram; the herb itself is yearly, coming up also of the shaking of the seed, the colour of the flower is carnation, resembling that of the lemon in form; the root yellow with many fillets, and thereto very small in comparison, if you respect the substance of the herb.

There is no doubt whatever from this description that Harrison had himself seen *N. tabacum* in cultivation. But who brought it into England? The accepted attribution by several of the tobacco historians and commentators is to Sir Francis Drake, but this is too late: Drake did not get back from his third voyage to the West Indies, where *N. tabacum* was the staple crop, until August 1573. Harrison is accurate about dates, and he was clearly already aware by 1573 not only of the botanical difference between *N. tabacum* and *N. rustica* but also of the different medical values ascribed to them—the former being useful for rheums and catarrhs, the latter for external application to wounds and sores. On the whole, it is safe to say that *N. tabacum* must have found its way to England before 1571, when Pena and de l'Obel's book was published. This is what they say of it:

> You will observe shipmasters and all others who come back from out there [the New World] using little funnels, made of palm leaves or straw, in the extreme end of which they stuff crumbled dried leaves of this plant. This they light, and opening their mouths as much as they can, they suck in the Smoke with their breath. By this they say their hunger and thirst are allayed, their strength restored, and their spirits refreshed. And they declare also that their brain is lulled with a pleasing drunkenness, and that an incredible quantity of phlegm is expelled. We have found, nevertheless, that while we drink this in, it does not inebriate quickly, nor drive one mad, nor benumb the senses as does hyoscyamus [i.e. true henbane] but it fills the ventricles of the brain with a certain vaporous perfume.[1]

The illustration which accompanies this valuably lucid description shows an enormous cigar being smoked by what looks like a juggler balancing a reeking cornucopia on his chin. We hear for the first time of sailors home from the sea smoking, and it is fair to claim that this is the earliest accurate account of the effect of smoking on the smoker.

Then, obviously not yet quite prepared to banish Nicotiana from the genus Hyoscyamus which holds the deadly hyoscine of Dr Crippen and probably of Hamlet's uncle's hebenon, the authors conclude:

> No proved harm is done to us by this yellow hyoscyamus, so truly called the *holy herb*, and its fame is now resounding everywhere. Our age has discovered nothing from the New

[1] Quoted as a translation from the Latin in Arents, Vol. I, No. 13.

World which will be numbered among the remedies more valuable and efficacious than this plant for sores, wounds, affections of the throat and chest, and the fever of the plague.

It will be noticed that the authors now claim for one herb the medical qualities which a few sentences earlier they had divided between what were later to be called *Nicotiana tabacum* and *Nicotiana rustica*. It seems clear, too, that the smoking which the authors obviously enjoyed was the smoking of *N. tabacum*. Thomas Pennant in his *Tour in Wales* (1810) wrote of William Myddelton, a Welsh poet of two centuries earlier:

> It is said that he, with Captain Thomas Price of Plâsyollin, and one Captain Koet were the first who smoked, or (as they called it) drank tobacco publicly in London, and that the Londoners flocked from all parts to see them. Pipes were not then invented, so they used the twisted leaves, or segars.

Pennant's authority for this statement were the unpublished Sebright manuscripts which had been lent to him. Myddelton was born *c.* 1556, and therefore this incident can hardly have occurred before 1580. It was Myddelton who in 1591 commanded the pinnace which "like a fluttered bird came flying from far away" to warn Lord Thomas Howard lying off Flores in the Azores of the immediate approach of an overwhelming Spanish fleet. It was then that Sir Richard Grenville in Drake's Armada flagship the *Revenge* insisted on remaining to take aboard his sick from ashore and to fight the Spaniards alone. William Myddelton's brother, Sir Hugh, traded in tobacco later, and in *Londinium Redivivum* (1801) J. P. Malcolm mentions a tradition in the city of London that he and Sir Walter Ralegh used to smoke together in the door of his warehouse.

Pennant was wrong in saying that pipes had not been invented when the three sea-captains excited the attention of the London citizens, but he was probably right in supposing that pipes had not yet reached London. When *did* they arrive?

In July 1565 Sir John Hawkins, looking for fresh water along the coast of Florida, found a French colony there, and in John Sparke's report of this when he returned home in September of that year we read:

> The Floridians when they travel, have a kind of herb dried, who with a cane and an earthen cup in the end, with fire, and the dried herbs put together, do suck through the cane the

smoke thereof; which smoke satisfieth their hunger, and therewith they live four or five days without meat or drink, and this all the Frenchmen used for this purpose; yet do they hold opinions withal, that it causeth water and steam to void from their stomachs.

If any of Hawkins's crew brought back to England either pipes or leaves or seed, it would have been the seeds of *N. rustica* that they brought; at this date *N. tabacum* was not growing anywhere on the mainland of North America north of Mexico. There is no justification for the confident statement of so many historians that pipes and tobacco in England date back to this second West Indies voyage of John Hawkins. It is easier to believe that both *N. tabacum* and *N. rustica* were growing as rarities in gardens and that any experiments made in smoking their leaves were made in the interests of science, botanical or medical. Pennant's observation about the pipe's not having been invented when those three sea-captains, no doubt primed with wine, smoked 'segars' in the streets of London suggests that the authors of the manuscript he read knew nothing about pipes. The curious anxiety of some tobacco historians to deprive Ralegh of all credit for introducing tobacco leads them occasionally into rash assertions. I have seen it stated in print that the Statute of Labourers in 1563 laid down that no man or woman might be employed in making clay tobacco-pipes without serving a five-year apprenticeship in the craft. What the Statute of Labourers laid down was a five-year apprenticeship for any craft, and the London pipe-makers appealed to it to stop the Bristol pipe-makers cutting them out. But that was years later.

It was in April 1584 that Sir Walter Ralegh sent his first expedition to North America under Captain Philip Amadas and Captain Arthur Barlowe. They sailed up by way of the coast of Florida and took possession of Roanoke Island and other land in what is now called North Carolina. At that date all the eastern coast of North America from Newfoundland down to Florida was known as Virginia in honour of Queen Elizabeth I.

Amadas and Barlowe brought back with them what King James I would one day call two or three 'poor barbarous savages', who smoked for the gaping Londoners and soon died far from home. Ralegh may have already had experience

of tobacco in a pipe while he was serving at La Rochelle with
the Huguenots from 1569 to 1572, and it seems a reasonable
conjecture that when in 1585 he equipped his second expedition, this time to found a colony, he enjoined upon the leaders
the desirability of bringing a good store of tobacco to England.
Sir Richard Grenville was in command of the transport;
Ralph Lane was to be the first Governor; Ralegh's mathe-
matical tutor Thomas Hariot, then only twenty-five years old,
was despatched as surveyor. The colonists landed at Wokoken
Island in North Carolina, whence they explored the country
inland. Soon they were in difficulties with the natives and with
provisions. Therefore when Sir Francis Drake arrived in the
spring of 1586 on the way home from his West Indian raiding
expedition the colonists asked him to put them aboard. Grenville arriving not long afterwards with supplies found Roanoke
and Wokoken Islands both abandoned.

An account by Hariot of the expedition equipped by Ralegh
was published in 1588, and his remarks on tobacco are helpful:

There is an herb which is sowed apart by itself and is
called by the inhabitants *Uppówoc*. In the West Indies it hath
divers names, according to the several places and countries
where it groweth and is used : the Spaniards generally call it
Tabacco. The leaves thereof being dried and brought into
powder, they use to take the fume or smoke thereof by sucking it through pipes made of clay into their stomachs and
head ; from whence it purgeth superfluous steam and other
gross humours, openeth all the pores and passages of the
body ; by which means the use thereof not only preserveth
the body from obstructions, but also if any be, so that they
have not been of too long continuance, in short time breaketh
them ; whereby their bodies are notably preserved in health,
and know not many grievous diseases wherewithal we in
England are oftentimes afflicted.

This *Uppówoc* is of so precious estimation amongst them,
that they think their gods are marvellously delighted therewith. Whereupon sometime they make hallowed fires and
cast some of the powder therein for a sacrifice ; being in a
storm upon the waters, to pacify their gods, they cast some up
into the air and into the water : so a weir for fish being newly
set up, they cast some therein and into the air : also after an
escape from danger, they cast some into the air likewise : but
all done with strange gestures, stamping, sometime dancing,

clapping of hands, holding up of hands, and staring up into
the heavens, uttering therewithal and chattering strange
words and noises.

With similar reverence was wine, that other divine gift to
man, celebrated. As yet the mere fringes of the mighty North
American continent had been here and there explored; the
future would reveal that all over it the Red Indians treated
tobacco with reverence, and that since how many years ago
they had been doing so archæological excavation would in due
course hazard guesses: it was certainly an immensely long
time.

To us of to-day the concluding paragraph of Hariot's
relation is the most vital:

> We ourselves during the time we were there used to suck
> it after their manner, as also since our return, and have found
> many rare and wonderful experiments of the virtues thereof,
> of which the relation would require a volume of itself: the
> use of it by so many of late, men and women of great calling
> as else, and some learned Physicians also, is sufficient witness.

Drake came back in 1586 from that plundering voyage of
his with a good store of *N. tabacum* which the inhabitants of
Dominica had surrendered, and the fact that he thought this
worth-while transporting home suggests that there was already
some demand for tobacco in England. Nevertheless, it was by
those disheartened colonists who brought back *N. rustica*, and
more important still the clay pipe, that the passion for smoking
which would presently seize England under the example of
Walter Ralegh was kindled.

A footnote De l'Escluse added to his abridged translation of
Monardes, in 1605, confirms Hariot's account:

> In the year 1585 . . . they found that the Inhabitants did
> frequently use some Pipes made of clay, to draw forth the
> fume of Tobacco leaves set on fire; which grew amongst
> them in great quantity, or rather to drink it down, to pre-
> serve their health. The English returning from thence
> (Virginy), brought the like pipes with them, to drink the
> smoke of Tobacco; and since that time, the use of drinking
> Tobacco hath so much prevailed all *England* over, especially
> amongst the Courtiers, that they have caused many such
> like Pipes to be made to drink Tobacco with.

In the summer of 1587 another expedition which Ralegh helped to finance carried colonists to Virginia; when supplies ran out, John White in command of the expedition sailed away to obtain more, leaving behind eighty-nine men and seventeen women, including his own daughter and her child. In the opening of 1588 Ralegh fitted out a relief expedition of two ships, but the captains turned it into a privateering adventure, and after being knocked about by some La Rochelle warships came back to England. When in 1589 a relief ship did reach Virginia, there was no sign of any colonists and no trace of them was ever discovered: they may have tried to explore the interior in search of gold.

Ralegh had spent over £40,000 on a dream; we could call it half a million to-day. As late as 1603, when he himself would very soon be a prisoner in the Tower for many weary years, he was still preoccupied with the future of Virginia.

It is a tribute to the larger view of life that smokers in general were able to take compared with non-smokers that they recognized who it was that more than anybody made tobacco a vital contribution to the greatness of that magical alloy of peoples we call British. Whatever the meticulous and grudging historian may declare, it is to Sir Walter Ralegh that we owe the popularity of tobacco. That he never went to Virginia himself is beside the point. That he may never have smoked tobacco until his friend and tutor Thomas Hariot taught him how to smoke one of those clay pipes brought back with him from Virginia in 1586 does not detract from his influence. Until Ralegh's surrender to tobacco as a profitable pleasure for the body and mind of man, the main importance of tobacco was medicinal.

> We ourselves . . . used to suck it . . . as also since our return, and we have found many rare and wonderful experiments of the virtues thereof, of which the relation would require a volume of itself.

Ralph Lane may have endorsed what Hariot was to write about the pipe, and the story that he presented Ralegh with an Indian pipe may well be true, but it may also be true that when Captain Amadas and Captain Barlowe returned from that expedition which took possession of Virginia in the name of Queen Elizabeth they introduced Ralegh to the pipe.

We may recall that Harrison as early as 1573 had seen tobacco smoked in 'little ladells' for medicinal administration, and that for this reason some have attempted to give Sir John Hawkins the credit of introducing pipe-smoking to England as early as 1565. The fact remains that it was not until Ralegh discovered the delight of smoking a pipe that England began to follow his example, and the testimony to this comes from his remorseless enemy King James I, as we shall see presently. To disprove the authenticity of the story about Ralegh's servant trying to extinguish him when he was smoking does not invalidate the tradition that Ralegh was the first man to make smoking popular, not merely in England, let it be added, but through the English example in other parts of Europe.

That tale about extinguishing the smoker was a bit of domestic folk-lore recurrent everywhere during the early part of the seventeenth century, and it was not pinned on to Ralegh until 1708 in an ephemeral periodical called the *British Apollo*. Nevertheless, it should be recognized that no bit of domestic folk-lore survives unless it is, as the Italians say, *ben trovato*. It may not *be* true, but it *could* be true. Canute and the incoming tide, King Alfred and the burnt cakes, Ralegh and his pipe, and many such another tale may err against probability, but not like too many writers of tales against possibility.

It is not worth discussing the claims of the half dozen or so houses in which Ralegh smoked his first pipe; it is worth recording that he certainly planted tobacco and potatoes at Youghal, his house in the south of Ireland, and that to him the Irish owed the potato, which was still hardly known in Scotland or England at the beginning of the eighteenth century.

The tobacco grown at Youghal was *Nicotiana rustica*, and Ralegh is said to have arranged for its curing at Durham House, which stood near where the Adelphi stood and where now rises the great concrete pile of Shell-Mex. He seems to have genuinely preferred English tobacco, and his taste for it endured to the end.

John Parkinson in his *Theatrum Botanicum* in 1640 would write:

I have in my former book [the famous *Paradisi in Sole*, published in 1629] given you the knowledge of divers sorts of Tobacco, such as for their flowers' sake might be fit to be nursed up in gardens.

These had been what was then called Indian tobacco
(*N. tabacum*). He now goes on to speak of what

we do usually call in England English tobacco . . . because
it is more commonly growing in every country garden almost,
and better endureth than the other . . . This kind of Tobacco,
although it be not thought so strong, or sweet for such as
take it by the pipe, and yet I have known Sir Walter Ralegh,
when he was prisoner in the Tower, make choice of this sort
to make good Tobacco of, which he knew so rightly to cure as
they call it, that it was held almost as good as that which
came from the Indies, and fully as good as any other made in
England.

By this time the growing of tobacco in England had become
a serious problem, having started after the return of the first
colonists from Virginia in 1586, but that story must wait for a
while.

The tale that Ralegh invited Queen Elizabeth to try a pipe
is usually considered apocryphal, but there is abundant
evidence from contemporary sources that the ladies of Queen
Elizabeth's court did smoke pipes. The tale was that the Queen
took two or three whiffs and was then seized with a nausea,
observing which some of the Earl of Leicester's faction whispered that Sir Walter had certainly poisoned her. "But Her
Majesty in a short while recovering, made the Countess of
Nottingham and all her maids smoke a whole pipe out among
them."

Ralegh himself made only a single reference to tobacco in
his books. This was in *The Discoverie of the Large Rich and
Bewtiful Empire of Guiana, with a relation of the Great and Golden
Citie of Manoa (which the Spaniards call El Dorado). Performed in the
yeare* 1595 *by Sir W. Ralegh Knight, Captaine of Her Majesties
Guard, Lord Warden of the Stanneries, and Her Highnesse Lieutenant
Generall of the Countie of Cornewall. Imprinted at London by Robert
Robinson.* 1596.

From that voyage up the Orinoco through the middle of
Venezuela, Ralegh returned with gold and the first mahogany
to reach England. His enemies put it about that the voyage was
a fiction; *The Discoverie* was written to refute them.

The allusion to tobacco, though brief, is significant. It occurs
in the description of

A quayside scene in old Virginia showing tobacco being shipped for England

the Tivitivas that dwell upon the branches of Orenoque. . . .
Those called Cupuri and Macureo are for the most part
Carpenters of *Canoas*, for they make the most and fayrest
houses, and sell them into Guiana for golde, and into *Trinedado*
for *Tobacco*, in the excessive taking whereof they exceed all
nations, and notwithstanding the moistness of the aire in
which they live . . . in all my life either in the Indies or in
Europe did I never beholde a more goodlie or better favoured
people, or more manlie.

His thoughts may sometimes have turned to those tobacco-
smoking Indians when he was immured in the Bloody Tower
for those fourteen weary years, and compared them not un-
favourably with the tobacco-hating King James. He was to
sail once again to Guiana when he was released, still under
sentence of death, to find gold for James. Everything went
wrong: even his son and heir died up the Orinoco. He came
back to England and to death.

Ralegh's only other reference to tobacco is in a note he made
in his will on October 29th, 1618:

> Sir Lewis Stukeley sold all the tobacco at Plimouth of
> which, for the most part of it, I gave him a fift part of it, as
> also a role for my Lord Admirall and a role for himself. . . .
> I desire that hee may give his account for the tobacco.

It was Stukeley, his treacherous cousin, who as Vice-
Admiral of Devon had arrested the old hero on his return from
that last fatal voyage to Guiana. He had also foiled Ralegh's
escape to France, and he became the Sir Judas Stukeley of public
indignation. To everybody's delight he and his son were
charged a few months later with clipping coin, for this was a
hanging matter. Stukeley was found guilty, but King James
pardoned him; even he could feel grateful to Sir Judas for the
part he had played first by preventing his enemy's escape and
then by giving hostile evidence against him at the trial.
Stukeley became an outcast from society, and at last he fled
from popular hatred to the isle of Lundy, where in 1620 he
died raving mad.

Ralegh smoked in the Bloody Tower and worked there for
seven years at his noble *History of the World*, in which may be
read what will serve as his own immortal epitaph:

> O eloquent, just and mighty Death! Whom none could
> advise, thou hast persuaded; what none hath dared thou hast

done ; and whom all the world hath flattered thou only hath cast out of the world and despised. Thou hast drawn together all the far-stretched greatness, all the pride, cruelty, and ambition of man, and covered it all over with these two narrow words : *Hic jacet*.

One of the glories of English prose was penned by the greatest Elizabethan of them all, who as he wrote *hic jacet* must have laid down his quill and picked up his pipe.

Aubrey, writing some fifty years after the execution of Ralegh, says that he smoked a little before he went to the scaffold—"which some formall persons were scandalized at, but I thinke it was well, and properly donne to settle his spirits."

As he smoked his farewell pipe he may have thought of that last speech to his judges when he declared:

> I shall speak of the imputation laid upon me through the jealousy of the people that I had been on persecution of my lord of Essex; that I rejoiced at his death, and stood in a window over-against him when he suffered, and puffed out tobacco in defiance of him ; when, as God is my witness, that I shed tears for him when he died.

When he had smoked that final pipe, Ralegh walked with a firm step to the scaffold. "He was the most fearless of death that ever was known; and the most resolute and confident, yet with reverence and conscience." On the scaffold he asked for the axe, and running his finger along the edge said: "This is sharp medicine, but it is a sure cure for all diseases." The headsman, dismayed by Ralegh's tranquil courage, hesitated. "What dost thou fear?" Ralegh asked. "Strike, man, strike!"

The curious can see Sir Walter's pipe-case to-day in the Wallace Collection, which may be part of the tobacco-box described by Ralph Thoresby, the Yorkshire antiquarian, in whose possession it was until his death in 1725. He says:

> Sir Walter Ralegh's tobacco-box, as it is called, but is rather the Case for the Glass wherein it was preserved, which was surrounded with small wax candles of curious colours. This is of gilded Leather, like a snuff-case, above half a foot broad and 13 inches high, and hath cases for Sixteen Pipes within it.

The object in the Wallace Collection is a pouch of red

leather containing two clay pipes, each in two parts, with silver mounts, and a tobacco stopper of bone in the shape of a finger.

There is an inscription from Cicero cut into the leather, *"Comes meus fuit in illo miserrimo tempore"* ("It was my companion in that most wretched time"). Under that within a heart are the initials W. R. and the date 1617.

A piece of paper enclosed with the pouch affirms in modern handwriting: "This was the last gift of the honourable and learned knight Sir Walter Ralegh to his loving friend Sir Henry Spelman, Ralph Whitfield, Barbican." On the other side is written, "Spelman, Sir Walter's friend, Ralph Whitfield, Spelman's son-in-law. In his family, till bought by deceased husband of present owner." [1]

Apperson says that when excavations were being made round the foundations of Ralegh's house at Youghal a clay pipe-bowl was dug up which in size and shape was exactly like the pipes in the Wallace Collection, but he does not give the authority for this statement. Apperson sets on record that in November 1911 a wooden pipe carved with dogs' heads and Red Indian faces was put up for sale at Stevens's Auction Room in Covent Garden and described as the pipe that Ralegh smoked "on the scaffold". It was said to have been given by Ralegh to Bishop Andrewes, in whose family it remained for many years, and to have been for some 200 years in the family of the owner who sent it to the sale. According to legend the pipe had been presented to Ralegh by the Indians. That is obviously a myth. The auctioneer told the bidders that unfortunately an old parchment with the full history of the pipe had been lost some years ago and that if only that parchment could be produced the lot would fetch £500. In the end the pipe was knocked down to a trustful bidder for 75 guineas. The auctioneer and the owner did well in the circumstances.

When I read that I began to regret having given away that silver churchwarden reputed to belong to Dr Johnson, particularly after hearing that Ralegh himself enjoyed smoking a silver pipe. And then I consoled myself. So great a man and so great a smoker as Ralegh would never have enjoyed smoking a silver pipe. Peace to his ashes, his own and his tobacco's. 'This was the noblest Roman of them all.'

[1] G. L. Apperson, *The Social History of Smoking* (Martin Secker, 1914).

Chapter 3

I T does not appear that smoking made much progress during
the sixteenth century anywhere in Europe except England.
Presumably people were smoking cigars in Spain, but we do
not hear of them. However, when Ralegh started the fashion of
pipe-smoking round about 1586, within a decade it had become
a craze. Many continental observers have left their impressions
of what seemed to them the extraordinary volatility of the
English and their readiness to take up with enthusiasm anything
new. While other European countries still regarded tobacco as a
medicine rather than a recreation, London was in a cloud of
smoke, and very soon the rest of England followed suit.

In 1598 Paul Hentzner, a German lawyer who was acting as
tutor to a young German nobleman, spent a fortnight in
London with his charge. Here they visited theatres and other
amusements like bull-baiting and bear-baiting.

> At these spectacles, and everywhere else, [he recorded[1]],
> the English are constantly smoking the Nicotian weed, which
> in America is called *Tobaca*—others call it Paetum—and
> generally in this manner : they have pipes on purpose made of
> clay, into the farther end of which they put the herb, so dry
> that it may be rubbed into powder, and lighting it, they draw
> the smoke into their mouths, which they puff out again
> through their nostrils, like funnels, along with it plenty of
> phlegm and defluxion from the head.

It is to be noted as a sign of how far England was ahead with
smoking that Hentzner's *Itinerarium* was not published until
1612 when evidently pipe-smoking was still enough of a rarity
in Germany to require explanation.

Perhaps some of the anti-tobacconist feeling—tobacconist at
this date was the word for the drinker of tobacco as he was
called—which inspired so much pamphleteering against smoking
was the jealousy of the medical profession. Apothecaries did
not want to lose the monopoly they had enjoyed at first, and
that monopoly was vanishing fast. When we laugh to-day at
the preposterous claims made for tobacco as a panacea, we
should do well to remember that it occupied a place in the

---

[1] Rye's translation of Hentzner's *Itinerarium* (Nuremberg).

British pharmacopœia until well into the twentieth century. It was no longer said to cure *anything* from cancer and syphilis to a nasal catarrh, but it was still indicated as a remedy for tetanus.

It was not for its soothing effect upon the human mind that the poet Spenser hailed 'Divine tobacco'. If it had been we might have been left lines the magic of which would compare with:

> *Not poppy, nor mandragora,*
> *Nor all the drowsy syrups of the world*
> *Shall ever medicine thee to that sweet sleep*
> *Which thou owed'st yesterday.*

For Spenser, whose *Faerie Queene* was published in 1590, tobacco was a vulnerary vouched for by the physicians of the day. Belphoebe went forth in search of healing herbs for Timais:

> *Into the woods thenceforth in haste she went,*
> *To seek for herbs that mote him remedy;*
> *For she of herbs had great intendiment,*
> *Taught of the Nymph which from her infancy*
> *Her nurséd had in true nobility:*
> *There whether it divine Tobacco were,*
> *Or Panachaea, or Polygony,*
> *She found and brought it to her patient dear,*
> *Who all this while lay bleeding out his heart-blood near.*

> *The sovereign weed betwixt two marbles plain*
> *She pounded small and did in pieces bruise,*
> *And then atween her lily handes twain,*
> *Into his wound the juice thereof did scruze*
> *And round about, as she could well it use,*
> *The flesh therewith she suppled and did steep,*
> *T' abate all spasm, and soak the swelling bruise,*
> *And after having searched the intuse deep*
> *She with her scarf did bind the wound from cold to keep.*

The elegant euphuism of John Lyly the poet, who was a smoker himself, did not play around tobacco as a pleasure. For him, too, it had to be a medicine. In his play *The Woman in the Moone* (1597), Pandora, after sticking a spear into her lover, sends a servant for herbs:

Gather me balm and cooling violets,
And of our holy herb nicotian,
And bring withall pure honey from the hive,
To heale the wound of my unhappy hand.

Almost the first work in English about tobacco was written by Anthony Chute. It was entitled *Tabaco* and was published in 1595, in which year the author apparently died.[1] While paying tribute to tobacco from a medical point of view, Chute recognizes its attraction for smokers:

> Drinking of tobacco . . . is more vulgarly received with us now than ever, and although it seems that the Indians use to take this *Tabacco* in other manner of pipes than we, yet I think we shall not need to think our earthen or silver pipes more unapt than those which the Indians make of Palm leaves and such like.

Chute's pamphlet is the first to mention silver pipes. Those palm-leaf pipes sound more like the cigar of Cuba and His-paniola; Chute seems unware that the English earthen or clay pipe came from pipe-smoking Indians. The pamphlet gives the first illustration of a white man smoking. The clay pipes then in use had small bowls at a forward angle from the stems, which varied in length from six to twelve inches; the bottom of the bowl was flat so that the pipe could rest on its base. The pamphlet was dedicated

> "To the Heroical minded Gentleman,
> Master Humphrey King".

In it Chute implies the existence of a kind of co-operative society of smokers—the "smoakie Societie"—banded together under the presidency of "His Excelsitude" Humphrey King so that "hoarding apothecaries might be glad to abate their prices of their mingle mangle which forsooth they will not sell, under unreasonable rate, when there is scarce good to be got".

The price of tobacco at this period fluctuated, most of it being smuggled from the Spanish West Indies. When privateers had good captures the price dropped. English tobacco [*N. rustica*], already being grown in Gloucestershire, was frowned upon by the connoisseurs as bitter.

[1] The authorship of Chute was established by Dr Robert Kane of Harvard in a thesis published in 1929.

In 1597 a a pound of tobacco cost 35s.; in 1598 it was at 12s. at the beginning of the year, but shot up to £4 10s. by the end of it. One may multiply these figures by about twelve to get the comparative price to-day.

Humphrey King, a shadowy figure who occupies three-quarters of a column in the *Dictionary of National Biography*, was also the inscript of Thomas Nash's *Lenten Stuffe*, which was published in 1599:

To his worthy good patron, Lusty Humfrey, according as the townsmen do christen him, little Numps as the nobility and courtiers do name him, and Honest Humfrey, as all his friends and acquaintance esteem him, King of the Tobacconists *hic et ubique*, and a singular Maecenas to the Pipe and the Tabour (as his patient livery attendant can witness) his bounden orator T. N. most prostrately offers up this tribute of ink and paper. . . .

Nash was always in acute poverty, and it might be that he hoped King, who was a tobacco-merchant, might repay him in kind for his dedication. We authors do not write fulsome dedications to patrons nowadays, but we are willing to praise good stuff for advertisement.

Humphrey King himself published a book of verse entitled *An Halfe-penny-worth of wit, in a Penny-worth of Paper*, of which no copies of the first or second editions have survived; the third is dated 1613. There is only one allusion to tobacco in the volume, and that is in the preface. In it the author says that he has forsworn wine-pots until Michaelmas, but not "the new wine of Peru, that is made of no grape, but a strange fruit in the West Indies, and is more comfortable to the brain and stomach than any restorative or cordial whatsoever".

Some attention has been paid to this little man because he was obviously a forceful character, and because he may have hoped not only to counteract the extravagance of the contemporary way of smoking, but also to get tobacco out of the hands of the apothecaries who, on account of its reputation as a curative, had been the first people to sell tobacco in England.

"Seller of smoke (fumi vendulus) is the best epithet of an apothecary" was a contemporary saying, and indeed many druggists did a far bigger trade in tobacco than in medicine; Dekker describes one apothecary who had no customers at all "for any phisicall stuffe", but whose shop was a rendez-vous for a great many gentlemen who "came to take their pipes of the divine smoke" upon his premises.

But the apothecaries did not retain a monopoly in the tobacco trade for long. Barnaby Rich, in his *Honestie of this Age* (1614), says:

> It is a commodity that is nowe as vendible in every tavern, wine and ale-house, as eyther wine, ale or beare; and for apothecaries' shops, grocers' shops, chandlers' shops, they are (almost) never without company that from morning till night are still taking of tobacco. What a number are there besides, that doe keepe houses, set open shoppes, that have no other trade to live by, but by the selling of tobacco.
>
> I have heard it told that now very lately there hath been a catalogue of all those new houses that have sett up that trade of selling tobacco in London, and neare about London; and if a man may believe what is confidently reported, there are found to be upward of seven thousand houses that doth live by that trade. I cannot say whether they number apothe-caries' shops, grocers' shops and chandlers' shops in that computation.

These shops were not known as tobacconists. Until the begin-ning of the eighteenth century the term 'tobacconist' was used to describe the smoker not the vendor of tobacco.

Ben Jonson parodies the extravagance of the fashionable devotees of tobacco in several of his plays. His first play, *Every Man in his Humour*, was produced in 1598 at the Globe, which meant that Shakespeare played one of the parts and we smokers can wish that the Bard with his independence of anachronism had made Falstaff a smoker, because Captain Bobadill, though he lacks Falstaff's humour in our use of the word to-day, is the only figure of the Elizabethan and Jacobean drama of com-parable comic stature.

Captain Bobadill is described in the *dramatis personæ* as a Paul's man; that is to say, he was a frequenter of the middle aisle of St Paul's, which at this date was half mart, half fair, the resort of every rascal in London. Bobadill is lodging in the house of Oliver Cob, a water-bearer, who is soliloquizing in the lane outside his house about the oaths he has learnt from the Captain:

... "by the foot of Pharaoh!" There's an oath! How many water-bearers shall you hear swear such an oath? O, I have a guest—he teaches me—he does swear the legiblest of any man christened: "By St George!—the foot of Pharaoh!—the body of me!—as I am a gentleman and a soldier!" such dainty oaths! and withal he does take this same filthy roguish tobacco, the finest, and cleanliest! it would do a man good to see the fume come forth at's tonnels.

The habit of all pipe-smokers at this date was to expel what tobacco smoke they did not swallow through their 'tonnels' or nostrils.

The second scene of Act 3 is set in the warehouse of the merchant Kitely. Bobadill is addressing Master Stephen, a country gull.

> *Bob.* Sir, believe me, upon my relation, for what I tell you, the world shall not reprove. I have been in the Indies, where this herb grows, where neither myself, nor a dozen gentlemen more, of my knowledge, have received the taste of any other nutriment in the world, for the space of one and twenty weeks, but the fume of this simple only: therefore, it cannot be, but 'tis most divine! Further, take it in the nature, in the true kind, so, it makes an antidote, that, had you taken the most deadly poisonous plant in all Italy, it should expel it, and clarify you, with as much ease, as I speak. And for your green wound, your Balsamum and your St John's wort are all mere gulleries and trash to it, especially your Trinidado; your Nicotian is good too. I could say what I know of the virtue of it, for the expulsion of rheums, raw humours, crudities, obstructions, with a thousand of this kind; but I profess myself no quacksalver. Only thus much, by Hercules, I do hold it, and will affirm it, before any Prince in Europe, to be the most sovereign, and precious weed, that ever the earth tendered to the use of man.

Edward Kno'well comments:

> This speech would ha' done decently in a tobacco-trader's mouth.

Bobadill's claim to have smoked seven pounds of tobacco in a week is on a par with the rest of his braggart lying. It is to be noted that he extols Trinidado as the best tobacco, but allows some merit to Nicotian (*N. rustica*), which is what at this date was being shipped from Virginia and also being grown in England. Cob now enters, and Bobadill asks Cash, Kitely's cashier, where was the match he had asked him to light. Cash exits muttering

> would his match, and he, and pipe, and all were at Sancto Domingo!

At this point Cob speaks:

> I mar'le what pleasure or felicity they have in taking this roguish tobacco! it's good for nothing but to choke a man, and fill him full of smoke, and embers: there were four died out of the house, last week, with taking of it, and two more the bell went for, yesternight; one of them, they say, will ne'er scape it: he voided a bushel of soot yesterday, upward, and downward. By the stocks, an there were no wiser men than I, I'ld have it present whipping, man or woman, that should but deal with a tobacco pipe: why, it will stifle them all in the end.

Bobadill takes exception to this, and the onlookers have to separate the pair.

Presently Cob complains to Justice Clement of Bobadill's assault:

> *Clement.* How began the quarrel betwixt you, ha? speak truly, knave, I advise you.
> *Cob.* Marry, indeed, an't please your worship, only because I spake against their vagrant tobacco, as I came by 'hem when they were taking on't; for nothing else.
>
> .   .   .   .   .
>
> *Clem.* What? a thread-bare rascal! a begger! a slave that never drunk out of better than piss-pot metal in his life! and he to deprave and abuse the virtue of an herb so generally received in the courts of princes, the chambers of nobles, the bowers of sweet ladies, the cabins of soldiers!— Roger, away with him! By God's precious—I say, go to.

Ben Jonson's second play, *Every Man Out of His Humour*, was produced in 1599 at the Globe, and one of the performances was honoured by the presence of Queen Elizabeth. In the third act he laughs at the extravagances of the tobacconists. The scene is the Middle Aisle of St Paul's thronged by bullies, swindlers and what to-day we call 'spivs'. Shift, a 'threadbare shark', has managed to set up his placards, advertising himself as a professor of smoking.

Presently Puntarvolo, a 'vainglorious knight', comes along and begins to read the placards in the company of Carlo Buffone:

Punt (*reads*). If this city or the suburbs of the same, do afford any young gentleman . . . , whose friends are but lately deceased, and whose lands are but new come into his hands, that, to be as exactly qualified as the best of our ordinary gallants are, is affected to entertain the most gentlemanlike use of tobacco: as first, to give it the most exquisite perfume: then, to know all the delicate sweet forms for the assumption of it: as also the rare corollary, and practice of the Cuban ebullition, Euripus, and Whiff, which he shall receive, or take in, here at London, and evaporate at Uxbridge, or farther, if it please him. If there be any such generous spirit, that is truly enamoured of these good faculties; may it please him, but, by a note of his hand, to specify the place, or Ordinary, where he used to eat and lie; and most sweet attendance, with tobacco, and pipes of the best sort, shall be ministered.

Now arrives Sogliardo who has just bought a coat-of-arms from the heralds. The author describes him as

an essential clown, yet so enamoured of the name of a gentle-man, that he will have it, though he buys it. He comes up every Term to learn to take tobacco, and see new Motions.

Plus ça change! The Motions were puppet shows, the Movies of once upon a time.

Puntarvolo and Carlo presently introduce the newcomer to Shift:

Shift. Sir, if I should deny the manuscripts I were worthy to be banished the middle aisle, for ever.

Carlo. This gentleman . . . is most desirious to become your pupil. Signior Insulso Sogliardo, this is the professor.

Sog. In good time, sir; nay, good sir, house your head: do you profess these sleights in tobacco?

Shift. I do more than profess, sir, and, if you please to be a practitioner, I will undertake in one fortnight to bring you, that you shall take it plausibly in any Ordinary, Theatre, or Tilt-yard, if need be, i' the most popular assembly that is.

Punt. But you cannot bring him to the whiffe, so soon.

Shift. Yes, as soon, sir; he shall receive the first, second, and third whiffe, if it please him, and upon the receipt, take his horse, drink his three cups of canary, and expose one at Hounslow, a second at Staines, and a third at Bagshot.

From that last claim we can presume that the whiff was inhaling, but what the Cuban ebullition or the Euripus was nobody knows. One guess is as good as another.

Carlo. They have hired a chamber and all, private, to practise in, for the making of the 'patoun', 'the receipt reciprocal', and a number of other mysteries not yet extant. I brought some dozen, or twenty gallants this morning to view 'hem, as you'ld do a piece of perspective, in at the key-hole: and there we might see Sogliardo sit in a chair, holding his snout up like a sow under an apple-tree, while th' other opened his nostrils with a poking-stick, to give the smoke a more free delivery. They had spit some three, or fourscore ounces between 'hem, afore we came away.

Punt. How! spit three or four score ounces?

Carlo. Ay, and preserved it in porrengers, as a barber does his blood, when he opens a vein.

By *Patoun* obviously *petum* or *petun* is meant, for the word was still competing with tobacco. One or two editors of Ben Jonson have been baffled by it altogether or made unconvincing suggestions. Arents suggests that the making of patoun might mean the rolling and smoking of a cigar, and this seems plausible. Arents also suggests that the 'Receipt Reciprocal' may mean "the exercise of expelling smoke in rings, each increasing or decreasing in size". This is less convincing: it might mean blowing the smoke into one another's mouths.

Spitting occurs continually in early references to tobacco. One of its merits as a medicine was its ability to make the patient get rid of phlegm. Some fashionable smokers at this date carried about with them small silver spittoons.

In scenes as tedious as the wisecracks of British comedians trying to emulate their American exemplars, the verbal play about tobacco goes on. It is worth noting that a Court lady is offered a pipe by one of the characters.

With the exception of *Sejanus*, all the later plays of Ben Jonson contain references to tobacco, but when we reach *The Alchemist*, first performed in 1610, we find Abel Drugger, a leading character, described as a tobacco-man, and we realize

that smoking has definitely gone on from what many had
believed was no more than a passing craze to become a permanent feature of the national life. Abel Drugger himself was a
symbol of honest dealing, and more than a century hence
would figure as the sign of many a tobacconist's shop. Subtle
the alchemist enters followed by Drugger.

> *Subtle.* What is your name, you say Abel Drugger?
> *Drug.* Yes, sir.
> *Sub.* A seller of tobacco?
> *Drug.* Yes, sir.
> *Sub.* Umph! Free of grocers?
> *Drug.* Ay, an't please you.
>
> . . . . . .
>
> *Re-enter Face.*
> *Face.* What! My honest Abel?
> Thou art well met here.
> *Drug.* Troth, sir, I was speaking,
> Just as your worship came here, of your worship:
> I pray you speak for me to master doctor.
> *Face.* He shall do anything. Doctor, do you hear?
> This is my friend, Abel, an honest fellow;
> He lets me have good tobacco, and he does not
> Sophisticate it with sack-lees or oil,
> Nor washes it in muscadel and grains,
> Nor buries it in gravel, under ground,
> Wrapped up in greasy leather, or pissed clouts:
> But keeps it in fine lily pots, that, opened,
> Smell like conserve of roses, or French beans.
> He has his maple block, his silver tongs,
> Winchester pipes, and fire of juniper:
> A neat, spruce, honest fellow, and no goldsmith.

Subtle's desire to know whether Drugger was free of the
grocers suggests the competition at this date between them and
the apothecaries over selling tobacco. The habit of adulterating
tobacco with other substances was as much a device to cheat
the Customs as the customer. We shall hear more about that.

In Jonson's *Bartholemew Fair*, Ursula, the pig woman who
"can but hold life and soul together with a whiff of tobacco"
calls upon Nightingale the ballad-maker to see that the tapster
she has sent for tobacco will

discharge his place of trust. Threepence a pipe-full I will have made, of all my half pound of tobacco, and a quarter of pound of coltsfoot mixt with it too, to eke it out.

However, Face's tribute to Drugger's treatment of tobacco refers rather to the condition in which it was kept. Virginia tobacco was imported in the leaf and tied in loose bundles; most of the Spanish tobacco was imported in carottes, tightly packed leaves which had been soaked in molasses and bound with pack thread in the shape of an enormous carrot. There were also balls, the size of a man's head made of tobacco coarsely spun into a thick twist. Cane tobacco was in the shape of a small cylinder, sweetened with rum or molasses. Pudding tobacco was a sausage-shaped roll, also sweetened. A roll was like our twist of to-day; it was also called 'pigtail' and 'cord'. Tobacco which had turned musty was buried in gravel to get rid of the unpleasant smell. Tobacco which had become too dry was treated as mentioned above or, as not mentioned, often wrapped in sheep's skin. When the leaf tobacco was required for smoking, it was dried and rubbed to a powder. The carotte and the ball were cut into small pieces on a block of maple wood with a knife, and the smokers rubbed these finer with their hands as you will see smokers of twist do to-day. The lily-pots were white jars, often imported from Holland like the golf-balls of the period. Juniper wood was kept burning in a kind of chafing-dish, and the customer would take up a glowing ember with the silver tongs to light his pipe. Winchester pipes were clay pipes made at Winchester, and at this date considered the best in the country. Face's commendation of Drugger as 'no goldsmith' meant that he was not used to ensure himself against bad debts by overcharging customers.

Chapter 4

WE have run ahead rather with Abel Drugger, for by 1610 much of the extravagant anti-tobacco propaganda had died down, and so, too, had some of the extravagance of the smokers themselves.

Spanish tobacco was arriving regularly in England in spite of the war. Some time after 1590 Elizabeth, in accordance with the first statute of her reign which had granted her a subsidy on all imported goods, levied a duty of twopence a pound on imported tobacco. It was not a heavy impost, but it infuriated the Cornishmen, who were getting hold of as much Spanish tobacco as they could and making a good profit out of its sale. In November 1597 a French ship and a Flemish ship came into Penryn and disposed of £2,000 worth of tobacco. When the excisemen came along to collect the Queen's twopence a pound, the masters of the ships and those who had bought their tobacco refused to let them examine the cargoes. The local justices took the side of the importers and denied the existence of any duty on tobacco. The collector, Randall Ingarson, tried to stop one Thomas Spaye from landing his purchases, and in a letter to his superior at Plymouth he reported:

I offering to make stay of that, he with his company did forcibly draw their weapons and did swear if I did not depart presently, they would kill me and he did thrust his naked rapier to my breast about a dozen times.

Further in this letter Ingarson named several 'gentlemen' who had been buying in bulk, and pleaded that an example should be made of the ringleaders. The fact that Ingarson urges the advisability of publishing the duty on tobacco suggests that it had only recently been imposed.

The first official figures of 'tabaco' importation were given in 1602, when 16,128 pounds of tobacco entered the Port of London, at which date it was being retailed at 16s. to 33s. a pound. Elizabeth's twopence does not seem an excessive duty on such an expensive luxury, and it was obviously imposed to remind subjects of the royal rights rather than for the immediate revenue it brought in. The circumstances of war made it very difficult to be sure of a supply of Spanish tobacco, and in spite of Sir Walter Ralegh's example, the smokers would not be content with English-grown tobacco. It is disagreeable to reflect that Sir Robert Cecil was doing his best to get hold of Spanish tobacco at the time when through his agents in Scotland he was poisoning the mind of King James VI against Ralegh. Among the Hatfield House manuscripts is a letter to Cecil from Alderman Watts under the date December 12th, 1600:

> According to your request, I have sent the greatest part of my store of tobaca by the bearer, wishing that the same may be to your good liking. But this tobaca I have had this six months, which was such as my son brought home, but since that time I have had none. At this present there is none that is good to be had for money. Wishing you to make store thereof, for I do not know where to have the like, I have sent you of two sorts.

Soon afterwards, on January 26th, 1601, Sir John Stanhope was writing to Sir George Carew:

> I send you now no Tabacco because Mr Secretary [i.e. Cecil], Sir Walter, and your other friends, as they say, have stored you of late, neither have I any proportion of it that is good, but only am rich in Alderman Watses' promise of plenty, wherewith you shall be acquainted. God willing.

Tobacco from a fashionable pastime or panacea has become the consolation of harassed soldiers and statesmen. It is good to recall that Sir George Carew pleaded with King James for the life of Ralegh. One may be allowed to wonder whether Sir Walter was always loyal to English tobacco when he was smoking with Carew, his friend of thirty years; that letter from Stanhope suggests otherwise.

The notion that tobacco could give pleasure to man was enough to rouse disapproval in Puritan circles. A scribe writing under the pseudonym Philaretes published in 1602 a pamphlet called *Worke for Chimney-sweepers* which bitterly attacked those "smoky gallants, the Tobacconists" and was to be sold "at the great North door of Paul's".

> *But hence thou Pagan Idol: tawny weed.*
> *Come not within our Fairie Coasts to feed,*

Earliest known picture of an English tobacco shop, 1617

Our wit-worn gallants, with the scent of thee,
Sent for the Devil and his Company,
Go charm the Priest and Indian Cannibals,
That ceremoniously dead sleeping falls,
Flat on the ground, by virtue of thy scent.

The arguments mustered against tobacco are similar to those that James I would be using, but lacking the King's sour-mouthed eloquence. Roger Marbecke, an urbane physician in his sixty-sixth year, soon published *A Defence of Tobacco: With a Friendly Answer to the late printed Booke called* Worke for Chimney Sweepers.

He argues for the medicinal value of tobacco, but without making exaggerated claims for it. And then he defends the smell of it, which Philaretes had called a horrible stink:

> Men of great learning and judgment, men of right good bringing up, men of fine and dainty diet, men of good worth, and worship, yea, men of right honourable estate and calling, do like of the smell of Tabacco well enough. Why then should it be so mightily condemned by you for such an horrible stinker? For I can tell you, that this is held for an infallible rule, and to be one of the most perfectest signs of good Tabacco, that it be sweet, and yield a kind of pleasing, fragrant, aromatical smell.

Dr Marbecke goes on to say that the inhabitants of "the most famous Island in Christendom" are at the mercy of a climate that induces rheumatism; in addition to which they are great eaters and excessive drinkers, and are inclined to idleness. What could be better for such people surfeited with watery humours than tobacco?

As for the contention that tobacco came from the Devil, surely "it were a more charitable motion, to think that it came from God, who is the author of all good gifts".

Sir John Beaumont, the elder brother of Francis, was next in the field before he was twenty with a poem dedicated to Michael Drayton called *The Metamorphosis of Tabacco* (1602).

The verses are full of ingenious Elizabethan conceits, with a delightful origin for tobacco in a Virginian nymph pursued by Jupiter and turned into a herb by Juno. Jupiter endows the plant with heavenly powers, and in due course Æsculapius

> *did devise a pipe, which should assuage*
> *The wounds, which sorrow in our hearts did fix.*

But the most noteworthy lines are those which first celebrate in verse the pipe-dream:

> *How many cowards base and recreant,*
> *By one pipe's draught were turnéd valiant,*
> *And after in an artificial mist*
> *Have overthrown their foes before they wist:*
> *How one that dreams of a Tabacco roll,*
> *Though sick before, was straight made perfect whole.*

James VI of Scotland was hardly seated upon the throne of England as James I than he launched in 1604 *A Counterblaste to Tobacco.*

It is probable that the King's hatred of Sir Walter Ralegh gave more inspiration to this work than his dislike of tobacco, by which in Scotland he could not have been much offended, since the habit there hardly existed as yet. That learned and treacherous sycophant, Henry Howard, the younger brother of the Duke of Norfolk, had been the prime mover against Ralegh by poisoning James's mind, but Robert Cecil cannot be exonerated from associating himself with this intrigue. Howard had been suspected of treasonable correspondence with Mary Queen of Scots, but Elizabeth considered him "too mean a man for Mary's liking". James sent him a ruby from Scotland when Elizabeth died as a token of his good will, and Howard was successful in getting Ralegh condemned to death and himself created Earl of Northampton.

So let it be realized that *A Counterblaste to Tobacco* is the hatred of a man expressed in terms of hating a herb. It was published anonymously, but the King's authorship was an open secret and in 1616 it was acknowledged.

The royal pamphleteer begins by testifying to the value of kings as monitors, and then plunges into the attack:

> That the manifold abuses of this vile custom of Tobacco taking, may the better be espied, it is fit, that first you enter into consideration both of the first original thereof, and likewise of the reasons of the first entry thereof into this Country. For certainly as such customs, that have their first institution either from a godly, necessary, or honourable ground, and are first brought in, by the means of some worthy, virtuous, and

great Personage, are ever, and most justly, holden in great
and reverent estimation and account, by all wise, virtuous,
and temperate spirits: so should it by the contrary, justly
bring a great disgrace into that sort of customs, which having
their original from base corruption and barbarity, do in like
sort, make their first entry into a Country, by an inconsider-
ate and childish affectation of novelty as is the true case of the
first invention of Tobacco taking, and of the first entry
thereof among us. For Tobacco being a common herb,
which (though under divers names) grows almost everywhere, was first found out by some of the barbarous Indians,
to be a Preservative, an Antidote against the Pox, a filthy
disease, whereunto these barbarous people are (as all men
know) very much subject, what through the uncleanly and
adust constitution of their bodies, and what through the
intemperate heat of their Climate: so that as from them was
first brought into Christendom, that most detestable disease,
so from them likewise was first brought this use of Tobacco,
as a stinking and unsavoury Antidote, for so corrupted and
execrable a Malady, the stinking Suffumigation whereof
they yet use against that disease, making so one canker or
venom to eat out another.

And now good Country men let us (I pray you) consider,
what honour or policy can move us to imitate the barbarous
and beastly manners of the wild, godless, and slavish Indians,
especially in so vile and stinking a custom? . . . Why do we
not as well imitate them in walking naked as they do? in
preferring glasses, feathers, and such toys, to gold and
precious stones, as they do? yea, why do we not deny God
and adore the Devil, as they do?

Now to the corrupted baseness of the first use of this
Tobacco, doth very well agree the foolish and groundless
first entry thereof into this Kingdom. It is not so long since
the first entry of this abuse amongst us here . . . both the
first Author, and the form of the first introduction of it
amongst us. It was neither brought in by King, great Con-
queror, nor learned Doctor of Physic.

With the report of a great discovery for a Conquest, some
two or three savage men, were brought in, together with this
Savage custom. But the pity is, the poor wild barbarous men
died, but that vile barbarous custom is yet alive, yea, in
fresh vigour: so as it seems a miracle to me, how a custom
springing from so vile a ground, and brought in by a father
so generally hated, should be welcomed upon so slender a
warrant.

A father so generally hated! Whoever may have been the first man that introduced tobacco into England, there is no doubt at all who was regarded as the popularizer of it. James could not have slobbered out that vicious denunciation on a legend not much more than ten years old unless it was justified.

The counterblast is now directed for several pages against the false claims made for tobacco as a medicine, and one is bound to admit that in this respect the savage ridicule and irony are justified.

Such is the miraculous omnipotency of our strong tasted Tobacco, as it cures all sorts of diseases (which never any drug could do before) in all persons, and at all times. It cures all manner of distillations, either in the head or stomach (if you believe their Axioms) although in very deed it do both corrupt the brain, and by causing over quick digestion, fill the stomach full of crudities. It cures the Gout in the feet, and (which is miraculous) in that very instant when the smoke thereof, as light, flies up into the head, the virtue thereof, as heavy, runs down to the little toe. It helps all sorts of Agues. It makes a man sober that was drunk. It refreshes a weary man, and yet makes a man hungry. Being taken when they go to bed, it makes one sleep soundly, and yet being taken when a man is sleepy and drowsy it will, as they say, awake his brain, and quicken his understanding. As for curing of the Pox, it serves for that use but among the poxy Indian slaves. Here in England it is refined, and will not deign to cure here any other than cleanly and gentle-manly diseases. Omnipotent power of Tobacco! And if it could by the smoke thereof chase out devils, as the smoke of Tobias fish did (which I am sure could smell no stronglier) it would serve for a precious Relic, both for the superstitious Priests, and the insolent Puritans, to cast out devils withal. Admitting then, and not confessing that the use thereof were healthful for some sorts of diseases; should it be used for all sicknesses? should it be used by all men? should it be used at all times? yea, should it be used by able, young, strong, healthful men? Medicine hath that virtue that it never leaveth a man in that state wherein it findeth him: it makes a sick man whole, but a whole man sick. And as Medicine helps nature being taken at times of necessity, so being ever and continually used, it doth but weaken, weary and wear nature. What speak I of Medicine? Nay, let a man every hour of the day, or as oft as many in this country use to take Tobacco, let a man, I say, but take as oft the best sorts of nourishments in meat and drink that can be devised, he shall with the continual use thereof weaken both his head and his stomach: all his members shall become feeble, his spirits dull, and in the end, as a drowsy lazy belly-god, he shall evanish in a Lethargy.

And from this weakness it proceeds, that many in this kingdom have had such a continual use of taking this unsavoury smoke, as now they are not able to forbear the same, no more than an old drunkard can abide to be long sober, without falling into an incurable weakness and evil constitution: for their continual custom hath made to them, *habitum, alteram naturam*: so to those that from their birth have been continually nourished upon poison and things venomous, wholesome meat are only poisonable.

So as early as James I we have this exaggerated fear of any drug that can lead to addiction. It never seems to occur to those who wish to abolish alcohol or heroin or hashish or opium that the natural addict of any drug will always seek a substitute. The addict is born not made. Prohibition of alcohol or of any other drug has never exerted anything but a corrupting influence.

And now the natural adversary of liberty rolls into a diapason of rodomontade against the danger of addiction:

Thus having, as I trust, sufficiently answered the most principal arguments that are used in defence of this vile custom, it rests only to inform you what sins and vanities you commit in the filthy abuse thereof. First are you not guilty of sinful and shameful lust? (for lust may be as well in any of the senses as in feeling) that although you be troubled with no disease, but in perfect health, yet can you neither be merry at an Ordinary, nor lascivious in the Stews, if you lack Tobacco to provoke your appetite to any of those sorts of recreation, lusting after it as the children of Israel did in the wilderness after Quails? Secondly it is, as you use or rather abuse it, a branch of the sin of drunkenness, which is the root of all sins: for as the only delight that drunkards take in wine is in the strength of the taste, and the force of the fume thereof that mounts up to the brain; for no drunkards love any weak, or sweet drink, so are not those (I mean the strong heat and the fume), the only qualities that make Tobacco so delectable to all the lovers of it? And as no man likes strong heady drink the first day..., but by custom is piece and piece allured, . . . So is not this the very case of all the great takers of Tobacco? which therefore they themselves do attribute to a bewitching quality in it. Thirdly, is it not the greatest sin of all, that you the people of all sorts of this Kingdom, who are created and ordained by God to bestow both your persons and goods for the maintenance both of the honour and safety of your King and Commonwealth, should disable your selves in both? In your persons having by this continual vile custom brought yourselves to this shameful imbecility that you are not able to ride or walk the journey of a Jew's Sabbath, but you must have a reeky coal brought you from the next poor house to kindle your Tobacco with? whereas he cannot be thought able for any service in the wars, that cannot endure oftentimes the want of meat, drink, and sleep, much more then must he endure the want of Tobacco. In the times of the many glorious and victorious battles fought by this nation there was no word of Tobacco. But now if it were time of wars, and that you were to make some sudden Cavalcado upon your enemies, if any of you should seek leisure to stay behind his fellow for taking of Tobacco, for my part I should be sorry for any evil chance that might befall him. To take a custom in any thing that be left again, is most harmful to the people of any land. Mollicies and delicacy were the wrack and overthrow, first of the Persian, and next of the Roman Empire. And this very custom of taking Tobacco (whereof our present purpose is), is even at this day accounted so effeminate among the Indians themselves, as in the market they will offer no price for a slave to be sold, whom they find to be a great Tobacco taker.

A physical coward like James was hardly the man to lay down the law about fighting. Yet within a few years of his counterblast, the Thirty Years' War would begin and do much more to spread the habit of smoking than any Ralegh. Every war hence onward would intensify and spread the habit of smoking, as we shall see in due course.

In his last invective we may perceive that James genuinely did dislike tobacco smoke. Ralegh is now forgotten in the expression of his own distaste:

> And for the vanities committed in this filthy custom, is it not both great vanity and uncleanness, that at the table, a place of respect, of cleanliness, of modesty, men should not be ashamed, to sit tossing of Tobacco pipes, and puffing of the

smoke of Tobacco one to another, making the filthy smoke and stink thereof, to exhale athwart the dishes, and infect the air, when very often, men that abhor it are at their repast? Surely Smoke becomes a kitchen far better than a dining chamber, and yet it makes a kitchen also oftentimes in the inward parts of men, soiling and infecting them, with an unctuous and oily kind of Soot as hath been found in some Tobacco takers, that after their death were opened.

The discovery in *post mortem* examination that the insides of smokers were covered with oily soot was a domestic fable which enjoyed a lively currency at the time, and perhaps James really did believe it.

The public use of this uncivil trick, . . . at all times, and in all places, hath now so far prevailed, as divers men very sound both in judgment, and complexion, have been at last forced to take it also without desire, partly because they were ashamed to seem singular . . . and partly, to be as one that was content to eat Garlic (which he did not love) that he might not be troubled with the smell of it in the breath of his fellows. And is it not a great vanity that a man cannot heartily welcome his friend now, but straight they must be in hand with Tobacco? No, it is become in place of a cure, a point of good fellowship, and he that will refuse to take a pipe of Tobacco among his fellows, (though by his own election he would rather feel the savour of a Sink) is accounted peevish and no good company, even as they do with tippling in the cold Eastern Countries. Yea, the Mistress cannot in a more mannerly kind entertain her servant than by giving him out of her fair hand a pipe of Tobacco. But herein is not only a great vanity but a great contempt of God's good gifts, that the sweetness of man's breath, being a good gift of God, should be wilfully corrupted by this stinking smoke, wherein I must confess, it hath too strong a virtue: and so that which is an ornament of nature, and can neither by any artifice be at the first acquired, nor once lost, be recovered again, shall be filthily corrupted with an incurable stink, which vile quality is as directly contrary to that wrong opinion which is holden of the wholesomeness thereof, as the venom of putrifaction is contrary to the virtue Preservative.

Moreover, which is a great iniquity and against all humanity, the husband shall not be ashamed to reduce thereby his delicate, wholesome, and clean complexioned wife to that extremity that either she must also corrupt her sweet breath therewith, or else resolve to live in a perpetual stinking torment.

James was evidently anxious to discourage the habit of female smoking, and it must be admitted that in those last words he did so with considerable tact.

And so we come to the last famous paragraph of the *Counterblaste*. Note that the King is able to denounce his own "dear country men" for shocking foreign observers by their devotion to tobacco:

> Have you not reason then to be ashamed, and to forbear this filthy novelty so basely grounded, so foolishly received and so grossly mistaken in the right use thereof? In your abuse thereof sinning against God, harming yourselves both in persons and goods, and taking also thereby the marks and notes of vanity upon you: by the custom thereof making yourselves to be wondered at by all foreign civil Nations, and by all strangers that come among you, to be scorned and condemned. A custom loathsome to the eye, hateful to the nose, harmful to the brain, dangerous to the lungs, and in the black stinking fume thereof, nearest resembling the horrible Stygian smoke of the pit that is bottomless.

And now it is time to learn what practical steps King James took to abolish smoking in Great Britain.

Chapter 5

KING JAMES did not wait long to load his counterblast with a cannon-ball, which was fired on October 17th, 1604, from Westminster:

James, by the Grace of God, etc., to our right Trusty and right Wellbeloved Cousin and Counsellor, Thomas, Earl of Dorset, our High Treasurer of England, greeting . . . we do will and command, and hereby also warrant and authorize you to give order to all Customers, Comptrollers, Searchers, Surveyors, and other officers of our Ports, that, from and after the six and twentieth Day of October next coming, they shall demand and take to our use of all Merchants, as well English as Strangers, and of all others who shall bring in any Tobacco into this Realm, within any Port, Haven or Creek belonging to any of their several Charges, the sum of *Six Shillings and Eight Pence* upon every Pound Weight thereof, over and above the Custom of Two Pence upon the Pound usually paid heretofore.

It should be borne in mind that all the tobacco imported into England at this date came from Spanish sources and that with the end of the long Spanish war in this year, 1604, a much heavier importation of tobacco could be expected. Six and tenpence may not seem so heavy, but let it be remembered that six and tenpence at the beginning of the seventeenth century was the equivalent of at least £4 to-day.

What James did not foresee was the future of Virginia. The abortive attempts of Ralegh to colonise that part of it which would later be known as North Carolina did not destroy the impulse in England to play a part in the New World. In 1607 another expedition of hopeful colonists set out with the backing of the Virginia Company of London formed in emulation of the East India Company. Jamestown was founded. At first the colony was not a success. By 1610 the colonists had decided to abandon it and set sail for Newfoundland. At the mouth of the James River they met the incoming relief expedition of Lord Delaware, bringing more colonists and much-needed supplies. It was in the following year that John Rolfe, who married the Princess Pocahontas and by doing so mitigated the hostility of

the Indians, secured from Trinidad and probably later from
Caracas seeds of *Nicotiana tabacum*. There has been speculation
about the way in which Rolfe managed to get hold of the seeds.
It may be noted that in 1610 Don Fernando de Berio, the
Spanish Governor of Trinidad, was accused of trading with the
enemies of his Catholic Majesty and in that year relieved of his
office. Rolfe established by trial that the species would grow as
well in the sandy soil of the peninsula round Jamestown as the
Nicotiana rustica which was abundant all over Virginia. This was
"of a biting taste" according to William Strachey. Ralph Hamor
was secretary at the time to the settlement and gave Rolfe all the
credit for the experiment, the success of which may be saluted
as the foundation of what is now the greatest power on earth—
the United States of America.

Not that success came so easily. An experimental shipment
to England was made as early as 1613, but the planters had
not fully mastered the art of curing and the connoisseurs at
home were in no hurry to admit that such "pleasant, sweet
and strong Tobacco", as Hamor calls it, could compete with
the Trinidado, Orinoque or Varinas favoured by them. Sir
Thomas Roe, writing to the Earl of Salisbury (Robert Cecil)
in 1611, referred to the great trade carried on between England
and Trinidad, and told him that there were sometimes as many
as fifteen ships of other nations in Port of Spain, all waiting for
tobacco. Don Alonzo de Belasco, the Spanish Ambassador in
England, informed the King of Spain in the same year that one
ship had reached London from Guiana and Trinidad with
16,000 pounds of tobacco which had been sold at six reales a
pound (about 8s.).

Gradually, however, the sweet scent of Virginia tobacco, to
which was added the guarantee of its purity by exporting it in
leaf, began to attract the English smokers. It was improving,
too, all the time by cross-breeding with other varieties of
Nicotiana tabacum and better methods of curing. In 1615–16
the Virginia planters exported 2,300 pounds to London; in
that same period 58,300 pounds were imported from the
Spanish dominions. Less than two years later the colonists
exported 20,000 pounds. Captain Samuel Argall, the new
governor, reported on his arrival in 1617 that there were only
half a dozen houses in Jamestown, and that the church had
collapsed because the market-place, the streets and every spare

bit of ground were planted with tobacco, and that the colony
was "dispersed all about, planting tobacco". The new governor
took strong measures ; he even made it a capital offence not to
attend the rebuilt church.

There was another man with the vision of a Ralegh, and that
was Robert Harcourt of Stanton Harcourt who in 1609 tried to
achieve the colonization of Guiana. He published his *Relation of
A Voyage to Guiana* in 1613 and in it occur some remarks which
seem to give the author the status of a major prophet :

> There is yet another profitable commodity to be reaped in
> Guiana, and that is by Tobacco, which albeit some dislike,
> yet the generality of men in this kingdom doth with great
> affection entertain it. It is not only in request in this our
> Country of England, but also in Ireland, the Netherlands,
> in all the Easterly Countries, and Germany; and most of all
> amongst the Turks, and in Barbary.

We have yet to learn what smokers had to endure before
Harcourt could make that remark.

> The price it holdeth is great, the benefit our merchants
> gain thereby is infinite, and the King's rent from the custom
> thereof is not a little. The Tobacco that was brought into
> this kingdom in the year of our Lord 1610 was at the least
> worth £60,000. And since that time the store that yearly
> hath come in, was little less.
>
> It is planted, gathered, seasoned, and made up fit for the
> Merchant in short time, and with easy labour. But when we
> first arrived in Guiana we altogether wanted the true skill
> and knowledge how to order it, which now of late we happily
> have learned of the Spaniards themselves whereby I dare
> presume to say . . . that only this commodity Tobacco (so
> much sought after and desired) will bring as great a benefit
> and profit to the undertakers, as ever the Spaniards gained
> by the best and richest Silver mine in all their Indies con-
> sidering the charge of both.

Harcourt took possession of "the whole Continent of Guiana,
lying betwixt the rivers of Amazon and Orinoco", and handed
over a mountain to an Indian who had lived in England for
fourteen years with a stipulation that a tithe of the tobacco and
what else he raised on it should be handed over to the King.

Alas, there were few in England with the vision of Ralegh or

Harcourt. Otherwise Venezuela, the three Guianas and a large piece of Northern Brazil might have been British to-day. The Dutch exploited Guiana; we collared a piece of it, and at the Treaty of Breda in 1677 exchanged it for New Amsterdam which we renamed New York. British Guiana we got from the Dutch at the settlement after the Napoleonic Wars.

The Bermudas and St Kitts competed for a time with Virginia in tobacco, but by the middle of the century St Kitts had taken to indigo, cotton and sugar, and early in the twentieth century the curing of tobacco had ceased in the Bermudas.

By 1608 James decided that from a financial point of view the heavy tax on tobacco was a mistake. Smuggling had become more and more prevalent, and home-grown tobacco, although not the true Trinidado, was on the increase. The impost on tobacco was reduced to a shilling, and about this time he granted a patent to Philip Herbert, a disagreeable but extremely good-looking young man whom he created Earl of Montgomery, to collect the impost.

By 1613 James was again in need of money and considered a project "for increase of the King's revenue by his resuming into his own hands the grant of sole importation of tobacco, and regranting it to an agent, who will yield him half the profits, estimated at £15,000". In March 1615 the impost on tobacco having been raised to 2s. a pound, James granted two patentees, who were to pay him £3,500 the first year and £7,000 a year afterwards, the sole power to import tobacco. So in spite of the *Counterblaste* James had discovered by now that tobacco was a profitable monopoly. Indeed, he was beginning to rely for so much of his revenue on it that he bought back from Montgomery the patent he had granted him by paying him £3,000 a year for twenty-one years.

Smuggling on a large scale continued, and in 1620 an order went out that all tobacco sold in future must bear the Government stamp. Finally, in 1624 tobacco was made a royal monopoly. The Virginia Company had resisted the application of those orders to colonial imports, but in 1620 it agreed to a duty of one shilling on the pound, which was half the duty on Spanish tobacco, provided that steps were taken to enforce the regulation against growing tobacco in England. This preferential treatment accorded to Virginia tobacco over Spanish tobacco might have been a landmark in the colonial policy of

Great Britain, but Empire Preference had to wait for three centuries to pass.

The words in which King James declared a Royal monopoly are worth recording:

> Whereas it is agreed on all sides that the Tobacco of these Plantations of Virginia and the Somers Islands [as the Bermudas were then called], which is the only present means of their subsisting, cannot be managed for the good of the Plantations unless it be brought into one hand, whereby the Foreign Tobacco may be carefully kept out, and the Tobacco of those Plantations may yield a certain and ready price to the owners thereof, we do hereby declare, That to avoid all differences and contrarieties of opinions, which will hardly be reconciled between the Planters and Adventurers themselves, we are resolved to take the same into Our Own Hands and by Our Servants or Agents for us, to give such Prices to the Planters and Adventurers for the same as may give them reasonable Satisfaction and Encouragement.

Much of the prosperity of the young colony of Virginia was due to the importation there of negro slaves, which began in 1619 when John Rolfe noted the arrival of a "Dutch man of warre that sold us twenty Negars", paid for with tobacco. In that same year James I deported a hundred dissolute persons to Virginia, which marked the beginning of the transportation of white felons who, with Negro slaves, would provide forced labour for long enough.

In August 1605 King James paid a state visit to the University of Oxford, of which the public orator Isaac Wake, aged only twenty-five, wrote an account in Latin under the title of *Rex Platonicus*—the Platonic King. By 1605 James had not appreciated what a treasure tobacco was going to be and was congratulating himself on having checked the spread of smoking by his six-and-tenpenny impost. For the third day of the royal visit a debate was held to decide whether "the frequent smoking of exotic tobacco is salutary for the health", following upon a debate whether "the morals of nurses are imbibed by infants with the milk".

Bartholemew Ward and Sir William Paddy, the King's Physician, were against tobacco, although the latter who lived to eighty was known to be a great smoker himself; it was he who first hailed James as another Solomon, after writing an elegy for Queen Elizabeth which begins with one of the most barbarous hexameters ever penned. However, he was a good and genial man, and within the narrow limits of his time an able physician.

The King himself followed Paddy with an appeal not to admit medicines which offended against the precepts of Hippocrates and Galen.

Then John Cheynell, an Oxford physician, spoke up for tobacco, holding in his hand a pipe. Wake says that his learned and jocular speech delighted the audience because it showed clearly that he was at heart an enemy to tobacco; whether or not Cheynell was being jocular, he produced a Roundhead fanatic of a son who never smiled at all.

The King now spoke again, and the young public orator in recalling the occasion later was unwilling to add "as much as a drop of ink to the ocean of applause" that hailed the royal effort. The fulsome reception of King James by the University of Oxford included the prohibition of smoking by under-graduates while he was in the city. It may be that the prohibi-tion of smoking when in cap and gown dates from this occasion. But do not let Cambridge men feel superior. When King James visited Cambridge the tenth regulation issued by the University authorities for the guidance of undergraduate behaviour read :

> That no Graduate, Scholar, or Student of this University presume to resort to any Inn, Tavern, Alehouse, or Tobacco-shop at any time during the abode of His Majesty here; nor to presume to take tobacco in St Mary's Church or in Trinity College Hall, upon pain of final expelling the University.

So already some Jacobean tobacconists in Oxford and Cambridge may have been discussing with their undergraduate clients the comparative merits of Winchester and Bristol clays.

Nevertheless, the tobacco war continued. In 1607 Samuel Rowlands published sixpennyworth of epigrams after Martial —directed against smokers, which if not so good as his Roman masters are not bad.

Cornutus, dazed with drink and believing himself to be at death's door, summons his friends to hear his last testament :

I here bequeath, if I do chance to die,
To you kind friends, and boon companions all,
A pound of good Tobacco, sweet and dry,
To drink amongst you, at my Funeral.

The continual references to the quality of dryness as so desirable for tobacco suggests how much the first smokers had to contend with in the preservatives and adulterants of the time.

Samuel Rowlands in his *Knave of Clubs*, a collection of light verse published in 1609, has a poem called *The Devil's Health-drinker*, in which he writes:

The leaf green, dry, steept, burnéd, dust,
Have each their special praise.

Only home-grown tobacco could have been green, and dust suggests snuff; indeed, Rowlands does mention snuff as an alternative to the pipe. However, popular though it was already in Scotland and Ireland, snuff did not make much headway in England before the eighteenth century.

That poem of Rowlands has eight lines which although they have been quoted in every book about tobacco cannot be left out:

But he's a frugal man indeed,
That with a leaf can dine,
And needs no napkin for his hands,
His fingers' ends to wipe,
But keeps his kitchen in a box,
And roast-meat in a pipe.

Another poem misquoted in almost every book about tobacco in half a dozen different versions has been wrongly attributed by several writers to George Wither. Fairholt thinks that Wither's willingness to praise tobacco showed how he "despised the servility which would have tended to his advancement at court". He ignores the fact that in his *Abuses Stript and Whipt* published in 1613 (for which the authorities shut him up in the Marshalsea for a while at the prompting of one or two men of influence who thought he had libelled them), Wither had attacked tobacco. He was not at that date a smoker, having been born and brought up at Bentworth in Hampshire, in whose 'beechy shadows' the present writer smoked more

forbidden tobacco than anywhere else in his boyhood. Wither
wrote some charming lyrics, but wasted too much of his talent
on second-rate satire. In 1621 another volume again got him
into the Marshalsea for libel, but after a month or two he was
liberated without trial, for which he was indebted to the kind
offices of the Princess Elizabeth to celebrate whose marriage
with the Elector Palatine he had composed a volume of
Epithalamia and thereby given that delightful young woman
much pleasure. During the Great Rebellion, Wither fought
feebly and wrote tediously in support of the Roundheads, and
in 1660 after the Restoration, being by now seventy-two years
of age, he was arrested and lodged in Newgate, whence he
was sent to the Tower to await impeachment. Finally he was
released in 1663, and lived on in the precincts of the Savoy
until he died in 1667 in his eightieth year.

Wither, who had taken to smoking soon after he published
Abuses Stript and Whipt, gave it up ten years later, but took to it
again to console himself during his last imprisonment. In 1661
he wrote:

> *Here, all alone, I by myself have took,*
> *An Emblem of my Self, a Pipe of Smoke :*
> *For, I am but a little piece of Clay*
> *Fill'd with a Smoke that quickly fumes away.*
> *This Vanity our Climate never knew*
> *Till near the time, in which, first breath I drew,*[1]
> *And otherwise, it is of wholesome use*
> *(Though for the most part subject to abuse :)*
> *Since first I smoked it, after (it come hither)*
> *I laid it by, nigh thirty years together,*
> *And for my health's sake, then, did reassume*
> *That Bauble wherewith we Tobacco fume.*

That is not a bad lyric for a man who has reached the allotted
span and written since his youth page after page of turgid
polemics and self-righteous sermons. It is typical of the old
Roundhead that when he does take to smoking again he
should claim that he did so only for the sake of his health, not
of course for enjoyment.

So much for George Wither. Now for that beautiful little
lyric for which he was undeservedly given the credit. This was

[1] 1588.

written by Thomas Jenner, author, publisher and engraver; he was recommended in his last capacity by Evelyn to Pepys. The poem first appeared in *The Soul's Solace or Thirty and one Spiritual Emblems* written and published, and in a later edition engraved, by Thomas Jenner:

31. Tobacco

The Indian weed witheréd quite,
Green at noon, cut down at night;
Shows thy decay, all flesh is hay,
Thus think, then drink Tobacco.

The Pipe that is so lily white
Shows thee to be a mortal wight,
And even such, gone with a touch,
Thus think, then drink Tobacco.

And when the smoke ascends on high,
Think, thou behold'st the vanity
Of wordly stuff gone with a puff:
Thus think, then drink Tobacco.

And when thy Pipe grows foul within,
Think on thy soul defil'd with sin,
And then the fire it doth require,
Thus think, then drink Tobacco.

The ashes that are left behind,
May serve to put thee still in mind,
That unto dust, return thou must,
Thus think, then drink Tobacco.
Answered by G. W. thus,
Thus think, drink no Tobacco.

We may surmise either that George Wither had been displaying a good deal of spiritual pride over giving up smoking or that this was an allusion to Wither's attack on tobacco in *Abuses Stript and Whipt*. The former seems more likely.

This little poem, which is the only lyric about tobacco that can compete with Anacreon on wine (Herrick, alas, was not a smoker [1]), was mauled about for nearly two centuries.

[1] Since making that statement the final text of Herrick's verse has been published by the O.U.P., in which a hitherto unprinted poem about tobacco appears. This will be quoted in my epilogue.

S.T.—9

The quantity and the venomous quality of the writing against tobacco would suggest to anybody dependent upon them for his knowledge of the conquest of England by the pipe that the anti-tobacconists were in a large majority. Perhaps the smokers, guided by a muse who may not have been one of the original Nine but who now is certainly of their company on some Parnassus revealed by relativity, were counselled to keep their breath for their pipes of whose melodies Apollo would never be jealous.

Yet, in spite of the royal disfavour, from time to time a voice was raised in defence of tobacco, and I am conscious of a flow of civic pride when I boast that the first sober plea for tobacco was written by a Scotsman and published in Edinburgh in the year 1614.

William Barclay was a brother of Sir Patrick Barclay of Towie who went to study at the University of Louvain, where he took the degrees of M.A. and M.D. For a time he was Professor of Humanity in the University of Paris, whence he returned to Scotland to practise medicine. Perhaps he found his native land out of touch with humanity at that date; anyway, he went back to France and settled in Nantes.

Nepenthes or The Vertues of Tabacco, which the *Dictionary of National Biography* by an unusual blunder treats as appearing two years before the *Counterblaste* instead of ten years after it, is an urbane and tolerant tract. The author may seem to attach too much importance to the stock curative virtues of tobacco, but his title suggests what in his heart he felt was the herb's real virtue.

Barclay, as a doctor not as a Puritan, warns his readers against the abuse of tobacco. They are

not, as the English abusers do, to make a smoke-box of their skull, more fit to be carried under his arm that selleth at Paris *du noir à noircir* to black men's shoes than to carry the brain of him that cannot walk, cannot ride except the tobacco pipe be in his mouth.

Barclay writes racily about the medical uses of the herb, and insists that only West Indian tobacco is any good. He dismisses the variety (*N. rustica*) grown in many gardens in England and on the Continent, and he denounces those merchants who through greed dress up European plants in

"Indian coats, and install them in shops as righteous and legitimate tobacco". He has no use for Florida tobacco (*N. rustica*), and what he says about that would have been equally true of Virginia tobacco a couple of years earlier. He does not realize, however, that Florida tobacco was not the same plant as other West Indian tobacco, but attributes its inferiority

> because either it is exhausted of spirituality, or the radical humour is spent and wasted, or it hath gotten moisture by the way, or it hath been dried for expedition in the sun, or carried too negligently. Treating it with black spice, galingale, brandy, Spanish-wine, aniseed or lavender will not make it good tobacco.
> The most fine, best and purest is that which is brought to Europe in leaves, and not rolled in puddings, as the English navigators first brought home.

That observation is a clue to the supremacy Virginia tobacco would achieve within a few years.

And no doubt it was in due course stocked by William Anslop

> an honest man dwelling in Bishopsgate Street, hard within the gate, that selleth the best Tobacco in England, and useth it most discreetly.

Dr Barclay added several sonnets to his tract, one of which was inscribed to the Bishop of Moray:

> *The stately rich late conquered Indian plains,*
> *Foster a plant, the princess of all plants,*
> *Which Portugal, after peril and pains,*
> *To Europe brought, as it most justly vaunts:*
> *This plant at home the people and priests assure,*
> *Of his goodwill, whom they as God adore,*
> *Both here and there it worketh wondrous cure,*
> *And hath such heavenly virtue hid in store.*
> *A stranger plant shipwreckéd in our coast,*
> *Is come to help this cold phlegmatic soil,*
> *Yet cannot live for calumny and boast,*
> *In danger daily of some greater broil:*
> *My lord, this sacred herb which never offendit*
> *Is forc'd to crave your favour to defend it.*

The earliest allusion I have been able to find to growing tobacco in Scotland is in *The Genealogical History of the Earldom*

of Sutherland compiled between 1615 and 1630.[1] He is writing
of Dunrobin Castle:

> A house well seated upon a mote hard by the sea, with
> fair orchards, where there be pleasant gardens, planted with
> all kinds of fruits, herbs and flowers, used in this kingdom,
> and abundance of good saffron, tobacco and rosemary.

That tobacco was undoubtedly *N. tabacum*.

As I sit over this book in the New Town of Edinburgh I like
to think of that predecessor sitting over his book in the Old
Town of Edinburgh all but three and a half centuries ago, and I
echo the final couplet of one of Dr Barclay's sonnets which,
although penned by one who in his own words was "a valley
poet . . . I never having slept in Parnassus", is a charming
pendant to the sober prose of the tract.

> *Tobacco neither altereth health nor hue,*
> *Ten thousand thousands know that it is true.*

[1] Quoted by Archbishop David Mathew in *Scotland Under Charles I.*

Chapter 6

BARCLAY's salute to the part played by Portugal in the introduction of tobacco was no doubt inspired more by his belief in it as a medicine than his admiration of it as a narcotic; but he was right. To England belongs the credit for the spread of pipe-smoking through Europe; Spain can be praised for the cigar. Portugal, however, carried pipe and cigar round the world. One tribe in South Brazil used pipes with nut-shell bowls and stems of hollow wood or reeds. In passing, we may recall that the English peasantry for a while used a walnut-shell and a straw as a pipe.

The first place to which Portuguese mariners brought tobacco was the west coast of Africa. By 1607 William Finch [1] could write of Sierra Leone:

> Tobacco is planted about every man's house, which seemeth half their food: the bowl of their tobacco pipe is very large, and stands right upward, made of clay well burnt in the fire. In the lower end thereof they thrust in a small hollow cane . . . through which they suck it, both men and women drinking the most part down.

The welcome tobacco received from the natives suggested a use for it in trade, and that the abominable slave trade. In due course the price for an unhappy Negro kidnapped in the interior by slave-traders on the Guinea Coast was six or seven rolls of Brazilian tobacco. We can reflect with a sigh that a human being was weighed against tobacco and dragged from home to misery. The Dutch followed the example set by the Portuguese, and when they were exploiting Cape Colony they were able to cheat the Hottentots out of cattle and lands with rolls of tobacco.

The Portuguese brought tobacco to India, and when it is remembered that India is now the third largest tobacco-producing country in the world, some of the Indian indignation about Goa might be mitigated. Tobacco was first grown in the Deccan about 1605. Edward Terry, who spent two years and a half in Malwa and Gujerat (1616–19), writes in his memoirs:

[1] *Purchas, IV.*

They sow tobacco in abundance, but know not how to cure and make it strong as those in the West Indies.

The Portuguese introduced tobacco to Ceylon early in the sixteenth century, but as a cure for beri-beri not as a recreation. With the smoking of tobacco, the eating of pork was prescribed and the drinking of palm-wine. The soldiers were prejudiced against tobacco, as they would be some centuries later by mepacrine, because the rumour ran that it injured virility. The Captain-General had to set an example to his troops by smoking a pipeful in public every day.

The Spaniards brought tobacco to the Philippines, but the indomitable navigator, Ferdinand Magellan, who discovered them was a Portuguese, and it was only the ingratitude of his country that drove him into the service of Spain.

Corti says that it was Magellan who brought tobacco to the Philippines. It is difficult to believe that during the miraculous voyage of ninety-eight days across the ocean he named Pacific, when his crew was rotting with scurvy and those that had survived had been driven to eat rats and sawdust, any tobacco they might have had on board would not have been chewed away long before the greatest navigator that ever sailed reached those islands where he was to meet his end.

The Portuguese certainly brought tobacco to Indonesia before the Dutch, and from Macao they introduced it to Canton and Southern China, where the habit spread so rapidly that by the end of the sixteenth century the Emperor was astonished to find smoking had become as much of a habit as the drinking of tea. In 1641 the last Emperor of the Ming Dynasty issued an edict against smoking, no doubt suspecting it of an influence as deleterious as opium. However, three years later Peking fell to the Manchus who, having already taken to smoking themselves, encouraged the habit which led to China's becoming a nation of smokers.

Japan, however, was the first Oriental country to welcome tobacco, and that was due to the Portuguese. In 1542 a Chinese junk on the way from Siam to Macao with three Portuguese on board was blown out of its course by a typhoon and made land on a small island off Kyushu, the southernmost island of Japan. They were hospitably received by the inhabitants; commercial intercourse between the Portuguese and the Japanese began.

Ever since Marco Polo wrote, "Chipanzu is an island towards the East in the high seas. . . . The people are white, civilized, and well favoured . . . and I can tell you the quantity of gold they have is endless", Japan had been an eldorado dream for European adventurers : Columbus hoped he was near it when he landed on San Salvador in 1492.

The Portuguese merchants brought tobacco with them, and in Japanese archives there exist accounts of the way they taught the people of Kyushu to smoke. In 1596 the Mikado was sent seeds of *N. tabacum*, and plants were grown in the gardens of the Imperial Palace at Kioto. About the same time cultivation of tobacco went on round the southern seaports, and a doctor of Nagasaki recorded how the *Nañbaño*, or Southern Barbarians, had taught the people how to smoke.

After Hideyoshi occupied Korea tobacco reached Manchuria, and as mentioned above led to the encouragement of smoking when the Ming Dynasty was destroyed by the Manchus. When Jeyasu became Shôgun in the reign of Hideyoshi's son, smoking was prohibited almost at the same time as King James published his *Counterblaste*; in 1609 the cultivation of tobacco was made a penal offence. Yet smoking could not be suppressed. Three years later Jeyasu ordered that anybody caught selling tobacco should hand over his property to the man who caught him, and that anybody who arrested a vendor carrying it on a horse should be entitled to seize the horse and the tobacco for himself. Yet smoking persisted. By 1615 the officers of the Shôgun's own bodyguard were smoking, in spite of an order that any man in the army discovered smoking was liable to have all his property confiscated. And still they smoked. In 1616 imprisonment and heavy fines were made the penalty for smoking. It was no use, and at last the leaders of the military aristocracy took to tobacco themselves, on which the opposition gave up. In 1625 permission was granted to cultivate tobacco except in the ricefields and vegetable gardens, and by 1639 smoking was the recognized accompaniment of the formal cup of tea offered to a guest. Tobacco had won. So much for the Far East; in the rest of the Orient the way of the smoker was hard for a long time.

We do not know who brought tobacco first to Turkey, but mariners enough of various nationalities brought merchandise to Constantinople, and we may guess that smoking was an established habit some time before the end of the sixteenth century.

The Ottoman Empire, which had threatened Europe with the prospect of being conquered by the barbarous Turk, was now showing signs of a merciful decline. However, he was still a menace to civilization. The muftis, who had much in common with the fanatical ministers of puritanism, declared that smoking like the drinking of wine violated the teaching of the Koran, and in the reign of Ahmed I, who succeeded Mohammed III as Sultan in 1603, smoking was prohibited. George Sandys who visited Constantinople in 1611 relates:

> The Turks ... also delight in Tobacco, they take it through reeds that have joined unto them great heads of wood to contain it: I doubt not but lately taught them, as brought by the English: and were it not sometimes looked into (for Morat Bashaw not long since commanded a pipe to be thrust through the nose of a Turk, and so to be led in derision through the City) no question but it would prove a principal commodity. Nevertheless they will take it in corners, and are so ignorant therein that that which in England is not saleable, doth pass here amongst them for most excellent.

If Morat Bashaw is Murad III who died in 1595, why did he send some dried leaves of tobacco to the King of Poland as a special gift? Perhaps he approved of tobacco as medicine but disapproved of smoking as a recreation. Sandys states positively that the English taught the Turks to smoke pipes; it is to be noted that Thomas Dallam recorded in his diary that when the ship he was in met the galleys of the Turkish navy in the Dardanelles the captain of one of them came on board and "desired to have some tobacco and tobacco-pipes".

The real trouble for Turkish smokers came when Murad IV was Sultan. At the age of fourteen he succeeded a feeble uncle who abdicated, and nine years later he established himself as the most bloodthirsty tyrant that even Turkey had known. By now an imaginary prediction made by the Prophet had been invented to the effect that there would come a time when some Moslems would smoke a weed called tobacco and that such people would not be true Moslems. The muftis even made an effort to find that coffee was also forbidden by the Koran.

A great fire which burnt half Constantinople in 1633 gave Murad IV his chance. A ship at anchor in the harbour was set alight by fireworks being let off in honour of the birth of a son to the Sultan, and there was much resentment among the people. Murad IV used to emulate the Caliph Haroun-al-Raschid, and while visiting tobacco- and coffee-houses in disguise he overheard a great deal of grumbling at him and his officials. Having ordered that all such places should be levelled, he went on to make indulgence in tobacco, opium and coffee a capital offence. Drinking wine was already punished by death in spite of his own drunkenness. Thousands were executed. Before he died in 1640 at the age of twenty-nine, of gout aggravated by drink, this horrible creature of immense physical strength had put to death over 100,000 of his subjects.

The edict against smoking remained in force during the reign of his feeble successor Ibrahim I, but fortunately Mohammed IV, who succeeded him, smoked himself, and the edict was repealed. No doubt the muftis wagged their heads when Mohammed IV's army was broken by the charge of Sobieski and his Polish cavalry at the siege of Vienna in 1683 and muttered that such a disgrace was to be expected of a Sultan who defied the Prophet. But the Turks smoked in peace and, what is more, grew some of the best tobacco in the world in Thrace, from which they would derive much financial benefit in the years to come.

Some say that tobacco first reached Persia when Murad IV went to war with Persia; it is more likely to have been brought in through the ports in the Persian Gulf by Portuguese mariners much earlier. The Shah Abbas tried to extirpate the fashion with the usual bloody penalties. We are given a vivid picture of the Shah's methods in young Sir Thomas Herbert's racy *Relation of Some Yeares Travaile* (1634). Herbert was in the suite of the British Ambassador, and made an extended tour through the interior of Persia during 1628.

The King of Persia got into Cazbeen two days before us. . . . At the time forty camels loaden with tobacco, out of India, came hither, which Mahomet Allibeg the Favourite hearing acquaints the King with it, who, commanded forthwith the camel-men to have their noses and ears cut off. The forty load of tobacco . . . was put into a large earthenware pipe . . . and fired, whose black vapour gave the whole city infernal incense, two whole days and nights together. It seems some later edict had forbid it, and then 'tis death or as bad as death to drink it, for he sometimes tolerates and forbids the same thing three or four times in two years as the humour pleases him.

Shah Abbas himself smoked sometimes. He once called for tobacco, and because the attendant did not bring it quickly enough the Shah cut off his hand.

Twixt meals they meet often in houses like our taverns. Where is vendible wine, arrack, sherbet, tobacco sucked through water by long canes or pipes . . . they spit but seldom (the Jews less) and that liquor which most delights them is coffee.

The Shah's severity impressed the Great Mogul at Delhi. Jehangir decided to be equally severe and forbade smoking under the penalty for smokers of having their lips slit. Shah Abbas was succeeded by Shah Sefi in 1629. He, like his grandfather, was subject to sudden attacks on tobacco. Jean Tavernier, a translation of whose *Six Voyages*, which began in 1631, was published in English in 1676, writes of Persia:

The plains are planted with tobacco which is transported into Turkey, for which they have a very great trade.

In spite of this smokers were not safe.

The Persians both men and women are so addicted to take tobacco, that to take their tobacco from them, is to take away their lives. So that if the King should prohibit Tobacco for any time, he should lose a good part of his revenue. However, Shah Sefi in a humour having once forbidden tobacco to be taken in any part of his dominion his spies (that are in every city) found in the Indian inn two rich merchants of that nation smoking their noses. Immediately they were seized, bound and carried to the King, who commanded forthwith that justice should be done upon them, which was that they should pour melted lead down their throats till they were dead.

Tavernier has much more to say about tobacco, but he can be allowed only two more excerpts:

They sing very little in their cups, but they recite a vast number of wicked verses, which they rehearse with a great deal of gravity.

What Tavernier called being in their cups apparently was smoking a hubble-bubble and drinking a dish of coffee.

And lastly, although Tavernier himself was not a smoker, he once had to accept a pipe as a present from a "young man of good family . . . who rode upon an ass, the hinder part of which was painted red".

To-day we should suspect that young man of being a fellow-traveller.

Evidently neither Mogul nor Shah was any more successful than King James in extirpating tobacco.

By 1625 homeward-bound East Indiamen were bringing back tobacco from India as part of their cargoes. Dr John Fryer, in *A New Account of East-India and Persia*, which recorded his travels between 1672 and 1681, described how a number of thugs smoked tobacco on their way to execution.

And of Persia Fryer wrote:

> The coffee-houses are modelled after the nature of our theatres, that every one may sit around, and suck choice tobacco out of long Malabar canes, fastened to crystal bottles, like the recipients of bolt-heads of the Chymists, with a narrow neck, where the bowl or head of the pipe is inserted, a shorter cane reaching to the bottom, where the long pipe meets it, the vessel being filled with water. After this sort they are mightily pleased; for putting fragrant and delightful flowers into the water upon every attempt to draw tobacco, the water bubbles, and makes them dance in various figures, which both qualifies the heat of the smoke, and creates together a pretty sight.

Probably the chief prejudice against tobacco in the minds of Moslem rulers was created by the recurrent accusation of its discouraging virility. This was an accusation widely spread, and was levelled as often in Europe as in Asia. The elementary state of medicine allowed physicians to attribute to smoking a drying influence on the human body with the obvious corollary, and the sedative effect of tobacco confirmed suspic-ions of its anaphrodisiac quality. Virility is more highly esteemed in the Moslem code of ethics than in any other religious system. To this day an elderly Pathan will dye his hair and fierce moustache with henna out of respect to the traditional colour of the Prophet's beard to proclaim that in spite of his years he is still a force to be reckoned with. Remarkable virility as a sign of Divine favour occurs in the Old Testament. It was an inheritance of the children of Shem which they regarded with reverence, and when the Moslems conquered non-Semitic peoples that Semitic tradition coloured their point of view. As time went on without smoking's having any apparently deleterious effect on human fertility, conservative opposition gradually weakened and finally disappeared.

The austere code of morals originally imposed by Sikhism, which in its attitude towards orthodox Brahminism has parallels with the attitude of the Reformers to Catholicism, demanded abstention from both wine and tobacco. When their enemies in the North-west accepted abstention from wine but surrendered to smoking, the Sikhs allowed wine but continued to forbid smoking, and even to-day no orthodox Sikh will smoke so much as a cigarette. Some orthodox Hindus use their hands as a funnel to avoid bringing their lips into contact with fire, one of the five elements held sacred.

Many strict Moslems in Pakistan still disapprove of smoking; I have seen a Pakistani senior officer puff a hurried cigarette in the passage like a schoolboy because he did not dare smoke in front of his father, it being considered disrespectful to smoke in front of one's elders.

One achievement of tobacco in the Orient should never be overlooked. It was able to compete with harmful narcotics like opium and hemp. It is not extravagant to claim that the resurgence of the East owed much to the displacement of those harmful narcotics by beneficent tobacco.

And now we must leave the Orient for home, with a salute to Portugal for the part she played in making tobacco world-wide.

Chapter 7

JAMES I did his best to persuade the colonists of Virginia to cultivate other crops than tobacco. He thought that silk would be a good idea, and mulberries were sent out to be planted for the silkworms. He had the same idea for London; the present grounds of Buckingham Palace are on the site of the old mulberry garden. The London project was a fiasco because the wrong kind of mulberry for silkworms was planted; probably the wrong trees were planted in Virginia. Nothing availed to dissuade the colonists from committing their future to tobacco, and, however distasteful tobacco might be to him, James was astute enough to grasp the financial possibilities of the noxious herb.

In 1619 King James granted a charter to the Company of Pipe Makers, whose arms were to be:

Argent on a mount in base vert, three plants of tobacco, growing and flowering all proper. Crest: A Moor, in his dexter hand a tobacco-pipe, in his sinister a roll of tobacco, all proper. Supporters: Two young Moors proper, wreathed about the loins with tobacco-leaves vert. Motto: *Let brotherly love continue.*

Following upon this the manufacture of pipes was limited to London, which had already been made the sole port of entry for tobacco. Bristol, which had been cutting out Winchester as the centre for the pipe-making industry, was not pleased, for by this London monopoly its growing industry was ruined. Nor was Bristol pleased by the tobacco staple's being fixed in London, because with the development of the Virginia trade the mercantile marine of Bristol had flourished.

At this point attention may be paid to *An Advice How to Plant Tobacco in England*, by C. T., published in 1615.

It should be borne in mind that when this pamphlet was written the results of the great Virginia experiment were not yet apparent. The author is concerned to discourage the importation of Spanish tobacco, for although James had been successful in making friends with Spain, Spain in the eyes of popular opinion was still the enemy.

I have heard it reported by men of good judgment, that there is paid out of England and Ireland, near the value of £200,000 every year for tobacco; and that the greatest part thereof is bought for ready money. Sure I am, that when our Englishmen for these seven or eight years traded for it at Trinidado, or in Orinoque, that great store of gold, silver, coin and plate was carried hence, and given to the Spaniard there in exchange. For besides the ill exchange made for this fantastical merchandise, and besides the extreme rate, and price of the Indian tobacco, of which the greatest part is sold for ten times the value of pepper, and the best of it, weight for weight, with the finest silver, it is hard to find one pound weight in five hundred that is not sophisticate. The black colour which it hath and for which our shopkeepers praise it, is artificial; yea, all the tobacco (the leaves of Hispaniola excepted, which we call Saint Domingo tobacco) is nointed and slubbered over with a kind of juice, or syrup, made of salt-water, of the dregs of filth of sugar, called molasses, of black honey, Guiana pepper, and lees of wine, to which in some places they add a red berry called Anotto, and other tawny berries, with which the Indians paint their bodies and their beds. This they do to give it colour and gloss, to make it the more merchantable, and to give one and the same countenance to all their rotten, withered and ground leaves, which they wrap up in the middle of their wreaths, covering them on the outside with one that is good.

It looks as if C. T. possessed first-hand knowledge of the tobacco trade. Anotto or Annatto is not poisonous. A dye from it is still used to colour cheeses, and in the preparation of chocolate. It is made from the berries of *Bixia orellana*, a beautiful West India tree with panicles of peach-coloured flowers. C. T. says that tobacco stained with these berries has been imported into England in bulk and that recently the Portuguese residing in London had been selling a "filthie leafe".

The natural colour of tobacco is a deep yellow, or a light tawny: and when the Indians themselves sold it for knives, hatchets, beads, bells, and like merchandise it had no other complexion, as all the tobacco at this day hath, which is brought from the coast of Guiana, from Saint Vincent, from Saint Lucia, from Dominica, and other places, where we buy it but of the natural people, and all these sorts are clean, and so is that of St Domingo, where the Spaniards have not yet learned the art of sophistication. . . .

C. T. goes on to argue that tobacco even stronger than the imported Spanish tobacco can be grown in England, and gives some advice to English growers of *N. rustica*:

> You must not so love your own as to take it green; for if when you cut it and dry it, how strong soever it prove in the taking of it, the greatness [?greenness] shows that either it wants ripeness or fermentation; it must look yellow at the least, otherwise it may prove equally harmful with that which is sophisticate. I must also advise you, not to slubber your English with Melrosarum[1] and other trumpery, as many of our own artificers do, thereby to bring it to the Indian colour: it is an impious practice to play with the health of men, and to make profit by their destruction. Your English tobacco if you give it time to ripen, and time to ferment, will change colour, and cast off all her naughty and unwholesome moisture, and change her green garment for that which is perfect yellow or tawny, without any art or addition.

However, after C. T. has given expert advice to the English planter about growing and curing, he evidently feels that it is going to be difficult to wean the average smoker from West Indian tobacco, and contents himself with advising him to forbear the black drugged tobacco and that from the Bermudas.

> For conclusion, because there hath been much dispute about this herb, whether it be wholesome or harmful, I will let my countrymen know, what by long experience, and conference with others, I find.
> It is taken in all America, even from Canada to the straits of Magellan, in all Africa upon the coast, from Barbary to the Cape of Good Hope . . . also used in most of all the kingdoms of the East Indies.

This is convincing testimony to the extent to which tobacco had spread by the beginning of the seventeenth century. The author then goes on to speak of the virtues ascribed to it by the natives everywhere, and by the Spaniards.

> The people of the south parts of Virginia esteem it exceedingly . . . they say that God in the creation did first

---

[1] This was a teaser to hunt out, but at last it was run down as 'melrose', which the *Oxford English Dictionary* describes as a mixture of honey, powdered rose-leaves and alcohol, but gives no example of its use except with muriatic acid!

make a woman, then a man, thirdly great maize, or Indian wheat, and fourthly, tobacco.

Finally C. T. utters, and not without good cause, a protest against the confusion of the botanical classification of tobacco. He is naturally annoyed when *N. rustica*, the tobacco being grown in England, is called henbane. He also inverts the usual order by avowing that tobacco should not be smoked with wine because the wine spoils the good effect of the tobacco. What would the devotees of port who managed to keep club dining-rooms clear of tobacco smoke until quite recently have replied to that assertion?

In 1616 King James acknowledged the authorship of the *Counterblaste* which had been an open secret for ten years, and this acknowledgment inspired several attacks on tobacco obviously written in the hope of royal favour, but the battle against tobacco was lost by this time and the accusations become tedious.

Richard Braithwait brought a dump of ponderous satire to bear in *The Smoaking Age* (1617), almost the only entertaining page of which is a frontispiece that provides us with the first illustration of a tobacco-shop. Three "renowned and unparallel'd Heroes, Captaine Whiffe, Captaine Pipe, and Captaine Snuffe" are shown in a private room behind the shop, the curtains being drawn back. They are seated behind a table supported by three tobacco casks, and puffing away hard at 3*d.* a pipeful, the smoke being covered with Latin quips like the bubbles in a comic strip.

By 1619 King James had become aware of the threat of home-grown tobacco to the profitable trade that by now was evident from the success of the Virginia experiment, and he consulted the College of Physicians about the quality of English tobacco. The physicians produced a courtier's opinion that English tobacco as it was now usually taken could not but be very hurtful and unwholesome, because it fell far short of the perfection of other tobaccos brought in from more southern parts where it had its natural maturity, vigour and efficacy.

On receiving this opinion James sent a letter to the Justices of Middlesex in which he said that he had been informed that many private yards and gardens in the neighbourhood of London and Westminster heretofore planted to grow vegetables were now being leased at high rents to grow tobacco. The Justices were therefore prayed to put an end to such cultivation and insist that tobacco was to be grown in places farther away.

Probably at this date tobacco was already being grown in Gloucestershire; indeed, it has been stated that such tobacco-growing was started by the colonists who were brought back by Drake from the first Virginia fiasco. This may well be true, but there does not appear to be any authority for such a statement. It is equally probable that tobacco-growing in Gloucestershire started as a result of raising the duty on it from twopence to six shillings and tenpence.

The Virginia Company, which had been contesting the King's action in raising the duty above that specified in the original charter, agreed to pay a higher duty if tobacco-growing in England was suppressed. So in 1620 James renewed a proclamation of six months earlier "for restraint of the disordered trade for tobacco".

The prohibition to grow tobacco in and round London was extended to the whole country. All plants of tobacco were to be destroyed, and the officers entrusted with the task were to execute it on pain of Star Chamber.

Next year James wrote an angry letter to the Lord Mayor and Aldermen of London to complain that in contempt of His Majesty's Royal authority both Englishmen and strangers had persisted in growing tobacco. His Majesty was resolved not to endure such an insolency, but to let these offenders know what it was to contemn his princely pleasure. All tobacco planted in the city was to be sequestrated into safe hands, and such measures were to be taken with the offenders as would restrain them from such transgressions in the future. Copies of this letter were sent to the High Sheriffs and Justices of the Peace of Middlesex, Surrey, Kent and Essex.

Efforts were now made by the Virginia Company to prevent the importation of any Spanish tobacco. There was a currency crisis at this time, and an economist, Edward Bennett, published a tract to show that £100,000 of the silver reserve was going annually to Spain. The House of Commons by a unanimous vote passed a Bill forbidding the importation of any tobacco after October 1621, except from Virginia and Bermuda, and the planting of any tobacco in England after that date.

S.T.—10

The King was to receive sixpence a pound to compensate him for the loss of revenue. The merchant was not to sell tobacco for more than eight shillings a pound and the retailer was not to charge more than ten shillings. "But such as sell tobacco by the pipe may make the most they can."

This Bill failed to become an Act because the House of Lords did nothing about it. However, in 1622 James granted the Virginia and Bermuda Companies a monopoly of the importation into England and Ireland of the tobacco produced by those colonies, with a promise that not less than 40,000 pounds and not more than 60,000 pounds of the best Spanish was to be imported by them. The companies did not like this, but James was firm. He refused to deprive "the better sort" of tobacco with a higher duty for which they were prepared to pay.

The agitation to exclude all foreign tobacco from England continued, and in 1624, not long before he died, James despite the "dislike we have ever had of the use of tobacco in general" issued a proclamation forbidding the use of any foreign tobacco after May 1st, 1625. All colonial tobacco was to pass through the London Customs Quay; none was to be landed elsewhere, and none was to be imported in "foreign bottoms". This led to a great increase in smuggling because the "better sort" were still unwilling to admit the merit of Virginia tobacco. Nevertheless, it was winning favour all the time. In 1617, 19,388 pounds were imported from the English colonies; ten years later the amount had risen to nearly 400,000 pounds.

Charles I, who succeeded his father in 1625, had no love for tobacco, but he was aware of the economic importance of the product to the many colonies, and he was resolved to prosecute the efforts to suppress the cultivation of tobacco in England, where it was being smoked all over the provinces and by the poorer classes.

It was about now that Gloucestershire became the main tobacco-producing area in England.

We have a record in the Gurney manuscript under the date 1627 of one speculator in London whose mother came from a long line of Gloucestershire landowners:

John Stratford, citizen of London, took a long lease of a house within the site of the Abbey of Winchcombe. . . . About five years past he fell to plant tobacco, and having the first year gained well thereby, he was so greedy after more gain thereby that he engaged his whole estate for tobacco, of which he had so much, was valued to be worth £20,000. His sale failing thereof he was by use of money worn out of his estate; hath sold all his land and hideth his head and hath undone many of his friends.

It is to be noted that in that same year, 1627, warrants were issued to William Bedo and William King to destroy all English and foreign tobacco in Gloucestershire, Worcestershire and Wiltshire. Forty places were particularly noted in Gloucestershire, ten places in Worcestershire, and Wootton Bassett in Wiltshire was denounced.

But cultivation in England continued. In July 1631 the Privy Council sent a reproachful letter to the Justices of Gloucestershire and Worcestershire:

> We could not have believed that after so many commands by His Majesty, and by his royal father of blessed memory by their royal proclamations, grounded upon such weighty reasons as are therein expressed, any men would have presumed to have planted or maintained any English tobacco.

William King was empowered to superintend the work of destruction, and he reported to the Council that in his efforts to displant and destroy the tobacco crop in Gloucestershire he

> received many great affronts in divers places. The offenders having gathered their tobacco, daily bring it to London by secret ways, and sell it for Virginia and Bermuda tobacco.

Not Spanish be it noted, which suggests the progress Virginia tobacco was making in popularity:

The next step taken to control tobacco was the decision to make retailers register themselves and pay a licence.

A royal proclamation was issued in October 1633:

> The plant or drug called tobacco scarce known to this nation in former times, was in this age first usually brought into this realm in small quantity, as medicine, and so used . . . but in process of time, to satisfy the inordinate appetites of a great number of men and women it hath been brought in in great quantity, and taken for wantonness and excess, provoking them to drinking and other inconveniences, to the great impairing of their healths, and depraving of their manners, so that the care which His Majesty hath of his

people hath enforced Him to think of some means for the preventing of the evil consequences of this immoderate use thereof.

His Majesty's paternal solicitude for the health, morals and manners of his people was expressed by deciding that "none but men of sufficiency . . . sell or utter any Tobacco by retail".

The first 1,928 licences issued during the next two years brought in a total of £12,460 and the expectation of a yearly rent of the same amount.

It need hardly be added that every effort was made by the population to evade the payment of these licences. Our present willingness to pay mammoth taxes is sad evidence of the decline of our native vigour. Graft, of course, was rampant: the Vice-Chancellor of Cambridge was complaining in October 1634 that he was not allowed the patronage of applicants, whereupon the Privy Council revoked the original licences and gave the Vice-Chancellor the nomination of any successors on death or withdrawal with a guarantee that not more than six Cambridge licences would be granted. The Vice-Chancellor ceased to complain.

By 1637 the total number of licences in England and Wales was 2,063 at an average rent of £5. Devon had most with 162, followed by Middlesex (119), Cornwall (116), Somerset (101), Norfolk (97), Gloucestershire and Yorkshire (92), Kent (90) and the City of London with 84. Rutland had 4 and the only county without any was Dorset. It is interesting to note the strength of the West Country, and particularly gratifying to see Devon, the shire of the sea-dogs that brought tobacco to England, with such a handsome lead. In spite of the monopoly, London makes a poor showing compared with Bristol or Plymouth.

That London monopoly was bitterly resented by the merchants of Bristol and Plymouth. Smuggling was carried on with determination, and fraud was rampant. One of the problems that worried the Government was the trade steadily growing between the English tobacco plantations in America with Holland. A letter from Sir John Pennington to the Lords of the Admiralty of August 7th, 1634, reports that he "met a great Holland ship, the *White Greyhound* of Rotterdam, laden with tobacco and cotton, and bound for Holland. Yet there were

twenty-eight English aboard, planters, and 2/3rds of the lading
belonged to them, so sent her into Plymouth by one of the
whelps to Sir Jas. Bagg". He admitted that his warrant for that
business (i.e. holding up foreign ships) does not stretch to the
Dutch, but he was sure that the Government would endorse
his action in this case because it would bring "at least £1,000"
to the Treasury. It was obvious that the 2/3rds of that cargo was
intended to be secretly landed somewhere in the West Country.

In 1638 the monopoly of the Port of London was rescinded,
and the right to import tobacco was granted to Bristol, Dart-
mouth, Southampton and Plymouth. Thence onward the
Government could count on the help of the civic authorities of
these ports to aid their efforts to stamp out the West Country
growers of tobacco.

Among the Bledisloe Papers discovered in 1949 in an old
chest at Lydney Park, where they had been lying since 1635,
was a petition from five London importers to the King,
complaining of the damage to their trade in supplying the new
licensed retailers that was being done by the home growers:

> The Merchants that trade much in tobacco complain that
> their trade is greatly impaired, since the Restraint of the
> general sale. . . .
> . . . Upon enquiry they find that the country complains that
> they can get little or no tobacco fit to be taken from the
> Patentees there, but that all is mingled, and basely and un-
> wholesomely compounded, wherein is a main part of
> English tobacco planted in Gloucestershire, Worcestershire
> and Herefordshire and worse things not to be discerned, by
> reason of their beating of it in mortars and otherwise, and
> thereby incorporating it into a body like tobacco. . . .
> So as long as the stream runs in this current the merchants
> are hopeless of their trade, and then as the old saying is
> (what's gotten in the Shire is lost in the Hundred) so what
> His Majesty gets by licence, he will in short time lose in his
> customs, and by the base and noisome tobaccos the old
> Takers of it will quickly be suffocated, and the coming gener-
> ation not allured to taste such unwholesome compositions.

In 1650 the merchants of London and Bristol appealed to
Parliament:

> The Humble Petition of the Merchants and others of the
> cities of London and Bristol most humbly sheweth . . . the

great prejudice this Commonwealth doth suffer by the planting and growing of tobaccos in England, both in relation to their several Foreign Plantations, whereupon thousands of families English depend abroad, as also to the manifold traffic which mutually accrueth thereby to the people here at home, by taking off a great part of the manufactures of this land, besides the interest of the State, both in the increasing and maintenance of shipping and navigation, and for advancing the Public Revenue thereof in Customs and Excise, and at the same time shewing both how unwholesome the tobaccos growing at home are to the body, compared with the foreign, as also how impossible it is to plant enough in England, if it could be made so good, sufficient for the consumption of the nation, without far greater prejudice to the arable grounds of this land.

A quarter of a century earlier Francis Bacon, a supporter of tobacco, had written:
"The English tobacco hath small credit, as being too dull and earthy." But, be it added, Bacon had no more use for Virginia tobacco at that date. He suggested a possibility of making English tobacco more 'aromatical' by growing it as mush-melons were grown in a hot bed.

Cromwell and his men were too busy at first to pay heed to the petitions; but after the defeat of the Royalists at Worcester, when several hundred MacLeods taken prisoner in that battle were shipped off to plantation slavery in Barbados, Cromwell turned his attention to the moans of Virginia planters and English merchants. In April 1652 an Act was passed by which a fine was to be imposed for every pole of ground planted with tobacco, half to go to the Commonwealth and the other half to the informer. Finally the Act authorized anybody to "grub, cut up, destroy and utterly to consume all and every such Tobaccos". The merchants of Bristol might petition Parliament, but when officers arrived from London to enforce the law there was serious rioting in the neighbourhood of the city, and petitions, one of them signed by the Mayor of Bristol, pleaded for mitigation of the new law. Parliament became nervous, and in September 1653 it was resolved that planters might enjoy the tobacco planted or cured for this year only, on condition that every buyer paid threepence a pound to the Excise. In other words, home-grown tobacco had been legalized if only for a year. Encouraged by this victory, the tobacco-growers planted a larger crop than ever in 1654. The Virginia merchants were furious, and the Bristol M.P.s were told to make every effort to stop further plantation. "Vast quantities having been planted this year are daily brought into the city, to the great prejudice of the local trade." So an Order in Council was drawn up in March 1654 that all tobacco growing in England must be destroyed immediately.

By June the men of Winchcombe had raised 300 horse and foot to resist the soldiers and invited all tobacco-growers to rally round. The more cautious of them sent emissaries to plead with Cromwell for this year's crop with a promise not to plant again without licence, although it had been their trade for forty years. Surely, if the historians are right who claim that tobacco-growing in England started when the first colonists came back with Drake, seventy years would have been claimed for the trade. However, it may well be that Hariot grew a supply for himself when he settled in Gloucestershire. Cromwell, anxious to avoid any more domestic trouble, consented to let the people of Winchcombe harvest their crop.

In the following year the President of the Council informed the Justices of the City and County of Gloucester that His Highness (Cromwell!) had learned that the well-being of the colonial trade and plantations had been damaged by the continuation of planting in England, the result of which had been that the colonies could not buy the usual amount of goods from this country. Therefore His Highness and the Council were resolved to put the Act of 1652 into execution forthwith.

Nevertheless, the Act was again suspended for 1655; there were too many whispering that the King would come to his own again. Letters to the Secretary of Charles II declared that 1,400 Bristol men would march to join him within four days of his landing. Letters from Gloucester promised that the gates of the city would be thrown open by loyalists, who could count on the support of 600 tobacco-planters.

The men of Winchcombe planted again in 1657 and again in 1658; the local authorities seemed powerless.

A letter to one of the Commissioners entrusted with the destruction of the tobacco crops in that year is illuminating:

Our hopeful proceedings are clouded, for this morning,

I got together 36 horse, and went to Cheltenham early, and found an armed multitude guarding the tobacco field. We broke through them and went into the town, but found no peace officer, but a rabble of men and women, calling for blood for the tobacco, so that, had there been any action, blood would have been spilt. The soldiers stood firm and with cocked pistols bade the multitude disperse, but they would not, and 200 more came from Winchcombe. . . . Ten men could not in four days destroy the good tobacco about Cheltenham. The cornet would not act, and some of the country troop are dealers and planters. I was forced to retreat. The Justices of the Peace rather hinder than help us. The soldiers say, if this be suffered, farewell all levies and taxes, and farewell the Virginia trade for tobacco. . . .

It would be jolly to be able to record that after the Glorious Restoration those obstinate tobacco planters who make our tax-payers of to-day seem such docile slaves to paper were encouraged by King Charles II. Clarendon, however, was as much determined upon an Imperial policy as Cromwell, and with a preamble that stressed the importance of encouraging the plantations in America in 1661, an Act of the Privy Council prohibited the growing of tobacco in England and Ireland with heavier fines for contravention than in previous acts. However, no steps seem to have been taken to enforce it, for in the following year the Governor of Virginia was asking for orders to be given to the Sheriff that the Act should be made immediately effective. At the same time, owing to the increasing demand for English tobacco, the customs receipts were falling.

Mr Secretary Nicholas, no longer concerned to stir up discontent on his master's behalf, wrote one or two sharp letters to the High Sheriff of Gloucester, urging him to do his duty by destroying the tobacco crops. The High Sheriffs and Justices of Worcester and Hereford received similar orders. Little was done, and in 1663 tobacco was being planted in Oxfordshire and Monmouthshire as well. Another Act was passed, raising the fine by an additional £10 for every pole planted, one-third to go to the King, one-third to the poor of the parish and one-third to the informer. Further penalties were imposed for resistance, and the Sheriffs of the offending counties were ordered to assist Mr Thomas Delaval, Surveyor to the Farmers of His Majesty's Customs and such persons as he shall employ, in the destruction of the tobacco crops. In January 1664, a special letter was sent to the bailiff of Winchcombe, the hot spot of the resistance.

In 1664 the Lord-Lieutenant of the County of Gloucester was ordered to assist the Sheriff. In June the Lord-Lieutenant was protesting that he had not enough horse for the job. The Sheriffs of Gloucester and Worcester had been met with such active opposition in Winchcombe and Evesham that they could not carry out their task, and a troop of horse from the Earl of Oxford's regiment was asked for. Nevertheless, in 1666 planting went on as before. The Sheriff of Gloucester tried to interfere, and barely escaped being killed in the Winchcombe and Cheltenham district. The Lord-Lieutenant was ordered to assist the Commissioner with all the militia he deemed necessary, and a troop of horse was despatched to Tewkesbury in support. Planting seems to have been extended; letters were now sent to the Sheriffs of Warwick, Oxford and Brecknock in addition to the others.

Old Rowley himself was 'wearied':

His Majesty is wearied with continual complaints and cannot but observe that his clemency is abused, and the stubborn spirit of nonconformists improved in that they continue to dig up new grounds for planting this illegal crop.

It was no use. In 1667 letters were being sent to the Sheriffs of York and Essex where planting was now going on. To Gloucestershire were despatched 120 Life Guards to help the *posse comitatus*.

Samuel Pepys noted in his diary on September 19th:

My cozen, Kate Joyce . . . tells me how the Life-Guard, which we thought a little while since was sent down into the country about some insurrection, was sent to Winchcombe, to spoil the tobacco there, which it seems the people there do plant contrary to law, and have always done, and still been under force and danger of having it spoiled, as it hath been often times, and yet they will continue to plant it. The place, she says, is a miserable poor place.

The Farmers of the Customs were at their wits' ends, and swore an affidavit before the Mayor of Bristol that the Sheriffs and the Justices of the Peace in their own interest would not enforce the law. By the following year Warwickshire, Shropshire and Flintshire had joined the planting counties.

In 1671 the officials were empowered to destroy crops without waiting for information. The only result of this was that in 1672 much new ground was dug up and prepared in Gloucestershire, Worcestershire, Herefordshire and Wiltshire.

In 1674 the Duke of Monmouth had a rehearsal for Sedgmoor by being sent to Gloucestershire with a troop of horse. Planting and harvesting went on. Much may have been destroyed, but enough was left to give the planters a profit that made it worth while to defy the law. In 1676 the records show that a good deal of tobacco was destroyed in Yorkshire and Nottinghamshire, and in the following year Lincolnshire was planting. Gloucestershire, however, was still the biggest planter and the core of the resistance. The Duke of Monmouth had another rehearsal for Sedgmoor in 1678. Soon afterwards he was in rebellion himself, and during the reign of James II the tobacco-planters were left undisturbed. With the fall in price of Virginia tobacco and the improved quality, during the 1680's there was a steady decline in planting, which by the first year of the reign of William and Mary had been practically reduced to Gloucestershire and Worcestershire. The last record of action by the authorities against the growers is in 1692, when nine plantations extending over 1,300 roods were discovered and destroyed.

In *The True English Interest* (1674), Carew Reynell was declaring that:

What would bring infinite wealth to this nation (if the law would permit it) is the planting of tobacco; it would employ abundance of people, would raise the value of the land from 10s. to £3 the acre, the tenant making a profit of £30 to £40 an acre; before the severity of the laws against its planting, it went well forward; those counties where it began to be planted are believed to be willing to allow the King the common rent of the ground, or more, to be permitted to plant again. There were reputed to have been 6,000 plantations in Gloucestershire, Devon, Somerset and Oxfordshire; if not so good as foreign-grown, it found plenty of purchasers, because people must have tobacco. Some preferred it to the foreign; being strong they could cure it to their own taste, it had often been sold for Spanish in London. . . .

We should consider ourselves before the interest of
Virginia. It would really be better to move Virginia and
New England further south; then they could trade with us,
while now, we and they have the same commodities, and
they export them also to the West Indies. It would be better
for Virginia to plant mulberries, vines and olives, as they
begin in Carolina. If they wished to continue their tobacco
trade we should leave them liberty so to do, and they say
theirs is so much better. The customs and shipping would
not be hurt because the tobacco would fetch in so many
other commodities. Indeed, it would be better to supply the
King some other way than by prejudicing the common good.
The whole of the South of England is fit for it. The more
home industries we have the more foreign trade we should
have.

In 1685 there was a debate in Parliament to consider raising
the duty on tobacco. A document in the British Museum
protesting against the proposed increase gives a picture of "The
Advantages of the Tobacco Trade at that date":

1. It employs near two hundred Sail of Ships, from one
hundred to five hundred Tons, and breeds many Mariners.
2. It vends vast quantities of English manufactures and
other things for clothing, building, furniture, etc.
3. It pays yearly from one hundred thousand, to one
hundred and thirty thousand pounds custom to the King.
4. It is sent from hence to most parts of Europe, and thereby Shipping is employed, and the stock of the Kingdom
increased by return of money and commodities.
The inconveniences that will follow, by laying a greater
Imposition are,
1. Great quantities of tobacco have been left in warehouses,
for that the custom, freight, etc., are more than oftentimes
the commodity yielded.
2. It hath been found by experience, that when the duty
hath been more, the revenue was less, and the Custom
book tells us, that His Majesty hath yearly received more
at two pence the pound, than in former times when it was
higher.
3. It will discourage the Importation, and encourage the
defrauding of the Custom, especially in the Out Ports and
Creeks.
4. A new tax will make it dearer, and so less quantities

will be imported, and will occasion the cutting of stalks amongst it, which are usually cast away, or sold for little.

5. As the tobacco trade hath of late been managed, it hath drawn the whole almost from other nations.

6. It will encourage the planting of tobacco in Ireland, Germany, France and Holland, and put them upon finding out ways to transport it privately hither to supply the nation.

7. The importation being less, the exportation of our native manufactures will be so likewise, and many families that depend upon them, and fitting tobacco for sale, will be ruined.

8. The great ships built and employed by the traders will be laid aside as useless, and no more built for want of employment, and so navigation weakened.

9. The tobacco will be carried into other nations where the duties are less, as Holland, Zeland, Hambrough and Flanders, where it pays not above one half-penny per pound, from whence the Planters will be supplied with all necessaries, or they will be necessitated to leave their own and go to the Dutch and French plantations where they may find better encouragement.

10. Necessity will cause the Inhabitants of the Plantations to turn their lands to the increasing of provisions, and employ their hands in making those manufactures which they have hitherto been supplied with from England.

Our knowledge of the long struggle to grow tobacco in England that lasted almost throughout the seventeenth century is wretchedly meagre, dependent indeed entirely upon State Papers. The excerpt from Carew Reynell quoted earlier sheds almost the only flicker of light upon an obscure byway of our nation's history. In none of the private letters of the period printed so far is there any reference to what must have been a large and lucrative trade. We do not know anything about the methods of curing or distribution, but we do read in Fuller's *Worthies* (1661) of "the great care and cost in planting, re-planting, transplanting, watering, snailing, suckering, topping, cropping, sweating, drying, making, and rolling it".

To-day not a tale remains in the folk-lore of Gloucestershire about those sturdy smokers of once upon a time. All that is left of that prolonged and obstinate struggle by Englishmen to grow what they wanted to grow is a field outside Winchcombe on the Cheltenham road. It is called 'Tobacco Close'. Two centuries were to pass almost to a year before tobacco was again grown in England.

During the war with the American Colonies, tobacco was grown in a few places in Scotland, but in 1782 the Act of 1660 prohibiting the home-growing of tobacco was formally extended to Scotland.

In 1778 an Act of Parliament had been passed permitting the growing of tobacco in Ireland, but for fifty years little or no advantage was taken of it. Then, when there were signs of a revival of an Irish tobacco-growing industry, a Select Committee of the House of Commons reported that permission to grow tobacco must either be withdrawn from Ireland or extended to the whole of Great Britain, and that the detriment to the Revenue would outweigh any advantage to be gained from the extension of tobacco-growing in the British Isles. Accordingly in 1831 the 1778 Act permitting tobacco to be grown in Ireland was repealed.

Between 1886 and 1889 the Government, with a notion of helping agriculture, allowed a number of approved persons to make experiments whether tobacco could be grown successfully in the United Kingdom. These experiments were not a success. The tobacco produced was ranker in flavour and poorer in quality than the cheapest varieties of imported leaf, and the Government's advisers reported that tobacco grown in this country could not compete successfully with tobacco grown in warmer climates. Inasmuch as the same duty was levied on this home-grown effort as upon imported tobacco, it is not surprising that the experiments failed to be profitable and were abandoned.

With the turn of the century, however, efforts to revive home-growing were renewed. In Ireland growers were allowed a rebate of one-third of the duty on tobacco grown for experimental purposes, and Americans were called in to give advice. This was followed by the Irish Tobacco Act, 1907, and the Finance Act, 1908, which repealed the 1660 Act so far as Ireland was concerned, and made possible there the unrestricted growth of tobacco for commercial purposes; assistance was given to the growers by way of technical instruction and the payment of an acreage bounty. In Scotland the Tobacco

Growing (Scotland) Act, 1908, and the Finance (1909–10) Act, 1910, permitted the experimental growing of tobacco on a maximum area of fifty acres, and allowed the growers a rebate of one-third of the duty. Very little advantage was taken in Scotland of this concession.

Similarly in England the Act of 1660 was finally repealed under the authority of the Finance (1909–10) Act, which allowed the experimental growing of tobacco on plots not exceeding 100 acres with a rebate of one-third of the duty. Both in England and Scotland the rebate was ended on March 15th, 1914, and assistance was given to the tobacco-growing industry through the British Tobacco Growers' Society, a non-profit-making association sponsored by the Government for this purpose.

When Imperial Preference was introduced in 1919 home-grown and Colonial tobacco both received the benefit of this preferential rate of duty, i.e. five-sixths of the normal duty. The British Tobacco Growers' Society was then wound-up and responsibility for the experimental growing of tobacco passed to the Ministry of Agriculture. Continuity of policy was ensured by the appointment of an Advisory Committee, including leading members of the Society, and by the retention of the services of an expert officer employed by the Society. The Ministry took over the Society's tobacco-curing barns and re-handling plant, and set up an experimental tobacco-growing and handling station at Methwold in Norfolk. Tobacco was bought from farmers and smallholders in the district who had formerly grown for the Society, and re-handled at the Methwold estate. However, owing to the great fall in prices, the venture was unprofitable and by 1922 no tobacco was being grown at Methwold.

In 1923 a Committee was set up by the Treasury to consider the position and prospects of commercial tobacco-growing in Great Britain and whether Government assistance should be given to it. They reported that, owing to unfavourable climatic conditions, tobacco grown here could not compete in quality or yield with tobaccos produced under more suitable conditions abroad, and that, moreover, the quality and yield of the British crop would always be uncertain. They added that in their opinion there were other forms of assistance to agriculture to which support might more profitably be given. In the circumstances they unanimously recommended that there should be no further expenditure of public funds to assist the industry of tobacco-growing in Great Britain.

Between the two world wars the Government of Ireland tried to revive tobacco-growing in that country by paying a bounty to growers and re-handlers of Irish tobacco and by forcing manufacturers to use a proportion of Irish-grown leaf. The home-grown leaf, however, proved unpopular with Irish smokers, and eventually the Irish Government acknowledged failure by withdrawing the obligation on manufacturers to use Irish-grown leaf, the commercial production of which has ceased.

In Great Britain shortage of tobacco supplies and the high rate of duty stimulated an interest in the home-growing of tobacco during and following the Second World War, and the Government was repeatedly pressed to reduce the duty on home-grown leaf. This they refused to do on the grounds adduced by the Committee appointed by the Treasury in 1923, that climatic conditions in this country were unsuitable for the commercial growing of tobacco and that, moreover, the land in this country suitable for tobacco production could be more advantageously used for growing other crops. In April 1948, however, a concession was made to amateur home-growers, who are now allowed to produce small quantities for personal consumption without payment of duty. Later it was announced that amateur growers might have up to twenty-five pounds of dry leaf each per year cured co-operatively without payment of duty.

That is the position to-day (1956).

Chapter 8

WITHOUT any doubt one of the major achievements of the English was teaching the rest of Europe to smoke. This was acknowledged in 1685 by a Dutch physician called Cornelis Bontekoe, who admits to his astonishment that the English had made the three great discoveries of the age— smoking, the circulation of the blood and the circumnavigation of the world. He is an enthusiastic supporter of tobacco and wishes that women would take to smoking as they do in England. He declared that when tea was being served everybody should smoke. Bontekoe's disciple Worb was almost a keener enthusiast for tobacco. He was sure that everybody, men and women, should smoke in order to be happy. Twenty pipes a day was a reasonable allowance, and it was better not to spit. Tea-time would be perfect when all women smoked.

The Dutch were the first Europeans who took up smoking as enthusiastically as the English. The many English students at the Dutch universities were ardent missionaries of the herb. When the Virginia plantations got going the Dutch became, outside England, the largest importers of tobacco, which they purchased with Negro slaves. Von Rusdorff, the Palatine Ambassador at The Hague, was protesting in 1627 against the extraordinary fashion lately introduced from America of swallowing the smoke of a plant they called Herba Nicotiana. This diplomat, like many another since, was behind the times. By 1620 tobacco had already crossed the Rhine, and the Thirty Years War spread the habit of smoking, the first examples being set by the English troops sent by James I to help his son-in-law the King of Bohemia and also by the Spanish troops. When the Swedes entered the war, they too learnt to smoke.

English sailors brought tobacco to the Baltic ports, and so Russia started smoking and continued to smoke in spite of the brutal knoutings and mutilations inflicted upon smokers by the Tsars, in which they were encouraged by the Orthodox clergy.

The Thirty Years War may have spread the habit all over Germany, but in 1649 the Elector of Cologne was "graciously and solemnly" commanding "Our Subjects in general, strictly to forbid the sale and purchase and use of tobacco everywhere, under pain of incurring Our High displeasure and punishment, together with the confiscation of the tobacco and the pipes." [1]

The Electorate of Saxony followed suit in 1653, blaming on smokers a fire in the cellar of the Dresden town-hall. Three years later tobacco was under an official interdict in Württemberg. Yet smoking persisted. In Bohemia a proclamation of 1662 announced that in spite of all the steps which had been taken to stop it, smoking was to be seen even in the streets, while the common people were wasting their few pennies on several pipes a day.

Official Switzerland was as much against tobacco as official Germany. After the Peace of Westphalia, which brought to an end the Thirty Years War, the independence of Switzerland was finally confirmed, and the theocratic ideals of Calvin which had inspired Scotland encouraged a stern interference with morals. Prohibition was imposed on tobacco, and it is to be noted that in all the edicts issued against tobacco attention was drawn to the extent that women were indulging in it.

Catholics were as intolerant of tobacco as Protestants. For years it was forbidden in Austria. The Bull of Pope Urban VIII forbidding the use of tobacco and snuff in the churches of the archdiocese of Seville was not an attempt to prohibit either elsewhere; it was an effort to check a local ecclesiastical abuse. That was in 1642. Some of the tobacco historians have gloated over this example of Papal intolerance, but it was an effort to preserve ecclesiastical discipline. Urban VIII was disliked in Spain on account of what was believed to be his French sympathies, and the archdiocese of Seville required keeping in order. Eight years later Pope Innocent X had to forbid smoking in or about St Peter's in Rome. The propriety of snuffing in church came into it also, and there was the question whether snuffing or smoking could be indulged in without breaking the pre-communion fast. When later Pope Benedict XIII revoked the penalty of excommunication for taking snuff in St Peter's, he insisted that the clergy should abstain from offering snuff to one another in the choir. To-day a priest may smoke before he says Mass, and that privilege has been a great boon to a priest who may have to wait until noon, fasting, and perhaps make a long journey before he reaches the church he is serving.

[1] Corti, op. cit., p. 110.

S.T.—11

Pages might be written about the persecution which tobacco
had to endure in that seventeenth century during which persecution of every kind flourished so vigorously. Not even in
North America was it immune. The economic future of Virginia
and Maryland might depend upon tobacco: Connecticut at
that date had not discovered how well it could grow it. In 1650
the General Court of Connecticut decided that nobody under
twenty-one should be allowed to smoke "nor any other that
hath not already accustomed himself to the use thereof". Even
the hardened smoker was not allowed to light his pipe until he
had obtained a doctor's certificate that smoking would be
"useful for him, and also that he hath received a licence from
the Court for the same". Yet even then he was at the mercy of
restrictions, for no man in Connecticut was to be allowed to
smoke publicly "in the streets, highways, or any barnyards, or
upon training days in any open places, under the penalty of
sixpence for each offence".

All over New England smoking was forbidden on the Sabbath
within two miles of the meeting-house. Almost the only place
where a smoker armed with a medical certificate and a licence
could light a pipe was in his private house.

In spite of their objection to smoking, these New England
colonists, both in Connecticut and Massachusetts, presently
tried their hands at tobacco planting in a small way, but we
must not suppose that the Act of Parliament during the Protectorate which alluded to the large importation of 'New-
England leaf' means the leaf was grown in New England.
Planters in Virginia and Maryland had been shipping their
crops in New England vessels because there was no duty on
tobacco from the northern colonies. The Act of 1650 imposed
the same duty on tobacco coming from any of the colonies.
The colonists of Virginia protested to no purpose that over
forty thousand people were being "impoverished to enrich little
more than forty merchants who, being the only buyers of
tobacco, give us what they please for it". Maryland at first
was allowed to export its tobacco known as Orinoco to other
countries than England, and had found good markets in
Holland and Scandinavia, but this freedom did not last. The
Navigation Act of 1651 followed, which required that tobacco
should be carried only in English or colonial ships and landed
first in England. This was particularly directed against the

Dutch and to some extent against the Scots. Another and
severer Navigation Act was passed in 1660 against which the
Scots protested to the Privy Council, who exempted them from
the maritime restrictions imposed by the Act until the Commissioners of the Customs had made their report. This was unfavourable. "The Scotch would . . . overthrow the essence of
the Act of Navigation, and they must not be allowed to trade
from port to port, for they are strangers and their bond is not
sufficient security." On this the Privy Council revoked the
exemption.

The Scots had upset the ring of English merchants by paying
a higher price to the planters; naturally the planters took
advantage of this. Thanks to the enterprise of the Scots merchantmen tobacco was cheap and plentiful in Scotland. They
also took care to bring the goods that the colonists most
needed.

The household accounts of the Rev. William Hamilton, the
minister of Eastwood near Glasgow, show that he smoked at
least a pound of tobacco a week at five shillings a pound Scots
sterling.[1]

Charles I as early as 1634 had tried to cure his Scottish
subjects of heavy smoking and snuffing by granting a monopoly
to Sir James Leslie and Thomas Dalmahoy with power to
appoint licensed vendors of tobacco. Evidently it had not had
much effect.

By 1701 Pennsylvania was growing tobacco and Colonel
Robert Quarry, the Judge of the Admiralty there, was reporting:

> Four times the tobacco was made there that year than
> had been made before, and all of it engrossed by the Scotch,
> as almost all other trade there was. No one who designed to
> trade fairly could give the extravagant rates they did, being
> not less than double what was given in Maryland.

Even after the Union the Scots traders were still a headache
to their English competitors; before the treaty was signed they
brought in as much tobacco as they could carry under the
lower duty in Scotland and then undersold them. During the
eighteenth century Glasgow became the greatest tobacco centre
in the world, as we shall see presently.

[1] Quoted by Apperson, op. cit., p. 61.

The Spaniards were finding the competition of Virginia tobacco a serious threat to their trade, but connoisseurs still thought their tobacco was the best and much smuggling into England went on, the cargoes being carried in Dutch bottoms.

Cigar-making was general in Italy and in Spain itself; elsewhere in Europe the pipe ruled. For snuff, which will be dealt with later, the Virginia and Maryland tobacco was most popular.

The first two Stuart kings may have disliked tobacco, but the way they turned it into revenue set an example which almost every government in the world has followed ever since.

In 1629 Richelieu, who disliked smoking, imposed a duty equivalent to 1s. 3d. on every pound of tobacco imported into France. The excuse, as usual, was that if tobacco was too cheap and too easily obtainable the country's health would be damaged. Only tobacco from the French West Indies was exempt.

The Duke of Mantua in 1627 granted to a patentee a monopoly of spirits and tobacco for a yearly rent of 16,900 lire. Lombardy and Savoy followed during the next decades, but it was the Venetian Republic that perfected the monopoly as a source of revenue in 1659. The exclusive right to import, manufacture and deal in tobacco was leased to a patentee for three years at 8,000 ducats. The Seven Communes were allowed to grow tobacco, but the monopoly had the right to regulate their supply. In 1655 Pope Alexander VII imposed a penalty of six scudi on every pound of tobacco imported or grown in the Papal States, having farmed out a monopoly for Rome and its neighbourhood. Two years later he granted a monopoly of manufacturing tobacco to the Jews of Ferrara. Silesia and Bohemia began with taxes, and went on to adopt the monopoly system.

In 1662 "Ferdinand Karl, by God's Grace Archduke of Austria, Burgundy, etc., Ruler of the County of Tyrol", graciously gave and granted to "Gideon May, the Jew", a monopoly of tobacco and snuff in the County of Tyrol. In 1668 the Estates of the Tyrol petitioned the Emperor Leopold I to prohibit the importation and smoking of tobacco, and caught the Emperor in the right mood to listen to them. One of the guards in the Hofburg at Vienna had used a live coal to light his pipe and managed to set fire to the Leopold suite which was destroyed. The private chapel was burnt out, and some of the archduchesses were nearly burnt with it.

So the Emperor issued an edict in August 1668 that in future tobacco was not to be bought or sold in the Tyrol except in apothecaries' shops for medicinal purposes because smoking was injurious to the health, took a lot of money out of the country and was the cause of many fires.

In those days before matches were invented smoking undoubtedly did cause many fires. An extract from *The Lord High Admiral's instructions to the Principle officers and Commissioners of Her Majesty's Navy and Subordinate officers of the Yards and Ships* reminds them at the beginning of the reign of Queen Anne of the regulations:

> The smoking tobacco in his Majesty's Yards and Ships in the Docks is absolutely prohibited by an Order of the 15 of March 1663, and by other orders it is not to be admitted in Ships-afloat, otherwise than over a Tub of Water, by warrants of the 19 November and 31 January 1662, and 21 of May 1670.

In 1670 the Emperor was anxious to enjoy a grand *battue*—the French word is used in deference to the feelings of English sportsmen who when they are a little ashamed of something they enjoy always prefer to use a French word for it—in Upper Austria. The game were to be driven into the woods and prevented from escape by narrowing their refuge with fences and strips of linen. The Chief Huntsman, Count Khevenhiller, pointed out the expenses involved, but the Emperor, unwilling to give up his treat, told Khevenhiller that he must find out some way of raising the money. Khevenhiller suggested the grant of a monopoly to import tobacco into Upper and Lower Austria, and went on to propose himself as the grantee, so that he might give His Imperial Majesty good hunting. He undertook to provide the country with sufficient tobacco out of his own capital at a reasonable price, and merely asked that anybody who infringed his monopoly by dealing in tobacco should have all his goods confiscated. If His Imperial Majesty would graciously accede to this request the money for the fences could be found without spending any of His Imperial Majesty's ordinary revenue.

On hearing of this proposal the provincial Estates protested strongly against putting tobacco at the mercy of a 'greedy monopolist'. The Emperor, however, wanted his *battue*, and the monopoly was granted. When some time later the Emperor was in funds Count Khevenhiller surrendered it for a cash payment.

The Habsburgs continued to grant tobacco monopolies to nobles, Jews and Italians until a State monopoly was instituted by the Austro-Hungarian Monarchy and carried on by the Austrian Republic. An extract from the report of the Exchequer on the application of an Italian for a monopoly in Styria, Carinthia and Carniola expresses exactly the attitude of the British Treasury to-day:

> Although tobacco be not necessary to the sustenance of man, yet have matters gone so far that many are of a mind that they would rather lack bread than tobacco.[1]

And with the comforting reflection that tobacco is still a luxury, one Chancellor of the Exchequer after another takes advantage of the fact that it is to-day more than ever it was a necessity. We are such a docile people nowadays that no Chancellor has been obliged to issue an apology such as the Emperor Leopold I felt was owing to His Imperial conscience when he decided to profit from tobacco:

> Following the example of other sovereigns and republics, for the good of Our General Treasury, We have graciously determined, in virtue of our Imperial, royal and princely power and sovereignty, . . . to draw a revenue from tobacco, whether smoked or taken as snuff. This commodity is not needful for the sustenance of mankind—rather has it become an arbitrary though almost universal habit. For this purpose we have determined, through Our Imperial Exchequer, either Ourself to take over the trade in such tobacco, or, according as We may think most profitable to our Treasury, to lease or farm it out to one or more persons.[2]

In September 1674 His Most Christian Majesty Louis XIV was announcing from Versailles his intention to follow the example of other princes by introducing a tobacco monopoly to help the revenue.

> We have considered the plan laid before us the more reasonable, in that tobacco is not a food needful for health

---

[1] Quoted by Corti, op. cit., p. 157.
[2] Quoted by Corti, op. cit., p. 158.

or nourishment, and may be a means of making it easier for
Our People to bear a part of the extraordinary expenses of
the present war.[1]

Perhaps it was poetic justice that tobacco should help to
pay for war, because through the years the popularity of tobacco
was always spread by war. That French monopoly was eventually to be handled by the *Fermiers-Généraux*, and would be the
most ruthless and dishonest but also the most efficient of all.

Louis XIV hated tobacco and would have been glad to
prohibit both smoking and snuff-taking, but the revenue it
brought in was too valuable for a King with such expensive
tastes not to take advantage of it. Autocrat though he was, he
was unable to keep tobacco out of his Court. Indeed, he could
not even prevent his own daughters from smoking. One night
when he was sitting late at cards his brother Philip of Orléans
left him to go to his own apartments. On his way he noticed the
smell of smoke coming from a room, and entering found two of
his nieces smoking pipes they had obtained from the guard-
room of the Swiss Guard. Philip warned the Princesses that
their father would be coming along presently and advised them
to stop smoking at once. However, the King noticed the smell
and, though he scolded his daughters next day, no doubt they
continued to smoke—like everybody else in Europe by now.

Although by the end of the seventeenth century the general
spread of tobacco had slightly impaired its reputation as a
panacea, belief in its value as a prophylactic and antiseptic
helped to spread its use when epidemics of the plague swept
Europe at intervals. In 1646 a Dutch physician called Diemer-
broek wrote of the value that smoking pipes of tobacco had
been to him when the stench in the sick-room became unbear-
able, and added he had been told that all the owners of tobacco
shops in London had escaped the infection during a bad
epidemic of the plague. His own experience in Nimeguen from
1635 to 1637 had not confirmed this, but it was true that neither
Thomas Peters, an English tobacco-merchant, nor any of his
many relatives and dependants living in the same house, had
been stricken.

[1] Quoted by Corti, op. cit., p. 160.

In 1665 Thomas Kemp, in his *Brief Treatise . . . of the Pestilence*, was definite about the value of tobacco as a purifier of the air, and was obviously in step with popular opinion:

> The American Silver-weed, or Tobacco, is very excellent for this purpose . . . being smoked in a pipe, either by itself, or with Nutmeg shred, and Rue seeds mixed with it, especially if it be nosed, for it cleanseth the air, and choketh, suppresseth and disperseth any venomous vapour. It hath singular and contrary effects, it is good to warm one being cold, and will cool one being hot. All ages, all sexes, all constitutions, young and old, men and women, the sanguine, the choleric, the melancholy, the phlegmatic, take it without any manifest inconvenience; it quencheth thirst, and yet will make one more able and fit to drink; it abateth hunger, and yet will get one a good stomach; it is agreeable with mirth or sadness, with feasting and with fasting; it will make one rest that wants sleep, and will keep one waking that is drowsy; it hath an offensive smell to some, and is more desirable than any perfume to others, that it is a most excellent preservative, both experience and reason do teach; it corrects the air by fumigation, and it avoids corrupt humours by salivation; for when one takes it either by chewing it in the leaf, or smoking it in the pipe, the humours are drawn and brought from all parts of the body to the stomach, and from thence rising up to the mouth of the Tobacconist [smoker] as to the helm of a sublimatory, are voided and spitten out.

Samuel Pepys had not read Kemp's treatise on that day of unexampled heat, June 7th, 1665, because it was not published until a month later. Therefore the prophylactic value of tobacco must already have been a generally diffused belief.

> This day, much against my will, I did in Drury Lane see two or three houses marked with a red cross upon the doors, and "Lord Have Mercy upon us" writ there; which was a sad sight to me, being the first of the kind that, to my remembrance, I ever saw. It put me into an ill conception of myself, and my smell, so that I was forced to buy some roll-tobacco to smell and to chaw, which took away the apprehension.

Pepys' dread of the plague was stronger than any doubts he may have had about the virtue of tobacco, for on the previous May 3rd he had written:

Out to Gresham College, and saw a cat killed with the Duke of Florence's poison, and saw it proved that the oil of tobacco drawn by one of the [Royal] Society do the same effect, and is judged to be the same thing with the poison both in colour and smell and effect. I saw also an abortive child preserved in spirits of salt.

Pepys was never a smoker himself. Indeed, throughout his diary the only allusions he makes to it are to record an evening on board the *Royal James* when he left Lord Sandwich 'taking tobacco' with some of his Commanders, and an occasion when he saw a horse at Islington suffering from the staggers which was cured by puffing tobacco smoke up its nostrils.

Hearne, the Oxford antiquary, writing in 1721, declared he had been told that during the Great Plague of London all the London tobacconists escaped infection, and W. Hutton, in his *History of Derby* (1817), put on record that when the Plague reached Derby at the

Headless-cross . . . the market people, having their mouths primed with tobacco as a preservative brought their provisions. . . . It was observed, that this cruel affliction never attempted the premises of a tobacconist, a tanner or a shoemaker.

There is no record that the boys of Pepys's old school, St Paul's, were made to smoke as a prophylactic during the Great Plague, but the boys at Eton had to smoke every morning. One Tom Rogers told Hearne that he was given the severest flogging he ever had for not smoking.

Worcester like Oxford escaped the plague of 1665. Not only did they grow tobacco in Worcester; they smoked it heavily. A French traveller, M. Jorévin de Rochefort, has left an account of his travels in England during 1666, in the course of which he spent an evening with a friend in a Worcester inn:

The supper being finished they [the landlady and her daughters] set on the table half a dozen pipes and a packet of tobacco for smoking, which is a general custom, as well among the women as men, who think that without tobacco, one cannot live in England, because they say it dissipates the evil humours of the brain. . . . Whilst we were walking about the town, he [my friend] asked me if it was the custom in France, as in England, that when the children went to school, they carried in their satchels, with their books, a pipe of tobacco, which their mothers took care to fill early in the morning, it serving them instead of a breakfast; and that at the accustomed hour every one laid aside his book to light his pipe, the master smoking with them, and teaching them how to hold their pipes and draw in the tobacco; thus accustoming them to it from their youth, believing it absolutely necessary for a man's health. . . .

I have known several who, not content with smoking in the day, went to bed with their pipes in their mouths, others who have risen in the night to light their pipes, to take tobacco with as much pleasure as they would have received in drinking either Alicant or Greek wine.

Those Worcester enthusiasts would all have been smoking *N. rustica* grown in the neighbourhood. No wonder they escaped the plague and put up such a stout fight against Government interference.

Although tobacco was being grown in the Ukraine, which it had reached from the Levant, the savage edicts against tobacco were not revoked until nearly the end of the seventeenth century. Yet the possibility of such a change of mind in Russia must have been in the air, for as early as 1681, Lord Culpeper, the Governor of Virginia, worried by over production, was announcing that "the free importation of tobacco into Russia would revive our drooping spirits, for we want nothing but a vent".

In 1689 that fantastic creature Peter the Great, after being junior Tsar to his sister during his minority, became the sole autocrat of the Russias, and kept up the friendships he had made with various foreigners who lived in the German suburb of Moscow—a mixed society of Scots, English, Germans, Dutch and Swiss. All of them smoked, and it was probably General Patrick Gordon of Auchterleuchries who taught the young Tsar to smoke.

In 1690 the Patriarch Joachim of Moscow tried to have the foreigners expelled, and was particularly bitter against the 'heathen' Gordon. The latter was in fact a Catholic who, sick of a Puritan Scotland, had gone abroad to fight for the Poles and Swedes in turn, and finally with great distinction for the Muscovites. Peter the Great remained devoted to him until the day that Scottish soldier of fortune died. Within a year or two the Tsar was smoking openly, having put the Patriarch in his place by revoking the edicts against his people's smoking.

The planters of Virginia and Maryland, with the English merchants, petitioned William of Orange in 1697 to suggest to the Tsar that he should allow colonial tobacco to enter Russia. William was under an obligation to tobacco because he had borrowed the wherewithal for his invasion of England from the Dutch Government by pledging his tobacco revenue in England, and when he met Peter in Utrecht he did make the suggestion.

Peter the Great when he came to England was given the services of the Marquis of Carmarthen who, as Rear-Admiral of the Blue, had not long since mistaken the West India trade convoy for the French fleet and withdrawn to the security of Milford, with the result that the West Indiamen were all captured together with five valuable East Indiamen. The English merchants, perhaps surmising that the Admiral would be inclined to make up for his mistake, sent a deputation to Peter to ask him to allow tobacco to be imported into Russia. The Admiral, with whom the Tsar was by now on boon companion terms, supported the request, to which Peter agreed. The merchants formed a joint stock company and agreed to 'lend' the Tsar £13,000 for the sole right to import tobacco into Russia. English workmen were to go out to Russia and arrange for factories to manufacture the imported colonial leaf into the roll tobacco that the Russians preferred. Furthermore, the Tsar promised to prohibit the cultivation of tobacco in the Ukraine. The Russia Company, which had been unsuccessful in obtaining the privileges granted to this new company, claimed that they were entitled to the monopoly, and refused to let the Virginia merchants become 'freemen' on payment of the customary 'fine' of £60. The result was that the Virginia merchants, who had paid out £13,000 to the Tsar, were faced with having to import their tobacco into Russia through Holland or Sweden, which involved paying heavy duties. Parliament had already tried unsuccessfully to reform the Russia Company, but now they dealt firmly with the dozen obstructionists of whom it was composed, and an Act was passed giving any subject of the realm the right to become a 'freeman' by paying a 'fine' of £5.

When Peter returned home from England he confirmed the agreement and started a tobacco monopoly the patent for which he granted to his old playmate and friend Menschikov, who had once been a pastry-cook. The Patriarch was furious, but Peter was too much for him. Besides excommunicating any Russians who smoked, the Patriarch had once threatened to excommunicate any Russians who shaved. The Tsar now came back from England, clean-shaven, and when he was greeted by various magnates in the Kremlin he pulled out a pair of scissors and walked round the gathering, snipping off their beards, on growing which in future he levelled a tax.

The freedom to smoke anywhere in Russia meant a heavy demand for tobacco, and Peter did not keep his promise to prohibit tobacco-growing in the Ukraine. His excuse was that "he needed it and durst not destroy it".

After deciding that a Muscovite would smoke anything, the English importers sent all the stale and mouldy tobacco from the London warehouses to Russia, where they blended it with the Circassian product in rolls. Apparently the Russians became displeased with the manner in which the original concessionaires were carrying out the contract; it is hardly surprising. Anyway, in 1705 another group contracted to despatch ". . . as many Persons skilled in the spinning and rolling of tobacco as the Czar should require together with the instruments, engines, materials and liquors commonly used in that work, to be employed not only for the manufacturing of English tobacco thus imported, but even for the tobacco of the growth of Circassia. . . ".

The Virginia merchants who were not in on this deal were most indignant over it; they protested that it would involve revealing trade secrets to the Russians. Moreover, the use of Circassian tobacco was a breach of the original contract, the whole point of which was to provide a market for colonial tobacco. The Privy Council, afraid of repercussions on the other side of the Atlantic, advised Queen Anne to bring the workmen back. So they were recalled with orders to destroy the machinery they had taken out to Russia.

Shortly afterwards for some reason which is not clear the concession granted by the Tsar was revoked and tobacco imported from England was forbidden throughout Russia.

If Holland took to pipe-smoking with as much enthusiasm as England, Switzerland kept the Puritan flag flying with the sternest restrictions against tobacco. The population grew restless under the attempts of officialdom to suppress smoking. In 1686 there was trouble in Zürich, when some merchants who had been fined for dealing in tobacco refused to pay, arguing that the rest of the world was free to trade in tobacco.

The Town Council of Zürich was shocked by such insubordination, and was about to proceed against the refractory merchants with appropriate severity when Switzerland was overrun by refugees from Piedmont all of whom were great smokers. The Town Council was worried by the prospect of Zürich's being set on fire by such people. However, it was evidently impossible to stop them from smoking at all and the Town Council was content to prohibit them from smoking in the public streets and inns, with the proviso that if they must indulge in it they must do so outside the town walls in order to avoid giving offence to citizens who disliked the nasty habit.

The Swiss have never been noted for any failure to look at matters from the point of view of business, and presently it was proposed that instead of prohibiting smoking smokers should be fined, the money thus obtained being allowed to accumulate in order to buy weapons of war.

Berne was more severe than Zürich. Berne had a table of police regulations based on the Ten Commandments, and smoking was included in the prohibition against adultery, the penalty for which was imprisonment, fine and pillory. In 1675 a miniature Holy Office known as the Tobacco Chamber was instituted to tackle offenders on the lines of the Inquisition. This was not abolished until 1750, although its activity remained dormant after the first few years.

By 1702 Switzerland was perturbed by the flow of money out of the country to pay for imports of the prohibited tobacco, and it was proposed that tobacco should be grown at home. The opponents of tobacco were successful for a time in averting such a disgrace, but they were fighting a losing battle. In 1706 the 'unprofitable, lewd and feckless' habit of smoking was not absolutely forbidden, but a fine was to be levied on anybody who smoked where there was danger of fire, adding that God's mercy only was responsible for having saved every house in Switzerland from being burnt down by careless smokers.

Three years later the prohibition of tobacco was finally repealed because it had been found impossible to enforce it. In 1710 a heavy tax was levied on all smokers and snuff-takers. The compatriots of William Tell would not stand for this. They muttered so fiercely that the Government feared a revolution. A month later the tax was taken off, and permission was granted to grow tobacco in Switzerland itself. So the only result of the authorities' attempt to make smoking as heinous an offence as adultery was that the authorities were afraid at the end to draw a revenue from tobacco in Switzerland as every other state in Europe was doing at this time.

Chapter 9

IT is often stated by tobacco historians that the habit of snuffing like smoking was introduced into Europe from the American Indies by those who had observed the method in which the natives took a narcotic they called *cohoba*. Yet the habit of sniffing up medicinal herbs was ages old in Europe; no doubt the salutary reputation of the sovereign herb would have led the doctors to experiment with such a method of taking tobacco. The first we hear of snuff is when Jean Nicot advised the Grand Prior of France to send it to Catherine de Medici in the form of a powder for headaches. It may well be that this started a fashion for taking snuff among the aristocrats of the French Court, but Louis XIII and Louis XIV both disliked snuffing as much as they did smoking. We heard that the daughters of Louis XIV got hold of those forbidden pipes from the Swiss Guard; the courtiers disapproved of smoking because the pipe was a favourite of soldiers and sailors, and also of the peasants.

Probably the Spanish clergy, their example soon to be followed by the Italian, made snuff-taking popular.

In his entertaining *Letters*, written in the Fleet during a long imprisonment of eight years by the Roundheads and published in 1650, James Howell wrote:

> The Spaniards and Irish take it most in powder or *smutchin*, and it mightily refreshes the brain, and I believe there is as much taken this way in Ireland, as there is in pipes in England; one shall commonly see the serving maid upon the washing block, and the swain upon the ploughshare when they are tir'd with labour, take out their boxes of *smutchin* and draw it into their nostrils with a quill, and it will beget new spirits in them with a fresh vigour to fall to their work again. . . .
>
> If you want paper to light your pipe this letter may serve the turn, and if it be true what the Poets frequently sing, that *affection is fire*, you shall need no other than the clean flames of the Donor's love to make ignition. . . .
>
> So I wish you as to myself a most happy new year; may the beginning be good, the middle better, and the end best of all.   1 January, 1646.

Howell had been in Ireland in 1639, by which date snuff must have been for some time the recognized method of taking tobacco there.

'Smutchin' is an attempt to represent the equivalent English sound of the Irish Gaelic *smuiteán*, the equivalent of which in Scots Gaelic is *smuideán*, meaning dust. From Ireland snuff soon reached the Highlands, where it became the favourite way of taking tobacco and whence it spread to the Lowlands. The Scots Gaels called it *snaoiseán*, which was vulgarized in braid Scots as *sneeshin*. Burns speaks of a sneeshin-mill or snuff-horn. There is a small cave in one of the most southerly of the Outer Hebrides from which at certain states of the tide the sea sneezes in a shower of foam. This cave is called the *snaoiseanach* or snuff-taker.

Probably Irish seminarists returning from Spain introduced their flocks of the future to the pleasures of snuff. There was also considerable trade between Spain and the westerly Irish ports.

It is said that snuff was brought back with them from exile by the courtiers of Charles II who had learned to prefer it to smoking when in France. If that be true, it is strange that a Dutch name was given to it. True, the word rappee was used for a kind of coarsely grated snuff (*tabac râpé*), but there is no allusion to it before 1740. Snuff was evidently being used by the Roundhead soldiers, who were also great smokers. Samuel Butler says of a Roundhead:

> *He had administered a dose*
> *Of snuff mundungus to his nose;*
> *And powdered th' inside of his skull*
> *Instead of th' outward jobbernowl.*

Mundungus, from the Spanish word for tripe, was the name given to bad tobacco; jobbernowl was a word used for a while instead of blockhead.

Fairholt[1] gives the picture of a French tobacco-grater made of delicately carved ivory.

It represents Cupid instructed by Venus, whose costume indicates the date of its fabrication to have been about 1680.

[1] *Tobacco, Its History and Associations*, p. 245.

Above the figures ornamental scroll-work supports a canopy.

The form of this implement is semicircular; the flat side discloses the grater of brass fitted into a groove, and having a receptacle at each end for the tobacco-powder, which passes from beneath the grater, through a small aperture into each. If the snuff-maker wishes to fill his box, he rasped a sufficient quantity to fill the large receptacle at the bottom; if he wishes for a pinch "fresh and fresh" he shook out a small quantity into the little shell at the top, which was not large enough to admit the fingers for a pinch, it was therefore turned out upon the back of the hand, and so snuffed up the nose.

Snuff and perfumery were kindred trades. The earliest reference to snuff in the *O.E.D.* is taken from a *London Gazette* of 1683—"James Norcock Snuffmaker and Perfumer . . . sells all sorts of Snuffs, Spanish and Italian."

Spanish snuff was scented with musk, civet, bergamot and cedar. One kind called neroly was perfumed with the essential oil of the orange-blossom. A favourite Italian snuff was called Odeur de Rome, presumably under clerical patronage, and was made up of one pound of snuff, six ounces of musk, five ounces of civet to which was added a little sugar. Odeur de Malthe, which was also probably under clerical patronage, added to a pound of snuff six grains of civet and sugar, five grains of amber, and orange-flower water. Ginger, rue, marjoram, cummin, hellebore, betony white and black, even mustard and pepper were mixed with snuff to increase the power of the sneeze. Not only was the maltreated tobacco perfumed, it was also dyed, red and yellow ochres being most frequently used.

The English snuff-makers were not behind their continental rivals. Here is a recipe from round about 1700:

To make snuff, and how to cleanse it. Put your tobacco-dust in a strong linen cloth, soak your tobacco-dust in a pail of water, only once in twenty-four hours; then let the water out, and squeeze the snuff well in the cloth, then dry it on wicker hurdles in the sun, stirring it carefully whilst it's a drying; being dry, pour sweet water over it, as rose-water, or any other you like best, and make it as a paste; dry it again, and it's fit to receive what smell you please. Mint dried and powdered makes a pleasant snuff; or some rose-leaves and cloves distilled and powdered, and put to your snuff; or what herb or flower you please.

The result must have been more like pot-pourri than anything; one asks why it was worth while using any tobacco at all.

Scented snuffs came under suspicion for a while after the Duc de Noailles was suspected of poisoning the wife of the Dauphin with a box of Spanish snuff in 1712. A rumour went round that it was a Spanish habit to dispose of one's political opponents with poisoned snuff, and of course it was a commonplace method for the Jesuits thus to put their enemies out of the way.

Snuff-taking, as once upon a time smoking, was mostly confined to the London fops at first, but Ned Ward noted in *The London Spy* that "a parcel of raw, second-rate beaux and wits, were conceited if they had but the honour to dip a finger and thumb into Mr Dryden's snuff-box when he was sitting in Will's Coffee-house in Bow Street".

Mr H. Warner Allen has told us [1] that among his heirlooms is a strip of parchment in a Dresden snuff-box on which is written in an eighteenth-century hand: "This snuff went round the world with Lord Anson." Smoking had perforce to be discouraged on board ship, and by 1744 the year when that wonderful voyage round the world came to an end, snuff had to some extent displaced the chewed quid in the affections of the British mariner.

In 1702 a French fleet, escorting what was said to be the most valuable Spanish convoy that ever sailed from the West Indies, was lying in Vigo harbour protected by a boom and shore batteries. Admiral Sir George Rooke, the future victor of Gibraltar, in command of a powerful English and Dutch fleet reached Vigo Bay and decided to attack; this had to be done with the smaller ships of the line, the others drawing too much water. Vice-Admiral Hopson in the *Torbay* led the attack on the boom, only for the wind to drop suddenly and leave him under the fire of the shore batteries. Then the wind freshened again, and in the words of a contemporary report the Vice-Admiral

cut his cables, clapt on all his sails, and bearing up directly upon the boom, amidst all the enemy's fire, broke through

[1] H. Warner Allen, 'Snuff and the Navy', *The Navy*, June 1953.

it at once, cast anchor between the *Bourbon* and *L'Espérance*,
two French men-of-war, and with unparalleled resolution,
received several broadsides from them.

The wind dropped again and the rest of the third rates
attacking the boom could not move.

All this while Admiral Hopson was in extreme danger;
for being clapt on board by a French fireship, whereby his
rigging was presently set on fire, he expected every moment
to be burnt; but it very fortunately fell out that the French
ship, which indeed was a merchantman laden with snuff,
and fitted up in haste for a fireship, being blown up, the
snuff, in some measure, extinguished the fire, and preserved
the English man-of-war from being consumed.

Then the Dutch Vice-Admiral found the breach in the
boom made by the *Torbay*, and in due course the whole of the
convoy was captured. The booty was immense; gold and silver
coins to the value of some millions were taken, and among the
valuable cargoes were several thousand barrels of the best
Havana snuff. No less than fifty tons of this snuff were distributed among the officers and crews with permission to sell it
when they reached England as prize money. It was retailed at
the rate of fourpence a pound in all the southern seaports,
where it was known as Vigo snuff. One of the dealers was
advertising "Fine Seville Snuff from the Pearl Prize, sold by
Jas. Healey at the Black Boy, without Bishopsgate."

Richard Steele, who liked his pipe, wrote in *The Tatler*:

I am very willing to encourage young Beginners; but am
extremely in the Dark how to introduce this gentleman [a
mythical young correspondent called Jeffrey Nicknack]. I
cannot see either his person or his Habit in this letter; but
I'll call at Charles's and know the shape of his Snuff-Box,
by which I can settle his character. Though indeed, to
know his full capacity, I ought to be inform'd, whether he
takes Spanish or Musty.

Charles was Charles Lillie, a French perfumer who had
established himself in London at Beaufort Buildings where
Fielding lived. Their foundations lie now underneath the Savoy
Hotel.

In No. 101 of *The Tatler* an editorial note says:

Mr Lillie has snuffs, Barcelona, Seville, Musty, Plain, and Spanish, which may be taken by a young Beginner without danger of sneezing.

In No. 78, Steele advises the 'ingenious gentlemen' of London and Westminster who want to take up poetry, music and politics to frequent the Smyrna Coffee-house where they will receive instruction gratis.

The Disciples are to prepare their bodies with three dishes of Bohea, and purge their brains with two pinches of Snuff. If any young student gives indication of Parts, by listening attentively, or asking a pertinent Question, one of the Professors shall distinguish him by taking snuff out of his box in the presence of the whole audience.

Then one more extract from *The Tatler*:

Four pounds of scented snuff, with three gilt snuff-boxes, one of them with an invisible hinge, and a looking-glass in the lid. Two more of ivory, with the portraitures on their lids of two ladies of the town, the originals to be seen every night in the side-boxes of the playhouse. . . . There will be added to these goods, to make a complete auction, a collection of gold snuff-boxes and clouded canes, which are to continue in fashion for three months after the sale.

This recalls *The Rape of the Lock*:

> Sir Plume of amber snuff-box justly vain,
> And the nice conduct of a clouded cane.

It is tempting to digress at this point and celebrate the work of the craftsmen inspired by the snuff-box, but it would need a volume to do justice to such a theme. James Arbuckle, a student of Glasgow University, summed it up in his *Poem on Snuff*, published in 1719, when he was nineteen years old:

> What strange and wondrous virtue must there be
> And secret charm, O Snuff, concealed in thee!
> How bounteous Nature and inventive Art,
> Bedecking thee, thus all their powers exert;
> Their treasures and united skill bestow,
> To set thine honours in majestic show!
> But oh, what witchcraft of a stronger kind,
> Or cause too deep for human search to find,

Makes earth-born weeds imperial man enslave,
Not little souls, but e'en the wise and brave!

Hoffmann, the physician to the King of Prussia, was prepared
to accept snuff as valuable for clearing the nose, but thought
that it should not become a social habit. He also rebutted the
notion that the brains of snuff-takers could become sooty;
though he admitted he had been informed that the heads of
some executed criminals, known to be great snuffers, had on
dissection been found to be black with snuff, and that the heads
of Scottish soldiers killed in the Thirty Years War had been
found in a similar condition.

The addiction of women to snuff roused much indignation.
A Frenchman declared that it deformed the nose, stained the
skin and tainted the breath, and wanted to know what would
be thought of Venus and the Graces if they took to snuff.

Young Arbuckle, however, was all for women snuffing:

With Snuff the beauteous Celia shades her face,
And adds a foil to every obvious grace,
Her lips, o'erspread with dusky Vigo, speak
The brighter colour on her lovely cheek;
Nay, underneath the tawny shade they wear,
The lips themselves more beautiful appear,
For beauty mask'd, like the great few who shun
The praise and honour of their merits won,
By how much it denies its own applause
Or seems but so to do, a greater draws.
For, apt to imagine more than is conceal'd
The fancy heightens every charm that's veil'd.

It is surprising to find a young Scot of nineteen paying such
an eloquent tribute to a female moustache. Nevertheless, on
the whole, opinion was against snuff-taking by women.

Many charlatans exaggerated the benefits of snuff; one of
them in 1722 was vouching for it to relieve the pain of gout
under the name 'Cephalic tobacco'. The impudence of these
quacks was boundless. Here is Mr Samuel Major proclaiming
his snuff in the *General Advertiser* of June 21, 1749:

Once more I desire you to remember, I have published my
Imperial Snuff, for all disorders in the head, and I think I
might have gone further, and said, for all disorders of body

and mind. It hath set a great many to rights that was never expected, but there is but few, or none, that careth to have it published they were a little out of their senses, although it be really an ailment that none can help. . . . I hear it is reported abroad, I am dead, and that the world is imposed on; but, thank God, I am alive . . . but suppose I was dead, my Snuff is alive, and I hope it will live after I am dead, as it is capable of keeping the world in spritely life and health, which must be allowed to be the greatest blessing in the world. But what is riches without that? And what would some have given for some of these reliefs before it was advertised? But you are all heartily welcome at this price of sixpence, at present, but I should be glad of more from the rich. I do assure you it is sold at this price in regard to the poor only.

This Snuff is sold by George Horselyham, servant at Mr Ashley's Punch-house on Ludgate-hill, and at Mr Child's, Sam's Coffee-house, near the Custom-house; of whom you may have a true character of this Snuff, it having repaired his constitution. It is left at the bar of the said house for conveniency of merchants, masters of ships, and others, where you may have a book and a bill of directions.

By 1740 snuff had made such progress as a medium for tobacco that Wimble, the snuff-dealer, was able to offer forty-six varieties, from common Scotch at a shilling to Best Brazil at twenty-four shillings.

Chambers's Encyclopædia of 1727 says:

The kinds of snuff and their several names are infinite, and new ones are invented; so that it would be difficult, not to say impossible, to give a detail of them. We shall only say, that there are three grand sorts, the first granulated, the second an impalpable powder, and the third the bran, or coarse part remaining after sifting a second sort.

Rappee, which figures in sixteen of the items in Wimble's list, was originally the granulated kind, but probably by now it was powdery. Macabao (which is hardly ever spelt the same way twice running) was a highly scented snuff from Martinique. Strasburgh Violet consisted of rappee and bitter almonds finely ground and scented with ambergris and attar; it was a favourite with the ladies, and seems comparatively cheap at four shillings a pound. Much the most expensive are the three qualities of Brazil.

Wimble does not offer either Étrenne or Bureau. The former was the snuff chosen by Louis XV as the one he liked best for a New Year's offering made to him by the various manufacturers in France of their choicest brands. Bureau was another of the King's selections, and was used in the cabinets of the politicians. Hence its name. It should be introduced to Whitehall when the Civil Servants take to snuff because they cannot afford to smoke without feeling that they are paying for their own trousers.

The adulteration of tobacco had been a habit of the English merchants from the time that tobacco was first imported into the country, but with the growth of the popularity of snuff adulteration became a menace. The first Act of Parliament passed in the first year of the reign of George I may have been directed more towards protecting the Revenue than the health of George I's subjects, but it is of interest. It was entitled:

An Act to prevent the Mischiefs by Manufacturing Leaves or other things to Resemble Tobacco, and the Abuses in Making or Mixing of Snuff.

Several Evil Persons have Cut, Cured, Manufactured, and Sold Wallnut-Tree-leaves, Hop-leaves, Sycomore Leaves, or other Leaves . . . resembling Tobacco of the growth or Product of the British Plantations, to the Prejudice of His Majesties Plantations . . . and of the Navigation and Trade of this Kingdom, and of the Public Revenues. . . .

[For doing this penalties of fine and forfeiture are laid down, and the Act goes on to forbid anybody to] Make, Mix, or Colour . . . any sort of Snuff with any Sort of Okers, Umber, or any other kind of Colouring, except with Water Ting'd with the Colouring commonly called Venetian Red only or shall mix . . . with any Sort of Snuff, any Fustick, or Yellow Ebony, Touchwood, or any other sort of wood, or any Dirt or Sand, or Dust sifted from Tobacco.

Hugh McCausland, in his entertaining book *Snuff and Snuff-Boxes*, tells the story of how Lundy Foot, a Dublin snuff-maker, discovered by accident the attraction of toasted snuff. The assistant whom he left in charge of the kiln that was drying the tobacco from which the snuff was ground fell asleep under the influence of whisky, with the result that the stalks were almost charring when Lundy Foot arrived next morning. The proprietor in the hope of saving his loss by selling the damaged snuff cheap started to grind, and on trying the result found that the burnt or toasted flavour gave a new and pleasant tang to the snuff. His customers endorsed his opinion, and this was the origin of Lundy Foot High Toast, which became a famous and popular brand and survives to this day as Irish High Toast.

Fairholt says that Lundyfoot was also known as Irish Black-guard because Foot bought a large quantity of charred tobacco after a fire in a Dublin warehouse and ground it into snuff which he sold very cheaply to the poor of Dublin. A messenger from the Castle sent to buy snuff at Foot's shop tried a pinch of the charred snuff being sold in ha'porths and took some back with him to the Castle, after which it soon became the rage in Dublin society. Foot never forgot the poor, who helped to make his fortune; and a keg of Blackguard was always placed at his door for all-comers; a custom continued by his descendants.

The most popular snuffs both in Scotland and Wales were also toasted.

Jamieson, in his *Etymological Dictionary of the Scottish Language*, says:

> When tobacco was first introduced into this country, those who wished to have snuff were wont to toast the leaves before the fire, and then bruise them with a bit of wood in the box, which was therefore called a *mill* from the snuff being *ground* in it.

Undoubtedly the *mill* or *mull* was a better way of making snuff than the English rasp, and one never hears of scents or dyes being found necessary. Whether the Irish or the Scots first thought of using the tobacco stalks is not certain. The *mill* or *mull* has kept its name for the curved horn which was to be the receptacle for snuff generally used in Scotland. This could be quite an elaborate affair, with a variety of small tools attached to it by silver chains—a hammer to knock the side of the mull and loosen any snuff adhering to it; a bodkin to stir up the snuff if damp; a rake to gather it into a miniature shovel; and finally a hare's foot to brush away any particles from the nose.

Snuff became as closely associated with Scotland in the public mind as whisky and homespun are to-day. The snuff-taking Highlander who used to stand at the door of so many tobacconists lasted longer than any other shop-sign, except for a brief period of unpopularity caused by the panic into which the approach of the Jacobite army had thrown London in 1745.

In the museum of the Society of Antiquaries of Scotland there is an ivory *rappoir* or snuff-grater of Italian workmanship reputed to have belonged to Prince Charles Edward. I have not been able to trace any reference to the Prince's taking of snuff, and as a pipe-smoker I am delighted to testify to his devotion to the pipe.

When the royal fugitive, who had tramped through the teeming rain of June 30th, 1746, to Portree in the isle of Skye, desired to spend the night in the inn, Captain Roy MacDonald urged the danger of delay. But in the words of Captain Mac-Donald:

> The Prince called for some tobacco that he might smoke a pipe before he should go off. The Captain told him there was no tobacco to be got there but what was very coarse. The Prince asked what kind of tobacco they had. "Only roll tobacco," said the Captain. The Prince said it would serve the present turn very well, and desired to have some of it. The Captain ordered the landlord to fetch a quarter of a pound, which he did in the scales, at fourpence halfpenny. The Prince gave a sixpence, but the landlord was desired by the Captain to bring in the change. The Prince smiled at the Captain's exactness, and would not be at the pains to take the three halfpence. The Captain insisted he should take them because in his present situation he would find bawbees very useful to him. . . . The Prince, the Captain, and Neil MacKechan drank a bottle of whiskie while at Portree.[1]

It would seem that the Prince learned both to drink and to smoke during that great adventure of his. After crossing the Minch with Flora MacDonald, he spent the night of June 29th with Alexander MacDonald at Kingsburgh, and

> after he had made a plentiful supper, he called for a dram; and when the bottle of brandy was brought, he said he would fill the glass for himself; "for," said he, "I have learned in my skulking to take a hearty dram." He filled up a bumper and drank it off to the happiness and prosperity of his landlord and lady. Then taking a crack'd and broken pipe out of his poutch, wrapt about with thread, he asked

[1] *The Lyon in Mourning* (Scottish History Society), Vol. II, p. 23.

Kingsburgh if he could furnish him with some tobacco; for that he had learn'd likewise to smoke in his wanderings. Kingsburgh took from him the broken pipe and laid it carefully up . . . and gave him a new clean pipe and plenty of tobacco.[1]

When the Prince was crossing from Skye to the mainland with Captain Malcolm MacLeod, in the words of the latter:

> The Prince . . . then asked him if he could light him a pipe, for he wanted to smoke in the passage. The Captain desired him to have the cutty ready in his cheek, and that he should fall upon a method to light it. Malcolm took some tow out of his pocket, and snapping one of the guns held the tow to the part and kindled it. Then putting it to the mouth of the pipe he blew and the Prince smok'd. But the cutty being exceedingly short, Malcolm scarred the Prince's cheek with the tow. . . .
> Captain MacLeod took care to have one of the cutties the Prince had used, and carried it to London with him, where meeting with one Dr Burton of York, a prisoner, and chancing to tell the story of the cutty the Doctor begged as a great favour to have the cutty, which Malcolm gave him. The Doctor has made a fine shagreen case for it and preserves it as a valuable rarity.[2]

I have not been able to find out if that cutty is still preserved, and Kingsburgh's broken pipe has vanished. It is on a snuffbox that we find the commemoration of the hazardous crossing from the mainland to the Outer Hebrides after Culloden, when Donald MacLeod was at the helm of that eight-oared boat.

> Donald has got in a present a large silver snuff-box prettily chessed, from his good friend, Mr John Walkingshaw of London, which serves as an excellent medal of his history, as it has engraven upon it the interesting adventure, with proper mottos, etc. The box is an octagon oval of three inches and three-quarters in breadth, and an inch and a quarter in depth, and the inside of it is doubly gilt. Upon the lid is raised the eight-oar'd boat, with Donald at the helm, and the four under his care, together with the eight rowers distinctly represented. The sea is made to appear very rough and tempestuous. Upon one of the extremities of the lid there is a landskip of the Long Isle, and the boat is just steering

---

[1] *Lyon in Mourning*, (Vol. I, p. 119.
[2] Ibid., pp. 142–3.

into Rushness, the point of Benbicula where they landed. Upon the other extremity of the lid there is a landskip of the end of the Isle of Skye, as it appears opposite to the Long Isle. Upon this representation of Skye are marked these two places, viz. Dunvegan and Gualtergill. Above the boat the clouds are represented heavy and lowring, and the rain is falling from them. The motto above the clouds, i.e. round the edge of the lid by the hinge, is this—*Olim Hæc Meminisse Juvabit—Aprilis* 26 1746. The inscription under the sea, i.e. round the edge of the lid by the opening, is this—*Quid, Neptune, Paras? Fatis Agitamur Iniquis.* Upon the bottom of the box are carved the following words—*Donald MacLeod of Gualtergill, in the Isle of Sky, The Faithful Palinurus, Aet.* 68. 1746. Below these words there is very prettily engraved a dove, with an olive branch in her bill.

When Donald came first to see me, along with Deacon Clark, I asked him why he had not snuff in the pretty box? "Sneeshin in that box!" said Donald. "Na, the deil a pickle sneeshin shall ever go into it till the K—— be restored, and then (I trust in God) I'll go to London, and then I will put sneeshin in the box and go to to the Prince, and say, "Sir, will you tak a sneeshin out o' my box." [1]

Alas, that great moment never came.

It is good to be able to record that most of the eighty-eight Jacobite prisoners taken at Carlisle and transported in fetters to Virginia were helped by Virginia and Maryland gentlemen, who when they were put up for sale bought them at £9 10s. each, and set them free instead of exacting the seven years' labour in the plantations to which they were entitled. One or two of the transportees signed on with the 'buckskins' as those born in the Colonies were called and remained behind; but the others, all with money in their pockets provided by their generous sympathizers, reached Scotland again safely.

It is strange what scanty material exists for giving an account of the way the transported felons fared in the plantations; this peep afforded by a returning prisoner-of-war suggests that Jacobite feeling must have been strong both in Virginia and Maryland. We may close this chapter with the reflection that if the Prince had won the day instead of Cumberland, it is more than possible that the American Revolution would have been averted.

[1] *Lyon in Mourning*, Vol. I, p. 183.

Chapter 10

W HEN we read of the displacement of smoking by snuff-taking, we must bear in mind that this was only in fashionable circles or in circles that hoped by snuff-taking to appear fashionable. When we read of such a citizen as John Gilpin taking his wife and two daughters to supper in Vauxhall Gardens and being forbidden to smoke a pipe afterwards because it is "ungenteel to smoke, where any ladies are in company", we seem to be in Queen Victoria's reign already. Yet there was no displacement comparable to that which the pipe has had to suffer at the hands of the cigarette during the last fifty or sixty years. In Scotland, Ireland and Wales smoking and snuff-taking had been enjoyed by the same people for a century. In Oxford and Cambridge dons and undergraduates remained loyal to the pipe. So, too, did most of the squires and parsons. Thomas Warton pleaded in 1746:

> *Return, ye days when endless pleasure*
> *I found in reading or in leisure!*
> *When calm around the Common Room*
> *I puff'd my daily pipe's perfume!*
> *Rode for a stomach, and inspected,*
> *At annual bottlings, corks selected:*
> *And dined untax'd, untroubled, under*
> *The portrait of our pious Founder!*

A. D. Godley, who was a fellow of Magdalen when the present writer was an undergraduate, wrote and translated one of the Christ Church *Carmina Quadragesmalia* with his accustomed grace, as it set forth the daily life of an eighteenth-century Oxford don who

> *Ne'er swerves a hair breadth from the same old way,*
> *Always within the memory of men,*
> *He's risen at eight and gone to bed at ten:*
> *The same old cat his college room partakes,*
> *The same old scout his bed each morning makes:*
> *On mutton roast he daily dines in state*
> *(Whole flocks have perished to supply his plate)*

Takes just one turn to catch the westering sun,
Then reads the paper, as he's always done:
Soon cracks in Common-room the same old jokes,
Drinking three glasses ere three pipes he smokes:—
And what he did while Charles our throne did fill,
'Neath George's heir you'll find him doing still.

And it was not only in Common-rooms that Oxford smoked. Hearne the antiquary recalls a smoking match held on September 4th, 1723. A scaffold was erected "over against the Theatre in Oxford . . . just at Finmore's, an alehouse", and the contest was timed to start at 2 p.m.

Any man or woman who was able to smoke through three ounces of tobacco first without drinking or quitting the stage would receive twelve shillings.

> Many tried [Hearne relates] and 'twas thought that a journeyman tailor of St Peter's in the East would have been victor, he smoking faster than, and being many pipes before the rest: but at last he was so sick, that 'twas thought he would have died; and an old man that had been a soldier, and smoked gently, came off conqueror, smoking the three ounces quite out, and he told one (from whom I had it) that, after it, he smoked 4 or 5 pipes the same evening.

Fielding testifies in many a character to the pipe's hold. Whatever the beaux might do he himself remained a devotee of the pipe, and we can hear his own sentiments uttered by Sir Owen Apshinken in *The Grub Street Opera*:

> What a glorious creature was he who first discovered the use of tobacco!—the industrious retires from business—the voluptuous from pleasure—the lover from a cruel mistress—the husband from a curs'd wife—and I from all the world to my pipe.

The Grub Street Opera, which included that popular song *The Roast Beef of Old England*, also included some audacious hits at George II, Queen Caroline and Sir Robert Walpole, the Prime Minister; Fielding was a Jacobite at heart. The Freemason's Tune deserves to be remembered:

> *Let the learn'd talk of books,*
> *The gluttons of cooks,*

The lover of Celia's soft smack-o;
No mortal can boast,
So noble a toast,
As a pipe of accepted tobacco.

Let the soldier for fame,
And a gen'ral's name,
In battle get many a thwack-o;
Let who will have most,
Who will rule the roost,
Give me but a pipe of tobacco.

Tobacco gives wit
To the dullest old cit,
And makes him of politics crack-o:
The lawyers i' th' hall
Were not able to bawl,
Were it not for a whiff of tobacco.

The man whose chief glory
Is telling of story,
Had never arrived at the knack-o,
Between every heying,
And as I was saying,
Did he not take a whiff of tobacco.

The doctor who places
Much skill in grimaces,
And feels your pulse running rick-rack-o;
Would you know his chief skill?
It is only to fill,
And smoke a good pipe of tobacco.

The courtiers alone
To this weed are not prone;
Would you know what 'tis makes them so slack-o?
'Twas because it inclined
To be honest the mind
And therefore they banished tobacco.

That is what the pipe-smokers of two centuries ago felt about the snuff-taker whose habit was dictated by the fashion. The pipe-smoker of fifty years ago was inclined to view the cigarette-smoker with similar suspicion.

And now it is time to tell the tale of Walpole's Excise Bill of 1733.

In 1731 Sir Robert Walpole, the guardian angel or the unclean spirit of the Hanoverian Succession according to political prejudice, had made a bid to lure the landed gentry out of their latent Jacobitism by lowering the land tax from two shillings to one shilling in the pound. A year later he was determined to raid the sinking-fund to the tune of £500,000, and in order to avoid opposition from the country gentry, he let it be known that the alternative was to put the land tax back to two shillings. Having successfully achieved his object, Walpole now attempted to do with tobacco and wine what he had done successfully with tea and coffee ten years earlier without opposition. That had been to apply a compulsory warehousing system by a transfer of Customs to Excise. The proposal put before the House of Commons was to levy the full tax on tobacco (wine was left out) only when it was removed from the warehouses for sale. Imports for re-exportation would be free of tax. The former of these two measures would check smuggling because the importer "would never run any risk, or be at any expense to evade the Custom-house officers at the first gate, when at so many more afterwards he would be equally exposed to be catched by the Excise-officer". The second measure in Walpole's words would "tend to make London a free port, and in consequence the market of the world".

Excise had been levied in the past upon various necessaries of life, and the public had hated it. In Walpole's proposal they discerned the first step towards a general Excise like the odious purchase-tax of to-day. The Opposition took its opportunity and with the help of pamphleteers stirred up the public wrath. Petitions against the scheme poured into the House of Commons. The House itself was besieged by a "a most extraordinary concourse of people". The City of London prayed to be heard by counsel against the Bill, and its petition was escorted by a train of coaches that reached from Temple Bar to Westminster. Discontent threatened to become active disaffection. Rumour declared that the army could not be relied upon because the soldiers believed that the price of tobacco would be raised. The ministerial majorities in the House began to shrink. On March 14th, 1733, when the scheme was introduced the majority was 61; less than a month later it was 17. Walpole gave up. He moved that the Bill be read a second time on June 12th, or in other words never, for Parliament would not be sitting on June 12th. There was a tumultuous display of popular rejoicing all over the country. George II was furious, for he saw that his sixth share of the duty on tobacco granted to the Civil List in 1698 would not be increased. The Excise system with tea and coffee had brought in an extra £120,000 a year. He dismissed Lord Chesterfield, the Lord Steward, and other peers in public employment who had opposed the Bill, and he cashiered the two Colonels of the Household Cavalry, the Duke of Bolton and Lord Cobham.

The indignation of the tobacconists with the Excise Bill is intelligible because the Customs frauds which it was designed to abolish were so frequent and so flagrant that the Revenue was losing a very large sum annually. What is not so clear is the reason for the violence of the popular wrath, unless it reflect the important position which tobacco held in the affections of the public.

How long has tobacco been reckoned an article of pure luxury? [demanded *The Vintner's and Tobacconist's Advocate* in attacking the arguments put forward by the ministerial supporters]. Is it not good part of the subsistence of our poor? How many thousands in this city never taste a morsel of victuals till noon, nay very frequently till night, but a small dram [of gin] and a chew, or a pipe of tobacco? To raise the price thereof which would be infallibly the effect of an excise would therefore be as effectually starving these wretches, as laying a tax upon flesh-meat and bread corn.

We cannot to-day argue that tobacco is a substitute for food, but we have a right to argue that the towering tax levied upon smokers by the Government is a tax upon what is even more a necessity for the great part of the population to-day than it was two centuries ago. When it is realized that the burden of national defence is borne almost entirely by smokers and drinkers, we who indulge in tobacco and whisky have a right to demand a respectful silence from non-smokers and teetotallers about our habits.

It must be remembered that in 1733 the Hanoverian dynasty was still far from being securely seated on the throne. Walpole himself said when he capitulated:

Jackson's BEST VIRGINIA *at the* Highlander *in Long Lane near West Smithfield. NB. He Makes & sells Pigtaile, Scotch & all other Sorts of* Snuffs, *no better nor cheaper in* London

Petum optimum fubter Solem.

Le meilleur Tabac desous le Soleil.

The Best Tobacco under the Sun.

COCKBURN,
TOBACCONIST & SNUFF-MAKER,
at the Abel Drugger.
Nº 146, Fenchurch Street.
NB. Late Shopman at Sr Roger de Coverly's

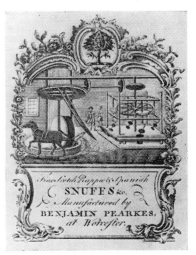

French Scotch Rappee & Spanish
SNUFFS &c.
Manufactured by
BENJAMIN PEARKES,
at Worcester.

Eighteenth century tobacco labels

The act could not be carried into execution without an armed force . . . and there would be an end of the liberties of England if supplies were to be raised by the sword.

Walpole's devoted faith in the Hanoverian Succession made him identify it with the liberties of England. It should be pointed out that the original impetus to the proposed transfer of Customs to Excise came from the Virginia Assembly. The planters had long standing grievances against the English merchants, and this was another campaign in the war still being fought between the producer and the distributor. However, the Virginia Assembly had cut itself free from British bonds before young William Pitt in 1789 succeeded in getting an Act passed which, although based on Walpole's abortive Bill, was much more elaborate and stringent. One of the most active opponents of Walpole's Bill was Ben Bradley, a London tobacconist, whose portrait was subscribed for by his admirers and distributed as a fine mezzotint with these lines below:

> *Behold the man, who when a gloomy band*
> *Of vile excisemen threatened all the land,*
> *Help'd to deliver from their harpy gripe*
> *The cheerful bottle and the social pipe,*
> *O rare Ben Bradley! may for this the bowl*
> *Still unexcised, rejoice thy honest soul!*
> *May still the best in Christendom for this*
> *Cleave to thy stopper and complete thy bliss!*

In the middle of this verse is a tiny etching by Hogarth, showing the British Lion and Britannia, the latter seated upon a cask of tobacco and both of them smoking pipes. Bradley used this design for his shop-bill with the motto: *The Best in Christendom without Excise.*

Hogarth was himself a heavy smoker, and the pipe may be seen in several of his pictures, notably in the mouth of the hangman sitting on top of Tyburn tree waiting for the arrival of the Idle Apprentice to be turned off. The tail-piece to his works, the last engraving made a few months before he died, shows Time expiring against a broken column, his scythe falling from his grasp and a long clay pipe breaking in two as it falls from his mouth.

Ben Bradley's shop-bill provides a good excuse to turn aside for some pages and look at a selection of the labels used by tobacconists. The examples described are to be found in the Ingham Foster collection of tobacco pipes now in the possession of the Imperial Tobacco Company. This was bought by Atkinson Bush at the sale of the late Ingham Foster in 1786, and presented to R. L. Pattenson by James Bush in 1876.

One of the first is:

Bradley's
Mild Virginia
at Ye Silver Lyon
In St Nicholas Lane
Lombard Street
London
1726.

The lion resembles the one that Hogarth engraved later, but it is not smoking.

His next label shows the Hogarth medallion with the addition of another lion, with his paw on a tobacco roll.

BRADLEY'S
Mild Virginia at the
White Lyon and Tobacco Rowle
Within Bishopsgate
London.

Whether Bradley had moved from Lombard Street or had opened a second shop is not known.

We shall come to the Highlander presently. Meanwhile, here is William Duke of Cumberland with

AUSTIN'S Best Virginia West Smithfield LONDON

on either side and, underneath, these fulsome lines for the man who was defeated by the French at Fontenoy:

What honest Briton that surveys this Face
Adorn'd with open Truth and manly Grace!
But must the importance of that Valour own,
That guards our Rights and aids his Father's throne.
No more shall France the Seats of Empire rend,
And where she lists her banefull Pow'r extend:
No more the Laws of Heav'n and Earth deride:
Another Marlborough lives to scourge her Pride.

We get him again in uniform with the star of the Garter, above and below a ring of bells and two tobacco rolls. The picture is inscribed 'Success to the Cumberland Youths', and beneath is this doggerel:

> *Ringing is a Curious Art,*
> *There is none can it exceed,*
> *The Cumberlands can hit in part,*
> *And BARTELL sells the best of Weed.*

Cumberland would have been more appropriate as a sign outside a butcher's shop.

Thomas Parr of Shropshire was reputed to have been born in 1483 and to have lived until 1635, expiring from too much unaccustomed rich food when Lord Arundel brought him down in a litter to London to show him to Charles I. Old Parr married his first wife at the age of eighty, and did penance when he was a centenarian for begetting a bastard child. The *D.N.B.* says there is no evidence that he became a heavy smoker in his latter days. Be that true or not, it was generally believed that he did, and we get:

> Thomas Parr who lived in X Kings and Queens Reigns
> Aged 152 years.

> Joseph Acton at Old Parr's
> Head, High Street, St Giles's.

One of the favourite signs for a tobacconist was the 'Tobacco Roll'. The rolls were usually painted in alternate rings of yellow and brown to suggest tobacco, but sometimes they were gilded all over.

> BEAUCHAMP'S
> Best Virginia at the
> Tobacco Roll against
> Token-house Yard in
> Lothbury, London.

The elaborate label of

> BARNARDS best
> VIRGINIA at the
> Tobacco Rolls in
> Queen-Street, London

shows a scene in Virginia, with a mountain in the background, a small settlement on the left, black boys packing tobacco into casks in the foreground, with a white overseer offering a 'hand' of tobacco to the owner of the plantation who is seated and smoking a pipe.

An indication that chewing was by no means confined to mariners appears in the label of Barnes, St Saviour's Churchyard. A well-dressed Englishman holds out a box, saying "Will you have a quid"; a Frenchman is holding out a box, saying "Voule [sic] vous de Rappee"; and between them a Dutchman smoking a pipe is saying "No dis been better". Underneath the picture are the words "These 3 unite in one Cause. This Smokes, that Snuffs, t'other Chaws".

Leach Baldwin of Greenwich has a black boy smoking a pipe and holding a roll of tobacco, underneath whom a verse declares:

> Life is a Smoke!—if this be true,
> Tobacco will thy Life renew;
> Then fear not Death, nor killing care
> Whilst we have best Virginia here.

The days when pipes were bought in quantity are recalled by a label of Bowler's Best showing three men sitting round a table, drinking and smoking, round about them on the floor several broken clay pipes. It was the custom for inns to provide 'parlour' customers with new pipes, which were afterwards cleaned by refiring and supplied to the customers in the tap-room.

In 1702 a judge on circuit was entertained by the City of Bristol when two gross of pipes were used to smoke two pounds, and at a banquet given by the Bristol County Council to celebrate the Coronation of George I two and a half pounds of tobacco were smoked in 216 pipes.

Charles Bosher in Bridges Street, Covent Garden, had a label showing a group smoking round a table. One is saying "It's a good tobacco." Another declares "Charming flavour'd"; a third "It smoaks well" and the fourth asks "Whose is it?"

One label has a figure like a nigger minstrel on the sands of a seaside resort, who is holding a flat hat on his head with one hand and in the other a churchwarden pipe. Round the figure are the words 'Haberdasher of HATS & TObaconist'. This is

GEORGE CORNELIUS

Successor to Mr Sly
the corner of Devereux Court
Without Temple Barr.

One asks why Carrington's Best Mild York River Tobacco should be advertised by a Freemason standing in a set-square under the medallion of mermaid inscribed below 'Aborigine Mundi'.

Turks appear at intervals. There is one label with an English gentleman selling tobacco leaves while a Turk holds a hand of tobacco from a cask of leaf by his side with the words 'It is Sweet Scented'.

These Turks suggest a considerable importation of tobacco from the Levant as early as this.

That Ben Jonson was still a household name in the drama is evident from one sign being called at the ABEL DRUGGER, and on several labels Captain Bobadill, in one of which he is shown smoking a pipe and saying "It is your Right Trinidado". One would have supposed that by the middle of the eighteenth century 'Trinidado' would have lost its Jacobean significance.

The DRUGGER'S HEAD, kept by Peter Cockburn, 'late Shopman at Sir Roger de Coverley's', indulged in verse:

At DRUGGER'S Head without a Puff,
You'll ever find the best of Snuff,
Believe me I'm not joking;
Tobacco too of ev'ry kind,
The very best you'll always find,
For chewing or for smoking.
Tho' A B E L when the Humour's in,
At Drury Lane to make you grin,
May some Times take his Station;
At Number Hundred Forty-six,
In Fenchurch-Street he now doth fix,
His present Habitation:
His best respects he therefore sends,
And thus acquaints his generous Friends,
From Limehouse up to Holborn,
That his rare Snuffs are sold by none,
Except in Fenchurch-Street alone,
And there by PETER COCKBURN.

No doubt it was in the composition of such verses that many of the Grub Street hacks eked out a livelihood.

Here is another specimen, from the Bull at Chiselhurst:

> *If you, in this calm Residence,*
> *To Smoking are inclin'd,*
> *Without a Jest, FAIRBARNS'S best*
> *Virginia here you'll find,*
> *With grateful Heart, he would impart*
> *Success to your concerns ;*
> *For, while you drink and fill your Pipe,*
> *You help to fill his Barns.*

Gaitskill's neat Tobacco at Fountain Stairs, Rotherhith Wall, displayed an aggressive colonialism which the present leader of H.M.'s Opposition would certainly disown. A small man, cutlass in hand, is reaching up to grasp a large Red Indian by the throat. There is a ship and a fort in the background. The legend runs:

CAPT SMITH the first Englishman who went ashore in Virginia taking the King of Paspahegh Prisoner.

Hollis of Islington, on a label showing Bacchus and a harvester with a sheaf of wheat, an owl on a barrel between them and the motto IN NOCTE, declares in rhyme:

> *Bacchus every Pleasure's heir*
> *Life of Joy and Death of Care,*
> *Bids us quit all fears and follies,*
> *For one pipe of honest Hollis,*
> *Then come ye Sons of soul and fun,*
> *Haste to Mirth and Islington.*

Tom Harbin has an elaborate label with scenes of hunting, music and preaching (*!*) inscribed:

TOM HARBIN'S
Superfine Sweet Scent
York-River Tobacco
RECOMMENDED
To Those who have Honour'd
him with their Friendship
Hic & Ubique.

J. W. Russell, No. 1 White X Place, Moorfields, makes a positive claim with his label for an Elizabethan adventurer:

RALPH LANE
Merchant of London
First introduc'd Tobacco in England Anno 1587.

A label with the date 1736 offers a puzzle. A man with a glass in his hand and the words 'Mundee's Mild' coming out of his mouth is standing by a tree, round which a vine is growing, that is being kicked down by a donkey. Below the picture is the motto 'Non Eradicabor' and the verse:

Pray Gentlemen See
Here's a Strange Prodigy
A Vine Sprung out of a Juniper Tree.

Riddles were not uncommon. William Moon of No. 120 Whitechapel has

Fashion	awkward	Nation	backward
the	seem	the	go
'tis	it	of	must
sure	you	way	you
be	to	the	Friend
yet	though	'tis	my

The solution is not insurmountable. Backward is the operative direction.

A label with a Negro in livery and a brick wall in the background is inscribed:

Richd Neale & Co's
Superfine—Ragg
on the Back
BRISTOL.

After that positive claim made by one sign for Ralph Lane, it is good to find

Preacher & Sainsbury's
Best Virginia
on Ludgate Hill,
London

proclaiming on their label

Great Britain to great Raleigh owes
This Plant & Country where it grows.

C. Periers Best, of Greek Street, St Ann's, Soho, produced a mysterious label showing liquor distilling out of pipes coming from three points on a globe marked Jamaica, Nantes and Holland (? rum, brandy and gin). The word 'Virginia' is in the background with a zephyr smoking a pipe stuck through the globe, under the gaze of the Man in the Moon.

Aggressive colonialism was not apparent in the label of Ricketts & Loads, Bristol, which showed a native with crown and sceptre on one side of a tobacco cask and a sailor on the other, both of them smoking.

A set of labels apparently commemorating the famous race-horse Dragon are of interest. The first shows two horses racing, the jockeys wearing black caps with ribbons and carrying long whips. One of the jockeys is saying 'WHY NOT beat DRA-GON?' This is for Marriott's Best Virginia from Crown Court, Broad Street, London. The second is similar, but the jockeys are smoking pipes and holding tobacco-leaves.

This comes from

Meridith Newmarket
The Best Smoker Wins the Day.

In a third a man is sitting in a chair with a spurred falcon at his side. Above is TREGONWELL FRAMPTON ESQR, and underneath is a man holding a horse with the word DRAGON above it. This label is for

TURPIN'S Best Virginia
at the Crown, St John's
Street Smithfield LONDON.

Tregonwell Frampton, "the father of the turf", died in 1727 in his eighty-seventh year, having been keeper of the running horses or, as we should say to-day, trainer to William of Orange, Queen Anne, George I and George II. He was the owner of the famous horse Dragon, and there is a letter from the Duke of York to the Prince of Orange written in 1678 in which he mentions a forthcoming match between the "famous horses Dragon and Why Not". The first label above seems to suggest that Why Not won. Frampton was also keen on falconry, coursing and cock-fighting. Dutch William always used to spend the afternoon of his visits to Newmarket watching his trainer's fighting-cocks.

Those labels must surely be very early examples, engraved when Dragon and Why Not were still familiar names.

Most of the verses attached to these labels may be doggerel, but occasionally they rise above it, as for example:

> Hail thou inspiring plant! thou balm of life,
> Well might thy worth engage two nations' strife;
> Exhaustless fountain of Britannia's wealth;
> Thou friend to wisdom and thou source of health;
> The mighty RALEGH first thy virtue taught,
> And prov'd himself thy gen'rous aid to thought.
> With thee shall live for ever RALEGH'S name,
> Nor thou the least of his immortal fame.

A favourite device was an idyllic view of a plantation with Negroes at work, and the owner sitting smoking under a brilliant sun with the stock legend "The Best Tobacco under the Sun". One ambitious dealer tried unsuccessfully to render this in Latin and French.

> Petum optimum subter Solem
> Le mellieur Tabac desous le Soliel [sic].

And here without any connexion with tobacco is an anagram:

> If you transpose what ladies wear,
> 'Twill plainly show what harlots are;
> Again if you transpose the same,
> You'll see an ancient Hebrew name;
> Change it again, and it will shew
> What all on earth desire to do;
> Transpose these letters yet once more,
> What bad men do you'll then explore.

Nor does the following rhyme appear a happy advertisement of Best Virginia London:

> ONE evening cold, as cold might be,
> With frost and hail, and pinching weather
> Companions, about three times three,
> Lay close in a pound together,
> One after t'other took a peat,
> And all dy'd that night in a sweat.

A dealer in Mild Virginia produced this riddle:

PRSVRYPRFCTMN,
VRKPTHSPRCPTSTN.

By adding a vowel to the above Letters, They will make two lines in verse.

They were written over the Ten Commandments in a Welsh church, and remained a whole century before the true sense was found, one vowel used seventeen times will provide the solution.

Perhaps those two lines remained so long unsolved because the solvers knew only Welsh.

The examples given above have been chosen from several hundred labels, and what a world away they seem from contemporary advertising!

One of the early signs used by tobacconists was inspired by the visit of Princess Pocahontas to England with Rolfe her husband. She had made a great impression on London. The courtyard of La Belle Sauvage off Ludgate Hill was called after her. Somewhere about 1616 a dealer in tobacco set up as his sign The Black Lady with a skirt of tobacco leaves, a feather headdress and in her hand the pipe of peace. The Black Lady was soon superseded by the Black o' Boy, who, when England sighed under the Protectorate, was considered insufficiently clad. His place was taken by the Black Prince (an Indian), the Turk, the Saracen and the Moor, all fully dressed, but none of them associated outwardly with tobacco. In due course these elaborate figures gave way to the Saracen's Head, no doubt for economic reasons. When a life-sized figure was wanted, the Sailor Boy, presumably costing less than a Saracen or Turk in full panoply, was used as a sign.

In due course the best-known and longest-lived sign of all appeared—the Highlander with his snuff-mull. I can recall two of those inspiring representatives in my youth. One stood outside a tobacconist's in Tottenham Court Road, and is probably now the mascot of one of the London University colleges; the other stood outside a small tobacconist's shop in Knightsbridge defying the Household Cavalry opposite until about 1890, when it vanished in one of those drastic rebuildings from which the health of London has benefited at the expense of almost all its personality. It will be a nice argument one day for social historians whether the German bombers or the London County Council did more damage.

The year 1719 was a bad one for Jacobite hopes. With the help of six hundred Spanish infantry in white (!) uniforms the Mackenzies and Macraes had fought a drawn battle with the Hanoverian troops in Glenshiel, but after that everything went wrong until at the end of 1720 an heir was born to the *de jure* James III and VIII, and Jacobite hopes revived. An Edinburgh man, David Wishart, who had opened a snuff-shop in Coventry Street, set up outside it the figure of a six-foot Highlander in doublet and trews with a targe on his arm and a claymore by his side. There was no snuff-mull in his hand, and he stood there in Coventry Street not to advertise David Wishart's wares but to let loyal gentlemen know that at the back of the shop they might discuss safely the prospect of the King's coming to his own again. Wishart's shop stood in Coventry Street until 1880, when it was moved to Panton Street.

With that superlative capacity for extracting romance out of commerce and, even more remarkably, commerce out of romance which has been the secret of Scottish vitality, the Scottish tobacco-dealers in London recognized the attraction of that Highlander outside Wishart's shop in the Haymarket; presently he was given the kilt instead of trews and instead of a targe and a claymore a snuff-mull in his hand, to become the recognized sign of the tobacconist who kept the best snuff in variety.

When the kilt and tartan were proscribed after the '45, the Highlander was under a cloud for a year or two.

An echo of that may be heard in a mock-petition:

> To the Powers that Be.
> We hear that the dapper wooden Highlanders who so heroically guard the doors of snuff shops intend to petition the Legislature in order that they may be excused from complying with the Act of Parliament with respect to the change of dress, alleging that they have ever been faithful subjects of His Majesty, having constantly supplied his guards with a pinch from their mulls when they marched by; and, so far from engaging in any rebellion, they have never

entertained a rebellious thought. Whence they humbly hope that they shall not have to be put to the expence of buying new clothes.

Mr Charles Rattray, that distinguished authority on tobacco, has elucidated the origin of the Highlander as a sign and disposed completely of the ill-informed notion that the Highlander was an adaptation of the Red Indian that once stood outside American cigar stores.

Chapter 11

SNUFF was making headway (almost literally) over smoking all over Europe during the eighteenth century. In 1725 Pope Benedict XIII, himself a snuff-taker, disapproving of the way some of the clergy had taken to vanishing from time to time from the chancel in order to take a surreptitious pinch away from the altar, annulled the Bull of Pope Innocent X and informed the Cardinal Archpriest of the Vatican Basilica that on the advice of physicians snuff-taking in St Peter's would in future be allowed. At the same time His Holiness warned the clergy that snuff must be taken with due discretion, and that none of them was to offer his box to another priest.

In 1701, when the Elector of Brandenburg assumed the title of King Frederick I of Prussia, he had instituted highly formal tobacco parties at which everybody sat round smoking in court dress. There is a picture of one of these occasions in which the Queen, dressed grandly enough for a coronation, is seen lighting the King's churchwarden pipe with a spill. Frederick William I, who succeeded his father, started a Tobacco Club for men only where everybody drank beer and smoked short Dutch clay pipes, the King's alone being silver-mounted. Dutch leaf tobacco stood on the table in wicker baskets, with pans of peat embers from which to light the pipes. The servants were dismissed so that the gathering could talk freely. Cheese and cold meat with bread and butter were at hand for the guests to help themselves. Sometimes the King and his friend the ex-King Stanislaus of Poland used to keep the party going from five in the afternoon until the small hours of the morning, smoking over thirty pipes each. The former used to complain that he lacked the advantage of the Polish King's leathern mouth.

His son Frederick the Great abolished the Tobacco Club and took to snuff. He issued edicts against careless smoking, and indeed the Germans, with their love of regulation, favoured the prohibition of smoking everywhere except indoors. Prussia was less severe than many other states. The fashion for snuff inspired a good deal of satirical writing, but the very fact of its being satirized is an indication of the progress it was making.

Christopher Smart, whose *Song to David* written when he was shut up in Bedlam was hailed by Browning, Rossetti and others as the greatest poem of the eighteenth century, wrote a delightful exchange in verse between a bag-wig and a tobacco-pipe published in his *Poems on Several Occasions* in 1752:

A Bag-wig of a jauntee air
Trick'd up with all a barber's care,
Loaded with powder and perfume,
Hung in a spendthrift's dressing-room;
Close by its side, by chance convey'd,
A black Tobacco-pipe was laid;
And with its vapours far and near,
Outstunk the essence of Monsieur;
At which its rage, the thing of hair,
Thus, bristling up, began declare
"Bak'd dirt, that with intrusion rude,
Breaks in upon my solitude,
And with thy fetid breath defiles
The air for forty thousand miles—
Avaunt—pollution's in thy touch—
O barb'rous English! horrid Dutch!
I cannot bear it—Here, Sue, Nan,
Go call the maid to call the man,
And bid him come without delay,
To take this odious pipe away, . . .

The pipe (for 'twas a pipe of soul)
Raising himself upon his bowl,
In smoke like oracle of old,
Did thus his sentiments unfold,
"Why, what's the matter, goodman Swagger,
Thou flaunting French, fantastic bragger?
Whose whole fine speech is (with a pox)
Ridiculous and heterodox.
'Twas better for the English nation
Before such scoundrels came in fashion,
When none bought hair in realms unknown,
But every blockhead bore his own.
Know, puppy, I'm an English pipe,
Deem'd worthy of each Briton's gripe,

Who, with my cloud-compelling aid,
Help our plantations and our trade,
And am, when sober and when mellow,
An upright, downright, honest fellow.
Tho' fools, like you may think me rough,
And scorn me, 'cause I am in buff,
Yet your contempt I glad receive,
'Tis all the fame that you can give.
None finery or foppery prize:
But they who've something to disguise;
For simple nature hates abuse,
And Plainness is the dress of Use.

This poem, which one may fancy implies a rebuke to snuff,
has not escaped the circumambient eye of Arents, but it is not
to be found in any of the popular books about smoking, and
being so far superior to most of the occasional verse about
smoking has been given here almost in full.

In 1736 Isaac Hawkins Browne published a volume entitled
A Pipe of Tobacco, which consisted of 'Imitations' of half a dozen
contemporary authors. These early examples of parody had a
vogue at the time and for long afterwards. They were praised by
Byron and were mentioned by Jane Austen.

The imitation of Colley Cibber is as dull as the verse of
Cibber himself. Neither the imitation of Pope nor of Swift is
really successful, but from the Popeian salute to the 'Blest Leaf'
may be quoted:

. . . the Critic owns thy genial aid,
While supperless he plies the piddling trade,
That tho' to Love and soft delights a foe,
By ladies hated, hated by the beau. . . .

In the imitation of Edward Young more evidence is afforded
of the disapproval of smoking among men and women of
fashion.

Coxcombs prefer the tickling sting of snuff;
Yet all their claim to wisdom is—a puff;
Lord Foplin smokes not—for his teeth afraid:
Sir Tawdry smokes not—for he wears brocade.

Ladies, when pipes are brought affect to swoon;
They love no smoke except the smoke of Town,
But courtiers hate the puffing tube—no matter,
Strange if they love the breath that cannot flatter.

. . . . .

Yet crowds remain, who still its worth proclaim,
While some for pleasure smoke, and some for fame.

It may well have been that the women of fashion whose elaborate headdresses were often kept without being taken down for a week objected to the smell of stale smoke in their hair. Washing was not a favourite occupation of the eighteenth century, and one is faintly surprised by the fuss made about the smell of tobacco at a time when noses had to accept so many affronts.

By far the best of the 'imitations' is the graceful parody of *The Splendid Shilling* by Ambrose Philips. Indeed, it is one of the best poems about smoking ever written:

Little tube of mighty pow'r
Charmer of an idle hour,
Object of my warm desire,
Lip of wax and eye of fire:
And thy snowy taper waist,
With my finger gently brac'd;
And thy pretty swelling crest,
With my little stopper prest,
And the sweetest bliss of blisses,
Breathing from thy balmy kisses.
Happy thrice, and thrice again,
Happiest he of happy men;
Who when again the night returns,
When again the taper burns;
When again the cricket's gay,
(Little cricket, full of play)
Can afford his tube to feed.
From the fragrant Indian weed:
Pleasure for a nose divine,
Incense of the god of wine.
Happy thrice, and thrice again,
Happiest he of happy men.

Eighteenth century tobacco labels

The churchwarden pipe is never seen to-day; the brier will be lucky if it should ever win such a comely epitaph.

Snuff was winning the battle against the pipe. In 1773 Dr Johnson could observe:

> Smoking has gone out. To be sure, it is a shocking thing, blowing smoke out of our mouths into other people's mouths, eyes and noses, and having the same thing done to us; yet I cannot account why a thing which requires so little exertion, and yet preserves the mind from total vacuity, should have gone out.

Dr Johnson himself took snuff which he kept loose in his waistcoat pocket, but he always had a respect for the sedative influence of smoking, and he was once heard to say that madness had grown more frequent since smoking had gone out of fashion. It would not be extravagant to claim to-day that smoking saves myriads from an exacerbation of the nerves that might well lead to an increase of insanity.

That formidable scholar Dr Samuel Parr, who was the nearest thing to Dr Johnson that the Whigs could produce, was a tremendous smoker. He maintained that tobacco preserved the memory, and as Dr Parr could remember being suckled by his mother his opinion must be respected. Parr's biographer was inclined to attribute his failure to be offered a bishopric to his smoking. "His pipe might be deemed in these fantastic days a degradation at the table of the palace." There is a portrait of Parr in the Combination-room at St John's College, Cambridge, in which the pipe he was holding has been painted out. Parr, who applied for the headmastership of Harrow when he was twenty-five, smoked all day from the moment he got out of bed. The ladies had to put up with his pipe or lose his company. One occasion after dining at the Bush Inn in Bristol he called for a pipe, to be told by the waiter that smoking was forbidden. Parr was furious, and when the landlord supported the waiter he roared:

> 'Why, man, I've smoked in the dining-room of every noble-man in England. The Duchess of Devonshire said I could smoke in every room in her house but her dressing-room, and here, in this dirty public-house of Bristol you forbid smoking! Amazing! Bring me my bill.'

Dr Parr had some excuse for his indignation at being forbidden one day to smoke in Bristol of all cities. He was to boast later that he had smoked a pipe with the Prince Regent at Carlton House; later, when he had not been given a bishopric, he became a fervid supporter of Queen Caroline.

The mighty Grecian Richard Porson was a friend of Parr's. In November 1789 the latter wrote to Dr Burney:

> The books may be consulted, and Porson shall do it, and he will do it. I know his price when he bargains with me: two bottles instead of one, six pipes instead of two, burgundy instead of claret, liberty to sit till five in the morning instead of sneaking into bed at one: these are his terms.

It was Porson who once declared that, when smoking began to go out of fashion, learning began to go out of fashion also. His memory was remarkable, but his constitution was delicate and he died on the edge of fifty. Porson, though Professor of Greek at Cambridge, lived most of his time in London. Perhaps he found the atmosphere of the Trinity Combination-room without tobacco unsympathetic. George Pryme in his *Autobiographic Recollections* says that in 1800 "smoking was allowed in the Trinity Combination-room after supper in the twelve days of Christmas, when a few old men availed themselves of it". A large silver tobacco-box was placed on the table with the wine and pipes, and Porson suggested that the box should be inscribed 'Τῷ Βάκχῳ' (To Baccho.)

That the pipe was in peril of extinction even in Oxford and Cambridge by the end of the eighteenth century is hard to believe, and yet the evidence is disagreeably recurrent.

About 1800 the older Fellows at New College

> not liking the then newly introduced luxury of Turkey carpets, often adjourned to smoke their pipes in a little room opposite to the Senior Common Room, now appropriated to other uses, but then kept as a smoking-room.[1]

Archdeacon Denison recorded:

> When I went up to Oxford, 1823-24, there were two things unknown at Christ Church, and I believe very generally in Oxford—smoking and slang.[2]

[1] G. V. Cox, *Recollections of Oxford* (1868).
[2] *Notes of my Life* (1878).

It is to be remembered that Christ Church at that date was by far the most fashionable college in a worldly sense, and Denison was unlikely to have seen much of other colleges. It is difficult to accept his sweeping statement. Denison himself, who invented the 'harvest festival', was always inclined to subordinate the facts to his own prejudices.

Tennyson, who was at Trinity College, Cambridge, in 1828–30, smoked hard as an undergraduate, and so did that remarkable group of his undergraduate friends who called themselves the Apostles. The dons, too, were still smoking. At Queens' College, the Combination-room had a sanded floor, and in the words of the poet himself the "table was set handsomely forth with long churchwardens".

However, it has to be admitted that when the new century came in smoking was becoming, indeed had already become, a plebeian habit.

Cowper could not be called a man about town, but in 1782 he was writing:

> *Says the Pipe to the Snuff-box, I can't understand*
> *What the ladies and gentlemen see in your face,*
> *That you are in fashion all over the land,*
> *And I am so much fallen into disgrace.*

The Elizabethan and Caroline ladies smoked; the daughters of Louis XIV smoked; indeed, women of every class everywhere had smoked. Yet by one of those mysterious exhibitions of unanimity which are periodically displayed by the female sex, outside the domain of dress where the phenomenon is persistent, English women decided for a century that they could not tolerate the smell of tobacco smoke. In spite of that, for a long time they continued to indulge in snuff. Queen Charlotte in Buckingham House was snuffing away. So why not her humble subjects?

Here is the will of a certain Mrs Thompson who lived in Boyle Street, Burlington Gardens:

IN THE NAME OF GOD. AMEN

I, Margaret Thompson . . . being of sound mind, do desire that when my soul is departed from this wicked world, my body and effects may be disposed of in the manner following. . . .

I also desire that all my handkerchiefs that I may have unwashed at the time of my decease, after they have been got together by my old and trusty servant, Sarah Stewart, be put by her, and her alone, at the bottom of my coffin, which I desire may be made large enough for that purpose, together with such a quantity of the best Scotch snuff (in which she knoweth I always had the greatest delight) as will cover my deceased body; and this I desire, and more especially as it is usual to put flowers into the coffins of departed friends, and nothing can be so pleasant and so refreshing to me as that precious powder. But I strictly charge that no one be suffered to approach my body till the coffin is closed, and it is necessary to carry me to my burial, which I order in the following manner:—

Six men to be my bearers, who are well known to be great snuff-takers in the parish of St James's, Westminster; and instead of mourning, each to wear a snuff-coloured beaver, which I desire to be bought for that purpose, and given to them. Six Maidens of my old acquaintance to bear my pall, each to wear a proper hood, and to carry a box filled with the best Scotch snuff, to take for their refreshment as they go along. Before my corpse I desire that the minister may be invited to walk, and to take a certain quantity of snuff, not exceeding one pound, to whom I also bequeath five guineas on condition of his doing so.

And I also desire my old and faithful servant, Sarah Stewart, to walk before the corpse to distribute every twenty yards a large handful of Scotch snuff on the ground, and to the crowd who possibly may follow me to my burial place, on condition I bequeath her £20. And I also desire that at least two bushels of the said snuff shall be distributed at the door of my house in Boyle Street.

I desire, also, that my funeral shall be at twelve o'clock at noon. And in addition to the various legacies I have left my friends in a former will, I desire that to each person there shall be given a pound of the best Scotch snuff, as it is the grand cordial of human nature.

Whatever we may think of eccentric old ladies like Mrs Thompson, we owe one debt to snuff, and that is the shop of Fribourg and Treyer, the two bow-windows of which have reflected the passers-by of London in the reigns of eleven Kings and Queens. It was opened in 1720 in the same year as David Wishart's snuff-shop close by in Coventry Street. It may have been started by the father of Peter Fribourg, who retired from the business in 1780 when Gottlieb Augustus Treyer came into it. Treyer married a Miss Martha Evans, and when he retired the business was looked after by her brother, Price Evans, two of whose sons succeeded to the business and premises at 34, Haymarket on the death of their aunt in 1815. There have been Evanses there ever since. Within my knowledge such a continuity combined of premises and proprietors is unique in London.

At first Fribourg and Treyer was almost exclusively a snuff-shop at the Sign of the Rasp and Crown. *"Makes and Sells Rappee and all other Sorts of Snuff Wholesale and Retail"* the oldest label announces. Then (and this contradicts Dr Johnson) a label of about 1780 shows above the Rasp and Crown a carotte of tobacco with the announcement: *"Sells all sorts of Snuffs and Tobaccos."* Finally a label of about 1800 shows the Prince of Wales's Feathers instead of the Rasp and Crown with the announcement in large capitals: *"Tobacconists to H.R.H. The Prince of Wales"* and underneath: *"Importers of Foreign Snuffs and Tobaccos also Lundy Foot's High Dried Irish Snuff. N.B. Have no concern whatever with any other Shop."* Over a century later a branch of Fribourg and Treyer was opened in Oxford to be patronized by another Prince of Wales. J. Fribourg had a snuff-shop in the colonnade of the Opera House where Her Majesty's Theatre stands to-day. There was also a firm called Fribourg and Pontet at 23, Haymarket, which no doubt provoked the wording on the label. Later the business was bought by a firm of cigarette makers and the shop in the Haymarket was closed. Finally Fribourg and Treyer bought the name Fribourg out of Fribourg and Pontet.

It is usually stated that the Prince Regent disliked smoking, but as already mentioned Dr Samuel Parr claimed to have smoked a pipe with him at Carlton House. Moreover, in 1800, when he first dealt with Fribourg and Treyer as Prince of Wales, he was frequently supplied with a tobacco called El Cham. This was an expensive Oriental tobacco costing eighteen shillings a pound. We may speculate that Beau Brummel persuaded him that smoking was vulgar. At any rate, the Prince of Wales became a devotee of snuff.

George Evans[1] wrote:

[1] An Old Snuff-House, 1720–1920.

It was the custom of fastidious snuff-takers to vary their snuffs more than once during the day, some kept a room specially for storing their snuffs and preparing them for daily use. King George IV kept a large stock of snuff in this way, and it was said that it was the duty of one of the partners in the firm to periodically inspect his stock. At the death of the King, the firm catalogued and arranged for sale the considerable quantity of this snuff stock. The greater part was bought by the firm and sold to its customers. There was naturally a great demand for this snuff and it commanded high prices.

In Lord Petersham's account, the following snuffs were selected in December 1830 from the late King's stock:

			£	s.	d.
18 lb. Old Bureau marked	1801		13	17	0
18 lb. Old Cologne	,,	1818	13	17	0
18 lb. Old Arras	,,	1818	13	17	0
12 lb. Old Havre	,,	1815	9	16	0
18 lb. Bureau D.G.	,,	1815	13	17	0
6 lb. French Prize	,,	1810	4	13	6
1 lb. French Prize	,,	1810	0	16	0
5 lb. Old Rouen	,,	1801	3	17	6

Not far away from a hundredweight of 'vintage snuff'. The suggestion of wine is heightened by the predominance of French names. Another favourite of George IV was Martinique and the King's Martinique was sold at 21s. per lb., three times as much as ordinary Martinique.

Martinique became popular from 1830 to 1840, and to quote George Evans, "customer after customer in the books of Fribourg and Treyer was supplied with it. . . . It had a distinct and very pleasant flavour, quite unscented; it was rather light in colour and also in character."

In view of that predominance of French snuff it is surprising to find Brummel writing from Calais, where he had fled to avoid his creditors:

Mr Brummel is very much obliged to Messrs Fribourg and Treyer for the snuff they have had the goodness to send him— it is excellent, and he will consider it a particular favour if they will from time to time when they have any really good Martinique or Façon de Paris, remit him a certain quantity —— Mr Brummel begs to assure Messrs Fribourg and Treyer that their recollection of him is not less seasonable than

flattering, for there is not a good pinch of snuff to be had
throughout France.

That last assertion would sound like a piece of affectation by
the Beau did we not know that in May 1819 Fribourg and
Treyer were sending fifty pounds of Carotte Bureau at half a
guinea a pound packed in "23 flat canisters" to King Louis
XVIII. Bureau (*gros*, *demigros*, and *fin*) was mentioned earlier
as a special French snuff favoured by His Most Christian
Majesty's Ministers. Tradition says that Napoleon, who disliked smoking but took snuff all the time, was supplied from the
Haymarket when he was in St Helena. Why the French wanted
to import French snuff from London is a puzzle.

The Prince Regent laid down others than French snuff in
that 'cellar' of snuffs at Windsor, where they filled a whole
room. Spanish Brown, the most expensive of all, cost £3 a
pound. A phial of Vinagrillo, a rose-scented vinegar, was always
sold with this, with which the snuff was freshly moistened when
required. It was a favourite with the ladies. Brazil was a
powerful and expensive snuff, unscented and coarse-grained.
It was used sparingly in mixtures, much in the way that
Perique is used in tobacco mixtures.

Masulipatam was an Indian snuff of strong and individual
flavour and, like Brazil, was used at the rate of a quarter or
half an ounce to a pound of snuff. It was packed in pint
bottles like claret bottles accompanied by a long iron skewer
to get it out, and sold at a guinea the bottle. It was a favourite
of Queen Charlotte's, and it often figures in her account with
'Colonel Taylor's sort (strong)'. She may have introduced it to
her eldest son. However, Morocco was the Queen's prime
favourite. It occurs repeatedly, ten or twelve pounds at a time,
in the ledger, sometimes to the account of Her Britannic
Majesty and sometimes simply to Her Majesty, the bill being
paid by the Queen's agent, Mr Compton of 6, Charlotte Street,
Pimlico. The price was usually 8s. 6d. a pound, the jar and
bung being three or four shillings extra. The poor Duke of
Sussex at a time when he was unmarrying himself from Lady
Augusta Murray opened an account with Fribourg and Treyer
in 1805. It may be significant that his badgered nerves required something more sedative than snuff. True, he was
ordering Étrennes, the snuff that Horace Walpole favoured,

but he was also ordering six pipes at the same time.

The first mention of cigars occurs in 1800, when two pounds of 'Havannah Sigars' were quoted at £2 12s. 6d., and then on October 8th, 1802, occurs the portentous entry "The Duke of Manchester, Cheroots, £1 1s. 0d."

A famous snuff-house in the City of London, James Taddy and Company, was established in 1740, and lasted until 1920, when the last Taddy gave up the business as his answer to what he considered an unreasonable strike.

The original John Hardham was already established in Fleet Street as a blender and retailer when James Taddy started. His most famous blend was No. 37, which became so popular that Hardham supplied it to many other retailers. He was a keen amateur actor and a friend of David Garrick, who is said to have given Hardham's 37 a fine advertisement by mention-ing it in a play. Hardham died in 1772 and left a fortune. His business was sold and changed hands several times in the course of the years, but the name was kept alive until the autumn of 1956 at the sign of the Red Lyon in another part of Fleet Street close to Ludgate Circus.

George Evans says:

> Snuff of the present day gives no idea of what it once was, and bears no comparison to that of former years. Its fragrance was derived by careful blending of snuffs made of various tobaccos, and not by the addition of scents or essences. Scented snuffs were sometimes taken; but the proportion was small in comparison to the quantity of unscented snuffs sold. Scented snuffs came more into vogue as the more refined varieties were dying out; the latter as time went on, and the demand for them lessened, were no longer made and are now unobtainable.[1]

Nevertheless, scented snuffs were always in great demand, particularly for the ladies. Macouba, which under various spellings has been in fashion for a century and a half, was strongly scented with Attar of Roses.

The French snuff *gros grain* was ground from James River (Virginia) and Amersfoot (Dutch) tobacco, and then treated with a sauce compounded of brandy, burgundy, salt, soda, cream of tartar and tamarinds. Morocco, which Queen Charlotte liked so much, was made by blending rose petals

[1] Op. cit., p. 14.

with snuff ground from the midribs and stalks of Virginia tobacco, and then blended again with twice as much snuff ground from St Omer tobacco. The result was moistened with salt and water to which were added cream and salts of tartar, the mixture being finally packed in leaden canisters until lead gave way to tin.

Tonquin beans hailing from Brazil and British Guiana have been and are still much used by blenders of snuff, and it was a habit to carry a Tonquin bean in a snuff-box. This association may date back to the time when snuff was first introduced to the rest of the world from Brazil.

Scottish and Irish snuff have already been mentioned. The two English towns which have always been particularly famous for snuff are Sheffield and Kendal. In the former Joseph Wilson was making snuff over two centuries ago, and his successors are grinding snuff in the mills to-day. Kendal Brown is known all over the world, and the mill there goes back to the eighteenth century. Probably the oldest snuff-mill in the country is that of E. & W. Anstie of Devizes. This firm can trace its history back to the latter half of the seventeenth century, when Richard Anstie was a grocer in Devizes. In 1740 his son, John Anstie, who had succeeded him in the family business, entered into an agreement with a snuff manufacturer for the purchase and sale of snuff, and a year later he bought the Whistley Mill at Potterne, Wiltshire, in order to manufacture his own snuff. A pair of French grinding-stones, brought from Whistley Mill to Anstie's present factory in Devizes nearly two hundred years ago, are still in use (1956). So is an old giant wooden-toothed wheel which is used to turn the stones. In the old days it was driven by a windmill, and when there was no wind a donkey supplied the motive power.

There is one other town which must be mentioned in con-nexion with snuff, and that is Mitcham in Surrey, where in the first half of the nineteenth century, almost all the snuff sold in London was ground in mills for which the mechanical power was provided by the water-wheels of the River Wandle. The use of steam made the water-wheels idle. No snuff is ground to-day in Mitcham; the lavender has outlasted it.

In the days before air-tight tins were thought of, snuff used to be packed in bladders like lard to preserve its freshness and perfume.

Chapter 12

WE penetrated into the nineteenth century in the last
chapter, but before penetrating any farther it will be
as well to take a look at the economic background of
tobacco in the eighteenth century. Until the American Revolution more tobacco was grown in Virginia and Maryland than
anywhere, with Carolina and, after the middle of the century,
Tennessee and Kentucky also on the tobacco road not so far
behind.

J. F. D. Smyth, who was an agent of the British Government,
made an extensive tour of the Colonies just before the War of
Independence started, and published a book in 1784 in which
there are some interesting facts about tobacco. He says the
rich and loamy soil of the James River district produced 1,660
pounds an acre, and the worst not more than 500 pounds. The
price paid was from sixteen to twenty shillings the hundredweight:

> There are seven different kinds of tobacco, particularly
> adapted to the different qualities of the soil on which they
> are cultivated, and each varying from the other. They are
> named Hudson, Frederick, Thick-joint, Shoestring, Thickset,
> Sweet-scented, and Oroonoko.

Smyth says that "immediately on the commencement of the
rebellion the inspectors of tobacco were all set aside and every
planter shipped or sold all the trash he could make and pack
up."

"Thus it has continued," he adds, "and in this hopeful state
remains the whole tobacco trade of the United States of
America at present."

Nevertheless, competition always seemed to be threatening
the predominance of Virginia and Maryland. The work of an
anonymous Dutch dealer in tobacco, published at Amsterdam
in 1770, gives a notion of the extent of it. In Holland itself a
great deal of tobacco was grown. The author adds sarcastically
that most of the places in Holland do not smoke their own
tobacco because "we all have the strange idea that our neighbour eats better than we do". He says that the French are

growing much less at home than formerly because, being
compelled to sell to the tobacco monopoly, they have to accept
whatever price is offered. The tobacco of Andouillé, with a
dry reddish leaf, was packed in large bales; the tobacco of
Dieppe, small and black, was packed in barrels. The French
were also growing tobacco in Louisiana and Canada. The
Spanish colonies had a monopoly of the leaf for cigars, and also
of the best tobacco for snuff. Two much-esteemed tobaccos came
from Colombia and Venezuela—Varinas and Canaster, the
latter called after the rush basket in which the twist was packed.
According to the anonymous Dutch author, Canaster was very
dry and the colour of a dead leaf.

Portugal depended on Brazil for its tobacco, the snuff made
from which commanded the highest price. The author paid a
tribute to the pleasant odour of the Indian tobacco and also
to that of Japan, but added that the Indian and Japanese
tobacco was often spoilt on the voyage to Europe. He spoke
disparagingly of the snuffs from Seville, Havana and Barcelona, noting that the snuff from Portugal was olive-coloured
with an unpleasant smell. He considered that the carottes sent
from Strasbourg made the best snuff; they were decorated with
gold foil, silvered nails and strips of marbled paper. A good deal
of tobacco suitable for snuff came from the Levant, Italy and
Malta. The rolls from Brazil were often covered with a green
skin, which preserved the tobacco. The English did not like the
'Oroonoko' tobacco from Maryland, but in Holland, Germany,
Denmark and Sweden they preferred it to the sweet Virginian tobacco. The colonists of Louisiana, in the opinion of this tobacco
merchant, were the most efficient cultivators of tobacco, and
Louisiana itself was the cheapest place in which to grow it.

The French Government had tried to encourage tobacco
growing in Louisiana as early as 1719, and by 1756 several
hundred thousands of pounds had been exported to France.
A French economist observed that tobacco was the only
production of the earth which gave England an advantage
over France and that Louisiana ought to be accepted as a pro-
vidential means if not to compete with the English tobacco at
least to be able to do without it; but before the century ended the
planters of Louisiana were concentrating entirely on sugar and
cotton, except those very few who were exporting Perique.

The anonymous Dutch dealer says that the whole of Russia

could be supplied with the Circassian tobacco grown in the Ukraine. The plants came originally from Turkey, but were less fragrant in Russia. The Persians preferred the milder flavour of unsweated tobacco; if it were properly cured, it could be as strong as Brazilian tobacco.

The competition was world-wide. Yet Virginia and Maryland, in spite of the recurrent economic crises from which no great industry is continuously free, put all their faith in tobacco. Writing in 1770, Adam Smith reflected on the absurdity of prohibiting the culture of tobacco in Europe for the sake of its tax value. He viewed with doubt the wisdom of colonies like Virginia and Maryland depending so exclusively upon tobacco and observed:

> I have never even heard of any tobacco plantation that was improved and cultivated by the capital of merchants who resided in Great Britain, and our tobacco colonies send us home no such wealthy planters as we see frequently arrive from our sugar islands. . . .

Yet there were many wealthy planters. When Robert 'King' Carter died in 1732 he owned 300,000 acres of good land and 700 slaves. Such magnates existed in sufficient numbers to create an aristocratic society in an agreeable climate from which they did not feel the least inclined to cut themselves off by coming back to England.

George Washington and Thomas Jefferson, themselves planters, were uneasy about the prospect for Virginia if tobacco was to remain the staple. Jefferson in the middle of the War of Independence was convinced that wheat must take its place. He argued that the soil was richer and the sun hotter in Georgia and Mississippi. Planters there would be able to undersell Virginia, and the Virginian planters would be obliged to forsake tobacco.

> And a happy obligation for them it will be. It is a culture productive of infinite wretchedness. Those employed in it are in a continued state of exertion beyond the powers of nature to support. Little food of any kind is raised by them; so that the men and animals on these farms are illy fed, and the earth is rapidly impoverished. . . .

Early in the seventeenth century, the General Assembly of Virginia, on account of the dearth of currency, had authorized the colonists to pay taxes and other debts in the products of field and forest. These in effect were tobacco, and for years everything in Virginia, even the stipends of the clergy, was paid for in hogsheads of tobacco. The tobacco shipped to England was converted into credit. A system of bills was started. The planters brought their crops to the warehouses along the rivers, where the value of each crop was rated by public inspectors who gave a bill on certificate for the amount, and these bills were negotiable either in the colony or abroad. In 1722 England as a great concession agreed to the issue of a copper currency in the American colonies in farthings, half-pennies and pennies. In 1754 Virginia issued paper money, which survived until the Revolution.

In the books of the planters and the English merchants there was a vast amount of money, but such a system could only end in making the planters too dependent upon the merchants, and complaints were incessant. A book could be filled with the ups and downs of the Virginia trade, the grievances of the colonists and the greed of the English merchants, or from the other angle the greed of the colonists and the grievances of the English merchants.

Here is a specimen of shopping with the hogshead as currency. It is taken from a fascinating collection of letters[1]:

To
Mr John Norton
Mercht. in London
By Capt. Lilly
Sir,
    By Capt. Lilly have sent you 4 hds. Tobo and shall be oblig'd to you, to send me the following articles on it viz: 3 Tooth brushes, a green silk Tippet, 1 pr. womens pattins, 1 pr. clogs, 1 fashionable muft with a hair tippet to it, a red Silk Bonnet and Cloke for a child three years old, three mourning rings according to the inclosed directions, a Silver lac'd hatt for a Boy four years old. These things shall be glad to have by the first ship in York or Rappak.
                    I am, Sir,
                    Your humble sert.
                    Augustine Smith.
                    Middlesex 4th Jany. 1767.
P.S. 2 fans at 2s. 6d. each for a Child 5 years old.

[1] *John Norton & Sons, Merchants of London and Virginia. Being the Papers from their Counting House for the years* 1750 *to* 1795. Edited by Frances Norton Mason. Richmond, Virginia, 1937.

Within less than a decade after that letter was written shopping with hogsheads of tobacco would have vanished for ever. Thomas Jefferson, who owed over £9,000 to merchants in London and Glasgow at the outbreak of the War of Independence in 1775, would observe:

> These debts had become hereditary from father to son, for many generations, so that the planters were a species of property, annexed to certain mercantile houses in London.

To somebody who consulted him about a proposed debt transfer he urged that it should be made.

But upon condition that the person giving the credit shall be satisfied to receive annually his interest in money and shall not require consignments of tobacco. This is the usual condition of the tobacco merchants . . . there was never an instance of a man's getting out of debt who was once in the hands of a tobacco merchant and bound to consign his tobacco to him. It is the most delusive of all snares.

It was the resentment against the consignment merchants which had given the Scots their opportunity and for a quarter of a century made Glasgow the central tobacco mart of the world.

The Scottish interest in tobacco had begun back in the seventeenth century when Scotland was considered a foreign nation. Scottish ships had tried to get a share of the carrying trade, but their ships not being the bottoms demanded by the provocative Navigation Act were excluded from any privileges.

The Scots, being excluded from legitimate trade, took to smuggling tobacco into England or carrying it to ports on the Continent. In 1671 an Act forbade Colonial tobacco to be landed in Ireland unless it had been shipped from an English port. Naturally that gave a fillip to free trade as smuggling was called. The Virginian collector of Customs at the end of the seventeenth century was complaining:

> I find that in these three years past there has not been above 5 ships trading legally in the rivers . . . above 20 Scotch, Irish and New England vessels within these 8 months have sailed out . . . with their loadings of tobacco for Scotland and Holland and the man-of-war had not discovered one of them.

The perfidy of the English Government, which had been one of the chief causes for the failure of the Darien scheme and the ruin of thousands of small investors in Scotland, on top of the refusal to allow any shipment by Scottish vessels from or to any English colony, confirmed the Scots in their belief that the English were determined to force them to accept the Treaty of Union by commercial blackmail. Before the Union the Scottish duty on tobacco was lower than it was in England, and the Scottish shippers managed to land considerable stocks, thanks to which astute piece of foresight they were able to start that under-selling of the English merchants which at one time threatened the prosperity of Bristol and Liverpool. If the Scots had possessed a mercantile marine of comparable size at the beginning of the eighteenth century, they would have done much more damage to English trade than in fact they did.

The Scottish merchants relied on something better than smuggling for wresting trade from their English rivals. In former days when they were debarred by the Navigation Act from trading they had paid a better price to the planter, and after the Union they recognized the force of the planters' complaint against the consignment system.

The Scottish merchants paid for their tobacco in goods that the planters, particularly the new immigrants, needed, and what was more attractive they continued to charge less for them than the English merchants. At first there was a lack of shipping on the Clyde, but to deal with this the Glasgow merchants chartered ships from Whitehaven until they could build their own. Whitehaven soon woke up to the fact that it had made a mistake. The merchants "from that part of Great Britain called England" by the English and South Britain by the Scots were finding the competition severe within ten years of the Union. In 1717 Bristol was protesting to the Commissioners of Customs in London about the Glasgow methods of trading, but the protest was disregarded as commercial jealousy. Four years later the tobacco merchants of London, Liverpool and Whitehaven presented petitions to the Lords of the Treasury accusing the Glasgow merchants of fraudulent practices, but their lordships in dismissing the petition decided that "the complaints were groundless and that they proceeded from the spirit of envy, and not from a regard to the interests of trade or of the King's revenue". The English merchants persisted and took their grievance to the House of Commons. Commissioners were sent to Glasgow in 1722 and reported to the House in 1723. Although the charges were explicitly answered, new officers were appointed at the ports of Greenock and Port Glasgow with private instructions to ruin the trade if possible. Gibson writes:

> . . . bills of equity were exhibited against the merchants in the Court of Exchequer, for no less than thirty-three ships' cargoes by which they were commanded to declare upon oath, whether or not they had imported in these ships any and how much more tobacco than what had been exported, or had paid the King's duty; vexatious lawsuits of every kind were stirred up against them, every species of persecution which malice, assisted by wealth and interest, could invent, to destroy the trade of Glasgow, were put into practice, and they in part succeeded; it languished until the year 1735 that it began to revive.[1]

Glasgow was by no means the only port in Scotland that was handling tobacco. In September 1715 a shipment from Maryland consigned to James Coutts reached Montrose after the outbreak of the Jacobite rising. When Coutts's agent applied to the Customs collector for entry papers they were refused. A week later the commissioners of Customs ordered the cargo to be discharged at Leith. Before the ship could sail it was seized by the Jacobites, who demanded that the duty should be paid to them. When Coutts refused, they disabled the ship and took Coutts off to Perth as a prisoner. Here in order to obtain his freedom he paid £500 to the Earl of Mar, and ordered that the tobacco which was left after the ships had been pillaged should be sold for what it would fetch. This involved him in a loss of £200 over what was sold. When the '15 Rising collapsed the Commissioners of Customs not only compelled the unfortunate Coutts to pay duty on what tobacco was left to him but also demanded a bond of £720 19s. ½d. (presumably the odd halfpenny was the cost of the red tape) for duty on the tobacco of which he had been robbed and over the sale of which he had made a loss.

The case dragged on for nearly thirty years before the Lords of the Treasury agreed to release poor Coutts from his bond. In 1752 an Act of Parliament had to be passed to relieve

---

[1] *History of Glasgow* (1777).

James Guthrie, with respect to the duties paid and secured upon a quantity of tobacco burnt at the port of Kirkcudbright.

What had happened was that the ship *Neptune*, loaded with 223,480 pounds of tobacco and bound for Dieppe, capsized in the harbour of Kirkcudbright. James Guthrie and Co., merchants of Dumfries, had already paid the duties on this, but the whole of the damaged tobacco was burnt by order of the Customs officers, who refused to refund the duty paid. There was a furnace at the London docks in which contraband and spoilt tobacco was burnt. This was known as the King's Pipe, but there are no records to be found of such a large bowlful as James Guthrie's tobacco.

Notwithstanding the anxiety of the English tobacco merchants, the competition of Glasgow did not become really serious until the middle of the century. The great opportunity came with the outbreak of the Seven Years War. The French, as is apparent in the Kirkcudbright story, needed Virginia tobacco. Neither the tobacco they grew at home nor the tobacco they obtained from Louisiana and Martinique satisfied them. The British Government was afraid that if Virginia tobacco was denied to their enemies, the French might be driven in despair to develop their own American plantations. So a gentleman's agreement was reached between the two nations at war with each other by which the French Government was to be allowed to buy what tobacco it wanted in Great Britain, such tobacco to be the product and manufacture of British plantations. The ships carrying it were to proceed from a named port in Scotland or England to a named port in France carrying nothing but tobacco, and were to return from France empty.

Here is a specimen licence under the date June 3rd, 1756:

Upon application made to His Majesty in Council, a Pass hath been ordered to be forthwith issued under the Great Seal for the following ship to export Tobacco to France, in like manner and form as was done during the last war with France [which came to an end with the Peace of Aix-la-Chapelle in 1748]. The *Marion* of Glasgow, British Built, Burthen one hundred and fifty tons or thereabouts, carrying Twelve men, Alexander Morrison, Master, Laden with two hundred hogsheads of Tobacco, to sail from Glasgow to Bourdeaux in France.

I am ordered to acquaint you with this information of the Commissioners of His Majesty's Customs, that the necessary directions may be given to the proper officers at the Port of Glasgow from whence the ship is to sail.

Three months were allowed for the round voyage and during 1756 and 1757 more than fifty passes were issued.

An explanation of why Glasgow was able to benefit from the Seven Years War more than their English rivals had been well summed up by Defoe over thirty years earlier:

The Glasgow vessels are no sooner out of the Firth of Clyde, but they stretch away to the north-west, are out of the road of the privateers immediately, and are often at the capes of Virginia before the London ships get clear of the channel. Nay, even in times of peace, there must always be allowed one time with another, at least fourteen or twenty days difference in the voyage both going out and coming in, which taken together, is a month or six weeks in the whole voyage, and considering wear and tear, victuals and wages, this makes a considerable difference in trade.

Presumably the Bristol and Liverpool merchantmen were able to make the voyage as fast as the thirty-seven days required from Greenock to North Carolina in peace-time; it was the ships from London that required the extra fourteen to twenty days. In war-time the speed of the convoy was that of the slowest ship, and the preliminary waste of time involved in assembling the convoy in the Downs often meant that the English merchantment were a month behind their Scottish rivals.

The Glasgow merchants were also one up over Bristol, Liverpool and London in that war-time arrangement with the French. A lawsuit between an Edinburgh merchant and a Greenock tobacco agent in 1758 sheds some light on this. Mr Alexander of Edinburgh charged Mr Miller of Greenock with having sold him tobacco from the River Raphahanack of "a mean or inferior quality" instead of James River Tobacco "superior in point of goodness":

The French pay the lowest price for Tobaccos of any nation in Europe. They have the art of manufacturing tobacco of the meanest quality, so as to conceal its original defect. Hence the French always decline purchasing Tobacco of a superior quality, at the high price requisite . . . and hence the merchants of Glasgow, who had dealt with the French for a number of years, came to have an opinion, that the meanest Tobacco was the most proper for supplying the demands of the French, and by consequence they imported great part of their Tobacco from the River Raphahanack, as being of an inferior quality, and of a low prime cost.

The reason why the French paid such a low price was the monopoly of the greedy *Fermiers-Généraux*, whose heads would one day pay on the guillotine for that ruthless greed. William Alexander and Sons of Edinburgh, whose case against Miller has been mentioned, were their Scottish agents for some years, but they failed to satisfy their principals later on, and the agency was given to William Herries, who "procured for himself the honour of knighthood" in order to make an impression on the Farmers-General. He took in as his partner James Hunter (afterwards Sir James Hunter Blair), who was continuously quarrelling with the Glasgow traders, one of whom, Robert Crauford, of Frisky Hall, fought a duel with him. At the time trouble was beginning to boil up in Virginia, Herries assured his French clients that it could come to nothing, and insisted that the Glasgow merchants who had raised their prices in the expectation of a shortage of tobacco presently would soon have to lower them. The Farmers-General suspected Herries of speculating in tobacco on his own account, and he was deprived of the agency.

The arrogance and ostentation of the Tobacco Lords of Glasgow during their heyday, lasting some thirty years, have become a legend. We are given a picture of them swaggering about the Trongate in scarlet cloaks and gold-laced hats, a small oligarchy that despised its fellow citizens. These tales were told by people who were infants when the Tobacco Lords were in their prime; there is no contemporary testimony. Perhaps they were not so odiously purse-proud as they have been represented. Anyway, that purse-pride came before a heavy fall. Nothing remains to-day of the splendid mansions they built for themselves in Glasgow; nothing remains to commemorate those days that started Glasgow on the flourishing career expressed in the city's motto; nothing except the name Virginia Street which behind its dreary exterior enshrines a golden dream. Who that now walks through the surging traffic of Buchanan Street remembers what the name Buchanan once stood for? James Buchanan planned the street on the four acres of land behind his mansion. Who now that sees Mount Vernon on a Glasgow tram knows that once upon a time it was the estate of Windyedge which was bought by James Buchanan's brother, George Buchanan, and renamed Mount Vernon out of compliment to his friend George Washington whose tobacco plantations adjoined his own on the banks of the Potomac? George Buchanan built the great Virginia Mansion with its vineries and gardens where Wilson Street runs to-day. He died in 1762 at the age of thirty-four. His brother James lived on to be ruined by the American Revolution; ending up, ironically, as a Commissioner of Customs in Edinburgh, all his fortune having been swallowed in the bankruptcy of Buchanan, Hastie and Co. and Andrew Buchanan and Co. in 1777.

The Glasgow merchants had not been blind to the situation in the Colonies; they had anticipated the outbreak of hostilities which started at Lexington in April 1775. In the previous year some fifty Glasgow firms had between them imported 36,212 hogsheads from Virginia, 8,610 from Maryland and 1,721 from Carolina. At an average weight of 850 pounds to the hogshead, this amounted to a total of 15,384 tons. When war came the warehouses in Greenock and Port Glasgow were packed full of tobacco and thirty-two ships still unloaded lay in the harbours. The price of tobacco rose at once from threepence to sixpence a pound. The firm of William Cuninghame and Co. were among the largest holders of tobacco stocks, and the senior partners decided to sell at sixpence, believing that the war could not last long. Young William Cuninghame, the junior partner, thought otherwise. He took over the whole stock for himself, giving security for his investment. As the British forces made more and more a mess of it, the price of tobacco rose to the unheard of figure of three shillings and sixpence a pound. Cuninghame, who did not sell until tobacco had nearly reached its peak price, acquired a large fortune. While other firms were crashing he was able to build the handsome Virginia Mansion, which is now embedded in the Royal Exchange.

When the war began, the Government bought up the Glasgow ships for transports. No doubt the owners were glad to be rid of them, for they had been mostly built in America of unseasoned timber with a life of at most ten years, and were already worn

out. There were several failures among the exporters of goods
in 1775, but it was not until 1777, when the Colonists repudiated
their debts and when the property of all British firms was confiscated, that the really severe financial crisis came. The shortage of tobacco in Great Britain became acute as the war dragged
on and the years went by.

Jonathan Carver in a tract published in 1779 argued that
English consumers of tobacco could not depend upon prizes
at sea for their supply, and that therefore it was only reasonable
that this 'essential vegetable' should be produced at home. In
1782 Yorkshire farmers turned over many acres to tobacco.
Presumably it was *N. tabacum* they sowed, not the *N. rustica* of
the Gloucestershire of once upon a time. Whichever it was, the
Government took strong steps to stop tobacco-planting. In the
previous year the Redcoats of Cornwallis marching through
Virginia had destroyed more than ten thousand hogsheads of
tobacco. Now a year later the Redcoats were marching through
Yorkshire to destroy the tobacco crops, the planters of which
were thrown into gaol or heavily fined. Scotland got away with
it for a while with considerable plantations round Jedburgh
and Kelso because the Acts of the preceding century against
tobacco-planting in England had not applied to Scotland before
the Union. However, it was not long before those prohibitory
Acts were made valid for Scotland and the plantations were
destroyed. In Ireland, however, tobacco-growing was allowed,
with the result that so many acres were put under cultivation
that in 1831 tobacco-growing was prohibited and caused one of
those upsurges of resentment which the English used to provoke
in Ireland from time to time while wondering what it could be
that made the Irish so unreasonable.

The ability of the Colonies to go on producing their staple
annoyed the British enough to make them try to destroy the
tobacco, and from 1776 to 1782 the Colonies succeeded in
exporting only 87,000,000 pounds, of which 34,000,000
pounds were captured. The shipments were mostly made by
way of the islands in the West Indies that belonged to neutrals.
After the War of Independence ended the Virginians went
back to their staple, but a clause in the Treaty of Paris provided
for the payment of the debts owed to British merchants. This
caused much distress in Virginia. By now the lead in tobacco-
growing had passed to Carolina and Kentucky. Moreover, the

difficulty of obtaining Virginia tobacco during the war had led to substitutes entering the markets seriously; tobacco from the Spanish colonies in America and from the Dutch East Indies made powerful headway, and domestic cultivation all over Europe increased. Great Britain when commercial relations were re-established was, characteristically we may say, the best customer of her revolted Colonies. In 1790 Great Britain took more than half of the whole American crop. Let bygones be bygones.

Jefferson, when he was representing the young United States as Minister at the court of Louis XVI, had made an effort to secure favoured treatment for the tobacco-planters, but the heads of the Farmers-General were still on their shoulders; they drove a very hard bargain with Robert Morris who, after a Scottish firm had failed to stand up to the mono-polists' price, obtained the exclusive right to import American tobacco into France. This agreement made in 1785 reduced the prime cost from forty shillings a hundredweight in Virginian currency to twenty-two shillings and sixpence. Morris, who had been one of the signatories of the Declaration of Inde-pendence and done much to finance the American Revolution, was denounced in the United States as a traitor to his country; but the planters had to give in. Morris, however, lost money on the contract, and it was not renewed. This was when the American planters, who had sworn they would never again deal with the English merchants, decided that a devil you know is better than a devil you don't know. So trade with London, Bristol and Liverpool was resumed. Glasgow, having enjoyed the prime of the trade in Virginian tobacco, would never again, as in 1772, import 49,000 of the total of 90,000 hogsheads imported into Great Britain; but Glasgow would be rescued by another product of the Southern States—King Cotton, to whose allegiance it would soon submit.

I have sometimes asked myself whether if British statesmen had continued to smoke their pipes instead of surrendering to snuff the American Colonies would ever have been lost. Snuff tempted men to action, even precipitate action. What George III and Lord North required was the sedative pipe, or the even more soothing cigar. What the churchwarden and the cutty had failed to do against the influence of snuff, the cigar was to achieve. Let a charming anonymous poem in *The Gentleman's*

Magazine of 1757 serve as an epitaph of the churchwarden clay pipe:

Chusing a Wife by a Pipe of Tobacco

Tube, I love thee as my life;
By thee I mean to chuse a wife,
Tube thy colour *let me find,*
In her skin, *and in her mind.*
Let her have a shape *as fine;*
Let her breath be sweet as thine:
Let her, when her lips I kiss,
Burn *like thee, to give me bliss:*
Let her in some smoke *or other,*
All my failings kindly smother,
Often when my thoughts are low,
Lead them where they ought *to go.*
When to study I incline,
Let her aid be such as thine;
Such as thine her charming pow'r,
In the vacant social hour
Let her love to give delight,
Ever warm *and ever* bright:
Let her deeds, whene'er she dies,
Mount as incense *to the skies.*

But before the tale of the cigar is told, some details must be given of Pitt's Tobacco Act of 1789. Pitt was responsible for introducing income-tax: his Tobacco Act was a landmark in tobacco legislation, and although the system of meticulous and vexatious Excise control he imposed was changed later, he was responsible for instituting the first effectual measures to safe-guard the revenue from the tobacco duties which became the milch cow of all future governments.

The main provisions of the 1789 Act were:

The method of levying the duty was altered. Instead of the duty's being levied as formerly wholly as a Customs import duty, part was levied as a duty of Excise which was considered less easy of evasion, and part as a Customs duty. Later the duty reverted to a Customs duty on importation. The total duty charge remained unchanged—1*s.* 3*d.* per pound on British plantation or American tobacco, and 3*s.* 6*d.* per pound on Spanish or Portuguese tobacco. The duty was payable when the tobacco was removed from the bonded warehouses, which is the practice to-day.

Stringent regulations were introduced to prevent smuggling. Vessels importing tobacco had to be not less than 120 tons burthen. The crews of vessels were allowed individually five pounds of loose tobacco each. Vessels with more than 100 pounds of tobacco or snuff found hovering or at anchor within four leagues of the coast (except in cases of distress) would be subject to forfeiture.

Elaborate regulations were framed to deal with the exportation of tobacco. The exporter had to enter into a bond with the Customs as a surety against defrauding the revenue. Leaf tobacco exported had to be in the original casks (which bore a Customs identification mark made at the time of importation) and could be exported only at the place of entry. Drawback (that is a rebate of the duty paid on the tobacco) was allowed on manufactured tobacco exported to foreign parts, except to the Danish islands of Faroe. Drawback was not allowed on exports to the Faroe Islands because earlier it had been found that tobacco shipped there had been relanded in England, and in 1765 an Act had been passed prohibiting drawback on tobacco exported to these islands.

Further elaborate regulations were devised for the manufacturers. Three days before manufacturing tobacco owners were to make proper entries of "any mill, press, engine, roller, stove, muller or spinning-wheel". Before a manufacturer began to strip or spin tobacco, or press tobacco for cutting, or make carrots, or flatten stalks for 'Spanish', the officer was to be given six hours' notice. No roll or cut tobacco for exportation might contain stalks. All persons were prohibited from cutting walnut, hop or sycamore leaves, etc., into the form or imitation of the usual sizes or cuts of tobacco, or to stain any leaves to resemble tobacco. Manufacturers would be allowed to possess the usual liquid dyes or stains for preparing short cut, shag, roll, carrot and 'Spanish'. Snuff-makers were to come under similar provisions against adulteration. Moreover, they must start making snuff within an hour of the time specified or give fresh notice. Excise officers might enter manufacturing or dealers' premises between the hours of 5 a.m. and 11 p.m. without a constable; at other times they must be accompanied by a constable.

All Thumbcut, Black Leaf Lug and Twist or Pig Tail Tobacco, shall be deemed and taken to be Roll Tobacco . . . all Tobacco Smalls sifted from Short Cut Tobacco, and Shag Tobacco, and all Returns of Spanish shall be deemed and taken to be Returns of Tobacco.

The manufacturers of tobacco and snuff presented a petition against the Bill to the bar of the House, but there was no Rare Ben Bradley to inflame popular feeling this time.

One of the clauses particularly resented was that which required a declaration of manufactured tobacco on hand and of stock already prepared. They pointed out that there was an unascertainable quantity of liquid in tobacco when in the process of manufacture which made it impossible to swear to the quantity of each ingredient during the various steps in making it up. Another clause the petitioners disliked was having to submit a sample of all their goods in process, because it would put them at the mercy of officers who might be bribed by rivals for the specimens.

Pitt had set up a Parliamentary Committee to hear the objections, to none of which did the drafters of the Bill pay the least attention. One manufacturer declared:

The particular sorts of Roll Tobacco which I have orders for are prepared as a substitute for Brazil Tobacco imported into this country from Lisbon, and shipped from hence for the use of the Indians in the back settlements in Canada—therefore if twopence is withheld in the drawback of this Roll Tobacco, this branch of trade will be entirely cut off—because I shall not be able to meet the Brazil Tobacco on a footing at the Canada market.

This witness was asked whether tobacco manufactured in Great Britain brought a higher price in foreign markets (which also imported leaf tobacco directly from America) than that manufactured there, and replied:

In many ports it does, particularly at Naples, at Genoa, Leghorn, Königsburg, Dantzig, Stockholm, Gottenburg, Hamburg, Bremen, and a great many other places; the reason why it commands that superiority is, in my opinion, the secret or mystery of mixing York River tobacco with James River tobacco, Carolina tobacco with Maryland tobacco, Raphahanack tobacco with Potowmack [Potomac] tobacco; in short, the sweet with the sour, the fat with the lean, and the moist with the dry, in such due proportions as to make it palatable and saleable in those foreign markets before mentioned.

To the tobaccos above he added when asked into how many sorts tobacco was distinguished: "Bright Maryland, Copper-coloured Maryland, Brown Maryland, Ordinary Maryland, Upland tobacco and Lowland tobacco."

Although Pitt's Act of 1789 was immediately successful in checking the more glaring abuses by which the Revenue was defrauded, it did not achieve its purpose of eliminating smuggling and adulteration. Moreover, the Excise survey and permit system proved complicated and cumbersome in practice, and the vexatious regulations hampered the honest manufacturer and tobacconist.

In 1825 the Excise duty on tobacco introduced in the 1789 Act reverted to a Customs duty, but the Excise survey and permit system continued until it was abolished by the Tobacco Act of 1840.

Under the 1840 Tobacco Act, which became known as the Mixing Act, the irksome restrictions which impeded the manufacturer in conducting his business were lifted. The mixing of leaves of trees, shrubs, plants and herbs with tobacco was prohibited, but the restriction on the use of sweetening matter and other adulterants was abolished. This immediately led to a great increase in sweetening, and the amount of sugar, honey, treacle, molasses, nitre, liquorice and salt added was often as much as 60 per cent., the dealers very often adding their own ingredients to the product of the manufacturers. The Revenue's receipts began to fall, and the Chancellor of the Exchequer in the Peel Government of 1841 found that he was paying the adulterators a drawback of 3s. a pound. Moreover, 6 per cent. less tobacco was imported in 1840 and 1841 than in previous years.

This state of affairs led to the passing of the Tobacco Act of 1842, sometimes referred to as the Pure Tobacco Act, which was repealed in 1932. By it the manufacturer was restricted to the use of tobacco and water only. Alkaline salts were allowed in the manufacture of snuff, and for Welsh and Irish snuffs lime-water as well. Snuff might be scented, and oil was permitted in making up roll tobacco. The penalty for adding "any other

material, liquid, substance, matter or thing" was forfeiture of
the tobacco or snuff and a fine of £200 besides. Any sugar,
honey, leaves, etc., found on entered premises were to be
forfeited, and officers were empowered to sample "at any time
they shall see fit". The manufacturers urged that from time
immemorial many articles had been used to colour and flavour
tobacco and snuff without the slightest stigma of adulteration.
Moreover, they argued that the adulterated goods could not be
detected.

This last assertion was a challenge to the Commissioners of
Excise, who instituted the Inland Revenue Laboratory, now
called the Government Laboratory. Before the year was out
seizures of adulterated tobacco had taken place on a large
scale; in Yorkshire and Lancashire alone 30,000 pounds were
seized. Besides sugar, rhubarb, hops and oak leaves were discovered, and in one snuff factory a ton of sand was seized.
Many retailers were convicted for selling the adulterated article.
Smuggling, however, and adulteration were rife, and the
trade agitated for a reduction of the tobacco duty as the only
remedy. In March 1844 a Select Committee was appointed
to enquire into the present state of the tobacco trade, in the
hope of remedying the evils complained of and, without damag-
ing the Revenue, of promoting the general interests of the trade.
The Committee sat for five months, in the course of which they
examined Excisemen, Customs officers, coastguards, chemists,
distinguished scientists . . . and even smugglers! In the end the
Committee was in such a muddle that it dissolved.

The tobacco manufacturers of repute were disappointed by
the empty result of the Committee's labours, and for some
years the leading manufacturers periodically brought their
dissatisfaction to the notice of M.P.s. They had no belief in the
ability of the Board of Excise to protect the trade against the
continuance of adulteration, and in 1851 the tobacco manufacturers of Glasgow formed a society to detect and expose the
adulteration of tobacco and snuff.

In 1856 the Admiralty took over the Coastguard service
from the Customs, and this at once effected an improvement
in dealing with the smugglers. Throughout the decade before
the American Civil War the struggle to stop adulteration continued, and by 1860 the Board of Inland Revenue was able to
report that "adulteration of tobacco is now seldom attempted".

The American Civil War caused a shortage of Virginia tobacco, and substitutes were imported from China, Japan and elsewhere in an effort to meet the situation, scents being used to disguise the inferior quality.

The prohibition of the use of sweetening matter in the manufacture of tobacco products in the United Kingdom, imposed by the Tobacco Act of 1842, placed the home manufacturers at a disadvantage beside their foreign competitors. This was remedied by the Tobacco Act of 1863, passed when Mr Gladstone was Chancellor of the Exchequer in the Palmerston Administration. Under this Act sweetened tobacco, known for the purposes of the Act as Cavendish and Negrohead, was permitted to be manufactured in a bonded factory.

Here it is appropriate to describe the difference between bonded and Excise factories. In bonded factories the tobacco is received duty-free, and the duty is paid when the manufactured goods are sent out for home consumption. The building has to be specially constructed and strongly secured by locks and bars to conform with the very stringent Customs and Excise regulations. The manufacturer must give a bond to the Crown in a sum that will cover any loss by robbery or fraud. Revenue officials must be in attendance while manufacture is in progress, and special accommodation has to be provided for them. In Excise factories duty has to be paid on the leaf before it can be brought to the factory for manufacture. The premises are subject to Excise survey and regulations, but as duty has already been paid on the tobacco in course of manufacture constant attendance of Revenue officials and the special security arrangements applying to a bonded factory are not required. With the standard rate of duty on unmanufactured tobacco now (1956) exceeding £3 a pound, the manufacturer has his own very good reasons for ensuring that there is no loss or wastage of this precious commodity.

It would require a whole book to deal in detail with the history of tobacco legislation in the United Kingdom. In 1952 the existing laws were repealed by a consolidating enactment, the Customs and Excise Act of 1952 which is in force to-day (1956).

Chapter 13

IN 1735 John Cockburn published the story of his adventures in Mexico and Central America under the title *A Journey Over Land*. On the way to Costa Rica the author met three friars:

These gentlemen gave us some seegars to smoke, which they supposed would be very acceptable. These are leaves of tobacco rolled up in such a manner that they serve both for a pipe and tobacco itself. These the ladies, as well as gentlemen, are very fond of smoking; but indeed, they know no other way here, for there is no such thing as a tobacco-pipe throughout New Spain, but poor awkward tools used by the Negroes and Indians.

This is the first time that cigars are mentioned in English, and that they are called 'seegars' is evidence of an attempt to reproduce the Spanish pronunciation of 'cigarro'. It is generally agreed that 'cigarro' was derived from 'cigarra', the Spanish word for the cicada, the body of which its shape, cylindrical with a conical apex, was supposed to resemble. Barcia in his *Great Etymological Spanish Dictionary* says "el cigarro figura una cigarra de papel". A cigar of paper? And of what size? Dalrymple writing in 1777 says:

The Marquis took out of his pocket a little bit of tobacco, rolled it up in a piece of paper, making a cigar of it.[1]

This was certainly a cigarette, but cigarette was a name not yet invented. In 1873 Mrs Romer writing about the Rhone country observed:

The beggars in the streets have paper cigars (called cigarettes) in their mouths.

Fairholt quotes Stephens in his *Incidents of Travel in Central America* who, writing presumably in early Victorian days, observes:

I am sorry to say that, generally, the ladies of Central America, not excepting Guatemala, smoke—married ladies *puros*, or all tobacco; and unmarried cigars, or tobacco

[1] *Travels in Spain and Portugal.*

wrapped in paper or straw. Every gentleman carries in his pocket a silver case, with a long string of cotton, steel and flint, and one of the offices of gallantry is to strike a light.

Fairholt in 1859 is still rather vague about cigars. He says that they are "classified into white made from the Havanna and Virginia leaf; and black made from Brazilian tobacco. The paper of which cigarettes are made is of a peculiar structure, porous like India paper, and smouldering without smoke. The best is made at Valencia". Presently he asserts that "straw cigars are also made here for ladies' use; the straw being inserted as a mouthpiece; a few years ago they were the only ones smoked in London, but are now seldom seen". He also mentions a small shape called Queens, which he says were smoked by women. No allusion to this female addiction appears anywhere else, and it may be that Fairholt meant to say that Queens and straw cigars were made in Spain for ladies' use and smoked in London as a fashionable whim of the men.

It may seem remarkable that the Spanish habit of smoking cigars should not have spread over the rest of Europe before it did. The servants of the East India Company must have developed a taste for cheroots during the eighteenth century. The first reference to these cited in the *O.E.D.* is taken from a manuscript of between 1669 and 1679. Modernized it reads:

> The poor sort of inhabitants, viz, the Hindus, Malabars, etc., smoke their tobacco, after a very mean but I judge original manner: only the leaf rolled up and light one end, holding the other between their lips. . . . This is called a bunko and by the Portuguese a cheroota.

This time there is no difficulty about the etymology. Cheroot comes from *shuruttu*, the Tamil word for a roll.

No doubt the original cheroots were primitive enough, but the Trichinopoly cheroots and others made in South India and Ceylon would become the favourite smoke of merchant and soldier alike. Best of all once upon a time, when Spain still held the Philippines, was the Manilla cheroot.

The cigar reached North America before Great Britain. Colonel Israel Putnam, when he returned to Connecticut after the British campaign of 1762 in Cuba, is said to have brought back a store of Havana cigars packed on the backs of three donkeys and "cigars of a sort were available in New York as early as 1765".[1]

At Conestoga, the Dutch colonists made very long thin cigars from leaf grown in Pennsylvania, and later on these were known as 'stogies'. In 1810 small businesses in Philadelphia manufactured twenty-seven million cigars. Many were imported from Cuba, but they were comparatively expensive, and the stock cigars smoked were the long-nine and the short-six; I mentioned in the prologue my great-grandfather's encounter with a long-nine in 1821. The effect on him is not surprising when we read:

> These had been known earlier as 'barnyard' and 'paste segars'. They could be made by anyone (and they were), but as winding was an imperfectly understood art, glue was frequently used to paste the wrapper on the filler.[2]

No doubt Spanish cigars reached Italy by way of Naples, but in 1779 Peter Wendler, a German painter in Rome, obtained from the Papal authorities the sole right for five years to make *bastoni di tabacco*, literally sticks of tobacco. In 1788 a cigar factory on the Spanish model was started in Hamburg. Fairholt says that cheroots "not made by hand, but wound on a wire, both ends being cut flat" were extensively imitated in France and Germany, the mildest Maryland tobacco being used and mustard-seed sometimes rolled in with them to strengthen the flavour. In Hamburg carraway and aniseed were sometimes used. The Germans still make considerable quantities of cigars, though the advance of the all-conquering cigarette has since diminished the output.

Yet it was not until the revolution of 1848 that Prussians were allowed to smoke in the streets. When the mob outside the royal palace were demonstrating, they shouted for relief of taxation, freedom of the Press and liberty to smoke in the streets. Young Prince Lichnowsky may have saved the palace from being stormed by jumping on a table and telling the mob that all their demands had been granted, including the right to smoke even in the Tiergarten. Lichnowsky had no authority for this announcement, but the authorities were wise enough to support him, and a few days later the ban on smoking in the

---

[1] Jerome E. Brooks, *The Mighty Leaf* (Little Brown, Boston), p. 201.
[2] Jerome E. Brooks, op. cit., p. 207.

streets of Berlin was repealed. This was a triumph for the cigar, because people could not walk about smoking those clumsy porcelain pipes that Germans favoured. The cigar would presently be denounced by old-fashioned opinion as the inspiration of radical discontent and the corrupter of youth.

In Lombardy and Venetia the Austrians had long ago allowed people to smoke in the streets, and in 1847 an order by Field-Marshal Count Radetsky permitted soldiers in uniform to do so. The popular smokes were the Virginia cigars of the Austrian *Régie*, which are still the popular cigars of Venice under the state monopoly of the Italian Government. They are long and thin, with a straw down the middle which one pulls out before lighting up.

In 1848, while the Prussians were demanding liberty to smoke, the Milanese decided to annoy the Austrians by refusing to smoke and thus deprive them of revenue. *Chi fuma per la via è tedesco o è spia* was the cry. He who smokes in the street is a German or a spy, and forthwith the Milanese started knocking cigars out of smokers' mouths. They did this even to Austrian officers and soldiers who were smoking. Field-Marshal Count Radetsky became angry and sent out patrols, all smoking. The people of Milan stoned them; the soldiers killed some of the crowd. Affrays were constant. A week later the students of Pavia were knocking cigars out of the mouths of the soldiers and two officers were killed. Thereupon the Colonel in command of the Austrian troops issued an order against his men smoking in uniform. This angered the Field-Marshal, who proclaimed martial law in Pavia. The students of Padua carried on the boycott of cigars. Students shouted to soldiers coming out of a café, "Drop your cigars, *porci Ungheresi*"—'Hungarian swine'. One of the soldiers demanded who had said that, and when a student stepped forward to claim the responsibility the soldier cut him down and killed him.

By the end of the month of January 1849 the agitation against cigars had reached Venice, where stores of Virginia cigars began to accumulate in the factory. Metternich in Vienna considered the whole business was childish, but thought that the Archduke Rainer as Viceroy should take strong measures. The Archduke was pessimistic. The cigar trouble was the prelude to more serious events. There was a general revolt in Lombardy and Venice, and Piedmont went to war. Radetsky had to evacuate

Milan, whereupon the smoking of which the Milanese had deprived themselves for a political end started again in a grand way, because the people looted the Austrian cigar stores. However, the rebellious provinces and Piedmont were defeated, and the House of Savoy had to wait until 1859 to expel the hated Austrians with the help of France.

It was in that year, 1859, that pipe-tobacco and cigars began to leave snuff behind as the main business of Fribourg and Treyer after running level during the previous decade. When we remember that as early as 1800 cigars and cheroots were being supplied to aristocratic customers, it must be admitted that snuff put up a long fight before it yielded its supremacy. Croker, writing in 1831, said that the taste for smoking had revived, probably from the military habits of Europe during the French wars, but that instead of the "sober sedentary pipe, the ambulatory cigar" was chiefly used. The war in the Peninsula may have given officers a taste for cigars, but there is no evidence of their being much smoked at home. The heavy duty of eighteen shillings a pound levied on imported cigars when Europe settled down to peace after Waterloo prevented their becoming equally popular. The Chancellor of the Exchequer in Lord Liverpool's government was trying out protection for home industries in 1823, and so far as tobacco was concerned this protection was not abolished in favour of Free Trade and is still in force. In 1830, after the halving of the duty on imported cigars, importations at once shot up to 253,882 pounds and steadily increased year by year after that. Fairholt gives a list of over seventy varieties and sizes, and adds that it does not include the Penny Pickwick . . . "from which low price the cigar smoker may rise until a shilling be given for a really fine cigar, though amateurs have paid even higher prices".

The Pickwick cigar was made in London, where by the 'forties of the last century there was an extensive manufacture. It is described in *Tobacco Talk*, a miscellany published by Redway in 1886, as "a neat little cigar . . . which still retains its popularity". It must have vanished by a decade later, or the present writer would have been able to express an opinion of its smoking value.

Byron first apostrophized the cigar in verse, and nobody has written any apostrophe as good since. It appeared in his poem *The Island*, founded on the mutiny of the *Bounty*:

. . . here the herald of the self-same mouth
Came breathing o'er the aromatic south,
Not like a 'bed of violets' on the gale,
But such as wafts its cloud o'er grog and ale,
Borne from a short frail pipe, which yet had blown
Its gentle odours over either zone,
And puffed where'er winds rise or waters roll,
Had wafted smoke from Portsmouth to the Pole,
Opposed its vapour as the lightning flashed,
And reeked, 'midst mountain-billows unabash'd,
To Aeolus a constant sacrifice,
Through every change of all the varying skies,
And what was he who bore it? I may err,
But deem him sailor or philosopher.

Byron puts a note at this point to say that "Hobbes, the father of Locke's and other philosophy, was an inveterate smoker—even to pipes beyond computation". Non-smokers may be reminded that Thomas Hobbes lived to be ninety-one. In December 1956 Sibelius, the greatest living composer, entered his ninety-second year; he still smokes ten cigars a day.

Byron goes on:

Sublime tobacco! which from east to west
Cheers the Tar's labour or the Turkman's rest;
Which on the Moslem's ottoman divides
His hours, and rivals opium and his brides;
Magnificent in Stamboul, but less grand,
Though not less loved, in Wapping or the Strand:
Divine in hookas, glorious in a pipe,
When tipp'd with amber, mellow, rich and ripe;
Like other charmers, wooing the caress,
More dazzlingly when daring in full dress;
Yet thy true lovers more admire by far
Thy naked beauties—give me a cigar!

One curious feature of the entry of the cigar was its shame-facedness. Walter Scott, for instance, noted in his Journal of November 1825 that he usually smoked a couple of cigars after dinner as a sedative:

I smoked a good deal about twenty years ago at Ashestiel; but coming down one morning to the parlour, I found, as the room was small and confined, that the smell was unpleasant, and laid aside the use of the *Nicotian weed* for many years, but was again led to use it by the example of my son, a hussar officer, and my son-in-law, an Oxford student. I could lay it aside to-morrow; I laugh at the domination of custom in this and many things.

However, Sir Walter continued to smoke, and on July 4th, 1829, he recorded in his Journal:

When I had finished my bit of dinner, and was in a quiet way smoking my cigar over a glass of negus, Adam Ferguson comes with a summons to attend him to the Justice-Clerk's, where, it seems, I am engaged. I was totally out of case to attend his summons, redolent as I was of tobacco. But I am vexed at the circumstance. It looks careless, and, what is worse, affected; and the Justice is an old friend moreover.

The smoking-rooms of London clubs were wretchedly small and uncomfortable about this date. Macaulay in a letter to his sisters in the summer of 1831 wrote from the smoking-room in the House of Commons:

I have left Sir Francis Burdett on his legs, and repaired to the smoking-room; a large, wainscoted, uncarpeted place, with tables covered with green baize and writing materials. On a full night it is generally thronged towards twelve o'clock with smokers. It is then a perfect cloud of fume. There I have seen (tell it not to the West Indians) Buxton blowing fire out of his mouth.

In July of the following year he was writing again to his sisters from the same smoking-room:

I am writing here at eleven at night, in this filthiest of all filthy atmospheres . . . with the smell of tobacco in my nostrils. . . . Reject not my letter, though it is redolent of cigars and genuine pigtail; for this is the room—

The room—but I think I'll describe it in rhyme,
That smells of tobacco and chloride of lime,
The smell of tobacco was always the same:
But the chloride was brought since the cholera came.

One gets the impression that Macaulay was deliberately writing in the smoking-room in order to play the prig and enjoy sisterly admiration of his superiority.

Dickens, who smoked himself, in his own words, "a cigar after dinner when I am alone", was inclined to be self-consciously facetious about smoking. Nevertheless, he deserved to have a popular little cigar called after his immortal work which was published in 1836, for *The Pickwick Papers* provide the most vivid abstract and brief chronicle of contemporary tobacco habits that exists.

At the ball in Rochester, Colonel Bulder and Sir Thomas Clubber offered each other snuff, and

> while the aristocracy of the place . . . were thus preserving their dignity at the upper end of the room, the other classes of society were imitating their example in other parts of it. . . . Dr Slammer, surgeon to the 97th . . . took snuff with everybody.

Mr Perker "took an argumentative pinch of snuff from an oblong silver box" when he was discussing the prospects of Bardell *v.* Pickwick with his amiable client. Mr Bantam, the Master of Ceremonies at Bath, as a successor of Beau Nash, of course took snuff—Prince's Mixture from a gold snuff-box.

John Smauker, Mr Bantam's footman, on his way to the swarry offered his snuff-box to Sam Weller:

> "Do you do anything in this way, Sir?" inquired the tall footman, producing a small snuff-box with a fox's head on the top of it.
> "Not without sneezing," replied Sam.
> "Why, it is difficult, Sir, I confess," said the tall footman. "It may be done by degrees, Sir. Coffee is the best practice. I carried coffee, Sir, for a long time. It looks very like rappee, Sir."

But the cigar was already asserting itself. Later on that evening at the swarry Mr Smauker smoked a cigar "through an amber tube". Fairholt in 1859 writes about cigar-holders as if they were a novelty, but if Mr Smauker was using one nearly twenty-five years earlier, they must have been in general use for some time.

Cigars had already appeared on the journey to Bath in the coach from the White House Cellars.

> There was one young gentleman in an India rubber cloak, who smoked cigars all day; and there was another young gentleman in a parody upon a great coat, who lighted a good many, and feeling obviously unsettled after

the second whiff, threw them away when he thought nobody
was looking at him.

At the Magpie and Stump when Mr Pickwick ran to earth
Lowten, his lawyer's clerk, "a gentleman in a checked shirt
and Mosaic studs, with a cigar in his mouth" hoped that Mr
Pickwick did not "find this sort of thing disagreeable". Mr
Pickwick with his accustomed benevolence assured him that,
although no smoker himself, he liked it very much. On this
another gentleman observed that smoke was to him board and
lodging, which made Mr Pickwick reflect to himself that if it
were washing too it would be all to the good.

The dissipation of Ben Allen and Bob Sawyer is meant to be
suggested by their sitting on either side of the fire in the kitchen
of Dingley Dell on the morning of their arrival, smoking cigars.
Bob Sawyer had "that sort of slovenly smartness and swaggering
gait which is peculiar to young gentlemen who smoke in the
streets by day, shout and scream in the same by night, call
waiters by their Christian names, and do various other acts and
deeds of an equally facetious nature". Neither Mr Tupman nor
Mr Snodgrass would have let themselves be seen smoking in
the street, but in the commercial-room at the Peacock Inn in
Eatanswill they smoked cigars in the company of a dirty-faced
man with a clay-pipe, a very red-faced man behind a cigar,
and a man with a black eye who filled a large Dutch pipe with
a most capacious bowl. Sam Weller's father smoked a churchwarden. When the second Mrs Weller flew into a passion he
used to break his pipe and step out to get another. On one
occasion after having given Sam some valuable advice, "Mr
Weller, senior, refilled his pipe from a tin-box he carried in his
pocket, and lighting his fresh pipe from the ashes of the old one,
commenced smoking at a great rate".

That method of lighting a pipe is a reminder that nothing
has been said yet about the way in which people were lighting
cigars and pipes by now.

They were using a tinder-box and wooden spills tipped with
sulphur to get a light in the days of the ancient Greeks and
Romans, and when smoking came in the same equipment was
all that was available for lighting a pipe unless there was a
taper handy or a glowing ember, juniper wood being held to
provide the ideal ember. The tinder-pistol was invented in the

seventeenth century, a miniature of the contemporary firearm. On the trigger's being pulled sparks from the flint ignited on some gunpowder in the priming-pan, which then kindled the tinder. The Germans had invented a popular tinder called amadou made from fungus which had been boiled, beaten and impregnated with saltpetre. From this the smoker lighted the sulphur-tipped spill. Those who remember the sulphur-tipped matches in the France of not so long ago will hope that he let the sulphur burn itself out before he put the spill to his pipe. Those pistols were costly affairs, and the ordinary man used the old tinder-box or tinder-horn with flint and steel. This remained the stock way of obtaining light right on through the eighteenth-century; no wonder people availed themselves of red-hot coals, and no wonder that fires were frequent.

In 1807 Richard Lorentz patented a 'fire-pistol' walking-stick, which had a tube inside the handle. This was withdrawn and a pinch of tinder put in. Then the tube was plunged in and withdrawn again, the tinder being kindled. Lorentz's patent was not enough of an improvement on the tinder-box to capture the allegiance of smokers, but in 1810 the 'Instantaneous Light Box' was introduced from France. This contrivance held a bottle of sulphuric acid and a bundle of large paste-board matches tipped with chlorate of potash. As soon as the match-head was dipped into the bottle, it was alight. This box was in fairly wide use for some years, but the acid was apt to spill and burn carpets or clothes. Sulphide of antimony was tried instead, but this weakened after some exposure and the Instantaneous Light Box vanished from the scene in favour of the Dobereiner Lamp invented by an Austrian in 1823. This was made of glass in the shape of a modern milk-bottle. On the top a metal figure held a cap that fitted over a nozzle. When the cap was lifted a jet of lighted hydrogen gas spurted out. The gas was generated by zinc and sulphuric acid, and when this touched platinum the latter became incandescent and lighted the gas. Perhaps the ingenuity of inventors might have produced a serviceable lighter earlier than it did if lighters had not been superseded for many years to come by the invention of the friction match.

John Walker had a little bow-windowed chemist's shop at 59, High Street, Stockton-on-Tees. He took an interest in searching for a means of obtaining fire easily. There were several chemical mixtures which would ignite by a sudden explosion, but nobody had yet discovered how to transmit such a flame to a slow-burning substance like wood. One day while Walker was preparing a lighting mixture a match which had been dipped in it took fire by being accidentally rubbed along the hearthstone. Walker cut out wooden and cardboard sticks which he coated with sulphur and tipped with a mixture of sulphide of antimony, chlorate of potash and gum, the sulphur serving to communicate the flame to the wood. On April 7th, 1827, Walker's ledger shows that he sold to John Hixon, a local solicitor, a round tin container costing twopence in which were fifty cardboard sticks and a piece of folded sandpaper costing one shilling. The match was inserted in the sandpaper, held lightly between the fingers of one hand and pulled out sharply by the other. It was not long before the people of Stockton were buying John Walker's 'friction-lights' in some quantity, and presently he began to sell wooden sticks cut for him by the inmates of a neighbouring almshouse in card boxes made by a Stockton bookbinder. The news of Walker's invention soon spread, but he refused all offers to exploit it commercially or even to patent it. He stopped making matches in 1830, and lived on until his eightieth year, leaving £3,000.

Samuel Jones, a young chemist of 201, Strand, London, heard of Walker's invention when Faraday mentioned it in the course of a lecture at the Royal Institution, and in 1829 he produced an imitation which he called a Lucifer, for which he failed to get a patent, and G. F. Watts, another Strand chemist, brought out the Watts Chlorate Match at sixpence a hundred. Jones was the first maker to use a label for his boxes, and he and Watts used to advertise their wares against each other. Here is Jones:

Directions For Using
S. Jones's
Lucifer Matches.

Among these he includes a warning not to inhale the gas that escapes from the combustion of the black composition, and a particular warning that "persons whose lungs are delicate should by no means use the Lucifers".
He then attacks his rival:

In justice to himself and the Public in general it may be proper to state that he has not authorised any person or persons to sell his Lucifer Matches, with any other name on the Box than S. Jones, Light-House, 201, Strand, without which they are Base Counterfeits. This caution being rendered necessary from the perpetual complaints of Ladies and Gentlemen who have purchased a spurious and defective article, foisted on them as genuine, by those who are unfairly availing themselves of the benefits resulting from his experiments.

This was not bad from somebody who had so generously availed himself of John Walker's experiments. Jones also advertised as a product of the Light-House in the Strand what sounds like an early type of fusee which he called 'Patent Prometheans'.

For producing instant light, without the aid of a Bottle, and warranted never to impair by keeping. This is the most simple mode of producing Light ever invented for lighting candles, and for Smokers in the open air they are unequalled, no wind being able to blow them out, and emit on being burnt a fragrant perfume.

Finally there were "S. Jones's New Philosophical Pastilles for disinfecting and perfuming Drawing-Rooms, Dining-Rooms or Bed-Rooms".

In 1832 Richard Bell started in Broad Street the first British match factory. The firm, incorporated with Bryant and May, still exists, and the Bell matchbox label is still used.

The next advance in matches came from France when a young student of chemistry, Charles Sauria, by adding phosphorus to the recognized mixture invented a match that would strike on anything. He was too poor to patent his invention, with the result that the Germans exploited it and by 1832 it was everywhere in Europe, being made in German and Austrian factories. In Great Britain it was called a Congreve, after Sir William Congreve, the controller of Woolwich Arsenal and Colonel Commandant of the Royal Artillery, who had invented a war rocket which did very little damage in battle but was believed to scare the enemy by its noise and glare. The indefatigable Mayhew in his *London Labour and London Poor* interviewed a match-seller who said: "I believe I was the first who hawked 'congreves' or 'instantaneous

lights'; they weren't called 'lucifers' for a good while after."
This has misled the *O.E.D.* into ascribing the invention of them
to Sir William Congreve, who died less than a year after
Walker discovered the friction match. That match-hawker
was muddled about dates by the time Mayhew reported him
in 1852. As late as 1854 the penny box of lucifers or congreves
was being celebrated as "a triumph of science".

Let us pause a moment to light a cheroot with a congreve.
It is 'A Manilla Sonnet', by S. D. Blanchard, written some
time in the 1830's:

> *Luscious leaf of fragrant savour,*
> *Mild cheroot of choicest flavour,*
> *Wafting incense to the sky,*
> *Like the gales of Araby,*
> *Let us press thee to our lips,*
> *As the bee the honey sips;*
> *Culling as our well-earned meed,*
> *Songs from thee—thou heavenly weed.*
> *Ere thy burnished lip we kiss,*
> *Let us thus enjoy the bliss,*
> *Lit by the Promethean spark,*
> *Kindled from the congreve dark;*
> *In summer-house or country villa,*
> *There's nothing like a good Manilla.*

Jones's Promethean was followed by the fusee, and this was
followed in 1849 by the Vesuvian made by John Palmer of
Camberwell. In a collection of London street photographs
taken in the mid-eighties and exhibited recently by the Greenwich Central Library, there is one of a ragged, barefoot boy
selling Bryant and May's Alpine Vesuvians. Ararat Vesuvians
would have been a more appropriate name for that product of
the Ark trade-mark.

It was round about 1849 that Richard Bell produced the
first match to use wax instead of wood; he called it the Vesta.
Beneath Vesta Victoria's card in the old *Stage* was her slogan "A
Vesta that will strike anywhere". It is surprising that wax vestas
had such a long run, for they were the worst kind of matches
to light a pipe or a cigar. They were short, however, and fitted
into neat little silver or gold match-boxes attached to a watch-
chain. Bryant and May realized that the wax spoiled a pipe,

and brought out the Swan vesta of the same size but of wood instead of wax.

In 1855 a Swede called John Lundstrum created a sensation by inventing the safety-match, the British rights in which were at once secured by Bryant and May. Some of us elderly smokers remember with regret the original size of Bryant and May's safety-match, a single one of which burned long enough to light the noblest cigar. But where are the snows of yester-year? In Scotland we all use Bryant and May's Scottish Bluebells, which have bright blue tips and, in defiance of the proverbial Scottish caution, strike anywhere like Miss Vesta Victoria once upon a golden time. It may interest Scots to know that H.M. Queen Elizabeth, the Queen Mother, provides Bluebell matches at Clarence House for her guests to light their cigarettes.

In 1871, Lowe, the Chancellor of the Exchequer, announced a tax of a halfpenny on every box of matches. What an outcry it raised! It was like the days of Rare Ben Bradley and the Excise proposals of Walpole. There were riots in the East End and a riotous assemblage round the House of Commons from a great procession that started in the Bow-road. One of the placards carried read:

> To the working men of London. Agitate, agitate, agitate, and insist on the withdrawal of this iniquitous tax on British industry. If it becomes law, it will throw thousands of poor families out of employment, paralyse trade, stop enterprise, and tax the poor for an article of daily consumption 300 per cent. Let us rise as one man.

The police were too handy with their truncheons on match-makers and spectators, and what had been in the words of the *Annual Register* "not an ill-behaved gathering" was converted into

> a resisting, howling mob. Mr Lowe passed into the House unobserved entering, it is said, by an underground passage . . . but Mr Gladstone, who was escorted by a policeman, being recognized was received with a hoot. Almost at the same moment Mr Disraeli was driven through the gates in an open carriage, and received a cheer.

In the Chancellor's Budget Speech he had facetiously observed that he was not proposing to tax matrimonial engagements and added that he had borrowed the idea of taxing matches from America "as a token of admiration of her finance and goodwill towards herself". Then with the fatuity that is a common accompaniment of the speeches of Chancellors of the Exchequer who are proposing to tax a necessity but want to make it appear a luxury, he argued that matches were so cheap that they were

> wasted in a most reckless and dangerous way, and were often the cause of most serious fires, as when matches were flung down into areas in which dry straw from unpacked hampers was lying.

Nevertheless, although the stamps were already printed the Government withdrew the proposal in deference to the general indignation, which was by no means confined to the East End of London. The motto for those stamps was to have been *Ex Luce Lucellum* ("out of light a little profit")—

> a joke not appreciated by the great majority of Mr Lowe's hearers, who had evidently forgotten that the diminutive of *lucrum*[1] contains no *r*—and he thought this would be more suitable to them than the rather watery device of a Noah's Ark, which is usually found upon match-boxes.

When Mr Lowe was forced to withdraw his proposal to tax matches, he added twopence to the income-tax.

It will be more suitable to tell the story of the lighter when we come to the triumph of the cigarette and return now to the cigar.

[1] How many honourable members to-day would have known that there was a diminutive of *lucrum*?

Chapter 14

IMPORTED cigars were originally sold by weight, the number of them in a pound varying. It can be said that about fifty cigars of the Corona shape and size went to the pound, and of course half as many again of smaller sizes. In the books of Fribourg and Treyer the earliest 'Havannah Segars' are quoted at £2 12s. 6d. a pound. At that price a Corona would cost about a shilling. In 1824, when there was a duty of 18s. a pound, 'Gold Havannah Segars' are quoted at £3 3s. A Spanish name does not occur until 1832 with 'Cazadores Segars', and in the same year '2 pounds old C.C. Segars' were £5 10s. It is to be noted that C.C. did not stand then for Colorado-Claro but 'Cedar-Chest'. In the following year '1 pound full Cabañas' cost £2 15s. These may have been Maduro, the darkest of all, which are never seen to-day. Indeed, Colorados (C) are rare enough. To-day the fashion is all for Claros (C.C.C.) of which more anon.

Lambert and Butler, a firm which has been established in Drury Lane since 1834, started as importers of cigars and pipe tobacco. Charles Lambert was considered the best judge in London of an Havana cigar, and cultivated the taste of his son Edward to become an equal authority. They do not appear to have imported Havana leaf to make cigars in London until the 'eighties when the Marcella appeared. However, at the Great Exhibition in 1851 there was a prominent display of British cigars.

I have not been able to discover out of what tobacco were made the cheap cigars of the nineteenth century in Great Britain, which as in the United States were the smokes of the great majority. Imported Havanas, if not as far beyond the range of the average purse as they are to-day, were always a luxury. The cigar-ring or band was substituted for a stuck-on label that once upon a time guaranteed the authenticity of an Havana brand. The disapproval of somebody seen smoking a cigar without removing the band may have been due to the appearance of ostentation such a habit suggested, but such disapproval was probably reinforced by the thought that so clumsy a smoker was endangering the flavour of a good cigar.

A paragraph writer of *The Glasgow Herald* in February 1954 asserted that it had been the correct thing to smoke a cigar with the band left on until King Edward VII received a special brand of cigar from Havana with no band, after which it became the fashion to remove the band before smoking. That sounds a phoney tale. Nor does the tale that the cigar-band was brought in to prevent the fingers from being stained by nicotine, although more probable, quite convince me.

The most famous district in the world for growing tobacco for cigars is the Vuelta Abajo (The Lower Turn) in the Province of Pinar del Rio, the most westerly in the island of Cuba. Here are grown all the tobaccos of the classic brands. There is a tobacco-growing district in the centre of the island called Remedios, but also known as Vuelta Arriba. A great deal of leaf from here is exported to the United States, and the rest is used for local consumption. Finally there is a district south-west of the city of Havana called Partidos, where most of the tobacco is shade-grown for wrappers, and afterwards fire-cured to produce the greyish-green wrapper called Candela which of late years has caught the fancy of the cigar-smoker in the United States; why it is hard to say, for the flavour seems dull and thin to British taste. The extravagant demand for Candela by U.S. buyers is a threat to the quality of cigars in the future, because in trying to keep up with that demand growers may neglect the traditional type of wrapper and make it increasingly scarce. The tendency of American cooking and catering has been to lower the standard of the flavour of food, and the example of America has already done much by old-fashioned notions to debase British taste.

A cigar consists of three parts: the filler, the binder and the wrapper. The filler is the core of the cigar and forms its body and shape. It is made of leaves blended according to the quality and character of the cigar. The binder is the leaf in which the filler or core of the cigar is wrapped to form what is known as the cigar 'bunch'. The binder is sometimes called the 'bunch wrapper'. The wrapper is the outer covering of the cigar; it must be strong and silky with very small veins and possess good flavour, body and burning properties. This is a difficult combination to achieve, and wrapper-leaf is the most expensive of all. The matching of the colour is another very serious matter, and experts are employed to match the colour in every box.

The Connecticut Valley and Florida produce shade-grown wrapper—mainly for domestic consumption—but the flavour is very different from that of a good Havana leaf. Sumatra produces light silky wrappers with a tendency to thin texture. The wrappers grown in North Borneo are similar in character but tend to have a stronger texture. Java produces wrappers of poor colour, and they are used mainly on the Continent. Strange to say, Jamaica up till now has not been able to produce good-quality wrapper, and Cuban leaf is used there.

The binder is chosen for smoothness of surface, so that the tightly drawn wrapper may lie evenly on the cigar. It is thicker than the wrappers, and it need not be as elastic. The burning quality is important, because a binder that burns poorly can smother a lighted cigar. Most of the binders used in British cigars come from Cuba, Borneo and Sumatra. India, Burma and Canada produce binders for domestic consumption. Java, Brazil and the Philippines produce binders for export. All the countries that produce binder produce filler, from which of course comes most of the flavour and aroma of a good cigar. It must burn well, and it must blend well with wrapper and binder. Good Havana filler is, of course, hard to beat. Jamaican filler blends excellently with Havana and Sumatra wrapper. It is in the blending of fillers and their marriage with binder and wrapper that the skill of the good cigar manufacturer lies.

I have been able to consult the prices current at the beginning of the century in 130 Havana cigar factories. This volume of nearly 400 pages was published in July 1901 when the cigar was at the peak of its glory. The first thing that strikes the contemporary cigar smoker is the incredible number of different shapes and sizes, each with its own name, which were then being produced.

H. Upmann had eighty-four different *vitolas* (shapes and sizes), the most expensive of which were called simply Upmanns and priced at 1,000 dollars for forty pounds, which works out at about two shillings apiece. Their smallest size was *Liliputanos* at 38 dollars for five and a half pounds or about 500 of them.

Henry Clay had no less than 154 shapes and sizes, the leaders being *Exclusivos de Henry Clay* at the same price as the Upmanns, and the cheapest being *Brevas Chicas* at four dollars a pound. Henry Clay was an American Senator, born two years after the Declaration of Independence; a year or two before his death in 1852 he went to stay in Cuba with Julian Alvarez, one of the leading cigar-manufacturers. Henry Clay had been the champion in the United States of the Spanish-American colonies bent on achieving independence, and Alvarez, who was dreaming of freedom for Cuba, not content to name a *vitola* after him, called a brand of cigars Henry Clay, when the old Senator died, as a symbolic expression of his dream. That brand of cigars became famous the world over, and is as famous as ever to-day.

The stars of Bock were *El Aguila De Oro* and *Mil Maravillas* sold at half a dollar each. These probably all went to the United States. La Intimidad called their stars *Prominencias*, and it is amusing to find among their sizes three called after Queen Victoria—*Reina Victoria Extrafina, Especial* and *Elegante*. Did the Prince of Wales ever venture to smoke an *Extrafina* at the cost of a shilling? The top of the La Corona list were not Corona *Coronas*, but *Cremas de Corona Ramero I*, which cost half a crown.

La Corona *Coronas* were seventh in a list of 186 shapes and sizes, which included *Reina Victoria Chica* squeezed between *Demócratos* and *Republicanos* with *Neoyorkinos* not far away. The *Corona* size and shape which originated with the La Corona brand is nowadays used by all cigar manufacturers. So, too, to a lesser extent is the size *Alfredo de Rothschild*. La Corona was originally established in 1845, and the label on the inside of the box represents an optimistic picture of a Spanish lady in yellow and red, attended by a benevolent lion, shaking hands with a younger Cuban lady. That lion was the symbol of the old Spanish Empire, and he was evidently anxious for the two ladies to be friends.

La Flor de Murias included not only *Reina Victoria* but also *Principe Alberto* and *Balmoral* in their list. I am under the impression that La Flor de J. S. Murias was a better-known brand in Great Britain, and it is still popular. Villar y Villar announced at the end of their price list that owing to the scarcity and high prices ruling for prime material they were compelled to increase their prices by 5 per cent. This was the only factory to do this.

The brand of Hoyo de Monterrey was introduced in 1860. It means literally Monterrey's Hole, he having been the owner of the land once upon a time. Its list of sizes was exceptionally short, and a note at the end said that the factory was using only tobacco of their own *vegas* in the Vuelta Abajo. The brand is now under the same ownership as Punch, which was founded in 1850. The first order the factory received from England was from the Mess of the Royal Engineers, and to this day on the band of most Punch cigars are the initials R.E. In this price list a trade-mark of Punch is called *La Hija del Regimiento*—the Beauty of the Regiment.

The full name of the famous Cabañas cigars is Hijas de Cabañas y Carbajal. This was the first factory to supply the King of Spain with cigars and appropriately its leading *vitola* was *Soberanos de lujo*—Luxury Sovereigns—at half a crown each. The original proprietor was Leopoldo Carbajal, the Marquis of Pinar del Rio.

Romeo y Julieta was established as long ago as 1834. The only other brand of to-day as old as this is Por Larrañaga which was started in the same year. Ramon Allones is only three years junior; *Sultanes* were their star performers in 1901, and one of their trade-marks was *Amor en Sueño*—Love in Idleness. Last but not least of the famous brands that flourished at the beginning of the twentieth century and still flourish is Partagás, whose full name is Flor de Tabacos (Partagás y Ca). They produced some expensive beauties as the notice in English at the end of their price list testifies:

> We place at the disposal of our numerous and intelligent customers the most exquisite tobacco grown on our Vuelta Abajo plantations, presenting them under the newest and most elegant styles; extra fine caskets from 2 dollars to 10 dollars; tasteful cabinets, with 500, 1,000, 10,000 and 12,000 cigars with a capricious and elegant variety of sizes, from 80 dollars to 1,200 dollars per mille.

Ten years earlier Rudyard Kipling had sung in *Departmental Ditties*:

> *For Maggie has written a letter to give me my choice between*
> *The wee little whimpering Love, and the great god Nick o' Teen,*
> *And I had been servant of Love for barely a twelvemonth clear*
> *But I have been Priest of Partagas a matter of seven year.*

And earlier in the same poem he had declared:

> *There's peace in a Larranaga, there's calm in a Henry Clay.*

We must hope that by the time Maggie was fifty, "grey and dour and old" as Kipling pictured her, she had taken to smoking cigarettes. Otherwise there would have been little calm, whatever brand of cigar he smoked, and it may be doubted whether a "harem of dusky beauties fifty tied in a string" would have given him that

Thought in the early morning, solace in time of woes,
Peace in the hush of the twilight, balm ere my eyelids close.

Kipling speaks in this poem of opening the old cigar-box, which apparently held anything from 'a mild Manilla' to 'a Cuba stout', and he must still have been buying his cigars in bundles tied with ribbon (not string, as he says) from those cedar-wood cabinets in which any number from 500 to 10,000 would be packed. To-day the bundles of cigars are packed in cabinets of plain cedar with a sliding lid. Such a box is called a *Corredera Boîte Nature.* No substitute has been found for the West Indian cedar (*Cedrela odorata*), a deciduous tree which is no relation to the cedar of Lebanon, but the wood of which has a similar aromatic scent and being light and porous is ideally suited to house cigars. Glass or plastic jars are usually lined with cedar, and cigars in the aluminium tubes favoured to-day are sometimes surrounded with a sliver of the wood. It might be held as an example of Providence that the perfect wood to preserve it should grow so close to the most aromatic tobacco on earth.

It is surprising that the cultivation of tobacco in Jamaica for cigars was not attempted until late in the nineteenth century; *Nicotiana tabacum* had been growing wild over the coastal plains from the days of Columbus. Jamaican cigars may be said to date from the time of the ruthless steps taken by the Spaniards to stamp out unrest in Cuba. In 1875 many of the inhabitants connected with the growing and manufacture of leaf emigrated to Jamaica and brought with them Havana seed together with the knowledge of how to grow and handle cigar tobacco and also how to make fine cigars. The incoming Cubans selected districts in St Andrew, St Catherine and Clarendon as the most suitable. The quality of Jamaican cigars improved slowly but steadily, and the acreage under tobacco increased as the Jamaican cigar made itself known. However, it was not until the Second World War that the Jamaican cigar was able to get a footing in the

British Isles. Then the United Kingdom had to cut down her dollar outgoings and, by the same token, to cut out all imports of cigars from Cuba. The Jamaican cigar industry developed rapidly, and by 1947 it was exporting about thirty million cigars a year. At present things are not going too well. Great Britain has readmitted Cuban cigars, and these have hit Jamaica hard. The preferential duty on imported Empire-made cigars is so little less than upon Havanas that the advantage is nugatory. Nor has the fantastic duty on tobacco in general been conducive to cigar smoking.

Mention was made in the prologue of Italian cigars. The tobacco for the Napoletano, the Toscano and the Venetian cigar called a Virginia is grown in Italy, but for the more pretentious Minghetti and Conte de Cavour Cuban tobacco is used. The result cannot be recommended to the normal cigar smoker; but *chacun á son goût*, as witness the fact that some Italian patriots import them to Soho where they are sold at 3s. 9d. each. They used to seem expensive at 3d. in Italy once upon a time. Napoletani are unobtainable in Great Britain, and indeed unless they were hand-picked, as already mentioned, they would not be worth importing.

Apart from the Havana-type cigars made in Britain—the best of which, like Embassy Emperor, are really good and can compare well with any Havana cigar—the Danish are the best within my experience. Everybody seems to smoke cigars in Denmark, and if the murderous grip of the duty on British cigars were relaxed there is little doubt that many who having abandoned the pipe miss something in the cigarette would be converted to cigar-smoking. British manufacturers are trying to encourage cigar-smoking with the whiff type of small cigar, for which in spite of the duty there is a growing demand.

Indian cigars can be excellent but they vary too much in quality, and an Indian cheroot is a safer bet for the smoker. Some Indian cigars have that peppery effect which was noted by the old adventurers when they tried smoking for the first time tobacco made from *Nicotiana rustica*.

The Burma cheroot does not always travel well. Freshly made and smoked 'green', it can offer an ennobling experience. There are some smokers who prefer freshly rolled Havana cigars. The 'green' cigars which Americans like are not freshly rolled; they are cigars wrapped in Candela.

It was presumably the opposition of the senior members of the London clubs in Victorian days that led to the institution of the cigar divan and smoking-rooms.

These were fitted up with comfortable chairs and sofas in what was believed to be an authentic Oriental style, and, to the accompaniment of Turkish coffee, men frequented them to smoke cigars. H. J. Nellar,[1] writing in 1832, speaks of there being six popular divans (independent of several obscure ones) in London. These were:

The Oriental Divan, Regent Street.
The Private Subscription Divan, Pall Mall.
The Royal City Divan, St Paul's Churchyard.
The Royal Divan, King Street, Covent Garden.
The Royal Divan, Strand.
The Divan, Charing Cross.

He goes on to observe that "the whole of these divans are fitted up in a style of Asiatic splendour and comfort, that produces to the uncultivated eye a very novel and pleasing effect; while upon a closer examination, the other senses are no less delighted". One or two of these divans growing shabbier with the years lingered on into the 'nineties, but by then the clientêle no longer consisted of clubmen in search of a comfortable smoking-room but of flash young men enjoying the pleasure of what they called 'going up west' and smoking not cigars but cigarettes while they discussed the programme for the evening.

The increase in the price of cigars rose slowly from 1800 to 1863, when the price for the best and largest, like Cabañas *Regalia*, was £6 10s. a hundred. Thence onward until 1914 that remained the limit. It was very exceptional to find cigars priced over £8 a hundred—about eighteenpence each. *O mihi præteritos!*

I recall as an undergraduate meeting Lady Ritchie, Thackeray's daughter, and on being offered a cigarette by the host asking if she minded smoking.

"Oh, not at all. I've always been used to smoking," she said with that enchanting smile of hers. I had not read then what she wrote in her book *Tennyson and his Friends*:

I can remember vaguely, on one occasion through a cloud

[1] *Nicotiana.*

of smoke, looking across a darkening room at the noble grave head of the Poet Laureate. He was sitting with my Father in the twilight after some family meal in the old house in Kensington.

Tennyson would have been smoking a churchwarden, or a cutty of his own design, Thackeray a cigar, and there could be no better conclusion to this chapter than a quotation from the latter's *Sketches and Travels in London*, which was published in 1853.

Honest men, with pipes and cigars in their mouths, have great physical advantages in conversation. You may stop talking if you like—but the breaks of silence never seem disagreeable, being filled up by the puffing of the smoke . . . the cigar harmonises the society, and soothes at once the speaker and the subject whereon he converses. I have no doubt that it is from the habit of smoking that . . . American Indians are such monstrous well-bred men. The pipe draws wisdom from the lips of the philosopher, and shuts up the mouth of the foolish: it generates a style of conversation, contemplative, thoughtful, benevolent, and unaffected: in fact. . . . I must come out with it—I am an old smoker. At home I have done it up the chimney rather than not do it (the which I own is a crime).

I vow and believe that the cigar has been one of the greatest creature comforters of my life—a kind companion, a gentle stimulant, an amiable anodyne, a cementer of friendship. May I die if I abuse that kindly weed which has given me so much pleasure.

And with Thackeray's praise of the cigar let Lord Lytton's tribute to the pipe be coupled before we postpone the approach of the all-conquering cigarette by a chapter about pipes and the tobacco thereof.

A pipe! It is a great soother, a pleasant comforter. Blue devils fly before its honest breath. It ripens the brain, it opens the heart; and the man who smokes thinks like a sage and acts like a Samaritan.

Chapter 15

I N 1849 Herman Melville published a romance[1] of Polynesian
adventure in which, when the fantastic King Media had
called for his subjects to bring pipes, the author soliloquizes:

Nothing so beguiling as the fumes of tobacco, whether
inhaled through hookah, nargil, chibouque, Dutch porcelain, pure Principe, or Regalia.

The last two indicated to Americans expensive Havana
cigars.

Tobacco in rouleaus we had none; cigar nor cigarret,
which little the company esteemed. Pipes were preferred.
. . . But not of the vile clay, of which mankind and Etruscan
vases were made, were these jolly fine pipes of ours. But all in
good time.
Now the leaf called tobacco is of divers species and sorts.
Not to dwell upon vile Shag, Pig-tail, Plug, Nail-rod, Negrohead, Cavendish, and misnamed Lady's Twist, there are the
following varieties:
Gold-leaf, Oronoco, Cimaroza, Smyrna, Bird's-eye, James-
river, Sweet-scented, Honey-dew, Kentucky, Canaster,
Scarfalati, and famed Shiraz, or Persian, of all of which
perhaps the last is the best.

Melville goes on with some nonsense about Shiraz, until
the pipes are brought in.

Soon we were all smoking so hard, that the canopied
howdah, under which we reclined, sent up purple wreaths
like a Michigan wigwam. . . . Among these calumets, my
lord Media's showed like the turbaned grand Turk among his
Bashaws. . . . Its mouthpiece an eagle's beak; its long stem
a bright, red-barked cherry-tree branch, partly covered with
a close network of purple dyed porcupine quills, and towards
the upper end streaming with pennons. . . .

Melville then describes the fantastic pipes smoked by King
Media's entourage. The King asks one of them, old Mohi,
about Froth-of-the-Sea (Meerschaum) as a material for pipes,
whereupon old Mohi gives a fanciful account of Froth-of-the-

[1] *Mardi and A Voyage Thither.* (Harpers.)

Sea which he calls Farnoo. Media asks how long such a pipe-bowl will last:

"My lord, like one's cranium, it will endure till broken. I have smoked this one of mine more than half a century."

"But unlike our craniums, stocked full of concretions, our pipe-bowls never need cleaning out," observed another counsellor.

"True," said Mohi, "they absorb the oil of the smoke to incrust . . . like a good wife a pipe is a friend and companion for life. . . . After many vexations, he may go home to that faithful counsellor, and find it full of kind consolations and suggestions. But not thus with cigars or cigarrets; the acquaintances of a moment, . . . their existence so fugitive, uncertain, unsatisfactory. . . ."

Herman Melville says he wrote this fiction in the hope that those who had mocked at his others might receive it as 'verity'. And indeed when we read about the sale of the effects of the Duke of Sussex in June 1843, King Media seems a less extravagant figure, and Melville's own list of tobaccos appears the normal experience of a pipe-smoker at this date.

The sale of the Duke's tobacco collection was announced thus:

Catalogue
of
The Unrivalled Collection
of
PIPES
Turkey, Persian, Marakiebo, and
Kanaster Tobacco,
and
Havannah Cigars and Manilla Cheroots,
of the Rarest Quality

The property of
His Late Royal Highness
The Duke of Sussex, K.G.

and removed from Kensington Palace

Will be sold by Auction by
Messrs Christie and Manson.

The sale lasted seventeen days, of which the last three were occupied by the Duke's tobacco, pipes and cigars.

The 146 lots of tobacco amounting to over four hundred-weight fetched £550. "Turkey Leaf 6½ lbs. very broad cut, 1842, from Lord Ponsonby" found a purchaser at £3 per pound. Other lots included: "A Box of Persian tobacco 3 lbs. 6 ozs. from the Duke of Hamilton; Djebel, 2¼ lbs. from Major Bagot; East India tobacco 5 lbs. from Sir Gore Ousley; Very old tobacco of dark colour, 4¾ lbs. brought by His Royal Highness from Vienna; six half-pound packets of Kanaster from Breal and Habernicht of Hanover." Louisiana Kanaster, which was presumably Perique; Marakiebo, which must have been Venezuela tobacco if it is the Maracaibo of to-day; Syria, which was probably Latakia; and South American stick were also offered; the last is not traceable to any particular place.

Besides the tobacco there were twenty-two lots of snuff, which fetched £45. After the sale of King George IV's huge cellar of snuff thirteen years earlier this seems an insignificant collection, and it is an indication of the return to favour of smoking among the *haut ton*, for which the cigar was mainly responsible. Nevertheless, if 480 pounds of tobacco could realize an average of twenty-three shillings a pound, there must have been plenty of wealthy pipe-smokers at work already, colouring meerschaums.

One of the daily papers commented thus on the last day's sale of cigars:

> The company was more numerous than on any previous day during the week . . . it will scarcely be credited that some of the rare lots among the cigars sold for more than 2/6 each; and it is a remarkable fact that three small parcels of the same realised a sum exceeding that fetched by the whole of the carriages belonging to the late Duke sold on Monday last by Messrs Tattersall. The principal purchases made during the day were by gentlemen, the prices ranging too high for the workers. Among the more important Lots were a box of 1,000 cigars presented to His Royal Highness by Lord John Churchill, £40 (Colonel Gurwood).

Colonel Gurwood also acquired three lots of 1,000 cigars each for £137, and on top of them 2,125 cigars for £148. In the course of the day over 50,000 cigars were sold, enough for His Royal Highness to smoke some fifteen cigars a day for ten years.

Two hundred and twenty pipes were put up for sale. The top price was reached by a "very beautiful pipe of carved wood with an engagement of cavalry and three groups of infantry . . . the cover of the bowl is a chased helmet of gold, surmounted by a Sphinx". That pipe fetched £33, and a "large bowl formerly belonging to John Sobieski, gold-mounted with a crown of Poland and carved in relief with a battle in which the King is introduced" was knocked down to Lord Dudley Stuart for £29. Seven guineas were paid for "an immense Courland bowl, the mount chased with animals", and four guineas for a "wooden bowl with a nymph seated on a lion, beautifully carved".

Mr R. C. Bruce Gardner[1] is the source of this information about what can be called the tobaccomania of the Duke of Sussex, and he adds an interesting personal note.

> In my possession is a meerschaum pipe with silver-gilt cover and gold chain which the Duke of Sussex gave to my great-grandfather. . . . The depth of the bowl from the tip of the cover to the bottom of the bowl is 5½ inches and the overall length, from the bottom of the bowl to the mouthpiece along the curve of the stem, is 21 inches.

Tradition[2] says that the first meerschaum pipe was made by a Hungarian shoemaker of Budapest round about 1730. A Count Andrassy brought him a lump of the hydrous silicate of magnesia found mainly at Eskisher in Asia Minor and asked Karl Kowates who, when he was not sticking to his last, carved wooden pipes for his customers, to make him a pipe of it. He had been presented with it in Turkey, where they used it for the bowls of their chibouques.

The shoemaker made two pipes out of the lump and kept one for himself. In due course he noticed that where he had held the bowl while smoking it had turned to a golden-brown colour, and it occurred to him that the reason for this was the cobbler's wax upon his fingers. So he waxed the bowl all over, and found that the deeper the colour the better the tobacco tasted in it. The meerschaum pipe, so much sweeter and cooler than the porcelain pipes of Germany, became the fashion in Austria-Hungary, and there was a steady importation of the 'sea-foam' from Turkey whence the bowls roughly shaped were exported to Vienna to be turned into luxury pipes.

[1] *Country Life*, March 29th, 1956.
[2] *The Pipe Book*, Alfred Dunhill. (A. and C. Black, 1924.)

In 1799 John Tomas, a mechanic of Erlangen, wrote an enthusiastic little book of technical instruction for the making of meerschaum and of praise for its superiority from the point of health over any other material. Meerschaum pipes were reaching England by the end of the century, and as noted in the prologue it was still a duty for the undergraduate when the twentieth century dawned to colour a meerschaum.

It is a pity that the Duke of Sussex did not live to see the introduction of the brier-pipe.[1] Some of those straight-grained briers of once upon a time would have given his friends a fine opportunity to gratify his collector's passion.

In the Dunhill collection of pipes there is a rough-looking specimen made out of the root of the gorse, and the countryman who made this experiment was closer to the solution of the right material for a wooden pipe than he realized, or indeed than anybody realized for many years to come. Wooden pipes were tried often enough, but nobody found the right wood. Tobias Smollett in 1765 wrote from Turin to his friend Dr S——, describing his encounter at the top of a mountain with a Quixotic figure, "very tall, meagre and yellow, with a long hooked nose and twinkling eyes" whose "mouth was furnished with a short wooden pipe, from which he discharged wreathing clouds of tobacco-smoke", and who turned out to be an Italian marquis. Smollett made no comment on the wooden pipe, and presumably it was not the first he had seen. The Duke of Sussex had some carved wooden pipes in his collection, but however well they may have been carved, they were no use for smoking because the right wood for the business was still unknown.

A correspondent of *Notes and Queries* was writing in April 1885 to claim that he had had the honour of having helped, however feebly, to introduce the wooden pipe to England in 1853:

"for in that year meerschaums and clays were the rule at both the English universities and in all shops throughout the land, and the art of making pipes of wood was either obsolete or wholly *in futuro*. But a college friend of mine, a Norfolk squire, possessed a gardener who . . . conceived the idea of making pipes of willow-wood, cutting the bowl out of a thick stem, and the tube out of a thinner one growing from

[1] Although 'briar' is now the more popular spelling, the *O.E.D.* still gives preference to 'brier', which as a corruption of *bruyère* is nearer to the original than 'briar'.

the bowl. . . . The pipes did not last long; but, . . . the young squire's friends bought them eagerly at eighteenpence a piece. A year or two after 1853 the so-called briar-root pipes began to appear in England. Thirty years have enabled these intruders to destroy short clays, ruin meerschaums, and even do much mischief to the venerable churchwarden."

Napoleon, like the Duke of Wellington and Lord Montgomery, may have hated smoking but he was indirectly responsible for conferring on pipe-smokers a priceless boon. It was a habit of pious Bonapartists in the middle of the last century to make a pilgrimage to the birthplace of their hero in Corsica. One year round about 1855 a French pipe-maker lost his meerschaum pipe somewhere in the *maquis,* and one of the peasants volunteered to cut him another pipe out of wood. It was such a success that the pipe-maker asked for some specimens of the wood, which turned out to be the root of the Mediterranean tree-heath (*Erica arborea*) or *bruyère.* Of these roots the Corsican peasants made pipes as long ago as that Englishman made a pipe out of the roots of the gorse. The French pipe-maker sent these roots to a factory at St Claude in a valley of the Jura Mountains where he was accustomed to buy wooden pipe-stems for his meerschaum bowls.

The inhabitants of St Claude had for ages been accustomed to turnery, their skill in which they had used on the box-wood which grew in abundance close at hand. Such a success had they had with their local craft that St Claude had grown into a prosperous little town, and as far back as the eighteenth century they had added pipe-stems to the other articles they made.

These brier pipes seem to have reached England in about 1856. The *O.E.D.* quotes as the earliest reference to the brier an advertisement from the *Tobacco Trade Review* of February 8th, 1868: "Health pipe: in Bruyer wood", and another from April 11th of the same year "Joseph Izod. Importer of Meerschaum and Bruyer Pipes" and from another advertisement in the same number "Brier Wood, Lava, Clay and China pipes."

A pipe of lava has defeated me. Even the encyclopaedic Arents, who deals with pipes of various stones from porphyry to steatite and of various materials from the claw of a lobster to the foot of an emu, has not one word about a pipe of lava.

Note the phrase 'health-pipe' in that first advertisement.

The alarmists were uttering warnings about the danger of cancer from smoking clay-pipes. The original briers from St Claude had been equipped with horn stems locally made, but in 1878 an English firm invented the vulcanite mouthpiece. The invention was taken over by the Germans, who perfected vulcanite and secured almost a monopoly of its manufacture. Shortly before the First World War a factory for making vulcanite mouthpieces was established in St Claude, and when the supplies from Germany were cut off they expanded and made not only mouthpieces but also ebonite parts necessary for electrical apparatus.

The amber mouthpiece is the most agreeable of all for a brier-pipe, but apart from the question of expense, which to-day is prohibitive, amber is no use to the smoker who holds his pipe too tightly, for it easily cracks. Horn was incapable of standing up to a tight grip, and the mouthpieces of such smokers were always bitten into at the end. So, too, was the early vulcanite. This bad habit is all too common, but the man who does not bite too hard on a pipe would have no difficulty with false teeth when his own have left him.

Writing in 1924 Alfred Dunhill says:

No fewer than thirty million pipes are turned out from St Claude in the course of a year, of which 90% are exported. . . . The bulk of the St Claude pipes come to England, which imports, according to official statistics, about twenty-five million pipes annually while exporting a quarter of a million superfine pipes of English make, besides twenty million English clays.[1]

Since those days a very high percentage of the cheap pipe trade has passed from St Claude to Italy. In the last war we suffered from the shortage of brier pipes, but there was no sign of a revival of the clay-pipe industry in consequence. Broseley, in the heart of Shropshire, which claimed to have made clay pipes since 1575, was not making so much as a single cutty when I visited it in 1950. The clay used for them was the same as that from which the famous Coalport china was made, the same indeed as was probably used to coat the outside of houses in Uriconium, the white city of Roman Britain that the Saxons destroyed. The clay pipes of Broseley had such a

[1] *The Pipe Book*, p. 245.

widespread renown that a Broseley became a synonym for a clay pipe.

Norman Douglas wrote in 1915 of the slopes of Aspromonte:

> To the firs succeeded long stretches of odorous pines interspersed with Mediterranean heath, which here grows to a height of twelve feet; one thinks of the number of briar pipes that could be cut out of its knotty roots. A British Vice-Consul at Reggio started this industry about the year 1899; he collected the roots, which were sawn into blocks and then sent to France and America to be made into pipes. This Calabrian briar was considered superior to the French kind.[1]

Calabria, Greece and Algeria are now the main source for the supply of briers, and nothing is an adequate substitute for the brier. Some people believe they are enjoying tobacco when they smoke it in a cherry-wood pipe, but they are rarities. The corncob claims adherents, but perhaps the failure of the pipe to establish itself all over the country which had the glory of producing pipes long before the white man set foot upon the Atlantic shore may be ascribed in part to the disillusionment of smoking a corncob. The calabash may be all right for Afrikanders, but it will never do in Europe; they do not smoke it even in Holland. The bamboo can be cut into all sorts of pleasant shapes; but it remains something to look at, not to smoke. If any young man should chance to read these words let him be urged by them to consider the glory that would be his if he could succeed in discovering a substitute for the brier so that when the scented white blossoms of the last tree-heath have been scattered pipe-smokers will not be starved of their richest pleasure. Fortunately there is no reason to suppose that the smokers of briers are in danger of being deprived of them within any foreseeable future.

In *Notes and Queries* of September 6th, 1913, G. L. Apperson, then in the throes of writing *The Social History of Smoking*, posed this query:

> Surtees in 'Ask Mamma', 1858, says:
> "The gorse was within a stone's throw of the 'Public', so Luff and some of the thirsty ones pulled up to whet their whistles and light the clay pipes of gentility."

[1] *Old Calabria* (Secker & Warburg), p. 281.

Were clay pipes in fashionable use in the 'fifties or 'sixties of the last century? The Luff mentioned was a Capt. Luff.

The answers are of interest.

Mr. Wm. E. Browning said:

Certainly clay pipes were in fashionable use in the middle of the last century. Two famous tobacconists of that time have been handed down to posterity as makers of such pipes —Milo, in the Strand, and Inderwick, near Leicester Square —in a certain burlesque poem of 1853, in praise of an old black pipe:

> Think not of meerschaum is that bowl: away,
> Ye fond enthusiasts! it is common clay,
> By Milo stamped, perchance by Milo's hand,
> And for a tizzy purchased in the Strand.
> Famed are the clays of Inderwick, and fair,
> The pipes of Fiolet from Saint Omer.

But alas! their lights have all been long since put out by the intrusion of briar-roots.

Colonel W. F. Prideaux said:

Before briar-root pipes came into common use clay pipes were of necessity smoked by all classes. When I matriculated at Oxford in 1858 . . . University men used to be rather particular about the pipes they smoked. The finest were made in France, and the favourite brand was 'Fiolet St Omer'. I do not know if this kind is still smoked, but it was made of a soft clay that easily coloured. . . . At Simpson's fish ordinary at Billingsgate churchwarden pipes were always placed on the table after dinner, together with screws of shag tobacco . . . of course, in those days no one ever thought of smoking a pipe in the presence of ladies.

Colonel Harold Malet said:

When I was a cadet at Sandhurst in 1855–8 Milo's cutty pipes were quite the thing, and the selection by cadets of a good one out of a fresh consignment packed in sawdust was eagerly watched by the 'Johns'. Of course we were imitating our parents.

Mr B. D. Moseley said:

The old pipe-rack with its long row of churchwardens and

Broseleys—at one time an indispensable fitting in most bar-parlours—has vanished. These pipes survived long after the sixties of the last century and the advent of meerschaums and briars. Professional men and tradesmen met nightly to smoke their long pipes and to discuss scandal and affairs of state. By an unwritten law working-men and their habiliments were excluded except under the wing of a protector. He was a bold man who would enter with a short clay pipe in his mouth. This curious notion concerning the appearance of the short clay still exists, although the enormous quantity of them sold shows it is a general favourite with smokers.

The cadets of Sandhurst and the undergraduates of Oxford could smoke cutties without losing cast apparently, but the respectable professional men and tradesmen of a provincial bar-parlour looked down the stems of their churchwardens at a labourer smoking a cutty. The cigarette has done a great deal to abolish class distinctions. No wonder the cheap cigars in the mouths of the populace were regarded with such distaste by the faintly apprehensive *bourgeoisie*. Ruskin thought that the prevalence of cigar-smoking among the youth of London was a sign of their moral collapse.

One curious effect was brought about by the introduction of the brier-pipe and that was the final discouragement of women from smoking a pipe. All the pictures of women smoking from the beginning of the seventeenth century until that delightful portrait of Madame Lebrun, "de la beauté le peintre et le modèle", which belonged to the late Mr Alfred Dunhill, who reproduced it in colour in *The Pipe Book*, portray them smoking clays. Madame Lebrun painted many of the most famous women in Europe from Marie Antoinette to Emma Hamilton. The portrait in the Dunhill collection, presumably a self-portrait, depicts her with a slim long-stemmed clay pipe in her right hand and her left hand resting on what looks like a kind of lighter, a jet of flame burning from a fat wick. Beside her is a table on which lie two or three clay pipes the bowl of one of which suggests by its colour that many pipefuls have been smoked in it. A quizzing-glass and a small bowl are beyond. What was that bowl for? For genteel spitting?

It is to be noted that Madame Lebrun who was born in 1755 lived to be eighty-seven. That was in 1842. Three years later Pheasy Molly, who had been a heavy smoker all her life, died

at Buxton at the age of ninety-six after setting fire to her clothes
when lighting her pipe at the fire. In 1856 Mrs Jane Garbutt
died in her hundred and tenth year at a village in the North
Riding of Yorkshire, and enjoyed her pipe until the end. Asked
by a newspaper reporter how long she had smoked, Mrs
Garbutt replied, "Very nigh a hundred years."

Just after I came across that story I read in a newspaper:

John Shaffer, a former Negro slave, celebrated his 110th
birthday yesterday at Leavensworth, Kansas. John . . .
started smoking when he was nine and is still at it.

The brier-pipe is not suited by a small bowl, and if Madame
Lebrun had smoked briers she would probably never have
wanted to paint herself in the act.

The first entries of 'Briarwood Pipes' in the books of Fribourg
and Treyer were in 1879 when they cost 7s. each; in cases 11s.
each. The mouth-pieces were presumably of horn, but the
pipes in cases may have had amber ones. There is not much
variety in the tobaccos sold for about a hundred years. In 1797
Virginia tobacco was quoted at 3s. 6d. a pound which the historian of the House thinks was probably shag, though he says
it was not called by that name until 1846. Joseph Fume writing
in 1839 [1] says that shag was originally used to denote all kinds of
tobacco cut into thin filaments. It was called shag because that
was the old name for short and matted wool or hair. Fume
adds:

The tobacco called *returns* is manufactured from the best
and mildest kind of common Virginia leaf, with the stalk
taken out. The name *returns* as applied to tobacco for smoking,
is of comparatively recent date. About forty years ago [1800]
short-cut was the favourite with those for whom the common
shag was too strong; and as this kind of tobacco, in order to
make it sufficiently small, was rubbed through a sieve, the
comparatively long shreds or outsiftings, which would not
pass through the wires, were called *returns*. The smoking
public having become tired of short-cut, on account of its
small particles frequently getting into the stalk of the pipe
and stopping the draught, the manufacturers tried them with
a sample of *returns*, under the name of *long-tails*. The quality
was approved of, for it was precisely the same as that of

[1] *A Paper of Tobacco* (Chapman & Hall, 1839).

short-cut; but as the appellation was not fancied—it was even worse than shag—the manufacturers changed it to the old trade name of *returns*.

Latakia was mentioned for the first time in the books of Fribourg and Treyer in 1846; a pound cost 12s. About this time Varinas Canaster was quoted at 10s. Varinas of which we never seem to hear to-day was a name to conjure with when smoking started in Europe. It came originally from a town and province in Colombia, and was imported in rolls formed of the leaves of the tobacco spun into a thick twist. Fume says that most of the Varinas imported (i.e. about 1839) into Great Britain came from Colombia and Guatemala, and that "by many smokers of unquestionable taste it is preferred to Turkey, from its being rather stronger, and having, as they say, more of a real tobacco flavour". Presumably it was not at all like Latakia. Fume puts the price at 10s. a pound which is what the Fribourg and Treyer books quote as its cost.

Evans, however, says that Varinas was of Dutch origin, rather broadly cut and suitable for smoking in a large pipe.

Canaster (also Kanaster and Knaster) as already mentioned derived its name from the *canastros* or large wicker baskets in which the finest tobacco from Spanish America used to be imported. The Germans and Dutch were particularly fond of it.

Melville makes Gold Leaf and Sweet Scented Honeydew separate tobaccos, but Gold Leaf Honeydew appears for the first time in the books of Fribourg and Treyer in 1863. Originally Honeydew seems to have been a mild Virginia tobacco soaked in molasses, but the Honeydew I recall in youth was a light fine tobacco not unlike Bird's-eye without the birds' eyes which, once upon a time, were the cut midribs of the stripped leaf. It first occurs in the books of 34, Haymarket in 1852.

The earliest mention of a tobacco mixture occurs in 1859, but Evans says that the tobaccos noted above were practically the only ones sold by his firm until 1890 "when the Mixtures now in use were added one by one". This sheds a light on Barrie's Arcadian Mixture in *My Lady Nicotine*; almost any kind of a mixture was still a novelty, and such a tobacco as Latakia had hitherto been smoked neat. When the Duke of Sussex amassed those four hundredweights of various tobaccos, so many of which were Oriental, nobody had thought of blending them with the tobaccos of Virginia and Maryland.

Tom Cribb's Parlour. The Champion smokes his churchwarden while friends admire the silver cup presented to him by the *Sporting World* on 2nd December, 1811

Negrohead was originally made from leaves of tobacco steeped in molasses and tightly twisted together. It was very strong and extremely sweet and, according to Joseph Fume, was seldom smoked alone. He writes:

A smoking friend of mine says that Orinoco and Maryland and even mild Kanaster is materially improved by a small portion of negro-head cut small and placed as a priming above the charge.[1]

Cavendish was another dark tobacco steeped in molasses, but I cannot ascertain whether it was called after the Elizabethan adventure or whether it was the name of the firm that first made it; both statements appear.

To-day, however, in the United Kingdom, the terms Cavendish and Negrohead are both used in two entirely different senses by H.M. Customs and Excise to apply to sweetened tobacco, and in the other sense to specific types of tobacco manufactured in the ordinary Excise factory, where the addition of sweetening ingredients in manufacture is not permitted.

To quote Fume once more:

The principal kinds of tobacco smoked in this country are:—Turkey, Varinas, and Kanaster, consumed by the more wealthy classes who can afford to purchase fine tobacco, and indulge in a real meerschaum; Orinoco and Maryland, chiefly in favour with incipient amateurs; Returns, the delight of steady, seasoned smokers; and Shag, the favourite of all who like 'a strong article'. Pigtail, or small twist tobacco, shred small, is not unfrequently smoked by many persons, but more particularly in Scotland; and a few iron-nerved smokers occasionally take a pipe of Negro-head.

The Scots are conservative smokers, and pigtail is still the favourite smoke in the Highlands and Islands for those who have not surrendered to the cigarette. I have experienced few sharper pleasures in life than lighting a pipe of pigtail about eight o'clock on a cloudless morning in June and lolling back in a small boat, with the sun on the port side and small green islands drawing nearer on the starboard bow.

When that smoking friend of Joseph Fume's added Negrohead to his Orinoco and Maryland tobacco he would have obtained an even better "priming above the charge" by adding instead

[1] *A Paper of Tobacco.*

Perique. Perique, however, does not appear to have reached us in this country by the middle of the last century. It has a romantic history.

In 1755 the British Governor of Nova Scotia suddenly expelled 6,000 French settlers. Some of these unfortunate Acadians in search of a new home reached as far as Louisiana, where they settled on low-lying alluvial land near the Mississippi some fifty miles north-west of New Orleans. The climate is hot and very humid, with a high rainfall. One of these settlers, Pierre Chenet, observed the method of curing tobacco which the Indians of the Chickasaw and Choctaw tribes practised, by pressing the leaf in hollow logs, using another log as a ram. Pierre Chenet, whose nickname was Perique, resolved to improve upon this method, and it is only within recent years that Pierre Chenet's method of pressing has been further improved by substituting screw presses for the wooden box presses in which the pressure was applied by means of long wooden fulcrum bars with lumps of rock.

The crop is planted out in March, and normally harvested towards the end of July. The whole plant is cut; a large nail is driven through the thick end of the main stem and the plant is suspended thereby from wires stretched from end to end of well-ventilated sheds or barns. When the leaf is adequately dried out and 'set', it is stripped from the main stem, softened by the addition of water and stemmed. The farmer makes up the strips into bundles, each bundle being tied with raffia (produced locally) and packed into barrels, the barrels being left open at the tops. The leaf is then pressed in the barrels by hand-operated screw presses—pressure being applied until it blackens and juice is expressed. It is left under pressure for several weeks, turned out of the barrel, loosened up, re-packed into the barrel and again put under pressure. Each barrel is turned out, re-packed and placed again under pressure twice during the first year, and is then handed over to the shipper for its final processing. He turns out the barrels, removes the raffia ties, re-packs, and replaces the leaf under pressure at least three more times before shipping.

Fermentation begins very soon after the first pressing by the farmer, and appears to continue to a diminishing extent up to the third or fourth turning out and re-pressing. No water is added after stemming, but great care is taken that the juices are retained and reabsorbed during processing. The process of fermentation and repeated pressing darkens the leaf to an almost coal-black colour, and it is during this time that the aroma peculiar to Perique is acquired. The art of producing Perique lies in knowing how long and how hard to press and when and how to turn the leaf without losing the juices. Until towards the end of the nineteenth century the production of Perique barely exceeded 22,000 pounds annually, but it was world famous among smokers. To-day the total annual production is around 150,000 to 200,000 pounds.

Those who use it claim that it has more aroma than any other type . . . that it has a rich, pungent odor, with a smooth, delicate and agreeable taste, and that it stimulates the action of the brain without impairing the organs of digestion, or affecting the nervous system.[1]

There is no doubt that when J. B. Killebrew wrote those words, he wrote them as a devotee of Perique, and the present writer affirms here that he agrees with every word of that eulogy.

And with the fragrance of this noble pipe-tobacco in our minds, of which so regrettably the Duke of Sussex seems to have been unaware, let us turn to the cigarette, in the earlier American varieties of which Perique was a popular constituent. Sometimes, indeed, it was smoked solo which Tennant[2] considers "must have smoked like shredded dynamite".

[1] J. B. Killebrew and Herbert Myrick, *Tobacco Leaf* (Orange Judd Company, New York, 1897).

[2] Richard B. Tennant, *The American Cigarette Industry* (Yale University Press, 1950).

Chapter 16

THE devotees of the cigarette who feel that its triumph was too long delayed by less perfect mediums for tobacco are always anxious to insist that its antiquity is contemporary with that of the cigar, the pipe and snuff. Let that be granted without further argument, but the present writer is not prepared to concede the claim of Young,[1] that what the two emissaries of Christopher Columbus saw being smoked by the natives of Cuba on that November day in 1492 was something nearer to a cigarette than a cigar. However, in Mexico, Brazil and elsewhere the equivalent of the cigarette was certainly noted by the earliest travellers, and probably the first cigarette reached Spain with the tobacco wrapped in the leaf of Indian corn. The substitution of paper as a wrapper may have originated from the manufacture of a particularly fine paper both in Barcelona and Valencia. The habit of smoking *papeletes* was sufficiently general by 1635 to incur the denunciation of one of those Dominican friars who at this date were as intolerant and intolerable as the most bigoted representatives of Geneva. Fra Tomás Ramon of Alcañiz, Preacher-General of the Order of Preachers and Doctor of Divinity, presented to the very illustrious Lord-Jurors of the Imperial and always August City of Saragossa a tract demanding their help in reforming such bad habits as wearing the hair long (the Roundheads felt the same about this) and a variety of other moral delinquencies, winding up with excess in the use of tobacco. He is particularly severe on the secular clergy for taking snuff and smoking *papeletes* at ecclesiastical gatherings, stigmatizing the latter as instruments of the Devil from whom the Indian priests had acquired the habit of smoking which they had taught to the natives. The denunciation of Fra Tomás does not seem to have had much effect, for seven years later Pope Urban VIII had to publish that Papal Bull prohibiting the use of tobacco in the churches of Seville.

The *papelete* did not pass beyond Spain for a long time. As late as 1768 Casanova thought it worth-while to record his having seen an inn-keeper in Spain smoking "a cigarette of

[1] W. W. Young, *The Story of the Cigarette* (Appleton, 1916).

Brazilian tobacco wrapped in a little paper tube, from which he blew great clouds of smoke with evident enjoyment". Casanova himself was a snuff-taker and recorded his belief that the chief pleasure smokers derived was from the sight of the tobacco fumes. Casanova was more often right than wrong: snuffers could argue fairly that without the sight of the fumes some of the pleasure of smoking would languish.

The Spaniards do not seem to have converted the Dutch to the cigarette, but it may be presumed that they were more successful in Naples, and that from Naples the cigarette reached the Levant and Russia. The Spanish supporting forces introduced cigarettes to Denmark in 1808. A contemporary account says: "Spanish warriors had small pocket-books containing pieces of a white paper, they used to tear such a piece of paper out of the book, wrap smoking tobacco in it in the form of a spill, put one end in their mouth and set fire to the other end." The Peninsular War is always given the credit for popularizing the cigar in Great Britain. Be that as it may, there seems little doubt that the *papelete* was brought into France after that war and there given the name which was to spread all over the world. According to Young "its form like its name was perfected in France, and by 1843 the Government had decided that it was worth-while to establish a monopoly in cigarettes".[1]

Whether those early cigarettes were the Caporals of to-day I have not been able to discover, but the fact that one of the earliest brand of American cigarettes was called Sweet Caporal suggests that they were.

It must be added that such a preference is by no means shared by all Frenchmen. N. M. Tilley[2] says that in the 'forties of the last century the Russians were smoking home-grown leaf blended with Maryland, Ohio and Kentucky leaf, but that with the introduction of Turkish leaf in 1850 the blended cigarette went out of fashion.

Cigarettes in very small quantities were being imported into England from Russia just before the Crimean War, but the evidence seems inadequate for the confident assertion repeated by so many tobaccologues that the Crimean War started the fashion for cigarettes in Great Britain. It is no doubt true that

[1] W. W. Young, op. cit.
[2] Nannie M. Tilley, *The Bright Tobacco Industry 1860–1929* (University of Carolina Press, 1948).

British troops were introduced to cigarettes by the French and Turks and by Russian prisoners-of-war, and equally true that when they came home enough of them had learned to smoke cigarettes to make the venture of Robert Peacock Gloag in manufacturing them at home a success. In an interview[1] with *Tobacco* in 1890 this Crimean veteran said that when he returned from the war he decided to manufacture cigarettes in the Russian style.

> The tobacco used was Latakia dust and the paper yellow tissue . . . the mouthpiece was of cane. The mode of manufacture was first to make the canes, into which the tobacco had been pressed. In order to keep the dust tobacco from escaping, the ends were turned in. The size of the cigarettes was that which is now known as an Oxford, and they were put up in bundles of ten, to be retailed at 6*d*.

Later on Gloag and Co. seem to have given up paper and specialized in cigarettes covered with leaf. In 1873 they introduced 'Don Alphonso Spanish Whiffs', put up in bundles of twenty-five for a shilling, but by then the cigarette of Virginian tobacco was at the beginning of what was to become its omnipotent sway.

The books of Fribourg and Treyer show that they sold hardly any cigarettes until 1866, when Russian cigarettes began to figure frequently, "nearly all mouthpiece and very little cigarette".

It is amusing to find that in 1854 an observer in New York was reporting that "some of the ladies of this refined and fashion-forming metropolis are using the silly ways of some pseudo-accomplished foreigners in smoking tobacco through a weaker and more feminine article which has been most delicately denominated cigarette".[2] Yet, when those words were written, already in Caswell County, North Carolina, the leaf which was to have as much influence over the future of tobacco as those seeds of *Nicotiana Tabacum* with which John Rolfe experimented in Virginia had displayed its gold.

Readers may remember how many of the eighteenth-century advertising labels proclaimed the tobacco sold to be sweet-scented York River. The original Trinidad or Orinoco seed

[1] *Tobacco*, Vol. X, November 1st.
[2] Quoted by J. C. Robert, *The Story of Tobacco in America* (Alfred Knopf, New York, 1952).

was sown in the rich soil along the James River, but it was soon
found that the tobacco grown in the thin sandy soil near
Yorktown produced a much milder leaf which caught the
fancy of European connoisseurs. This was originally air-cured;
that is, hung up in barns for about two months and exposed to
a passage of air. By the middle of the eighteenth century most
of the tobacco grown in America was fire-cured, wood-fires
being lighted in trenches round the barn and the smoke coming
into direct contact with the leaf; the result after from a week to
six weeks of such curing was a dark brown leaf and what
seemed a stronger tobacco. The tendency has always been to
search for milder tobacco.

Killebrew and Meyrick[1] attribute the discovery of Bright
yellow leaf to about the year 1852:

> The rise and progress of the yellow tobacco interest in the
> Piedmont regions of Virginia and North Carolina and especi-
> ally in the latter State, show one of the most abnormal
> developments in agriculture that the world has ever known.
> This leaf is mainly used for wrappers, chewing plugs, and
> also for making 'fine cut' tobacco and cigarettes. . . . Two
> brothers, Eli and Elisha Slade owned farms on a poor ridge
> in Caswell County, North Carolina. Upon this ridge . . .
> they planted tobacco and cured it with fires made of char-
> coal, regulated in a definite manner. They succeeded, by
> this means, in giving to it a beautiful lemon-yellow colour.
> Their neighbours caught the infection. . . . The lands which
> grew the finest tobacco had light cream-coloured soils, 93
> per cent. of which was siliceous matter. This porous, spongy,
> sandy earth, destitute of humus . . . became the cornerstone
> of a great agriculture. . . . Just before they were harvested,
> the plants turned to a beautiful color, like hickory leaves in
> autumn, and fields of tobacco at a distance looked more like
> those of small grain ready for the harvest than tobacco fields.

Miss Tilley[2] in her exhaustive researches has been able to
show that the Slade discovery was in fact made as early as 1839.
She relates that Abisha Slade (not Elisha) had an eighteen-
year-old Negro slave called Stephen one of whose jobs it was to
prepare charcoal for the farm smithy. One wet night when he
was watching a barn of curing tobacco he fell asleep and woke

[1] Op. cit., pp, 110–11.
[2] N. M. Tilley, op. cit., p. 129. Her authority was an article in the *Danville*
(*Va.*) *Register*, quoted by *Tobacco* (1886).

to find the wood fires almost out. Instead of stoking them with wet wood Stephen hurried to the charcoal pit and brought some charred logs to put on the embers. The result of this on the tobacco being cured was to make it yellower than any yet seen and to sell at four times the average price that tobacco was obtaining at the time.

It was not until 1860 that charcoal was superseded by an improved flue for curing. This consisted of sheet-iron flues running across the floor of the barn and connected with an exterior furnace so that no smoke came into contact with the tobacco leaves hanging on sticks in tiers. It was from the use of these flues that the Bright leaf became known as flue-cured type tobacco. To-day well over four-fifths of the tobacco used in the United Kingdom is flue-cured.

It was about 1852 that the news of the Slade brothers' (there were four of them, not two) discovery reached beyond their immediate neighbours. Land in Caswell County, which had been sold at two dollars an acre, now fetched twenty-five. Durham, which had hardly existed, grew rapidly into a prosperous town given up to the manufacture of tobacco. All was set for transforming North Carolina from a thinly populated waste of pines into a thriving agricultural area when the Civil War broke out and the development of the new Bright tobacco stagnated. The tobacco farmers of the Old Belt, as the stretch of land that included the southern counties of Virginia and the northern counties of North Carolina was called, were in dread of invasion. The blockade of the Confederacy sent foreign buyers to New York, which now became the headquarters of the tobacco trade. Throughout the Southern States the cultivation of leaf was greatly diminished, much to the advantage of the Yankee States.

In the South, stocks of leaf were rushed from the Old Belt centres to Danville, which was thought to be comparatively safe from the danger of invasion. But the principal Danville factories had been turned into army hospitals, and little manufacture could be carried on there. The main development therefore in tobacco manufacture during the Civil War was to the North, while cultivation expanded in Kentucky, Ohio and Missouri, and spread still farther south in the Carolinas.

After the end of the war both Northern and Western manufacturers returned to the Virginia-Carolina area to buy Bright leaf. Originally the Americans used it as a wrapper for plug tobaccos, and when they began using it in cigarettes it was to displace some percentage of the Turkish type of tobacco from which cigarettes had hitherto been made. Later the percentage of Turkish leaf was reduced still further, following the introduction of 'home-grown' tobaccos from other American States— particularly Burley tobacco.

The origin of White Burley deserves recording. In 1864 George Webb sowed some Red Burley seed on his farm near Higginsport, Ohio. The plants grew up with their usual appearance except in one bed, where they had a whitish, unhealthy look. Webb did not bother to transplant them at first, but finding himself short he finally did so. For two or three weeks these whitish plants hardly grew at all, and then suddenly they started growing with great rapidity, retaining their rich creamy colour, and ripening a fortnight ahead of all the other plants in the field. Webb cured them by air and, after curing, the underside of the leaves retained this whitish tinge whereas the upper side was golden yellow. Moreover, the texture of the leaves was so fine that the grower exhibited them in Cincinnati. They sold well, and Webb, who had luckily saved some seed, planted ten acres with it in the following year. The plants all came up true, and yielded 11,000 pounds of tobacco, which sold at the top price. What the flue-cured Bright tobacco did for North Carolina, White Burley did for the rich blue limestone regions of Kentucky and the drift soils of Southern Ohio; blue grass pastures, which had been the pride of stock breeders for a hundred years and more, were ploughed up and planted with White Burley, so great was the demand for it and such a high price did it fetch. The original attraction of this unaccountable 'sport' was its mildness, its comparatively small content of nicotine, and above all, its greater absorbent capacity than any other tobacco, a combination which made it the ideal filler for chewing-plug. When chewing began to give way to cigarettesmoking, Burley became a popular tobacco for the cigarette in America, making it particularly suitable for the Americanblended cigarettes, which contain sweetening material.

The new Bright flue-cured leaf found a ready market in England, where manufacturers soon began to use it in cigarettes. It may well be that the first all-Virginian cigarette was produced in England. Scottish and German manufacturers are said by Miss N. M. Tilley[1] to have found the new leaf too expensive. It may not have been only a matter of cost with the Scots: they probably regarded cigarettes with conservative suspicion.

But before we come to the story of the development of the cigarette trade in the United Kingdom, let us continue to trace the train of events in America.

When the Civil War broke out in America, Washington Duke, a hard-working, prudent and religious farmer of forty-three, twice a widower, owned a 300-acre farm four miles north of Durham. In 1865 he was conscribed into the Confederate Army, to be captured in the retreat from Richmond before Lee's surrender at Appomattox. In 1865 Washington Duke was released from Libby Prison, which had been a tobacco-factory in Richmond, and sent to New Berne in North Carolina. From here, after exchanging a five-dollar Confederate bill for half a dollar in hard cash with a Federal soldier, Duke set out in his ragged grey uniform to tramp the 137 miles between himself and home. He found when he reached Durham that his farm had been pillaged by the Federal troops except for a little Bright tobacco and some flour they had missed. To raise working capital Duke sold his farm and rented a few acres of it. Then he sent for his four children who had been living with their grandparents, and set to work with them in a little long barn, to beat and clean the tobacco which had been left him. When it had been broken up he packed it in muslin bags labelled Pro Bono Publico, and after loading with them and the flour left him a waggon drawn by two blind mules, Washington Duke set out for Raleigh. Here he sold his tobacco for enough money to buy a supply of bacon.

General Joseph Johnston and 30,000 Confederate troops in retreating from Raleigh had passed through Durham, hotly pursued by Sherman. In Durham the two generals discussed a truce, and there troops on both sides, grey and blue, began to spread the news of the fine tobacco to be had in Durham. John Green had a factory which had been looted by the Federals; Green changed the name of his product to Genuine Durham Smoking Tobacco with the picture of a bull taken from a trademark for an English mustard. When Green died in 1869 a former tobacco retailer called Blackwell bought the Bull Durham

[1] Op. cit., p. 327.

business, and by heavy advertising coupled with the popularity of the Bright tobacco made it for some time the most popular smoking tobacco in the world, and for a much longer time the most popular in the United States.

Washington Duke gallantly set out to hold his own with this powerful competition, and in 1866, with only the labour of his three sons to help, turned out 15,000 pounds of Pro Bono Publico in 1866, which was one of those granulated tobaccos that the Americans enjoy in a pipe, but which we on the other side of the Atlantic do not. In 1871 W. Duke and Sons were making a brand called Duke of Durham. Five years later they had built their own factory in Main Street, Durham. The youngest of those sons was James Buchanan Duke, who when he was put in charge of the factory decided that they could not compete. "My company is up against a stone wall. It can not compete with the Bull. Something has to be done and that quick. As for me, I am going into the cigarette business." And in 1881 'Buck' Duke, being now aged twenty-four, went into the cigarette business.

In 1880 the brothers Bonsack of Virginia had registered a cigarette-making machine which was reputed to reduce the cost of manufacturing cigarettes from 80c. to 30c. This machine ordered by Allen and Ginter was destroyed by fire on the way to the factory, and a new machine with improvements was constructed in 1881. "For a number of years this complicated mechanism was manufactured in Paris",[1] and from Paris it reached the United Kingdom, as we shall hear presently. The cigarette manufacturers had hesitated to take up the new machine, partly because they were afraid that smokers would suppose the machine-made article inferior to the handmade and partly because they feared labour troubles.

In 1884 Duke made a bargain with Bonsack to use his machines at a royalty of 24c. a thousand instead of 30c., and furthermore inserted a clause in the contract by which Duke's royalty was always to be 25 per cent. less than the standard rental. The first two machines Bonsack delivered did not work as well as had been hoped and the other cigarette-manufacturers were beginning to congratulate themselves on their own prudence when William O'Brien, a clever young mechanic from Bonsack, improved the two machines and made them able to turn

[1] Tilley, op. cit., p. 572.

out 200 cigarettes a minute. That seemed a miraculous performance at this date when a handroller of cigarettes produced
about 1,250 in a day. The machines of to-day operate at speeds
of 1,000 a minute and over. Duke's next step was to invent the
'slide-and-shell' box. Then he cut the price of his Duke of
Durham cigarettes from a dime for ten to a nickel, that is,
from fivepence to twopence-halfpenny. Finally he started
cigarette-cards, with pictures of actresses and athletes at first.
He had opened a small factory in a loft down east in New York
in 1884, worked all day superintending the manufacture of his
cigarettes, tramped around New York at night, counting the
empty cigarette-packets in the streets to judge the popularity
of various brands, and retired to sleep in a hall-bedroom in
the Bowery for which he paid two dollars a week.

In 1880 before Duke decided to go in for cigarettes Allen and
Ginter, Kinney Tobacco Company, William S. Kimball and
Co., and Goodwin and Co. sold about 320 millions of the 400
millions consumed annually in the United States. By 1889 the
total annual production was 2,188 millions, of which W. Duke
Sons and Co. made and sold 837 millions, leaving those four
firms to split between them the rest. Duke proposed to Major
Lewis Ginter a merger. The Major scoffed. A year later Allen
and Ginter with the three other leading firms agreed to create
a new corporation with a capital of 25 million dollars. Of this
new firm James Buchanan Duke was President; it was called
the American Tobacco Company. Buck Duke himself was
thirty-three years old.

It must not be supposed that cigarettes at this date were anywhere near to being the favourite medium for tobacco in the
United States. The American Tobacco Company had to
obtain control of the other mediums for tobacco, and of these
chewing was still dominant. In 1878 the *New York Times* had
said:

> As tobacco eaters we occupy the field alone, having, it is
> to be regretted, a monopoly of one of the most unwholesome
> and obnoxious of practices. The national mastication and
> expectoration are known all over the world, and do ample
> service in all conceptions and caricatures of Brother Jonathan.
> To see a landsman chewing tobacco anywhere abroad is to
> know him for an American, native or adopted.

It was against chewing that the following poem [1] was directed:

> *I'll never use tobacco, no :*
> *It is a filthy weed :*
> *I'll never put it in my mouth,*
> *Said little Robert Reed,*
> *It hurts the health;*
> *It makes bad breath;*
> *'Tis very bad indeed,*
> *I'll never never use it, no!*
> *Said little Robert Reed.*

By the time little Robert Reed had grown up the anti-tobacco societies were concentrating their attack upon the cigarette, and so successfully that during the 'nineties propaganda did succeed in seriously diminishing their consumption. In 1896 the output of cigarettes was twice as large as it had been in 1890, but after 1896 the output fell each year until in 1901 it was back where it was in 1890. Output began to rise in 1902, but it was not until 1906 that it was back to where it had reached in 1896. To an anti-cigarette propaganda which was responsible for obtaining prohibition in several states was added the handicap of an increase of taxation in 1897 and 1898 which knocked out the cheapest brands.

The Waterville *Banner of Health* observed about the venerable author of *Ben Hur*:

> General Lew Wallace, who died at the early age of seventy-eight, was another victim of the deadly cigarette habit. But for the filthy weed, he might have lived to an even hundred.

On the other hand the Jericho *Primitive Christian* declared sternly:

> General Lew Wallace, who posed as a Christian, died at seventy-eight, having prolonged his life beyond the Scriptural three-score and ten by the use of those devilish drugs— cigarettes and coffee. God made seventy the sacred limit of our years, and those who violate it by employing drugs will surely suffer.

And finally, as a poor nineteenth-century attempt to rival King James I, hear what Mr Reamy of Baltimore had to say to the Epworth League when encamped at Denver:

[1] Quoted by Tennant, op. cit.

Like the upas, which casts the viewless pall of death on all around it, the tobacco plant exudes ruin and destruction over the wide earth. The fumes of its burning are an incentive to immorality and a provocative to vice and perniciousness. The deadly cigarette rots the soul of the user and converts the guileless boy into an assassin. The nauseous cigar contaminates the body, mind, and soul of the smoker and drives him to the hospital, the asylum, the potter's field, and last of all, into the brazen portals of hell. The pestilential pipe poisons its millions annually and makes the world reek with infamy. Chewing tobacco is the cause of burglary, arson, grave-robbing, incest, and perjury. Snuff obliges people to lie, swear, steal, and rob chicken-coops. All tobacco farmers are scoundrels; all tobacco merchants villains; all tobacco dealers are rogues and all tobacco users scamps and fools.[1]

Whether or not James Buchanan Duke's anxiety over the decline in cigarette consumption in the United States from 1896 to 1900 influenced him at all in his decision to invade the British market is not clear. Undoubtedly the expanding British home trade and the increasing competition he was meeting in export markets from British manufacturers were the main reasons. What is clear is that he misjudged the strength of the British resistance.

But before we come to the Tobacco War of 1901–2, the story of the development of the cigarette trade in the United Kingdom must be told.

[1] Quoted in John Bain Jr., *Cigarettes in Fact and Fancy* (Simpkin, Marshall, 1905).

Chapter 17

ALTHOUGH no exact date can be given for the introduction of cigarettes into the United Kingdom, it is generally accepted that Robert Gloag was the first to manufacture them here. He started his factory at Walworth, London, in 1856, but, from his own admission, it is clear that the Russian-type cigarettes he produced at the outset were made of inferior tobacco and were extremely crude. Although Lambert & Butler have entries of cigarettes in their stock book even before 1856, British manufacturers as a whole did not become really alive to the possibilities of the cigarette until some ten years later. They then succeeded in obtaining specially-made fine-textured paper and, by using best-quality Turkish tobacco, produced an attractive cigarette. Yet the aromatic flavour of Turkish or Oriental tobacco has never been widely appreciated in Britain, and the demand for Turkish cigarettes was small and was likely to remain limited. At about this time, however, supplies of the new Bright flue-cured leaf began to become available, and manufacturers were soon trying it out in cigarettes. The British smoker liked its mild flavour, and it was the introduction of the Virginian cigarette that marked the beginning of the real popularity of cigarettes in this country.

One of the first of the leading British firms to take up cigarette manufacture was W. D. & H. O. Wills, which by that time had been established in Bristol as tobacco manufacturers for nearly a century. They entered the cigarette market in 1871 with a brand appropriately named 'Bristol' (not their modern brand of that name). We do not know what tobacco was used for the original Bristol cigarettes, but in view of the fact that for so many years the name of W. D. & H. O. Wills had been associated so closely with Virginian tobacco, it is tempting to speculate that the Bright leaf played a part in the new venture.

In a Wills price list of 1874 over twenty brands of cigarettes are quoted, including Passing Cloud, which is still on the market to-day. In 1877 Wills introduced Three Castles pipe tobacco and a year later Three Castles cigarettes appeared both with the motto taken from Thackeray's novel *The Virginians*—

There's no sweeter tobacco comes from Virginia and no better brand than the Three Castles.

And on the Three Castles packing you may still see depicted the *Young Rachel*, one of the pioneer ships of the Bristol tobacco trade. In 1879 Wills, who had introduced Bird's-eye pipe tobacco at least thirty years earlier, brought out Bird's-eye cigarettes made from Virginian tobacco. These they sold in quantity to the French Government, which charged 75 centimes for a packet of ten of them. And the arrangement was hailed by a West Country journal as a contribution to the Entente Cordiale—a phrase that was to be revived a quarter of a century later when King Edward VII was the diplomatic agent instead of Bird's-eye cigarettes.

It was around this time that manufacturers began to issue cigarette-cards with their well-known brands, starting a fashion for collecting them which began with small boys and eventually extended to Royalty. The cigarette-card, as those whose memories go back to the days before the Second World War will remember it, was a masterpiece of condensed information and illustration whose presence in a packet of cigarettes was chiefly an inducement to buy that particular brand. Originally, however, it served a more utilitarian purpose. In the early days of cigarettes some brands were sold in paper packets, and the contents were apt to become crushed before they were smoked. To avoid this, manufacturers inserted plain pieces of pasteboard to stiffen the packets—'stiffeners' as they were called, and as they have been known to the trade ever since.

The exact date when it occurred to some enterprising manufacturer to print advertisements on these plain pieces of card is not known, but it is believed to have been about 1878. In 1887 Wills introduced their first pictorial stiffener, printed in colour, advertising Three Castles cigarettes and showing a servant girl knocking on a door. On the back of the card was a list of the firm's current cigarette brands.

Few people bothered to collect these early, strictly practical cards, and as a result they are now scarce and much sought after by collectors. It was a different matter, however, when, in the 1890's, manufacturers began to issue cards depicting famous actresses and beauties of the day. These were immediately popular, and were followed by sets depicting famous soldiers,

Time Off for a Smoke. N.C.O.'s relaxing in a shell-hole. Poperinghe, 1917

sailors, ships, incidents and personalities in the Boer War and the First World War—and, in the 1920's and 30's, by a revival of the original theme, this time depicting film and radio stars, and even novelists. Other popular subjects included famous footballers and cricketers and various aspects of natural history. The production of these cards entailed a tremendous amount of work. Considerable research was necessary to ensure that the facts and illustrations on the cards were accurate. They were so reliable that on one occasion a cigarette-card was used in a police-court to show the difference between a salmon and a pike, while on another occasion a set of cards illustrating English period costumes was used by a film library to ensure that the clothes for an historical production were absolutely correct.

Several American tobaccologues have fancied that American cigarettes never reached the United Kingdom until they were sold there by American firms. For instance, John Bain Jr states definitely [1] that John Morgan Richards, an enterprising American, was "the first to introduce our cigarettes in England". In 1876 Richards established himself in London as agent for various firms, including Allen and Ginter, and later on W. Duke & Sons.

To quote Richards:

> Although a considerable advertising was at once resorted to, and travellers were employed to call upon retail tobacconists, I found the cigarettes made no headway, and the *Richmond Gems* were absolutely refused. . . . The smoking of cigarettes of any sort was extremely limited. . . . But I was determined not to be beaten, and as a last resort I conceived the plan of offering to purchase a tobacco dealer's licence for every chemist in the United Kingdom who would place American cigarettes on his counter and undertake their sale. In a short time this proposition turned out highly successful . . . and the retail tobacconists . . . suddenly awoke to the fact that the American cigarettes were appreciated and required in their country. . . .
>
> As soon as the retail dealers came to this conclusion I decided to give them the utmost support by advertising. . . . The first welcome given to these cigarettes did not come from the west, but the east of London, and dealers in the west doggedly refused to take up the sale.
>
> Thereupon a tobacco shop was rented at the Piccadilly

[1] Op. cit., p. 59.

corner of the Circus, and styled the Ole Virginny Tobacco Shop. . . . Allen and Ginter held the monopoly of American cigarettes for perhaps two years, but at the end of that time the demand for cigarettes became so enormous that every tobacco manufacturer in the United States entered the market, and began turning out cigarettes, shipping them to England.

Colour is lent to Richards' claim that American cigarettes were more popular east of Piccadilly by the slang use of 'Straight Cut' for a respectable girl: Allen and Ginter's Richmond Straight Cuts were as well known as their Richmond Gems. However, Lambert and Butler brought out a cigarette called Straight Cut, and it may have been these which passed into London slang.

Richards was probably right in claiming that the heavy advertising by American firms helped to popularize the American cigarette, but it must be remembered that a good deal of the difficulty of selling them was due to the fact that the cheapest rate at which they could be sold was fivepence for ten on account of the heavier duty on imported manufactured tobacco. The idea that English manufacturers began to manufacture cigarettes after the advertising campaign of Richards is a myth.

Undoubtedly the chief cause for the rapidly increasing popularity of Virginia cigarettes in the 'eighties was the cigarette-machine which enabled cigarettes to be produced so much more cheaply.

Duke's deal with the Bonsack machine has been mentioned, but before that in May 1883 two machines and the English patent were sold to W. D. and H. O. Wills for £3,450. The Wills price list of December 1883 included this announcement:

> We take this opportunity of calling your attention to the Revised List of Cigarettes, the prices of which are considerably reduced, owing to our having erected powerful machinery, by which a great saving is effected in the cost of manufacture.

By 1888 eleven Bonsack machines were working in Bristol, and a visitor to the Wills factory was reporting in *Tobacco*, June 1888:

> The whole of the operations are very interesting, especially to watch the cigarette machines, each of which makes from 85,000 to 100,000 a day.

According to Miss Tilley [1] Duke's Bonsack machines were producing about 85,000 cigarettes a day in 1889. Other machines were invented, but none of them could compare with the Bonsack in efficiency until the Baron machine appeared in the 1890's.

Nevertheless, a considerable quantity of cigarettes continued to be made by hand, and for years—indeed until 1939—were believed by some to be superior to the machine-made cigarette. To-day hardly any cigarettes are hand-made.

In 1883 Wills introduced their Gold Flake cigarettes, made entirely of Virginia tobacco, and five years later the machine-made varieties of this brand and of their Best Bird's-eye cigarettes were selling at 7s. a thousand cheaper than the hand-made cigarettes of the same brands.

In 1883 *Tobacco* records Player's entry into the cigarette market:

> Mr John Player, of the Castle Tobacco Factory, Nottingham, devotes much attention to the manufacture of fine tobaccos and cigarettes. . . .
> Mr Player has recently commenced the manufacture of cigarettes and has adopted the names of Our Heroes, Our Charming Belles, the Castle Brand, etc.

In 1886 Player's Gold Leaf Navy Cut cigarettes appeared; these cigarettes were the forerunners of the famous Player's Medium Navy Cut cigarettes, which were introduced in 1900.

Gallaher & Co. of Belfast had not surrendered to the machine in 1885. An account of a visit to their factory in July of that year in *Tobacco* speaks of the cigarette-making girls as "neatly dressed and intelligent looking" and of the dexterity they use in their delicate work. "The cigarettes are all made by hand as it is considered that, being thus made, they are superior to those made mechanically."

Then there were the 'roll-your-own' cigarette-smokers, and it has been recorded that the present writer's first cigarette was a 'roll-your-own'.

The anti-tobacco people were never quite so ridiculous in the United Kingdom as they were in the United States, but they were ridiculous enough, and a large body of opinion was convinced that the youth of the day was heralding the decay and

[1] Op. cit., p. 572.

dissolution of their country by reading Penny Dreadfuls and smoking cigarettes.

However, W. D. & H. O. Wills, unaware of the fillip they were giving to youthful depravity, brought out in that dark and sodden autumn of 1888, when Jack the Ripper was so busy, what it is fair to call the most famous cigarette in the world.

In their price list dated November 21st, 1888, Wills announced:

> We would also direct your special attention to the following new cigarettes, viz. *Cinderella*, 5 in a packet, to be retailed at 1*d*. *Wild Woodbine*, 5 in a packet, to be retailed at 1*d*.

Within ten years Woodbines had far outstripped the sales of any other cigarette in this country. Woodbines passed into the language. At Gallipoli the Russian cruiser with five funnels was known as the 'Packet of Woodbines', and there was Woodbine Willie, the famous Army chaplain. To-day Woodbines are still one of the best sellers in the world, but alas, owing to penal taxation they are no longer retailed at 5 for 1*d*.

Another famous Wills brand was introduced in 1893 when Capstan cigarettes, Mild and Medium, were put on the market. During the 1890's Ogden's of Liverpool had had a popular success with their Guinea Gold brand at 3*d*. for 10, and had entered into competition with Woodbines by putting Tabs on the market at 5 for 1*d*.

By now Duke's Cameos and Kinney's Sweet Caporal were competing with Richmond Gems and Straight Cuts No 1 in the British cigarette market, and by their heavy advertising undoubtedly helping to popularize the Virginia cigarette. Women, too, were smoking more and more. In 1887 the *Birmingham Gazette* was reporting:

> The cigarette is becoming painfully popular with the fair sex. A traveller smoking a cigar in a non-smoking railway-train compartment noticed three young ladies enter the carriage, and before he could get in an apology for smoking, each fair damsel produced a dainty case, and, selecting a cigarette, lit up and proceeded to enjoy the same with the utmost composure and sang-froid. The calm audacity of the proceeding showed that the girls, though young, were practised smokers.

Rhoda Broughton's fast young women had been smoking at croquet-parties since the 'sixties, and now in the 'eighties when lawn-tennis was displacing croquet they did not have to be fast to smoke, but I cannot find any reference to women smoking in London restaurants until 1898.

At this point it may be as well to make clear what the position of the Turkish cigarette was during that latter half of the nineteenth century when the cigarette was beginning its steady advance to captivate the smokers of the world.

When cigarettes first reached America they were Turkish; the word is used for all cigarettes from the Levant. During the 1870's and 1880's Egyptian cigarettes established an individual reputation for themselves. Originally Egyptian cigarettes were made from tobacco grown in Egypt, but when, in 1890, the growing of tobacco was prohibited in Egypt, except in two small districts, the tobacco from the Levant was used. The skilful Greek manufacturers, like Melachrino and Vafiades, who exported them, preserved the flat shape and the close packing, and of course they were all hand-made. In 1889 Anagyros began to export cigarettes called Egyptian Deities. Two years later he started manufacturing them in New York, and by 1900 he had built up a large business. However, it was not until after the new century came in that the taste for Turkish cigarettes rapidly developed in the United States. This change of fashion had not been contemplated by the Trust, as the American Tobacco Company was now generally called, and during the first decade the Trust was becoming worried at not controlling the domestic market as completely as they had planned. They set to work hard to buy the businesses of Turkish cigarettes, and began to manufacture pseudo-Turkish cigarettes of their own from blended cheap Virginia and Turkish tobacco, which had a considerable sale.

In the United Kingdom the division between Turkish and Virginia cigarettes was definite. The smoker preferred one or the other; he did not want a blend. However, at the beginning of the century the Virginia cigarette had established its domination over the Turkish, and that domination was to be made absolute by the First World War.

The Egyptian campaign in 1882 is stated by some to have spread cigarette smoking; this is possible. In 1889 the *Saturday Review* was attacking the cigarette as an unmanly way of smoking and warning people against the danger of the habit-forming effects of inhaling, particularly Turkish tobacco, because it was "diluted with foreign and deleterious substances".

When in 1911 the Tobacco Trust was broken up by the decision of the Supreme Court under the Sherman Act, R. J. Reynolds, who had joined the Trust unwillingly, was delighted. "Watch me," he said to Josephus Daniels, "and see if I don't give Buck Duke hell." This threat was carried out with the Camel cigarette.

The R. J. Reynolds Tobacco Company had not made cigarettes before this association with the American Tobacco Company, and therefore under the decree dissolving the Trust they were not awarded any of its many Trust cigarette brands. In the autumn of 1913 the Camel cigarette was introduced at Cleveland, and by 1917 Camel sales were 35 per cent. of the national output; by 1923 they had risen to 45 per cent. The new brand was made of blended Bright Virginia, Turkish and Burley, to which Maryland was added in 1916 for its burning quality.

Camels cost ten cents for a packet of twenty, which cut into the sale of Fatimas, another blended Turkish and Virgina cigarette that cost fifteen cents. Then the manufacturers of Fatimas brought out a Burley-blended cigarette called Chesterfield which had a considerable success, and the American Tobacco Company put its money on Lucky Strike.

Whatever be the cause, in spite of the opportunities which the Second World War gave for American blended cigarettes to become popular, over here they have failed to attract the taste of the British public.

However, when James B. Duke set out to conquer the United Kingdom in 1901 he was armed not with Burley-blended cigarettes but with the menacing powers of the mighty Trust which by now had swallowed up at least a couple of hundred smaller firms in the United States. Duke felt almost jauntily confident that he could conquer the British market.

John K. Winkler [1] says that Duke was worried by the fact that in England "rival manufacturers had induced the British Government to place heavy duties upon manufactured tobacco. As a result the sale of American cigarettes in England had been cut in half in two years." This is one of those reckless statements

[1] *Tobacco Tycoon* (Random House, New York, 1942).

in which American tobaccologues occasionally indulge. The difference between the rates of duty in the United Kingdom on imported manufactured leaf and on imported manufactured tobacco products dated from 1823, long before the Duke invasion.

James B. Duke, with a couple of associates in business, landed in England early in September 1901; none of them had ever been there before. Before the end of the month he had bought Ogdens of Liverpool for something over £800,000, but had failed to buy two other British tobacco businesses.

The British manufacturers moved as fast as the invaders. On September 19th, a day before the Ogden shareholders held a meeting to consider Duke's offer, thirteen of the British firms met at the Queen's Hotel, Birmingham, and expressed themselves in favour of combining to resist the invasion. On October 2nd and 3rd a provisional agreement to pool their resources was reached. By October 30th the Agreement had been ratified and on December 10th, 1901, The Imperial Tobacco Company (of Great Britain and Ireland), Limited, was incorporated and the thirteen businesses became one; they were joined by four more firms in the first half of 1902.

The original thirteen were:

W. D. & H. O. Wills Limited, Bristol.
Lambert & Butler Limited, London.
John Player & Sons Limited, Nottingham.
Edwards, Ringer & Bigg Limited, Bristol.
Hignett Brothers & Company Limited, Liverpool.
Hignett's Tobacco Company Limited, London.
William Clarke & Son Limited, Liverpool.
The Richmond Cavendish Company Limited, Liverpool.
Stephen Mitchell & Son, Glasgow.
D. & J. Macdonald, Glasgow.
F. & J. Smith, Glasgow.
Adkin & Sons, London.
Franklyn, Davey & Co., Bristol.

The others who joined them in 1902 were:

W. A. & A. C. Churchman, Ipswich.
W. T. Davies & Sons, Chester.
W. Williams & Company, Chester.
W. & F. Faulkner Limited, London.
The printing firm of Mardon, Son & Hall Limited, Bristol.

Some of these firms had been in existence for over a century, and traced their histories back to the days when the founders lived with their families over the little shops in which they carried on their trade. The oldest of them all, Stephen Mitchell & Son of Glasgow, had been founded as far back as 1723. The first Chairman of The Imperial Tobacco Company was Sir William Henry Wills, later Lord Winterstoke.

The fact that the British firms were able to close their ranks so rapidly has led American tobaccologues into writing rather contemptuously about their joint action as the result of a panic. Professor J. C. Robert for instance observes [1]:

> Thirteen frightened British manufacturers scurried to merge their resources into one large corporation . . . for the purpose of defending their markets from the Yankee invaders.

They fought very coolly for men in a panic, and they had to fight hard. The invaders lost no time in applying American methods of salesmanship. Five days after the Ogden business had been acquired it was offering a rebate of 3d. per pound on Coolie Cut Plug provided that with every 5 pounds of Coolie the tobacconist ordered 2 pounds of St Julien pipe tobacco in packets. With every 1,000 Guinea Gold or Tabs cigarettes an extra 200 Tabs were to be given free provided Guinea Gold were sold retail at not less than 2½d. for 10 and Tabs at not less than 1d. for 5. This was followed presently by a promise to hand over all the Ogden profits to the trade for a period of four years and the sum of £200,000 per annum over the same period, and the lowering of prices as a bait for the public. The Imperial Tobacco Company replied by an advertising campaign in which the threat to the future of British trade was stressed.

Then in the spring of 1902 the Imperial forces considered the strategic advantage to be gained by a counter-attack on the American market, and a small deputation was sent to the United States to ascertain what chance of success such a venture might have. The prospects were considered favourable, and a special board was summoned for July 1st, 1902, to decide what American businesses should be bought. Mr Samuel Untermeyer, a well-known American lawyer, came over to England to discuss the situation and act for the Imperial Tobacco Company.

[1] *Story of Tobacco in America* (Alfred Knopf, New York).

Duke now faced the prospect of the war's being carried into his own territory; moreover, although he had increased the sales of the Ogden and American brands in the United Kingdom, it was only at enormous cost and his United Kingdom business was showing a considerable loss. He was therefore ready to talk, but as usual when two parties are considering a truce, each is anxious to make it clear that it is the other side which is looking for peace. J. K. Winkler says [1] that T. F. Ryan (second in importance to J. Buchanan Duke in the Trust) received a letter from a nephew of Sir William Wills suggesting that he should come to England and discuss the possibility of ending the war. "Tom, we've got 'em," Duke is reported to have exclaimed with jubilation.

Meanwhile, Imperial Tobacco went ahead, and negotiations were beginning for the expenditure of up to £500,000 in acquiring an American business when in the middle of August T. F. Ryan arrived in London to negotiate terms. Three weeks later he was followed by Duke, and on September 26th, 1902, almost exactly a year after the war started, it came to an end. By the terms of peace the American Tobacco Company was to go back to the United States; the Ogden business was to be transferred to the Imperial Tobacco Company; the Imperial Tobacco Company was to trade only in Great Britain and Ireland; and a new company, the British-American Tobacco Company, was to be formed and registered in England to take over the export trade of both the American Tobacco Company and the Imperial Tobacco Company.

Several great manufacturing businesses did not join the Imperial Tobacco Company. Gallahers of Belfast and Godfrey Phillips, whose B.D.V. (Best Dark Virginian) was one of the most popular brands of pipe tobacco, were among them. So too was Carreras. The latter started business, at 7, Wardour Street, in 1788, and was for many years a fashionable tobacco- and snuff-house. The third Earl of Craven was a patron and after experimenting with the various tobaccos available in the shop he finally produced for himself Craven Mixture some time in the 1870's. After Lord Craven's death in 1883, his mixture was sold to the public under his name. Sir James Barrie discovered Craven Mixture, and sang its praises in *My Lady Nicotine* as Arcadian Mixture. Lord Craven, when he was

[1] *Tobacco Tycoon.*

experimenting at 7, Wardour Street with his blended tobacco, never dreamed that one day he would give his name to a cigarette—the Craven A. There was another rather stronger mixture than Craven, invented by Major-General John Hankey and known as Hankey's Mixture. Then there was Sil Phillips Mixture, originally packed for the personal use of Colonel Sil Phillips, but so much enjoyed by his friends that the Colonel asked Carreras to pack it for sale. There was a third mixture invented by J. Mugge, Esq., which was sold under the discouraging name of Mugge's Mixture.

In 1895 Bernhard Baron arrived in England from the United States and took out a patent for a cigarette-making machine which consisted "in a means, for forming loose tobacco into a rod, for applying the wrapper thereto and pasting the edges of the wrapper together and for cutting the continuous cigarette into suitable lengths". Bernhard Baron was able to sell his machines to various manufacturers who had not been able to use the Bonsack, of which Wills had acquired the sole rights in the United Kingdom. As already mentioned, Player's used a Baron machine.

The formation of the Imperial Tobacco Company was not beneficial to Baron, because independent manufacturers after combining were able to use machinery previously unavailable to them: on top of this was the time expiry of certain patent rights.

In 1903 Bernhard Baron joined the Board of the Carreras Company, and turned his attention to the production of cigarettes as well as the manufacture of machinery. In 1905 he invented a machine with an automatic feeder which did away with hand feeding, and at intervals for the next fifty years further improvements in machinery were made.

In 1909 a machine was adapted to make cartridges of tobacco to be used for filling pipes. These cartridges for pipes which were tried hopefully by the manufacturers were never successful because the bowls of pipes were of so many different sizes, and the efficiency of the cartridge depended upon a standard-sized bowl.

In Scotland the ancient firm of John Cotton remained outside the Imperial Tobacco Company. So did Dobie of Paisley. This firm was founded in 1809 by William Dobie who combined a business in tallow and tallow candles with manufacturing a roll tobacco in several thicknesses of spinning and several kinds of snuff. William Dobie was joined by his nephew, George Dobie, in 1832, and he subsequently acquired the business, which prospered exceedingly. In 1908 J. and T. Hodge, dating back to 1795, joined George Dobie and Son. The firm of Hodge had been the first to introduce cigarette machines to Scotland. Dobie's Four Square pipe-tobacco was followed by Four Square cigarettes, which are particularly popular in Australia. In 1953 Dobie's acquired a controlling interest in Pritchard and Burton, a London firm going back to the early nineteenth century. They produced the famous Boar's Head brand, which was a great favourite in public houses, being sold there in half-ounce packets. When Charlie Chaplin was a boy he was employed in the packing department of Pritchard and Burton weighing out those packets to be fed into the automatic packing machine. Tradition says that his clowning was too much for the foreman; anyway, the embryo comedian was sacked. This must have been in about 1904.

In 1956 the Dobie firm was wound up, and its brands were taken over by the famous old tobacco house of Godfrey Phillips.

Twelve years after the tobacco war came to an end the First World War began. As the war dragged on the stocks of leaf were exhausted and the importance of tobacco was recognized by the Government by granting the importation of shipping facilities and priorities such as were granted for foodstuffs and munitions. At the same time the Government took advantage of the fact that tobacco was a necessity by raising the duty during the war from 3s. 8d. per pound to 8s. 2d.

The same thing happened in the United States. General Pershing cabled to his Government—"Tobacco is as indispensable as the daily ration; we must have thousands of tons of it without delay."

And as in the United Kingdom, it was the cigarette that was now in greatest demand.

One effect of the war was to make the lighter the stock equipment of the cigarette smoker. During the Boer War a superstition had been developed that it was unlucky to light three cigarettes with one match. This had been due to the success of the Boer snipers in taking advantage of a match burning long enough to give them a good aim. In the mud and rain of Flanders matches were still a help to the sniper when they struck, but all too often they did not strike.

It was round about 1905 that an Austrian professor of chemistry, Dr Auer von Welsbach, who had made his name as the inventor of the incandescent gas-mantle, discovered that by fusing certain minerals together he could produce an alloy which gave off sparks when it was rubbed against a rough metal surface. This alloy was called cerium, and it is the basic substance of the lighter flint. The patent for cerium was taken out by the Treibachen factory in Vienna, and here the first cerium lighter was made. There was no wheel and the action was like that of an ordinary match. It was not until 1909 that the first petrol lighter with a wheel action was produced. The wheel was made possible by the invention of a hardened-steel wheel by a workman named Findeisl. In 1911 a semi-automatic lighter was produced by Russbacher, an Austrian engineer. This was a box type, with a lid that sprang open when a side-button was pressed. The Germans took up the manufacture of lighters, a few of which reached England before the First World War. The lighter used by our troops had no petrol: it was a tube with a striker wheel at the top and a length of tinder wick which could be blown into a smouldering glow. It was a perfect medium for lighting cigarette or pipe in the trenches, and it was equally good for lighting in an open car or on deck.

The Ronson art-metal works in America directed by Mr Aronson put their first lighter on the market in 1919. Some years later the Ronson Delight, the first lighter with a simple thumb lever action, was produced and did much to popularize the lighter. In the United Kingdom Beney produced a lighter in 1919, and in 1922 Dunhills produced their first lighter. Both of them were expensive compared with the cheap imported lighters from the Continent. At this date the Excise duty was 1s., but when Mr Winston Churchill was Chancellor of the Exchequer in the Baldwin Government of 1924–9 he lowered the duty on British lighters to 6d., keeping the 1s. duty for foreign lighters. In 1945 Ronson put on the market a lighter that was made in England, and the latest development has been the butane gas lighter. The first of these came from France, but Ronson had been experimenting with butane gas for some time and in 1953 came the Ronson Viking Jet.

To-day it is seldom indeed that one sees anybody light a cigarette with a match. There have been a number of self-lighting cigarettes, but none of them attained popularity. Nobody has yet managed to produce a lighter that will function successfully for a smoker who reveres his pipe.

After the First World War the consumption of cigarettes continued to increase steadily, both here and in the United States.

When the twentieth century arrived, about four-fifths of the tobacco smoked in Britain was consumed in pipes and only one-eighth in cigarettes. To-day over four-fifths of the total tobacco consumption in this country is in cigarettes.

Chapter 18

THE United Kingdom's principal sources of supply of leaf tobacco (excluding cigar leaf and Oriental tobaccos) are the U.S.A., Canada, the Federation of Rhodesia and Nyasaland, and India. Cigar tobaccos come mainly from Cuba, Sumatra, Brazil, North Borneo and Jamaica. Turkey and Greece supply most of the Oriental-type leaf.

At the beginning of the present century we were virtually dependent on the U.S.A. for supplies of leaf tobacco apart from the cigar and Oriental types. To-day nearly half of the tobacco used in this country comes from within the Commonwealth, and the development of the Commonwealth sources of supply has been one of the major achievements in the modern history of tobacco. The event of outstanding importance in this development was the introduction in 1919, following the Ottawa Conference, of Imperial Preference, under which a lower rate of duty was paid on Empire tobacco. Yet a long time before there was any preferential rate of duty tobacco-growing was being developed in Nyasaland. In 1893 one of the early pioneers introduced Virginian seed into the country and made a trial export of the crop. Progress was slow at first, and by 1900 exports amounted to only 5,000 pounds. In the next seven years production was increased to 500,000 pounds. Impetus was given to the development when in 1908 the Imperial Tobacco Company established a leaf-buying organization and erected its own leaf-handling and packing factory at Limbe, Nyasaland. By 1913 the crop had reached 3,750,000 pounds. At that time almost all the tobacco produced in Nyasaland was of the flue-cured type, and it was used in the United Kingdom mainly in flakes and plugs. From 1922 onwards, however, more interest was shown in Nyasaland fire-cured tobacco, and this is now the main type produced there. To-day Nyasaland supplies most of the fire-cured leaf used in the United Kingdom, in addition to some Burley, sun-cured and flue-cured leaf.

The Rhodesias, Nyasaland's other partners in the Federation, produce mainly flue-cured leaf. The commercial growing of tobacco there began in 1911. By 1914 production had risen from half a million to just over three million pounds a year. It fell away during the 1914-18 war years to about half a million pounds, but then rose again to just over the pre-war level. In the early days, the principal market was the Union of South Africa. The introduction of Imperial Preference in 1919 and the Empire Exhibition at Wembley in 1924 stimulated interest in Rhodesian tobacco in the United Kingdom. In 1926 production in Southern Rhodesia had reached $5\frac{1}{4}$ million pounds. Too rapid expansion based on too optimistic forecasts of the prospects led to over-production in 1927 and 1928, and a slump followed. There was a gradual recovery, and in the years immediately preceding the Second World War the annual production was in the region of 20 to 25 million pounds. In 1946 there was a crop of more than 40 million pounds, and the value of Southern Rhodesia's tobacco exports exceeded that of her gold exports for the first time. The need to limit dollar expenditure called for increased production, and by 1956 the total production of flue-cured leaf in the Rhodesias had reached 170 million pounds. Rhodesia is now the United Kingdom's largest sterling-area source of tobacco supply, and Salisbury, where the whole of the crop is sold, is the biggest tobacco market in the world; in the U.S.A. the tobacco sales are spread over many marketing centres.

India, where tobacco has been grown from about the end of the sixteenth century, is the third largest tobacco-producing country in the world, but most of the production is in the types of leaf used domestically and not suitable for the British market. In the last thirty years, however, the production of flue-cured tobacco has been successfully developed in India, mainly in Central Andhra, which was formerly part of the Province of Madras, and this has made a valuable contribution to India's export trade. India's total leaf-tobacco exports now range between 70 million and 100 million pounds a year, of which the United Kingdom takes about a third, mainly in flue-cured leaf.

Canada produces high-quality flue-cured leaf as well as Burley and other types, and is one of our most important sources of tobacco supply. But Canada, although a Commonwealth source of supply, is also a dollar country. Consequently, since the Second World War the amount of Canadian leaf we have been able to buy has been limited by restrictions on dollar expenditure. Canada's main tobacco-growing Provinces are

Ontario and Quebec, but British Columbia grows a small
quantity. The history of tobacco-growing in Canada goes back
400 years, some of the growers in Quebec being descendants of
early French colonists whose land has been handed down to
them through successive generations. But it was not until
comparatively recently that Canada achieved importance in
the World Tobacco Trade. The development of the Canadian
tobacco-growing industry since the First World War has been
remarkable. In 1920 less than a third of the tobacco consumed
in Canada was manufactured from home-grown leaf. Production at that time was mainly in Burley and fire-cured types.
The abolition in 1922 of the Canadian Excise tax on domestic
leaf, while imported leaf continued to be highly taxed, encouraged domestic production, and the introduction of
Imperial Preference, especially after the increase in the
Preference in 1925, stimulated interest in Canadian leaf in the
United Kingdom. This led to an expansion in flue-cured production, which was soundly developed. In 1927 the total
quantity of flue-cured leaf produced in Canada was just over
6 million pounds. Since then it has been increased to 170
million pounds. Canada can now supply all her own needs, and
in addition produce substantial quantities for export.

A comprehensive account of the cultivation of tobacco is
beyond the scope of this work, but a brief and necessarily
superficial account is owed.

The very fine seed of *Nicotiana tabacum* is sown in a sheltered
bed with a southern aspect in late winter or early spring
according to the climatic conditions. The soil should be friable
and sharply drained, and the seed-bed is sterilized either by
burning brushwood or by steaming the soil. When the seeds
have been sown, the bed is covered with cheese-cloth as a
protection against the weather.

The seedlings are ready to be transplanted when they are
four or five inches high with four to six leaves. When lifted,
the strongest of the young plants are put into baskets and
carried to the fields, where great care is taken to keep them
cool and moist.

During the winter the land to be planted is heavily ploughed
to allow the frost to get at the various enemy insects. Before

the seedlings are transplanted, the soil is broken up by repeated harrowings because the fragile roots of the tobacco, fine as hairs, dislike heavy and lumpy ground.

The seedlings are planted out at intervals of twenty to twenty-four inches in rows about three feet apart, and as they dislike too much water they are planted on ridges so that surface water will drain away quickly.

It is considered important for the growth of the young plants that as soon as they have taken root, a week or so after transplanting, careful hoeing should encourage a quick start. Now comes an anxious time for the planter, who has to watch his crop and protect it from the ravages of insects and disease.

Nicotiana tabacum is a very rapid grower, and about two months after planting flower-buds show themselves. These, together with the top leaves are 'topped', that is, pinched off to improve the quality of the remaining leaves—usually from sixteen to twenty-five in number. The lower the plant is topped the thicker and heavier will be the leaves produced. About a week or ten days after topping, the plant will throw out small shoots in the axil of the leaf and stalk; these must be removed when about three or four inches long, a process known as 'suckering'.

There are two methods of harvesting. The one much more usually followed is called 'priming', which means that the leaves are picked two or three at a time as they ripen. This involves going over the field several times before the harvest is finished. The gathered leaves are 'strung' on sticks and taken to the curing barn.

The other method of harvesting is to cut down the whole plant. The stalks are pierced near the bottom, and the whole plants are threaded on to laths, which are then conveyed to the curing barns. This method produces a tobacco with more 'body' than 'primed' leaf because much of the 'nature' contained in the stalk goes into the leaf during curing.

When the tobacco is thoroughly cured the planter opens the doors of the curing barns so that the leaves may absorb the moisture in the atmosphere naturally and become soft enough to be handled without breaking. The leaves are then carefully sorted into four or five different grades, according to their colour, quality and length, after which they are tied in bundles of about thirty leaves each and are ready for sale.

In the United States, Rhodesia and Nyasaland tobacco is sold by auction, the leaf being brought to the sales warehouse by the growers and laid out in rows of baskets or bales on the floor. The auctioneer and his assistant pass down one side of a row, the buyers down the other. The bidding goes on with what seems bewildering speed to the layman, as many as 400 baskets being sold in an hour, each of which contains on an average about 150 pounds of tobacco. I was once given an imitation of a tobacco auction by a Rhodesian planter on holiday in the Seychelles and I use the epithet 'bewildering' deliberately.

The auction system of selling tobacco does not operate in Canada, where most types of tobacco are bought direct from the farmer who sells his entire crop to one buyer.

From the sales warehouse the tobacco goes to a leaf-packing plant, where it is closely examined and the original grading by the buyers confirmed. In the case of stemmed tobacco, the stems and midribs of the leaves are removed by machinery or by hand. This operation must be carried on in a humid atmosphere; otherwise the tobacco becomes 'chippy' and easily broken. The 'soft' tobacco is now passed through automatic drying machines to remove the excess moisture. The leaves are then packed into casks, about 885 pounds to each cask, in which a hydraulic ram compresses them tightly together into a compact, solid mass which will travel without damage and in which the leaves can mature evenly. Finally the casks are marked with grade, weight, etc., and are taken to the seaport ready for shipment to the United Kingdom. When the leaf arrives it is deposited in bonded warehouses where, under the supervision of the Customs and Excise authorities, it is kept until required for use. There are bonded warehouses at all the principal tobacco ports, including Bristol, Glasgow, Liverpool, Manchester and London. The largest of them can store up to 70,000 casks, each of over 1,000 pounds gross weight. One can say that about two hundred million pounds of potential revenue can be stored in one of these bonded warehouses which are administered under a code of rules and regulations that make ordinary red tape look a very pale pink. The duty is paid when the tobacco is withdrawn from bond. The casks of African tobacco are usually smaller than the American, and contain from 725 to 830 pounds. Casks of tobacco are also known as hogsheads and tierces, the hogshead containing 900 pounds or more, the tierce less than 900 pounds. Cigar and Turkish leaf is packed in bales usually weighing approximately 120 pounds.

Normally a reserve of two to three years' stock is stored in bond, but stocks were seriously depleted during the Second World War, and it has not yet been possible to build them up to the pre-war level.

Once upon a time, duty on British Plantation or American tobacco (which can be regarded as the main rate of duty) used to be 1s. 3d. per pound. As a result of the heavy financial drain of the Napoleonic wars, it was progressively increased to 4s. per pound which was the rate in force from June 1819 until July 1825. It was then reduced to 3s. per pound.

Before this, in 1823, an important duty change had been made. From 1790 manufactured tobacco and cigars had been subject to the same rates of duty as unmanufactured tobacco. To help the home manufacturers the Government changed this and imposed a higher duty on the manufactured imports. This principle has been maintained.

In 1826 the previous practice of classifying leaf tobacco for duty purposes as either "British Plantation or American" or "Spanish or Portuguese" was changed, the new classifications being "From British Plantations in America" and "From other parts". In 1842 the dual classification was dropped and the same rate of duty applied to all unmanufactured tobacco.

In 1863 a duty distinction was made between leaf tobacco containing 10 per cent. or more of moisture on importation and leaf with a moisture content of less than 10 per cent., a higher rate of duty being applied to imported leaf containing less than 10 per cent. of moisture. This distinction is still in force. The lower of these two duty rates on unmanufactured leaf is the one usually quoted because this now generally applies.

In 1878 the Beaconsfield Administration, looking for money to finance the vote of credit called for by the Russo-Turkish War, increased the import duty on tobacco by 4d. a pound to 3s. 6d. Some retailers charged 3¼d. for an ounce of shag and thereby upset the working-man who refused to pay the extra farthing; moreover, it called for a large issue of farthings. So the retailers insisted that the manufacturers should supply them at the old price and pay the whole of the extra duty themselves. It was not surprising that some manufacturers bought inferior leaf and used a good deal of water. Until then no limit had been laid down for the amount of water that might be added to tobacco during manufacture, with the result that there was a heavy demand for inferior leaf capable of absorbing a great deal of moisture. Java, which could absorb 50 per cent. of water, was the favourite, and the Revenue suffered. So too did the reputable manufacturers, who agitated continuously for the 4d. added to the duty to be taken off. The Government refused to listen, and it was not until the Goschen Budget of 1887 that the "obnoxious 4d." was surrendered. The Chancellor of the Exchequer, with a rare candour, admitted that the 4d. had been a mistake.

When we reflect what we are paying to-day for our tobacco, it seems like an old fairy-tale to hear that a mere extra 4d. had burdened the trade, had produced a debased product and had decreased the consumption of tobacco per head. The Chancellor was anxious to guarantee that the working-man should benefit from the reduction of the duty by getting better value in tobacco for his money.

This is how he proposed to do it, to quote from his Budget speech:

The natural moisture of tobacco is from 15 to 17 per cent., and it is increased to 30 per cent. in process of manufacture. But now it is often sold containing 40 or 45 per cent. of water. In future we intend to make it illegal to sell tobacco containing more than 35 per cent. of water.

And then once more like a voice from fairyland came the Chancellor's hope "as in the case of beer, for an increased yield of duty, because more tobacco would be smoked".

In 1898 Sir Michael Hicks-Beach lowered the moisture limit from 35 per cent. to 30 per cent., which led to bitter complaints from smokers about their tobacco being too dry and therefore burning too quickly. However, by now the cigarette was making such rapid strides in overtaking every other method of consuming tobacco that the question of moisture content was less acute. Moreover, Hicks-Beach lowered the duty from 3s. 2d. to 2s. 8d. The advent of the Boer War destroyed that blessed alleviation. In 1900 the "obnoxious 4d." was reimposed, making the duty 3s. a pound.

In 1904 Austen Chamberlain as Chancellor raised the limit

of moisture to 32 per cent., at which it stands to-day. Yet from
the point of view of the trade some of the benefit of this was
cancelled by raising the duty by 3*d.* a pound on imported
stripped tobacco; that is to say, with the midrib of the leaf
removed. The rate of duty to-day on stripped leaf is a halfpenny a pound higher than on unstripped leaf. Owing to the
supremacy of the cigarette and the swing to milder tobaccos
with lower moisture content than the shags and rolls of the
last century, most of the tobacco consumed by the public nowadays contains much less moisture than the statutory amount.

The duty on tobacco remained at 3*s.* until the Lloyd George
Budget of 1909 when it was increased to 3*s.* 8*d.* This seems
trivial to-day, but at the time it was a severe blow to the tobacco
trade because it drove many people to give up the slightly
more expensive brands and make the best of the cheaper ones.
Manufacturers who had spent large sums on the advertising of
those brands were compelled to pay that extra halfpenny an
ounce themselves so that the retail price should not be raised.

The First World War gave Chancellors of the Exchequer a
chance to see how much the public would stand for in the
taxation of tobacco, and in September 1915 the duty was
raised by 1*s.* 10*d.* per pound. Encouraged by the patriotic
acceptance of this Mr Bonar Law in his Budget of May 1917
put on another 1*s.* 10*d.*, making the tax 7*s.* 4*d.* a pound. This
caused such a rumpus that in July Bonar Law halved the
increase, and until April 1918 the tax was 6*s.* 5*d.* On May 31st,
1917, the Board of Trade made an order under the Defence of
the Realm Act to control all the stocks of manufactured and
unmanufactured tobacco and prohibit the owners from dealing
with them except as authorized by the newly constituted
Tobacco Control Board, which was allowed an advisory
committee formed from members of the tobacco trade. By the
Tobacco Restriction Order the Control Board was empowered
to dispose of all the tobacco in the United Kingdom and to
fix the price of it at every stage. The owners of tobacco leaf
lying in bond were ordered to make a return of their stocks in
nine days, and rationing of supplies began on the basis of "not
exceeding the deliveries of 1916".

In April 1918 the Government increased the duty to 8*s.* 2*d.*
per pound, at which figure it remained until 1927.

The Imperial Preferential rate of duty was introduced on

September 1st, 1919. The rate of duty for Empire-grown tobacco was reduced to five-sixths of the import duty for American tobacco, and in 1925 this was still further reduced to three-quarters, which meant that the duty on Empire tobaccos was 2s. 0½d. per pound less than on American tobacco. The preference was stabilised at 2s. 0½d., in spite of increases in the standard rate of duty, until 1943, when it was reduced to 1s. 6½d., at which it still remains (1956).

To return to the standard rate of duty. In 1927 it was increased from 8s. 2d. to 8s. 10d., and in 1931 it was raised again to 9s. 6d., at which figure it remained until April 1939, since when, with the exception of two years, it has risen at first steadily and then after the Second World War by leaps and bounds.

Here is the hurdle-track:

U.K. standard rate of duty on unmanufactured tobacco per lb.

1931 to April 1939	.	.	.	9s.	6d.
April to September 1939	.	.	.	11s.	6d.
September 1939 to April 1940	.	.	13s.	6d.
April to July 1940	.	.	.	17s.	6d.
July 1940 to April 1942	.	.	.	19s.	6d.
April 1942 to April 1943	.	.	.	29s.	6d.
April 1943 to April 1947	.	.	.	35s.	6d.
April 1947 to April 1948	.	.	.	54s.	10d.
April 1948 to April 1956	.	.	.	58s.	2d.
April 1956	.	.	.	.	61s.	2d.

The U.K. Government's net revenue from the Tobacco Customs and Excise duties in the year ended March 31st, 1956, was £668 million.

One of the aims of Christopher Columbus was to discover gold: he was unconsciously successful, and one may hope that in Elysium he is gratified by the figures recorded above.

Chapter 19

MY last chapter shall be a patchwork-quilt pieced together from odds and ends of information which have been gathered about tobacco in America, Asia, Africa and Australasia.

Mexico, which might reasonably claim to be the original home of the cigarette, is to-day rather ashamed of the "crimped and corn-shuck" kinds which were the staple until after the Second World War. Mexico now prefers the Bright North American type of tobacco wrapped in paper, although one Mexican informant believes that the paper cigarette was invented by "the ill-famed English pirate Sir Francis Drake (!)". As the result of the Mexicans turning against their own dark tobacco, they were invaded by North American cigarettes and leaf. To quote from the informant mentioned above:

An energetic measure was therefore indispensable in order to acclimatize these types of bright tobacco in Mexico . . . the cigarette industry made experiments in the different regions of the country, and finally succeeded . . . this led to the displacement of American cigarettes and leaf tobacco for the market, to such an extent that at the present time their importation is practically nil.

It is proudly proclaimed that

among all Mexican industries the cigarette industry is the one that has reached a higher grade of modernization and organization; that due to the nobleness of the product this industry has been able to uphold its position better than others during critical periods; and that at the same time as it has continued improving the quality and appearance of the product the price of same to the public has been much reduced, thus increasing the demand for the product and, consequently, fiscal revenue.

From Mexico to Brazil. According to a Brazilian informant many women now smoke in Brazil, although "only a few years ago smoking by women was considered extremely bold and brazen".

For years Brazil was one of the largest exporters of tobacco.

In 1886 the State of Salvador alone exported 22,500 tons. This tobacco was mainly for the manufacture of cigars in the State of Bahia, where twelve factories were in active operation. To-day the quantity of Brazilian tobacco exported is "a mere trickle in comparison", and it is the cigarette industry which dominates the market.

The first cigarette factory in Brazil was started about 1880, but even as late as 1911, 17 million packages were the sum total manufactured. The great majority of smokers in Brazil rolled their own cigarettes from dark cord-tobacco. Even to-day many agricultural workers prefer to whittle their pieces of cord-tobacco and roll the flakes in a straw. However, the machine-made cigarette went as fast ahead in Brazil during the First World War as everywhere else. By 1938, 786 million packages were being consumed; to-day that figure has been almost trebled.

To quote that Brazilian informant:

> Tobacco in Brazil is a tremendous business. It incorporates and brings benefits to the farmer who is planting more and more tobacco—to the factories who collect the leaf and prepare it for the manufacture of millions of cigarettes a day —to the enormous printing establishments—to the paper factories . . . all these have come into being through men's desire to indulge in the pleasant and relaxing pastime of smoking, and all make their considerable contribution to the Federal Government Revenue which, in turn, uses this to better the facilities offered to the people of Brazil.

Honduras has more claim than any country to be hailed as the original place where the virtue of *Nicotiana tabacum* was apprehended. Here was the centre of the lost Mayan civilization, whose sculptures and reliefs recovered from the jungle are the first representations that exist of smoking man. To this day the Copán area of Honduras, in which was the very heart of that Mayan culture, produces most of that country's tobacco. Here in the valleys you may still see a three-year-old child puffing away at a cigar; here women of all ages still smoke cigars. Honesty compels me to exclaim 'alas!' as I set down on record that the custom of smoking cigars is rapidly disappearing before the overwhelming advance of the factory-made cigarette.

The cultivation of tobacco in Guatemala was developed by the Spaniards in the seventeenth century, and by the end of the eighteenth century the economy of the country was largely dependent on tobacco. After the Central American States broke away from Spain, a war started within the new Union over the control of the tobacco-producing zones—Santa Rosa de Copán in Honduras, Gracias a Dios in Honduras and Chiquimala in Guatemala. Later on coffee took the place of tobacco to a great extent. To-day Guatemala does not export tobacco, but produces 90 per cent. of its own consumption.

In Brazil the Portuguese missionaries, particularly the Jesuits, were for a long time hostile to tobacco, and indeed invoked the help of the Inquisition to deal with rich white colonists who persisted in smoking. In Central America the Dominicans, who were in charge of the Holy Office, were nevertheless more tolerant of tobacco.

Fray Francisco Jiménez wrote of *picietl* as tobacco was called by the natives of Central America:

It makes labour easier, it cures fainting fits, drives away death, promotes sleep, relieves pain, cures colds, and appears to bring about a certain light-headedness.

In Costa Rica the earliest recorded date of tobacco cultivation is 1529. This was a black, thick and strong variety called *chircagre*, the leaves of which were rolled up into large cigars and tied with sisal fibre.

There is no record of pipes being smoked by the natives of Central America except in Panama, where the residue that forms in the bottom of them is used to check the decay of teeth, and also to remove ticks and chigoes. Anybody who has experienced the sensation of a chigoe or jigger burrowing in his toe will hope that the pipe was foul enough to be immediately effective.

A curious habit used to prevail among the older women of Panama, which was smoking their hand-rolled cigars with the lighted ends inside their mouths. Nowadays this practice is rapidly dying out, but we shall hear of it again in Central Africa. It is also known in Venezuela.

An Indian tribe, the Chibchas, had been settled in Colombia long before the arrival of the Spanish Conquistadores. Their agriculture was of a high standard, and these Chibchas were apparently the first to plant tobacco in Venezuela. This tribe had been growing corn, cotton, potatoes, tobacco and other crops in the Andes mountains from time immemorial, and they had developed a system of terraces to avoid erosion. The Spaniards called these terraces *andenes*, which means a bridle-path, and from these *andenes* came the name Andes for the whole mighty range of mountains. The Chibchas made a type of chewing tobacco which is still used to-day and is still called by its original name *el chimó*. The inhabitants of Sagunillas, a town in the modern State of Mérida, made a speciality of *el chimó*, which at one time had as big a reputation as a stimulant as the *coco* of the Peruvians.

The Spanish colonists went in for an intensive cultivation of tobacco, and about the middle of the sixteenth century the first tobacco was exported to Europe from the plantations of Varinas, the quality of which soon became famous and the re-nown of which lasted for a very long time. Readers may recall the allusions to it in earlier chapters. As the export of tobacco from Venezuela increased during the seventeenth century, contraband kept pace with that increase. Tobacco plantations multiplied all over the extensive coastal regions and thrived on the growing and handling of contraband tobacco. The Spanish authorities, anxious about their exports from Cuba, took the extreme step of prohibiting tobacco-growing in Venezuela. The Captain-General, Mexia de Godoy, soon realized the mistake of such a drastic ban and authorized the planting of tobacco again on condition that the planters gave a bond as a guarantee that their crops would not be used for illegal trading. The exportation of tobacco increased throughout the seventeenth century until it was second only to cocoa. The chief markets for Venezuelan tobacco and cocoa in Europe were in Flanders.

Contraband trading did not stop, and at last in an attempt to check this a monopoly was created by which the commercial handling of all tobacco was placed in the hands of an enterprise known as the *Compania Guipzcoana*. By the end of the Spanish Colonial period, Venezuela was exporting to Spain over two million pounds of tobacco annually.

In 1777 a Royal Decree proclaimed a monopoly by which the Spanish Government controlled the planting, cultivation and distribution of all tobacco. Contraband, however, went on, one of the chief reasons being the taxes levied on interstate movements of tobacco. A tax was imposed on Varinas tobacco

when it was transported out of the state, and it was taxed
again when it entered the neighbouring state of Mérida.
Guard-posts were set up along all roads and from these soldiers
searched the mule trains and collected the dues.

By the time that Venezuelan independence was declared in
1811, tobacco had become a leading crop in other countries;
gradually Venezuelan tobacco began to lose its popularity in
the European markets, until finally only enough was grown for
home consumption.

Native black tobacco for the manufacture of cigars and
cigarettes was used exclusively until about 1938. Then one of
the largest local manufacturers of cigarettes began to experiment with seed imported from Canada. By 1943 enough of this
Bright leaf had been gathered and matured to start experimenting with the local manufacture of a Bright cigarette. The
smoking public took to this cigarette with enthusiasm, and
large-scale planting with imported seed was immediately
undertaken. To-day less than 10 per cent. of the cigarettes
manufactured in Venezuela are made with native (black) leaf.
The native leaf is used for cigars, but the trade in cigars has
declined steadily during the last few years, and in the words of
my Venezuelan informant "it is the general belief that as the
population becomes more educated people are turning from
native tobacco cigarettes and cigars to Bright leaf cigarettes".

Tobacco seems to have been planted first in Chile round about
the end of the seventeenth century, the variety of *Nicotiana
tabacum* being of the type grown in Paraguay. It was dried in the
open fields, and then granulated by driving horses round and
round over the dried leaves. Smokers rolled their own cigarettes
which were wrapped as elsewhere all over Latin-America in
corn-shucks. Later, little factories produced hand-rolled
'tucked-in-end' cigarettes, which were either wrapped in
corn-shucks or in a yellow wheat-straw paper imported from
Spain. According to a Chilean informant, machine-equipped
factories started at the beginning of this century, and as everywhere else the cigarettes of darker granulated tobacco are
rapidly disappearing.

The introduction of tobacco into China has been mentioned
in an earlier chapter. It was planted most freely in the province

of Fukien, where the famous Silk Cut was developed. This is of extraordinarily fine cut, soft as silk, bright in colour and very mild and fragrant. It was smoked by the upper classes in water-pipes made of silver, brass or zinc. A visitor would be offered one of these pipes to smoke after tea had been served. At home the older members and the young women of the well-to-do families were served with water-pipes by servants, who filled them with tobacco, lighted them with a paper spill and removed the ashes when the pipes had been smoked. It was the custom for women to be attended at the theatre or in their sedan-chairs by servants with water-pipes in order to show their social importance.

Another kind of pipe was the long bamboo, which was smoked by old men; this was long enough to be used as a walking-stick. The short bamboo pipe was used by agricultural labourers and farmers. The latter favoured bamboo water-pipes when they were resting after work. These pipes were kept for any-body's use in villages, but the smoker had to provide his own tobacco. Cigarettes were also smoked. They were hand-rolled in a shape like a narrow funnel, the pointed end being in the mouth. Even to-day, when the machine-made cigarette is supreme, many of the poorer classes smoke these pointed cigarettes as an economy.

The most highly esteemed pipe tobacco after the Silk Cut was the Yellow. This was young leaf raw cut and fire-cured; it was then mixed with pea-nut oil and red lead powder. Snuff enjoyed considerable popularity at one time, and the Chinese snuff bottles are much prized by connoisseurs.

Formerly the tobacco grown in North China resembled the American Bright; the tobacco of Central and Southern China was dark brown. Whatever their appearance, all these tobaccos were of very poor quality.

However, American experts thought that if good seed and skilled methods of growing and curing could be introduced, North China might produce tobacco as suitable for cigarettes as Bright and Burley. So in 1908 Chinese farmers were supplied with good seed from America, free of charge, to make the experiment. The result was so promising that a number of expert growers came over from the United States to teach up-to-date methods of cultivation and curing. During the Second World War even better tobacco from American seed was grown in Yunnan, at an altitude of over 5,000 feet, and this fetched a higher price than tobacco grown in any of the other provinces.

When the South Chinese began to emigrate in numbers to Malaya they brought with them the recipe for *Ang-hoon*, which became very popular.

Here is the recipe:

For 100 katties of dry tobacco leaf, use

Caraway seeds large	2	tahils
Caraway seeds small	2	,,
Bunga Pelaga (cardamom)	2	,,
Cloves	1	,,
Banksia rose petals	1	,,
Liquorice	4	,,
Cinnamon	4	,,
Orange peel, dry	2	,,

These ingredients are all boiled down to a liquid mixture of about 8 gallons, to which *samsu* (a liquor brewed from rice) is added. Groundnut-oil is used to make the mixture oily. Experiments with coconut-oil as a substitute proved unsuccessful because it affected the flavour. Then the mixture is dyed with red ochre because, for the Chinese, red is the colour of prosperity. The melon-seeds served at Chinese lunches are dyed red. *Ang-hoon* is still smoked, but it is fighting a losing battle with the machine-made cigarette.

The method of smoking *Ang-hoon*, at any rate in Indonesia, is to insert in the bowl one pellet equal in weight to a quarter of an ordinary cigarette, and after lighting it with a taper to inhale one puff. Then a couple more pellets will be puffed, after which the water-pipe will be handed on to another smoker.

In Java the local cigarette industry produces two types of cigarettes, both of which are known as *kreteks*. For these the tobacco is mixed with cloves in the proportion of three parts clove to ten parts tobacco. These cloves, specially imported from Zanzibar, are soaked in water for six hours, dried in the sun and then cut into very small pieces before being added to the tobacco. The mixture is then rolled by hand into the tough outer leaf of the maize cob and tied with fine string. In the other type the mixture is made up in cigarette paper. The name *kretek* is derived from the crackling noise of the burning cloves. As an economy, the experiment was made of soaking the tobacco in an infusion of clove leaves; but this did not make the admired crackling, and when the noise was imitated by adding small bits of dried noodles the taste of them spoiled the smoke. Other spices are sometimes used, but the clove is by far the most esteemed.

Chewing was for a long time the chief medium for tobacco in Java. A wad was taken immediately after chewing betel-nut, and in Bali was believed to clean the teeth. Chewing tobacco has gradually been displaced by what the people call 'white cigarettes' during this century, and since the Second World War the women and girls of Java have taken to smoking cigarettes, which was unheard of before that.

The Jaffna cheroots of Ceylon have long been much esteemed.

I knew a Dutch gentleman, [wrote J. W. Bennett] [1] a connoisseur in Tobacco, to whom several boxes of the best Havannah cigars had been presented, offer them to an officer of the medical staff for one basket of Jaffna cheroots, the price of which in the market would have been about 3 shillings or less "for [said he] in all the world there is no tobacco like that of Jaffna" and it is so much esteemed above the produce of Malabar that the Rajah of Travancore . . . contracted with the Government of Ceylon for all tobacco grown in the province for purposes of exportation. This was locally called the "Travancore investment" and the Rajah was enabled by the high price he charged for tobacco to pay a subsidy to the Government of Madras for the maintenance of a body of native troops under the command of an officer of the army of that presidency in Travancore.

A century later Miss Elsie E. Cook could write:

Tobacco cultivation in the Jaffna Peninsula is carried on with great skill, the soil being somewhat poor, and exceedingly dry for the greater part of the year . . . after December artificial watering is necessary. . . . This involves an immense amount of labour as the watering is done by hand . . . from wells. . . . After fermentation the tobacco is smoked over a slow-burning fire of coconut husks and palmyra nuts. It is then made up into the well-known Jaffna cheroot. [2]

I regret that I have not had an opportunity to smoke a Jaffna

---

[1] *Ceylon and Its Capabilities* (1843).
[2] *Ceylon. Its Geography, its Resources and its People.*

cheroot in Ceylon; it would have been interesting to compare it with the Burma cheroot smoked in its own country.

Information about tobacco in Burma has been elusive. Nobody knows when or how tobacco reached Burma. There is no resemblance between Indian and Burmese tobacco to-day, but that does not exclude the possibility of its having reached Burma from India. The astonishingly protean nature of *Nicotiana tabacum* makes its behaviour as unpredictable as the vine. Nevertheless, it is just as likely to have reached Burma from the Philippines, or from China, or from the Dutch East Indies. Only in Shwegyin, in northern Burma, is the tobacco similar in colour to Virginian leaf; everywhere else it is dark.

Plug is extensively chewed, mostly by the yellow-robed Buddhist priests or *hpongyis*, old men and old women. Buddhism, which disapproves of alcohol, regards tobacco with benignity. In the holy places one walks discalced, but one does not take one's cheroot out of one's mouth.

The water-pipe of Malaya, Indonesia and northern Vietnam is not used in Burma. Where tobacco is smoked in the pipe, which is usually made of bamboo with a curved mouthpiece, its shape resembles that of a European or American smoker. Pipes are usually smoked only by men, but in remote places women may be seen smoking them.

The cheroot made entirely of tobacco leaf, or *sai-byin-leik*, which we Westerners associate with Burma, is not smoked by the humbler classes. Their smoke is the *sai-baw-leik* of which there are two types, the only difference being the material used for wrapping the tobacco contents. The townsfolk generally use a tobacco leaf known as *shan-phet*, while the country folk use the leaf cover of the Indian corncob. The *shan-phet sai-baw-leik* is dark, cylindrical and of uniform thickness throughout, and indeed resembles an untidily made Burma cheroot as known to the West. The *pyaung-phet* (literally 'leaf of corn') *sai-baw-leik* is cream-coloured, smaller in diameter at the smoking end, and at least three times as wide at the lighted end. The content of the corncob leaf is generally chopped tobacco-stalk flavoured with tamarind and molasses. The *pyaung-phet sai-baw-leik* is the characteristic smoke of the women, and they will hand it round for their children to puff at in turn when they are watching one of those plays which go on all night. We may remember Kipling's Burma maid, "An' I seed her first a-smokin' of a whackin' white cheroot." I am not easily baffled by a smoke, but I must confess that I was baffled by a *pyaung-phet sai-baw-leik*. A powerful intake of breath is required. How children of three or four manage to get a puff is a puzzle.

Machine-made cigarettes are much enjoyed, but at present they are too expensive except for the well-to-do Burmans; no doubt they will conquer Burma as they have conquered every other country. That will be a pity, because nowhere except in Cuba and a little bit of Louisiana can the devotee of tobacco in its noble strength feel himself in such accord with his fellow-smokers, and it can safely be claimed that the peculiar charm of the Burman owes much to his being an inveterate smoker from early childhood to old age.

Yet in emphasizing the important part that tobacco has played in Burma, the equally important part it has played in India must not be forgotten. "Show me the man who can live without either chewing or smoking tobacco" is a popular saying in Bihar. In an earlier chapter some of the tribulations through which tobacco had to pass before it was recognized and accepted as a boon to humanity were mentioned. The honour of introducing it was attributed to the Portuguese towards the end of the sixteenth century, but further research has brought to my notice a Persian treatise, *Dara Shikohi*, which puts the date as early as 1505, and Watt, who in an earlier book (1891) gave 1605 as the date, says in his *Commercial Products of India* (1908) that it was 1508. The rapidity with which the cultivation of tobacco and the rich folklore about it spread all over India suggests that smoking had existed from time immemorial. Certainly a Sanskrit medical treatise of the first century A.D.— the *Charaka*—has much to say about the therapeutic value of smoking. So does the *Susruta* of the fourth century. This is not to accept the argument put forward by some writers that tobacco was indigenous in Asia. It was its arrival in the shape of *Nicotiana rustica* that was hailed as the perfect foundation for the mixture of spices and leaves that were already being smoked in India. *N. tabacum* arrived later. The earliest efforts to improve the quality of Indian tobacco began towards the end of the eighteenth century. Colonel Kyd's letter to the Court of Directors of the East India Company in 1776, proposing the institution of the Botanic Gardens in Calcutta, expressly mentioned tobacco as one of the plants for profitable improvement. The first seed from the United States used in experiments of which there is record came from Maryland and Virginia in 1829, and the tobacco grown from it was pronounced by dealers and manufacturers to be the best so far imported from India. Seed from Chios tobacco was sown in 1866; in 1892 further experiments with Maryland and Virginia seeds were made under the guidance of Captain Basil Hall, but it was not until 1904 that the real improvement came.

The latest figures for home consumption from April 1954 to March 1955 showed that of the total manufactured products 26 per cent. was smoked in the *hookah*, particularly in Uttar Pradesh West Bengal, East Punjab and Bihar; 25 per cent. chewed, the consumers being almost all in the south; 26 per cent. in *biris*,[1] all over India; cigars and cheroots, 10 per cent.; cigarettes, 12 per cent.; snuff, 1 per cent.

The British in India started to smoke the hookah, an elaborate hubble-bubble, early in the eighteenth century, and by the middle of it the habit was general, the women smoking as well as the men. Grandpré wrote that the highest favour a lady could confer on a gentleman was to smoke his hookah. And in *Price's Tracts* (1782) we read:

> When he observes that the gentlemen introduce their hookas and smoak in the company of ladies, why did he not add that the mixture of sweet-scented Persian tobacco, sweet herbs, coarse sugar, spice, etc., which they inhale . . . comes through clean water, and is so very pleasant that many ladies take the tube and draw a little of the smoak into their mouths.

The rules for the Calcutta Subscription Dances in 1792 provided:

> That *hookers* be not admitted to the ball-room during any part of the night. But *hookers* might be admitted to the upper rooms, to the card-rooms, to the boxes in the theatre, and to each side of the assembly room, between the large pillars and the walls.[2]

[1] A *biri* or *bidi* is tobacco wrapped in a funnel-shaped leaf, usually of the *tendu* tree, and puffed in from cupped hands.

[2] W. H. Carey, *The Good Old Days of Honble John Company* (Simla, 1882).

Major-General Keatinge recalled:

In former days it was a dire offence to step over another person's hooka-carpet and hooka-snake. Men who did so intentionally were called out.

The hookah was such an important adjunct to the life of a *sahib* that he had a servant called a *hooka-burdar*, whose sole duty was to attend to his master's hookah.

(1779) Mr and Mrs Hastings present their compliments to Mr ———— and request the favour of his company to a concert and supper on Thursday next. Mr ———— is requested to bring no servants except his Houccaburdar.[1]

The best story about a *hooka-burdar*, in which a pipe-dream came true, occurs in Sir Edward Colebrooke's *Life of the Rt Hon. Mount-Stewart Elphinstone*:

(1801) The Resident . . . tells a strange story how his hookah-burdar, after cheating and robbing him, proceeded to England, and set up as the Prince of Sylhet, took in everybody, was waited upon by Pitt, dined with the Duke of York, and was presented to the King.

The popularity of the hookah among the British in India began to wane very slowly after 1800. Smoking one is certainly a complicated process. The tobacco has to be cut small or reduced to a powder which is kneaded into a pulp with molasses and a little water. A flat cake is then put into the *chillum* bowl, on top of which is laid a flat piece of baked clay; on this charcoal from the tamarind tree is lit. The tobacco does not come into direct contact with the fire, but burns slowly when the *tawa* (the clay disc) becomes red hot. The base of the hookah contains a bowl half full of water. This bowl has two pipes, one, the inlet pipe, containing the stem to which is attached the *chillum*; the other pipe, sometimes several yards long, is the one from which the smoker draws. The mouthpiece is usually of silver, and on the *chillum* a perforated silver cover is placed to prevent the charcoal from falling off. The variety of tobacco smoked by the rich was, and still is, known as the *badsahi*, the 'queen' of Indian tobacco preparations.

The hookah was still being smoked by retired Anglo-Indians until the early days of Queen Victoria, but out in India the

—————
[1] Carey, op. cit.

younger soldiers and civilians were all smoking cheroots, and continued to smoke them until the majority surrendered to the cigarette.

The habit of *biri* smoking, which is general among the poorer classes, dates back to the seventeenth century. Writing in 1711 Charles Lockyer, an English trader, described it under the name of bunco:

> Tobacco for want of pipes they smoke in Buncos as in the Coromandel Coast. A Bunco is a little tobacco wrapped up in the leaf of a tree, about the bigness of one's little finger; they light one end and draw the smoke through the other; they are curiously made up and sold twenty or thirty in a bundle.

In South India the Dravidian hillmen twist a bunch of the *sal* tree into the shape of a straight-stemmed pipe which lasts for a few smokes before it burns away or falls to pieces. The Himalayas provide a curious method of smoking. Two holes are dug in a sloping bank and connected by an underground channel. The lighted tobacco is placed in one hole and the smoker crouches over the other, which involves a mighty effort of deep breathing.

The Naga women smoke water-pipes in order to provide supplies of nicotine-impregnated liquor to sustain their menfolk against fatigue on long journeys. In the Kulu hills the peasants use their sickles as pipes. The iron handle is hollow, and there is a small aperture at the base where it joins the blade. The hollow handle is filled with grass, leaving about half an inch of space for a little dry tobacco and fire provided by a soft inflammable jungle growth called *kaphi*, which is ignited by a flint. Tobacco burnt and ground into a fine powder to which a little camphor has been added is used as a dentifrice.

The tribesmen scattered all over India, whose antiquity of race is immense, have many legends about tobacco and its origin which seem to go much farther back than the actual date of its introduction; it is possible that legends about other plants with narcotic properties were later attached to tobacco.

The Gadabas in Orissa say that a goat ate some tobacco leaves the juice of which passed into her milk drunk by some Gadabas, who were intoxicated by a new pleasure. The Konds say tobacco was discovered when by chance some food was cooked in its leaves and inebriated those who ate it. The

Juangs say that a drummer resting during a tribal dance chewed the leaf of an unfamiliar plant and was inspired to drum as he had never drummed before.

There is a Muria story from Bastar which relates that once upon a time the people had to give rice to their guests. Rice began to worry about this because she feared it would mean the end of her tribe. So she ran away into the jungle and persuaded Tobacco to take her place. Since then the people have given their guests tobacco instead of rice, which has relieved the food situation.

The Bondos of Orissa have another story about Rice. They tell that Rice grew frightened when she found how greedily men devoured her and ran away to hide. As she ran, the brown love-charm tobacco was born from under her feet, spreading its leaves and fragrant flowers. Then Tobacco with folded hands stood before Rice and said, "Do not go away, but stay here with us. I will allow men to eat me first, and they will not eat you so greedily afterwards."

Another set of legends celebrate the beneficent effect of tobacco. The Ojhas relate that when the plough was first invented the tillers worked so hard that the bullocks, who in those days had four ears, were exhausted. Mahadeo coming down to earth saw what was wrong, cut off two of the bullocks' ears and threw them away. These ears took root and grew up into tobacco plants. Then Mahadeo showed the tillers how to smoke, after which they often had to stop ploughing to enjoy their pipes, and thus the bullocks got a little rest.

The Konds say that in olden days men never stopped working because they did not know what to do with their leisure. Then Mother Earth gave them tobacco and they were able to relax.

The calumet pipe of peace was a solemn pledge of good-will among the North American Indians, and it took the ingenuity of Birmingham to devise for traders a tomahawk which could serve equally for smoking or scalping. The Saora tribesmen in India recognized tobacco as a promoter of peace. They tell how once upon a time Rama and Bhima, heroes and brothers, quarrelled and refused to speak to one another. Both of them were heavy smokers and each had a tobacco patch behind his house. Brahma tried to reconcile the brothers, but without success. So he sent an untouchable to pull up the tobacco-plants in Rama's garden, with the result that Rama could not get anything to smoke. He was too proud, however, to ask Bhima for tobacco. Brahma now put it into Bhima's head to walk up and down in front of Rama's house smoking a cheroot. Rama watched his brother smoking, and the longer he watched the more he craved for a smoke himself. At last he could stand it no longer and, going out, he asked Bhima for a cheroot. Bhima at once lit one and gave it to Rama, after which the brothers became friends again. "And ever since that day," the Saora tale finishes, "the gift of tobacco has made men friendly to one another."

There is the legend that tobacco sprang from the body of a maiden whom nobody loved. In the Gadaba version she was the daughter of a Raja. Her eyes shone like fireflies, but she squinted; her face was as beautiful as a parrot, but she was a dwarf; she spoke as sweetly as the myna bird, but one of her arms was withered. The Raja did all he could to get his daughter married, but nobody had the courage to wed such a mixture of sweet and bitter, and at last she died, a lonely and disappointed virgin. After her death she went to Mahaprabhu (the Lord) who bade her ask him to give her what she wished for most. The maiden said, "When I was alive nobody wanted me. Now when I am dead turn me into something which all men will desire and without which they cannot be happy." On the maiden's funeral pyre was a fragment of bone into which Mahaprabhu breathed life so that it grew up as a tobacco-plant which men desire so much that they say "There is no difference between tobacco and a wife; we love them both equally."

The Muslims have a legend about the origin of tobacco which tells how Mohammed once cured a sick viper, in return for which the ungrateful reptile bit his wrist. The Prophet sucked the poison from the wound and spat it out upon the ground, whereupon "from out of these drops sprang the wondrous weed which has the bitterness of the serpent's tooth tempered by the sweet spittle from the Prophet's mouth".

Incidentally, it is a popular belief in some snake-infested villages in the Punjab that tobacco beside the bed at night will keep the snakes away. And in other parts of the sub-continent snakes are supposed to shun tobacco fields.

Finally there is a Hindu legend from South India which

pays an eloquent tribute to the virtue of tobacco. Once upon a
time the god Indra asked Brahma the creator what was the
best thing in the world. And Brahma replied by his four
mouths, "Tabaku, Pogaku, Hogesoppu and Pogele"; that is,
Tobacco (in Hindi), Tobacco (in Telugu), Tobacco (in
Kanarese) and Tobacco (in Tamil).

Here indeed is the wisdom of the East at its most eloquent.

It may seem strange to many that the Union of South Africa
has never achieved a reputation for its tobacco, but perhaps
no country is allowed to excel with both wine and tobacco.
The gods may have ruled that their two great gifts to man should
be divided.

On April 10th, 1652, four days after the first white man
settled in South Africa, Jan van Riebeeck wrote in his diary:

> Skipper Davit Conick together with two assistants and
> two soldiers with fowling-pieces and muskets, having gone
> on a fishing-expedition to the Salt River, encountered nine
> Saldania [aborigines] who adopted such an amicable and
> pleasant attitude that it was almost a wonder: they took the
> skipper round the neck as if with great joy and made signs
> that if we had copper and tobacco they would bring us enough
> cattle.

On December 6th, 1652, he wrote:

> If we had no tobacco there would hardly be any trade, as
> a whole cow would often be withheld for a finger's length of
> tobacco or a pipe. We should therefore be provided with
> 1,000 lbs. annually, which should moreover be of good
> quality, for if there is the least rot in the tobacco, they can
> taste it immediately and will not look at it, calling it stinking
> tobacco.

On December 20th, 1652, he was writing:

> To-day we bought a fine sturdy milch ewe for its length in
> twisted tobacco, not more than $\frac{1}{4}$ lb. in weight and only
> worth 11 doits.

That was about threepence, and other entries in van Riebeeck's diary in that December recorded that he had got two
elephant's tusks for a quarter pound of tobacco, two fine

partridges for a finger-length of twist, and two young ostriches for a couple of ounces of tobacco.

Tobacco was used as a bait to extract work from the European servants of the Dutch East India Company as well as the natives. Labourers were required to push 130 wheelbarrow loads a day. For a quarter pound of roll tobacco the labourers were willing to push an extra twenty loads a day; they were paid two ounces at once and the other two at the end of a fortnight.

There seems no doubt that the tobacco which the Portuguese introduced to West Africa was *N. rustica*, and that for at least a hundred years before Jan van Riebeeck landed at the Cape the natives had been growing it for themselves in West and Central Africa. Why was it not being grown in South Africa?

By July 1656 van Riebeeck was entering in his diary:

> This herb thrives here and seed has already been won. A suitable plot was marked out at Rondebosch and instructions given for it to be cleared of shrubs and other vegetation by the two men stationed there who have to guard the grain in any case and who, to occupy themselves, could manage a fair-sized tobacco plantation.

In the following year, when the first Free Burghers were allowed to settle along the Liesbeek and farm on their own account, they announced their intention to grow tobacco as well as grain.

However, the Dutch East India Company was unwilling to give up the extremely profitable barter in which they were indulging with tobacco, and the right to grow tobacco was granted only to persons in the service of the Company.

The Company restricted their own plantations, having found the south-east wind a serious handicap. In 1719 the Lords Seventeen decided to start growing tobacco on a wider scale, and an expert was sent out from Holland. Cornelius Hendricks failed to justify his reputation as an expert, and the tobacco he produced in the teeth of the winds had a rank flavour. So after three years the Lords Seventeen gave up their project.

Nevertheless the Free Burghers were still forbidden to grow tobacco. Graham Botha says:

> Smoking at the Cape was universal. Virginian, Brazilian and Mauritian tobacco was used, and this had to be bought

from the Company which prohibited under severe penalty the growing of tobacco.[1]

So long as the Settlement was confined to the Cape peninsula and its immediate surroundings, the prohibition was effective, but when the settlers moved inland they were able to grow tobacco secretly, and they used it as barter with the Hottentots for cattle and sheep.

John Barrow in 1797–8 [2] found "extensive plantations of tobacco" in the Long Kloof, 300 miles from Cape Town, near to the present tobacco-growing area of Oudtshoorn. The Dutch East India Company had just lost their control, and it was obvious that these plantations had been in existence for a long time.

In 1831 an anonymous contributor to the *South Africa Directory* wrote:

> Upon the whole I am convinced that the finest quality of American Tobacco can be raised in this Colony with much less trouble and with more certainty of a good crop than in America. . . . The caterpillar and other insects, so trouble-some and destructive in America, are unknown in this country. . . . The only enemy tobacco has here is the South-east wind but there are millions of acres that are wholly beyond its reach.

In 1861 James Barry Munnik, the tobacco merchant, wrote a treatise in which he stated that the tobacco grown in the district of Wynberg at Alphen and Stellenberg, as well as tobacco from Riversdale and Heidelberg, had been used by him in his business, and was as good as any ever imported. He reproached the farmers for not growing more tobacco.

In 1875 the total production of tobacco in the Cape Colony was over three million pounds, of which the District of Oudtshoorn produced four-fifths, double that of ten years earlier.

In Natal tobacco had been grown by the Bantus in small gardens for their own use, and by 1840 its production by whites in a commercial year was large enough to make the revenue from it one of the most important items in the Colony's income.

However, it was the opening up of the low veld in the Transvaal which was to provide the chief tobacco area in South Africa one day. In 1906 experimental stations were

---

[1] *Social Life in the Cape Colony in the 18th Century.*
[2] John Barrow, *Travels in Southern Africa.*

established at Rustenburg and Barberton in the Transvaal. Local manufacturers found that South African tobaccos were then unsuitable for cigarette making, and they were used in the manufacture of pipe tobacco. In 1909 the Transvaal Government sent young men to America to learn the art of growing and curing tobacco. When they returned from America they found that no attempt to grade tobacco was made, and one of them gave his first demonstration of how it was done in a disused church.

In 1922 about a dozen Americans with practical knowledge of growing and handling tobacco were brought from the United States to serve as extension officers among the tobacco growers. As everywhere else, the all-conquering cigarette had to be served.

When the first white man settled at the Cape in 1652, the Hottentots and the Bushmen were using the ground pipe for smoking. This consisted of a bowl in the ground and an underground duct connected to it, shaped in moist soil, with a short reed for drawing the smoke from the underground tube. A horn was often used as a bowl. When the mouthpiece was short, the smoker had sometimes to lie on his stomach to smoke. It is not surprising that the Hottentots and Bushmen welcomed the clay pipes which the Dutch settlers brought with them, and that these clay pipes should have been found a valuable means of barter.

The calabash pipe came later, probably from tribes in the interior of Africa. Livingstone found tribes whose utensils were all made of the calabash gourd, which is a relation of the pumpkin. One variety has gourds with a curve at one end, and these provided a ready made bowl when cut off.

In the late nineteenth century bedside pipes were in vogue. The pipe rested on a table in front of the bed, and the mouthpiece reached as far as the pillow. This allowed the smoker to lie back and smoke at his ease without any risk of falling asleep and setting the bed on fire. President Kruger had one which is still to be seen in his grandson's house.

The Portuguese brought tobacco to East Africa, where it was grown and cured by primitive methods for more than three hundred years before the Uganda Department of Agriculture launched some experiments in better culture in 1907. They were not highly successful; twenty years passed before the results achieved made it seem worth while to press the possibility of tobacco as a remunerative crop for the African farmers. Fire-cured leaf from Nyasaland seed known as Henry Western was the first method. Air-cured was then tried in the West Nile district, and then Uganda obtained seed from the United States and Canada to experiment with flue-cured. Presently the exportation of seed from America was prohibited, and it was imported from Southern Rhodesia.

It was not until 1937 that a tobacco company was formed in Kenya which, with the co-operation of the Kenya Department of Agriculture, started operations in the African reserves near Fort Hall, and around Kitui. African farmers began flue-cured leaf production in Uganda in 1944.

In Tanganyika most of the flue-cured crop is grown by European farmers.

It is interesting to note that until recently smoking in public in Uganda was the exclusive privilege of the old men and old women. If a young man wished to smoke he had to approach his maternal uncle, who would help him to get hold of a goat and a pot of beer, which the young man would then present to his father in return for his permission to smoke. If a girl wanted to be allowed to smoke she had somehow to get hold of a cow to propitiate her father. Modern parents in Great Britain might learn something from the Uganda Africans to their own advantage.

After the Portuguese brought tobacco to Africa it spread deep into the interior.

Stanley noted in 1887 near Irumu:

> Mostly all the huts contained large baskets of superior tobacco weighing from twenty to fifty pounds each, such quantities indeed that every smoker in the camp obtained from five to ten pounds . . . owing to the imperfect drying it is not fragrant, but it is extremely smokable. Fifty pipefuls a day of it would not produce so much effect on the nerves as one of the article known as Cavendish. But here and there among the leaves there were a few of rich brown colour, slightly spotted with nitre, which produce a different effect. Two of our officers experimented on a pipeful of this . . . and were inconceivably wretched in consequence.[1]

[1] H. M. Stanley, *In Darkest Africa* (1890).

The pipe-bowls in this region, it may be pointed out, held half a pint of tobacco.

Burrows writing about the Mang-bettou tribe says:

> There is a plantation of tobacco near every village, though the natives have no idea of preparing it. They simply take out the centre stalk of the tobacco leaf, which is shredded and dried in the sun; this is sometimes mixed with red pepper, and is moulded by the aid of oil into the shape, and nearly to the hardness of a brick . . . they only take two or three whiffs of the pipe, inhaling the smoke, and coughing violently always. When the chief sneezes it is customary for all those around him to pretend to sneeze also . . . when a chief smokes the whole crowd standing round him clap their hands in unison until he has finished.[1]

An agreeable legend is current among the Bushongo:

> Many years ago a Bushongo returned from a long journey and after surprising his companions by smoking persuaded them to try it with these words:
> "When you have a quarrel with your brother, in your fury you may wish to slay him: sit down and smoke a pipe. When the pipe is finished you will think that perhaps death is too great a punishment for your brother's offences, and you will decide to let him off with a thrashing. Relight your pipe and smoke on. As the smoke curls upwards you will come to the conclusion that a few hard words might take the place of blows. Light up your pipe once more, and when it is smoked through you will go to your brother and ask him to forget the past."[2]

The way in which tobacco has spread all over Central Africa since the Portuguese introduced *N. rustica* first about 1560 has tempted one or two writers to speculate that the Africans captured for slaves introduced it to the West Indies. There is no foundation for this theory, and the fact that some of the tribes of Central Africa believe that tobacco always grew there is no argument. We have seen how rapidly folklore gathered round tobacco in India.

One habit which may have been brought by the African slaves to America was that of smoking the cigarette with the lighted end in the mouth. This was noted earlier as a Panama

[1] Guy Burrows, *The Land of the Pygmies* (1898).
[2] M. W. Hilton-Simpson, *Land and Peoples of the Masai* (Constable, 1911).

habit. The reason given is that the smoker gets a more concentrated smoke this way. On the Angola coast the fishermen keep the lighted end in the mouth to avoid the cigarette being put out by the sea-spray.

Tobacco was not developed commercially in Nigeria until 1933 at Oshogbo, but production has already reached six million pounds of leaf annually from six Nigerian provinces, and it is consumed locally in the manufacture of cigarettes. This tobacco has been grown from imported American seed. Besides this, the Nigerian farmers produce about ten million pounds of tobacco from a variety of *N. rustica* prepared locally with some form of menthol for pipes, chewing, cheroots and snuff. It is also used for what are called 'Booki' cigarettes. These are hand made and wrapped in any paper available, including newspapers and the pages of old books. They are called 'Bookis' because they were first made from the pages of Bibles (The Book) that were distributed free by missionaries, not of course with the idea of their being made into cigarettes.

Unmanufactured tobacco has also been imported for the last twenty-three years from America, India and Rhodesia, for the local manufacture of machine-made cigarettes. There is another type of black and heavily 'treated' tobacco imported from America for use in the preparation of snuff, pipe and chewing tobacco. This is sold under the local and not extremely attractive name of Black Fat.

The water-pipe in its most elaborate form—the hookah—has been described. One of my informants gave an example of it in a simple and most ingenious form from darkest Africa.

A European beer-bottle had been pierced and a small conical wooden container had been attached to the hole in the side of the bottle, thus making the pipe-head; the bottle was half filled with water and the smoker drew his smoke through the neck of the bottle.

And finally a glimpse at tobacco in New Zealand. An examination of the nineteenth annual report of the Tobacco Board issued in July 1955 records the astonishing increase in tobacco-smoking during and after the Second World War. In 1938, 2,945,221 pounds of raw leaf were imported into New Zealand and 1,423,610 pounds of leaf were produced there. In

1954 7,339,483 pounds were imported and 4,135,921 pounds were homegrown. Over 11½ millions in all compared with less than 4½ millions only sixteen years before; in terms of money £(N. Z.)2,900,363 compared with £(N.Z.)674,957. The number of growers in 1955 was 412, the acreage 3,000 acres, which gave an average acreage per grower of 7·5. Roughly one can say that tobacco in New Zealand yields £(N.Z.)30 an acre.

In 1835 Sir William Yate, who was writing of New Zealand from 1828 onward, observed:

> The use of tobacco is almost unanimously adopted throughout the island: it is mostly consumed with the pipe. I do not regret the introduction of this article as far as the health of the people is concerned. When heated at night, I have known them come out of their little huts, and sit naked on the dewy grass, to cool themselves; and then retire to bed again; whereas, now, when they are in the most profuse perspirations, they rise, fill their pipe, light it, and sometimes smoke it in the house, which gives time for the perspiration to subside gradually, and they do not come reeking hot, from a highly-heated hut, into the cold, raw damp air of night; by this means many colds are avoided, and much sickness prevented; on this ground then, I do not regret the introduction and general use of tobacco, particularly as it has not hitherto led to the drinking of spirituous or fermented liquors.

The first seeds of *N. tabacum* are presumed to have reached New Zealand in the early years of the nineteenth century, and to have been brought by whalers or missionaries. The former class seems more probable, because it explains the swindles that were perpetrated on the Maoris by unscrupulous sailors. Darwin, who visited the Bay of Islands with the *Beagle* in 1835, says:

> The common dock is widely disseminated, and will, I fear, for ever remain a proof of the rascality of an Englishman who sold the seeds for those of the tobacco plant.

In 1845 Colenso recorded of a village on the east side of the Rangatiki River:

> I was surprised to find such an extensive and formidable growth of English docks (*Rumex obtusifolius*) 4–5 feet high and densely thick, so that in some places I could scarcely make my way through them. On enquiry I found when some of

these people had visited Whanganni to sell their pigs they had purchased from a white man there some seed which they were told was tobacco seed. In their ignorance they took their treasure back with them, and carefully sowed it in some of their soil, which they also had prepared by digging; and lo, the crop proved to be the horrid dock, which seeding largely, was carried down the rivers and filled the country.

G. M. Thomson says:

The same iniquitous trick had also been played with the natives of Poverty Bay as early as 1837, when at their request I visited some young plants they had raised from seed, fenced in and tabooed, believing them to be tobacco.[1]

There is no doubt that the dock was introduced to New Zealand and became a pest, but tobacco seed must have arrived first and the seed of the dock does not resemble the seed of tobacco. And why did even the most rascally seamen bother to carry out with him dock-seed from England? It is a queer story.

If the theory behind the Kon-Tiki Expedition be correct, tobacco may have reached Polynesia from America. Thor Heyerdahl[2] seems to think it possible, but there is no archæological evidence in the remains of primeval pipes, as there is in North America. A search through the many books about the South Seas in my library has not yielded any information that bears on the subject.

[1] G. M. Thomson, *The Naturalization of Animals and Plants in New Zealand.*
[2] *American Indians in the Pacific* (George Allen & Unwin, 1952).

Epilogue

THROUGHOUT the writing of this book the anti-nicotine crusaders have been pressing the case against tobacco with statistics supposed to establish a connexion between cancer of the lung and smoking. That is the latest form of attack. A hundred years ago Dr Samuel Solly was leading a ferocious onslaught in *The Lancet*. All sorts of preposterous arguments were produced, including an assertion that the increase of smoking in the Royal Navy since the Napoleonic Wars had to all intents and purposes made officers and men incapable of useful service. This was firmly contradicted by Dr Gallacher who, after fourteen years as physician to the Royal Navy, testified that in the whole of that time he had observed only a couple of cases in which too much chewing might have had a deleterious effect. Oxford undergraduates came in for a heavy cannonade from Dr Rankin, who was particularly distressed by the appearance of the choirboys in chapel, "their pale and meagre faces made more conspicuous by their white surplices". Those choirboys of 1857 must have been cigar addicts! Most of the doctors allowed that mental instability could not be attributed to smoking, because mental instability was more frequent among women, who rarely smoked at that date. Dr Green believed that tuberculosis of the lungs was caused by smoking, but *not one* of the numerous doctors said a word about *cancer of the lungs*; not even Dr Solly himself, who was prepared to argue that smoking was the cause of paralysis, apoplexy, dyspepsia, deaths from typhus and all the misery of the working-classes. He added with an audacious omniscience that outstanding men in "politics, law, strategy and medicine" did not smoke, and that if they did so they died prematurely. In spite of abstaining from tobacco, Dr Solly himself died suddenly when he was sixty-six.

There were plenty of eminent doctors to defend tobacco, and those that had been asserting it shortened the life of man were silenced temporarily by a doctor who quoted the case of a man who between the ages of eighteen and ninety-one had drunk more than 22,000 gallons of beer and smoked four tons of tobacco.

Even if I were convinced by indisputable evidence that tobacco was physically harmful to certain constitutions, I should still argue that the advantage tobacco has been to the mind of man has far outweighed any harm it might have (and that *might* is still highly problematical) done to a few bodies. I am sure that when Prometheus stole fire from Zeus and gave it to mortals, he with the foresight his name commemorates knew that one ultimate benefit of fire would be its use for tobacco. It is regrettable that *Nicotiana tabacum* did not grow in Europe and Asia beside the vine. What epic tales, far more truly poetic than any we do possess, might have been ours. As it is, we are dependent for our tobacco mythology upon the stories told by the Red Indians of North America and the original inhabitants of Central and South America, very few of which have the poetic quality we demand from a myth. We know that tobacco was smoked some thousands of years before the New World was discovered. We know that smoking had a religious significance, and we can presume from ancient carvings that among the Mayas in Central America the privilege of smoking was reserved for the priests.

There was one custom, however, among the North American Indians which more eloquently than any piece of mythology symbolizes the beneficent influence of tobacco upon human nature, and that was the solemn smoking of the great calumet, adorned with woodpeckers' beaks dyed scarlet and with eagles' feathers, that solemn pipe of peace which signified the restoration of amity among warring tribes. I believe firmly that the vine has done more good to man than harm, but it would be deliberate blindness to pretend that excess of alcohol in whatever shape it was imbibed has not been responsible for many crimes of violence and many acts of folly. What indictment can be preferred against tobacco for either? None.

J. M. Barrie argued in an oft-quoted passage of *My Lady Nicotine* that tobacco had enlarged the mind of man and given him his noblest inspirations. It is certainly true that the great majority of men of letters have been smokers, whether they were poets or dramatists, philosphers or historians, essayists or novelists. I recall only one supreme figure in literature who hated tobacco, and that was Goethe. I deeply regret this to me incomprehensible antipathy, because I revere Goethe so profoundly. Swinburne, in whose verse I took much delight when young, was another poet that hated tobacco. One day at the Arts Club in Dover Street in a moment of petulance provoked by the fumes of cigars or pipes in every room he entered he is said to have shrilled:

"James the First was a knave, a tyrant, a fool, a liar and a coward. But I love him, I worship him, because he slit the throat of that blackguard Ralegh, who invented this filthy smoking."

There is no tradition at the Savile Club of any Swinburnian diatribes against smoking, but there must often have been moments when the members wished that the fuzzy-haired poet would put a pipe in his mouth and stop talking in that high rasping voice of his. Edmund Gosse told me of Swinburne's arriving one evening in the old 'drawing-room' at 107, Piccadilly, and holding forth in a high-pitched monologue as he stood on a brass fender from which he kept slipping in the excitement of his own flow of words. Herbert Spencer, who was reading the *Contemporary Review*, looked up severely over the covers from time to time, his long upper lip growing longer and longer with disapproval of the poet's shrill clamour and brassy clangour. At last he put his hand into the pocket of his coat and took out a pair of silencers, which he adjusted on his head to exclude the sound of Swinburne's voice and feet. Then he returned to his perusal of the *Contemporary Review*, the individualism he had expounded in so many pages of dialectic defended, the philosopher secured against a poet's profane intrusion.

I had written thus far when an Archbishop came to dinner with me, and to him I told this story. Whereupon his Grace asked if I had ever heard the tale of Cardinal Newman's encounter with a traveller who insisted upon smoking in a non-smoking compartment after being asked to desist.

"And what will you do, Sir, if I continue to smoke?" the traveller demanded pugnaciously.

"You will make me sick, Sir," Newman replied. "And you will have to take the consequences upon yourself."

It must be remembered that smoking-compartments were few and far between in mid-Victorian days, and indeed until well into the twentieth century. Then they were gradually made more numerous, until to-day when an inconspicuous little triangle pasted on the window of a compartment announces that it is reserved for non-smokers; and those non-smoking compartments are as few and far between as the smoking compartments of once upon a time. The notification of a sanctuary for non-smokers is so inconspicuous that the smoker often gets into one inadvertently, and only realizes his mistake when he puts a cigarette between his lips and finds his lighter burning blue under the baleful eyes of his fellow-travellers. Most smokers have been caught this way, and I am sure all of them will agree with me that nothing is so lowering to the spirits as the enforced companionship of a bunch of non-smokers when travelling through flat country on a wet afternoon at autumn's end, nothing so poignant as the sight of an occasional bonfire of dead leaves in the back garden to remind them of the smokelessness of the staid compartment in which they are temporarily immured.

In our zest for egalitarianism, we have now turned all third-class carriages into second-class carriages. In Spain sixty years ago it used to be said that nobody travelled third-class except blind beggars who thought they were travelling second. Mention of Spain reminds me of the label there for a smoking-compartment—*Para Fumadores*.

What a noble ring of words! The Cid himself might have made it his battle-cry. Yet, I'm afraid that even such a noble ring of words would not have impressed the Duke of Wellington, who remained as firm an opponent of tobacco as Lord Montgomery to-day. In justice to the latter, it must be added that he did realize how much troops appreciated cigarettes, and used to carry round with him a plentiful supply for distribution on his visits to men in the field. I cannot see the Duke of Wellington riding through the lines of Torres Vedras with packets of cigarillos.

If Napoleon had smoked cigars instead of taking snuff, he might have stayed quietly in Elba. If Grant had not been a chain-smoker of cigars, he might not have kept his nerves sufficiently calm and steady to bring the American Civil War to a victorious conclusion for the North. Incidentally it may be noted that Lee was not a smoker.

Another eloquent opponent of tobacco was John Ruskin. What was the result? His marriage was dissolved and his former wife married Sir John Millais, who was such a devoted

smoker that he was said to have indulged in a clay pipe when
driving in the Golden Jubilee procession of Queen Victoria.
I do not believe this, but the fact that such a story could have
been invented plausibly about the painter shows what a
devotee of tobacco he must have been. The expression he gave
to the eyes of the boy Ralegh listening to the tales of the
Spanish Main in that famous picture was undoubtedly a
tribute to the reverence he felt for Ralegh, not merely as a
great adventurer but also as the man who first made the pipe
popular in England. And who would deny that the picture of
the little boy blowing iridescent soap-bubbles from a clay-pipe
was a sentimental idealization of Millais' own smoking habits?

Although Ruskin regarded smoking as a corrupting influence
upon the youth of England, it is fair to his memory to record
that in February 1865 he sent to that devoted smoker Thomas
Carlyle a box of cigars.

The letter of acknowledgment exists:

> Dear Ruskin, you have sent me a magnificent Box of Cigars; for
> which what can I say in answer? It makes me both sad and glad.
> Ay de mi.
>
> We are such stuff,
> Gone with a puff—
> Then think and smoke Tobacco!

In later years Ruskin disliked tobacco more and more, and
his guests at Brantwood were never allowed to smoke there
even when lovely Lake Coniston was obscured by sheets of
chilly rain.

Undoubtedly the absence of any reference to tobacco in
Shakespeare's works has been a source of much encouragement
to the tobaccophobes. The long line of poets, playrights,
historians, philosophers and novelists who have found in
Nicotiana a muse more powerful than Clio or Melpomene
count as nothing in presenting the case for tobacco so long as
the greatest of them can be cited as an example of a poet
independent of its inspiration. Let us admit at once that
neither external nor internal evidence allows us to suppose that
Shakespeare was a smoker. Nevertheless, although out of
deference to the feelings of his patron King James, Shakespeare
may have abstained from making tobacco an anodyne like
sleep and celebrating its virtue in magical verse, it is to be
noted that nowhere does he attack it. His fantastical fops do

not indulge in it to make themselves more ridiculous by their extravagant behaviour. His heroes and his villains both appear ignorant of tobacco. Let nobody fancy that this was done out of regard for anachronism. If Shakespeare had felt like it he would have put a pipe in the mouth of Macbeth, or even of Julius Cæsar.

Yet, for all we know, Shakespeare may have been a smoker. My own belief is that he took to tobacco when he retired to Stratford, and that his last play, *The Tempest*, was the result of the mental tranquillity which smoking helped to give him in middle-age. I feel convinced, if that fell sergeant Death had not come to arrest him so soon, we should have had from his sublime pen a series of plays in the mood of *The Tempest* in which we should have been rejoiced by immortal lines about tobacco.

We may remember that Lord Southampton, who was Shakespeare's dearest friend, was a Governor of the Virginia Company, and that he, Sir Edwin Sandys and Nicholas Ferrar were all full of those ideas about the future of the new colony which seem reflected in Gonzalo's speech in *The Tempest*. Ariel's allusion to Prospero's having once called him up at midnight "to fetch dew from the still-vex'd Bermoothes" shows that Bermuda was in Shakespeare's mind. Not that this linking of *The Tempest* with the New World is any justification for linking it with tobacco in particular. I only mention Southampton's governorship of the Virginia Company as a minute straw to show the direction in which Shakespeare's mind was gently blowing. We can add *Cymbeline* and *The Winter's Tale* to *The Tempest* to illustrate this contented and tranquil mood of the Bard. Tradition says that he indulged in one or two drinking bouts with Ben Jonson and Michael Drayton about this time, and I cannot believe that the jolly evenings were passed without pipes. Ben Jonson would hardly have put up with Shakespeare's sitting with a face on him like Macaulay in the smoking-room of the House of Commons.

Finally I pin my faith to the theory that Shakespeare took up smoking after he retired to Stratford by recalling Prospero's famous speech:

> *Our revels now are ended. These our actors,*
> *As I foretold you, were all spirits and*

Are melted into air, into thin air:
And like the baseless fabric of this vision,
The cloud-capp'd towers, the gorgeous palaces,
The solemn temples, the great globe itself,
Yea, all which it inherit, shall dissolve
And, like this insubstantial pageant faded,
Leave not a rack behind.

I believe that these words were written after a pipe-dream. And when at the end of the speech Prospero tells Ferdinand and Miranda to retire into his cell and repose themselves while he walks a turn or two to still his beating mind, I cannot help feeling that as he walked he was puffing away at a pipe.

To those who think my theory of Shakespeare's taking to tobacco towards the end of his life a mere display of fondness, I can only reply that, while I have no positive evidence to support my theory, the opponents of tobacco have not a tittle more of evidence to contradict it.

I had always hoped that Herrick was a smoker in spite of there not being a line in the *Hesperides* to justify such an assumption. Many pages back I expressed my regret that the lyric poet I love best of all did not sing the praise of tobacco. I am never likely to be able to secure evidence that Shakespeare smoked, but in the latest volume of Herrick's poetical works edited by L. C. Martin and published by the Oxford University Press, the poem about tobacco I had always felt Herrick must have written is printed for the first time. I have modernized the spelling:

The Tobacconist

Know you the garb? thus I accost you, what?
My noble blades, will ye evaporate?
Will you exchange a whiff or two! come, smother,
In clouds of smoke, envelop one another;
A match; you, sirrah, bring the best you can.
Or else I swear I am a gentleman.
Sit round, boon blades; shaver, light the taper
How like a child thou suck'st! More ample vapour
Must steam to such excess, as when the sun
Changes the air to exhalation.
Faugh! by Jove, this relishes plain Kitt,
A Saint and brook such bastard counterfeit.

Tobacco? sure, good man, thou hast been priz'd
At higher rates when thou wert canoniz'd,
Better't, you villain, else (would I were dead)
Thy shoulders shall go bare unto thy head,
Why, this is right; it hath a dainty touch,
Varina's self could never boast of such.
I'faith, we'll smoke it, I must see it spread,
The air blue coated, whiff about my head.
Could I but feed upon such air alone
I'd quit my nature, turn chameleon.
See how the azure vapour wreathes the skies,
We'll smoke out all those vulgar deities
Which lurk so close; as you have seen them
Drive the silly drones from their unpeopled hive.
For this Prometheus ransack'd heaven, these fires
Entic'd his hand to second his desires
E'en to a sacrilege, divinest flame,
Why, then, a fie upon all such profane
Tobacco! Satan's herb, so vile will pose
All the rhetorical language of the nose.
Thou varlet, how thy stinking breath doth stain
An herb of virtue styléd sovereign.
It is the poet's Moly, richest Nectar.
The gods' Ambrosia, our pure Elixir,
It is most precious. Know it will revive
Decaying nature, 'tis restorative
For wasted spirits, shames the Empiric
And his cauterian for the rheumatic;
This head with cataracts of Nile did run;
I stopp'd the streams by salivation.
It prompts the memory, invention
Clears, it quickens apprehension;
Good for obstructions, it opes the veins,
Fills them with spirits, closeth them again,
Provokes an appetite it whetteth on
The stomach, helps all crude digestion,
My grandam sure, b'yr Lady, us'd to call
The ashes for kib'd heels a cordial;
Exchangeth mirth for grief, doth antidate
Presuming hopes it doth exhilarate,
Prevents all poison (though old Galen wrote

Of no such herb), this the best antidote;
This I daresay so good to kill the fleas,
There's no collyrium in Hippocrates.
The fire a vestal flame, the ruby nose
God Bacchus' altar whereon incense glows;
It is all spirit, not to force belief,
It is the life of air, the air of life.

I am not clear whether Herrick was condemning St Kitts (St Christopher) island tobacco or merely tobacco that was pretending to be St Kitts. The St Kitts tobacco was in good repute for a while, and the Virginia planters disliked its competition. However, on St Kitts by the middle of the seventeenth century the growing of tobacco had been abandoned for indigo and cotton. One may presume that Herrick wrote this poem, which may be found in manuscript in a commonplace-book belonging to the Rosenbach Foundation in Philadelphia, when he was still in London.

I have an uneasy feeling that the poet-parson gave up smoking after he went down to his Devonshire vicarage. Otherwise there must surely have been some reference to it in the songs he wrote there.

"See how the azure vapour wreathes the skies." That is the authentic lyric note. So, too, is the last line of the poem "It is the life of air; the air of life."

Indeed, I cannot recall a better line in verse about tobacco, and am almost temped to exchange Byron's *Sublime Tobacco* for *The Air of Life* as the title of this book. How forlorn and dead is the air of an unsmoked-in room; I never light up my pipe in such a room without feeling that the room is grateful to me for giving it the air of life. Non-smokers are always inclined to suggest that their noses are in better trim than those of smokers. I do not believe this. Rose and lilac, heliotrope, honeysuckle, carnation and sweet-pea, all smell the sweeter to me because I am a smoker. And what perfume is more potent than that of night-scented Virginia stock and the tobacco-plant of our gardens mingling with the fragrance of a good cigar when in a summer twilight we stroll along a border of flowers in a dusky English garden? The air of life. . . .

And as I murmur those words to myself there rises before the mind's eye the spectre of that non-smoking lackey of death in his lavatory-attendant's uniform—Adolf Hitler. I have been fair. I have cited examples of non-smokers to whom the world owes much. I have made it clear I recognize that human greatness may be displayed by one who never smoked so much as half a Woodbine cigarette. I do not propose to attribute the evil that was Hitler to his antipathy against tobacco. Nevertheless, the ineluctable fact remains that the man who brought more misery to the world than any other human being hated smoking as in medieval days the Devil was said to hate holy water. Hitler dreaded the benign influence of tobacco. He must have known intuitively that if he surrendered to that sedative influence his ulcerous mind might be healed, and if once the inner rage that gnawed at him was allayed he must have realized he would be as commonplace as he looked. Yes, I am convinced that Hitler was afraid of tobacco, and murdered it as Macbeth murdered sleep.

It would be idle to argue that cruelty, violence and wickedness did not flourish after man began to smoke. They certainly did. It can be maintained, however, that with the spread of tobacco there was a perceptible relaxation of tension in the progress of the ordinary man through life. The Thirty Years War was a fearful disaster for Europe; if tobacco had not alleviated some of the horrors it inflicted upon those who suffered from its devastation, the set-back it gave to European civilization might have been even greater than it was. It is surely significant that every war since has increased the demand for tobacco. Leave war out of it. Reflect what might be the condition of everybody who is exposed to the ever-growing tension of modern existence if tobacco had never been discovered. Our hospitals are already inadequate for ills that not even the bitterest anti-tobacco fanatic will attribute to smoking. Without the aid of tobacco we must find twenty times the number of mental sanatoriums inadequate for the patients they would be called upon to house. It may be remembered that Dr Johnson foresaw an increase of madness if smoking should become obsolete.

I ask myself how many men or women I have seen in all my life of whom I could say that tobacco had been their ruin, and I confidently answer 'none'. I could not give the same reply to such a question about alcohol, however beneficial I may believe wine and spirits to be in moderation. The excessive

General Montgomery distributing cigarettes sent by people at home to men of the Eighth Army, 1943

smokers I have known were driven to excess by their own nerves—tobacco was not to blame for them.

However, if it be granted that the health of some people has been injured, what an infinitesimal few they are among the myriads and myriads to whom smoking has been one of the greatest boons ever conferred upon humanity.

It has been frequently observed that, although the work of writers has owed more to tobacco than any other kind of sedentary work, writers themselves have failed on the whole to celebrate worthily the muse who in draperies of diaphanous blue and grey attends upon their inspiration. Even as I pen those words, pipe in mouth, I feel with a sense of frustration the inadequacy of my own words to express my gratitude to that muse who has helped me so often to write a sentence of which when I read it again years later I do not desire to change a single word. Isaac Newton, the greatest mind of his century, who smoked continuously, did not illuminate with his light the mysterious world of tobacco. Nor did that other Izaac, the Compleat Angler, mention his pipe more than once or twice. Hobbes, who like Izaak Walton lived to be ninety and smoked hard all his years, described the life of man without government and social order as "solitary, poor, nasty, brutish and short", he never found five such eloquent adjectives to describe the life of man without tobacco. Calverley's *Ode to Tobacco* is thin stuff, but from it the *Oxford Dictionary of Quotations* has been able to extract the line "Smith, take a fresh cigar" as one of three allusions to the cigar in literature. The other two are from Kipling, "a woman is only a woman but a good cigar is a smoke" and "the sweet post-prandial cigar" from that wretched scribbler, Robert Buchanan. And for the cigarette the *only* quotation it can produce is from Oscar Wilde's *Portrait of Dorian Grey*:

A cigarette is the perfect type of a perfect pleasure. It is exquisite, and it leaves one unsatisfied. What more can one want?

And when it comes to pipes, the *Oxford Dictionary of Quotations* cannot be bothered to distinguish between musical pipes and smoking pipes in the reference index.

However, the blame rests on the smoking authors if they

have produced nothing memorable. Charles Lamb's *Farewell to Tobacco* yields one couplet worth quoting:

> For thy sake, Tobacco, I
> Would do anything but die.

Lamb was often on the point of giving up his pipe because he thought smoking injured his health. It may be doubted whether it was only the tobacco that upset Lamb—he was very fond of alcohol. However, anybody familiar with his life must rejoice that one of the best-loved figures in English literature should have found a nepenthe for much anxiety and sorrow. I am sure that the insanity which always threatened his peace of mind was kept at bay by smoking, and if I could own a collection of authors' pipes there would be none I should regard with more affection and regard than one which had been smoked by Elia.

It was a dereliction of poetic duty that Tennyson, who probably owed more to his cutty pipes than to the church-wardens of which we hear so much from his friends, was never inspired by tobacco to salute it in verse. What *is* the reason for this literary neglect of literature's greatest benefactor? I put forward as a suggestion that its dear familiarity makes the poet take it for granted. The present campaign against smoking, if it does not end very soon in smoke, may remind smokers that the battle against the 'anti-tobaccoites' is still being fought. I take 'anti-tobaccoites' from an entertaining little book by Andrew Steinmetz, Esq., of the Middle Temple, Barrister-at-Law, published in 1857, to counter the assault made by Dr Solly and his medical adherents in that correspondence in *The Lancet* a hundred years ago.

I cannot refrain from quoting one paragraph:

> If the various propositions of Dr Solly and his friends of the "Lancet" were well founded, it would follow that every third man at least of our population must have been suffering from all manner of diseases for the last two centuries—since the consumption of tobacco has kept pace with the increase of population: nay, it also follows that, instead of increasing in population at a great ratio, as proved beyond doubt, we have been suffering from sterility! And this in the face of the well-known fact that population increased last year at the rate of one thousand per day. And insanity, too, is ascribed to tobacco—whilst it is well known that the female lunatics

exceed the male by a considerable number. In short, nothing but the most glaring improbabilities are adduced, and the assertions are such as Dr Solly may make when he pleases to his pupils without fear of contradiction. I cannot but look upon the whole excitement as an exhibition of ill-conditioned prejudices—from whatever motive proceeding I know not;— but if Dr Solly gave up smoking, as he says, because he believed that it impaired his nervous energy, I am sorry to feel compelled to say that his letters in the "Lancet" evince very considerable nervous weakness—indeed, such a weakness as would believe implicitly in the existence of witches and hobgoblins.

And then counsel for tobacco adds words which I commend to the present campaigners:

> Smoking . . . is entirely a matter of idiosyncrasy of constitution. Thus, we are told that there are cases on record of persons killing themselves by smoking seventeen or eighteen pipes at a sitting . . . the same result might have arisen of as many dishes. And how comes it that I am at this moment thinking, writing, and smoking indefatigably, whereas I have been thus engaged since three o'clock this morning the hour being now four o'clock p.m.?

That smoking Marathon was performed with "mild Havannah cigars". I have myself worked from five in the afternoon until eight o'clock in the morning with an hour off for dinner, relying for my support not on cigars but on pipes. As I write these words at the age of seventy-three I can, if necessary, with the help of an ounce of tobacco and one cigar, work in my chair for ten hours at a stretch. I have made it a rule all my life never to assist work with whisky or any other form of alcohol. If I feel I could finish a chapter with the aid of a powerful whisky I take the whisky, but I quit my chair and make no attempt to finish that chapter.

One of the great virtues of tobacco from a writer's point of view is that it does not blur the critical faculties by inducing a deceptive ease of composition. At the same time I frankly confess that I am so dependent upon tobacco when I am writing that without it I am seriously handicapped. I have tried to analyse its effect, and I believe that a great part of it is the way that the smoke of one's pipe deters intrusive thoughts from impinging on one's concentration. If I were not smoking, the petty problems of everyday existence would interrupt composition. Somehow or other between them and it my pipe interposes what can be called a smoke-screen. I sometimes wonder whether, if I lost my eyesight, I should still find smoking as efficacious when I was dictating a narrative instead of writing it. I do know from experience that, although I always have my pipe at my side when I am taking part in a broadcast debate of any kind, I usually let it go out. When I am speaking, my mind is concentrated on an audience real or imagined, and I do not want tobacco smoke to come between me and my listeners. That I take to be the heightened concentration demanded for extempore speaking on which the petty problems of everyday existence do not have a chance of obtruding themselves, and therefore do not require the help of tobacco to banish them. Some twenty years ago I was on a platform with that great man and great orator Cunninghame Graham. Of my speech he said as we left the platform:

"Yes, you'll be able to do that until you're sixty. After that you'll want notes."

In spite of that warning I still challenge fate by refusing to use notes, and I have only once had a black-out. This was in the middle of the last war when I was talking to a packed audience of Service men at the Churchill Club about Robert Louis Stevenson. I had been speaking every night for nearly a week and was very tired. Suddenly I found myself in a parenthesis, and could not for the life of me remember what I had been saying when I entered it. In the Chair just behind me was W. S. Morrison, the present Speaker, and he, realizing that I was completely lost, whispered:

"You were talking about George Meredith."

I leapt out of the parenthesis at once, and went ahead with gratitude to such a wonderful chairman.

I remember clearly that when this momentary black-out occurred, I put my hand into my pocket to take out my cigarette-case with the object of camouflaging my state of aberration. This was an odd gesture for me to make because I did not have a cigarette-case in my pocket, but it does illustrate the importance of the cigarette in a moment of emergency, and ever since then I have tried to remember to take a cigarette-case with me when I have to speak.

I am not a regular cigarette-smoker, and therefore I may

seem to have been insufficiently aware of the predominant part that cigarettes now play in the pleasure of contemporary smoking. I believe that the supreme enjoyment of tobacco is provided by a good cigar followed by a pipe of dark fire-cured flake. At the same time I recognize that the vast majority of mankind (in which woman is respectfully included) has found in the Virginia cigarette its supreme enjoyment. I recognize, too, that the cigarette has done much more to promote kindliness than ever the pipe or cigar accomplished. Between friends intimacy is fostered by sharing the pleasure of smoking a cigar or pipe during friendship's intercourse, but the cigarette can make utter strangers to one another disposed to friendliness. The cigarette is a passport accepted by every country without a visa.

The Reverend Walter Cotton, whose date I cannot trace in any work of reference, thus apostrophized tobacco:

> *Thy quiet spirit lulls the lab'ring brain,*
> *Lures back in thought the flights of vacant mirth,*
> *Consoles the Mourner, soothes the couch of Pain,*
> *And breathes Contentment round the humble hearth;*
> *While savage warriors soften'd by thy breath,*
> *Unbind the Captive hate had doom'd to death.*

That last couplet may not have been penned by the reverend poet with the cigarette in his mind, but we, with our knowledge of what the cigarette has done for the victims of war, cannot help associating them particularly with the merciful cigarette in gratitude to Providence.

We have heard how from the Thirty Years War onward soldiers have turned more and more gratefully to tobacco for consolation in time of war. This fact alone should be enough to close the lips and restrain the pens of those who denounce tobacco as the enemy of mankind. I shall not be extravagant when I claim that neither of the last two world wars would have been endurable for the vast majority of combatants and non-combatants alike without the help of tobacco.

Devotee as I am of the pipe and the cigar, I readily admit that the cigarette has been the most powerful and the most universal medium in bringing the consolation of tobacco to our own time.

We have heard that the Crimean War was probably the beginning of the cigarette's vogue in western Europe, but the Crimean War was a war that did not affect profoundly the lives of people at home, whether British, French, Sardinian, Turkish or Russian. Forty-odd years later the same could be said of the South African War, though it did start the superstition of its being unlucky to light more than two cigarettes with the same match, that superstition being based on the skill of the Boer sharpshooters. During the last quarter of the nineteenth century the popularity of the cigarette increased steadily on both sides of the Atlantic. The First World War consolidated that popularity and made it seem, to say the least, improbable that either the pipe of the cigar, the plug or the snuff-box, would ever regain the position that one or other of them had once occupied in the world of tobacco.

In how many escape stories or tales of life in prison camps did the cigarette play a prominent part! Perhaps during that war the only place in the world where cigarettes were not of prime importance was in the eastern Mediterranean. I do not mean by this that they were not being smoked there, but inasmuch as the Turkish enemy had plenty of cigarettes they were no use as a bait. When I was trying to land agents or take them off from the coast of Asia Minor, the surest means my smugglers used to avoid too close a search by the Turkish coast-guards was to send in coffee with them. The Turks were prepared to close an eye to everything if coffee was in the hold, so scarce had it become.

One Turkish cigarette I recall still with gloomy memories. By the middle of 1917 it was extremely difficult to maintain communication with what agents we still had in Constantinople, and the only way was to post letters from there to a courageous Levantine Englishman who had remained behind in Smyrna. He had a service of Greek runners who carried the information to the coast. There was an internal censorship of the post at Broussa, but this was conducted casually and therefore the simplest form of invisible writing was used. One fatal evening the Turkish officer examining the post happened to knock off the end of his cigarette upon an opened letter and the heat revealed the hidden writing between the lines. Forty-eight hours later six of our Greek runners had been hanged and the Englishman in Smyrna had been condemned to death. How I managed to save his life cannot be told even yet, but his life was saved.

What tobacco, and particularly cigarettes, meant to people during the Second World War needs nothing more as emphasis than the reminder of how much in the way of taxation the Government was able to extract from smokers. Whether a Government is justified in taxing so highly a necessity might give another Aristotle an opportunity to speculate where ethics cnd and politics begin.

When the Gestapo had beaten up some unfortunate victim, we are told time after time that the first step towards a gentle if subtle interrogation has been the offer of a cigarette. In escape stories the vital importance of the cigarette is continually stressed, whether in the comfort it brought in moments of fearful anxiety or whether as a way to the hearts of men. In Germany after the war was over the cigarette became currency; with cigarettes almost everything could be bought. Even the Japanese guards in their horrible prison-camps could be softened for a while by cigarettes.

If cigarettes vanished from the earth to-day, I believe that the world would go to war again within a comparatively short lapse of time. The cigarette to-day expresses in a brief instant all that the great calumet bedecked with ribbons and feathers expressed in the solemn ceremony of peace to the Red Indian braves of once upon a time. Insignificant may seem the gesture with which somebody will pull out a packet of cigarettes and offer it to a stranger. Yet in that superficially insignificant gesture is a handshake. Yes, the cigarette is a talisman that the pipe can never be. True, one may offer one's pouch to a stranger, but if one does the odds are that he will look at the tobacco suspiciously even if he be a pipe-smoker, for pipe-smokers are intensely conservative and seldom welcome an opportunity to try the favourite mixture or flake of another smoker. However, I must be careful now, because the smoker of those cigarettes which all taste alike to me may be protesting that he is not prepared to accept any cigarette that is offered to him, and that he is just as conservative as any pipe-smoker once he has discovered *the* cigarette.

I was long haunted by the thought of the suffering caused to prisoners in our gaols through being deprived absolutely of tobacco. Wilfrid Macartney, a friend and former subaltern of mine, after he had endured a fantastic sentence of ten years' penal servitude inflicted upon him by the late Lord Hewart, penned at my instigation an account of the experience, to which I wrote an introduction. This book, called *Walls Have Mouths*, sold 87,000 copies, and was influential in securing additional smoking privileges for prisoners, the credit for instituting which belongs to Lord Templewood, who as Sir Samuel Hoare was Home Secretary from 1937 to 1939. I know that Victor Gollancz, who published *Walls Have Mouths*, is as proud of having contributed to the reform of the smoking rules in prisons as of any crusade in which he has fought. He is himself a lover of cigars, and told me not long ago the story of his first cigar. He had a relative who was a prominent figure in the tobacco industry and a great connoisseur.

"Victor," he said to the young Gollancz who was then fifteen, "it is time that you should smoke a cigar."

With this he led Victor Gollancz to the room in which he kept his cigars, box upon box of them on shelves, against which he put a ladder and climbed up it to run his eyes along the top shelf. Soon he found the box he wanted and brought it down. His young relation presumed that he was looking for a specially mild cigar to give him his first experience. Not at all. He opened the box and took one out.

"Here is a smashed cigar for you, Victor," he said. "It is not too badly smashed for you to smoke, I think."

I have many friends with whom I enjoy smoking a cigar, but none that I know smokes one with such obvious enjoyment as J. B. Priestley. Indeed, I could almost sit cigarless and watch Priestley smoking a cigar under the impression that I am smoking it myself. Not that Priestley would allow a guest to sit without a cigar if he thought he deserved one. However, like myself, he is cautious; he is determined to know whether a guest appreciates a good cigar before he offers him one as a matter of course. Neither of us can be blamed for such caution in these days when good cigars at sixpence are no longer to be had. Nothing exasperates me so much as the sight of a man betraying hospitality by maltreatment of a good cigar. If a man does not know that he is incapable of smoking a large Corona, he should refuse the offer of one and ask for a whiff instead. The sight of a discarded half-smoked cigar lying in an ash-tray is an insult to the host, and any friend of mine who treats a cigar like that is never again offered one by me. I am too soft-hearted to hurt even such a delinquent by lighting one for myself and ignoring him; therefore rather than give him a cigar I will myself smoke a pipe. Nor will I give a good cigar to a man who has smoked one too quickly, for I know that he was not worthy of what he was smoking, and I do not like such unworthiness to be thrust upon my notice. There are few sweeter pleasures that hospitality can give to a host than the sight of a guest savouring to the full the taste of one of his best cigars; there is no mortification sharper than the sight of a guest he had deemed worthy of his best cigar betraying his confidence by continually knocking the ash into the coffee-cup, or lighting the cigar without meticulous judgment, or smoking it as if he was inflating a bicycle-tyre.

Once upon a time in the company of two or three young men I was lunching with P. G. Wodehouse, and the butler offered me a cigarette but not the box of cigars in his other hand. These he did not offer until he reached the host at the head of the table.

"Aren't I allowed a cigar, Plummy?" I asked reproachfully.

"Oh, I am so sorry. Of course. But Jeeves has orders never to offer cigars to these young people because they are wasted on them."

One might not suspect Wodehouse of being such a barmecide over his cigars, but the iron hand of the austere connoisseur is there under the velvet glove of the genial host. I relate this story as a tribute to a great romancer's realistic approach to everyday life.

I have spoken of Priestley the cigar-smoker; it is equally agreeable to watch him smoking a pipe. The sight reveals above those lips, slightly aggressive even when a pipe is between them, the eyes of a dreamer of contented dreams. Every puff he draws in seems to be welcomed with tenderness, and every puff he blows out seems to be parted from with regret.

I quote from some words he wrote in a review nearly thirty years ago:

> There can be no doubt that smoking nowadays is largely a miserable automatic business. People use tobacco without ever taking an intelligent interest in it. They do not experiment, compare, fit the tobacco to the occasion. A man should always be pleasantly conscious of the fact that he is smoking.

That is one reason why I have always been content to suffer the gibes of my friends at my fickleness in the matter of pipe tobacco. I have never settled down to one tobacco, and I have no intention of doing so. I have tried at one time or another almost every brand in existence, have ranged from the Channel Islands to Central Africa, Kentucky to Asia Minor. I try to make the tobacco suit the occasions, the place and the work. If I go for a week or two's walking among the hills I take with me a tobacco (probably a good sound plug) that I should reject for a month's work among books.

Those are wise words from one of the best essayists that ever wrote in English, and it is a satisfaction to set on record that the Priestley of thirty years later still smokes a pipe as if, like stout Cortez, he was gazing at the Pacific from a peak in Darien.

I had no sooner written these words than read these by Priestley in his book of brief essays called *Delight*:

Even though the duty on tobacco mounts to such a height that I have to turn smuggler, I shall continue to sit in my own central American jungle, bright with the birds of my fancy, still silently worshipping the sun-god, offering him the dissolving blue shapes and the fragrance of my pipe.

I shall not deny that like my old friend I sometimes deplore the tendency of our time to ignore what seem to me the finer joys of smoking. And having admitted as much, I have to recognize that I may be missing something by ignoring what for so many myriads is the pleasure of inhaling the smoke of cigarettes. Tolerance is one of the virtues that tobacco inculcates, and no good smoker should allow himself to feel superior to anybody because he prefers one way of smoking to another. When I see a man maltreat a good cigar I do not feel superior, I am merely irritated.

I have often suggested to my women friends that they should try to cultivate a taste for what *I* call smoking, but they look at me with a kindly contempt. They have discovered in the modern cigarette something for which women, without knowing it, mercifully for them, were longing for years. To them tobacco speaks in other accents than those in which it speaks to me, but I am not foolish enough to suppose that my approach to life is better than the realistic approach to it of women. And, anyway, why should I encourage women to smoke cigars, and thereby involve myself and my friends in an addition to every one of the alarming bills which we have to pay for our lunches and our dinners to-day? Presently some doctor, perplexed to learn that women are less prone to cancer of the lungs than men, may discover some peculiarly feminine complaint which has been encouraged by feminine smoking. One charge, at any rate, no doctor has been able to level against tobacco—it cannot be accused of encouraging new germs to flourish.

But do not let me end upon a note of controversy. I have written this book as a token of my gratitude for the immense benefit I have derived from tobacco and in complete certainty that I have not derived from it the slightest harm. This book is my eighty-first, and without being a smoker I doubt if I should have written half that number. I know that at my age I could not be penning these words at three o'clock in the morning, after ten hours of work unbroken except by the briefest dinner and listening to César Franck's Symphonic Variations while I smoked a small cigar, unless I had been sustained by pipe after pipe. They lie strewn about beside me, for I keep half a dozen in action during a session like this, and the smoke from them floats backward to join the smoke of their predecessors through old age, middle age and youth to boyhood. I reckon that in the course of my life I have smoked 200,000 pipefuls of tobacco at the very least, and probably nearer a quarter of a million. The volume of smoke from those pipes might not disgrace Vesuvius when not in full eruption. My memory is crystal clear. My power of concentration is undiminished. My digestion is perfect. My heart is sound. I am assured by my oculist that neither the retinal hemorrhage in one eye nor the cataract in both eyes has anything whatever to do with smoking. I never drink while I am working because I know that the kind of work I do is damaged by alcohol. On the other hand, I know with absolute certainty that the harder I work the more I need to smoke, because tobacco is the handmaid of literature and needed to-day more than it ever was. That may seem special pleading, but I would argue as stoutly that every man, whatever his race, whatever his rank, whatever his profession, whatever his work, is helped by smoking.

The following lines, written about 1850 by one of the Forrester brothers under the pseudonym of Alfred Crowquill, perfectly express my own gratitude for the sovereign herb:

Gods would have revell'd at their feasts of Mirth,
With this pure distillation of the Earth—
The Marrow of the World, Starre of the West,
The Pearle whereby this lower Orbe is blest—
The Joy of Mortals, Umpire of all Strife,
Delight of Nature, Mithridate of Life—
The daintiest dish of a delicious Feast,
By taking which Man differs from a Beast.

3.20 a.m. August 29th, 1956.

A Much Abbreviated Bibliography

TOBACCO—ITS HISTORY. Illustrated by the Books, Manuscripts and Engravings in the Library of George Arents, Jr., together with an introductory essay, glossary and bibliographic notes by Jerome E. Brooks. (Five volumes.)

THE SOCIAL HISTORY OF SMOKING, by G. L. Apperson. (1914.)

A HISTORY OF SMOKING, by Count Corti. (1931.)

THE PIPE BOOK, by Alfred Dunhill. (1924.)

TOBACCO—ITS HISTORY AND ASSOCIATIONS, by F. W. Fairholt. (1859.)

THE EARLY ENGLISH TOBACCO TRADE, by Professor C. M. MacInnes. (1926.)

TOBACCO, by A. E. Tanner. (1950.)

THE GENTLE ART OF SMOKING, by Alfred Dunhill. (1954.)

CIGARETTES IN FACT AND FANCY, by John Bain.

TOBACCO IN SONG AND STORY, by John Bain.

THE MIGHTY LEAF, by Jerome E. Brooks.

A DAY IN A TOBACCO FACTORY, by George Dodd. (1843.)

THE OLD SNUFF HOUSE OF FRIBOURG AND TREYER, by G. Evans. (1920.)

TOBACCO AND ITS USE IN ASIA, Field Museum of Natural History. (1924.)

TOBACCO AND ITS USE IN AFRICA, Field Museum of Natural History. (1930.)

THIS SMOKING WORLD, by A. E. Hamilton. (1928.)

SNUFF AND SNUFF-BOXES, by H. McCausland. (1951.)

JOHN NORTON AND SONS, MERCHANTS OF LONDON AND VIRGINIA, by Frances Norton Mason. (1937.)

SOME EARLY BOOKS ON TOBACCO, by A. C. Potter (Address contained in Harvard Library Notes). (1936.)

TOBACCO TALK AND SMOKERS' GOSSIP, by A. C. Potter.(1886.)

TOBACCO PIPES AND SMOKING CUSTOMS OF AMERICAN INDIANS, by G. A. West. (1934.)

THE SEVEN SISTERS OF SLEEP, by M. C. Cooke. (1860.)

TOBACCO TYCOON (The story of James Buchanan Duke), by John K. Winkler. (1942.)

THE AMERICAN CIGARETTE INDUSTRY (Yale Studies in Economics), by Richard B. Tennant. (1950.)

TOBACCO—ITS HISTORY, CULTIVATION, MANUFACTURE AND
ADULTERATIONS, by Andrew Steinmetz. (1857.)

PRICE LISTS OF THE CIGAR FACTORIES OF HAVANA 1901 (Boning
and Krause, Havana).

THE HABIT OF SMOKING, by W. Koskowski. (1955.)

TOBACCO LEAVES, by John Bain, Jr. (1903.)

TOBACCO LEAF, by J. B. Killebrew and Herbert Myrick. (1900.)

THE BRIGHT TOBACCO INDUSTRY, 1860–1929, by Nannie M.
Tilley. (1948.)

THE STORY OF TOBACCO IN AMERICA, by J. C. Roberts. (1952.)

Index

Abbas, Shah, 125–6
Africa: slave trade, 121; Rhodesias and Nyasaland, 290–1; Union of S. Africa, 314–17; East Africa, 317–19; Nigeria, 320
Allbutt, Sir Clifford, 29–30
American Tobacco Company, 272, 285
Arbuckle, James, 168–9
ash-trays, 31–2
Athens, incident of 1916, 43–5
Austria, 152–4, 228–9

Barclay, William, 118–20
Baron, Bernhard, 286
Barrie, J. M., 324
Bateman, Hezekiah Linthicum, 7–8
Bateman's cigarettes, 27–8
Beaumont, Sir John, 101–2
Bedfordshire Regiment, 1st (Herts) Volunteer Battalion, 21–3
Belgium, 75
Bennett, Arnold, 50–1
Berenson, Mrs Bernard, 57
Bermuda, 112–13
Bewsher, James and Samuel, 4
Brazil, 20, 74, 207, 299–301
Bright yellow leaf, 267–9, 275
Bristol, 68, 129, 136–8, 211, 214, 275–6
British-American Tobacco Company, 285
Browne, Isaac Hawkins, 195

Brummel, Beau, 202–3
Bryant and May, 236–8
Burley leaf, 269, 282, 304
Burma, 307–8: cheroots, 59–60
Byron, Lord, 229–30

Cambridge, 176, 197–9
Canada, 291–2
Caporal cigarettes, 20
Carew, Sir George, 100
Carreras, 285–6
Cartier, Jacques, 69–70
Cavendish tobacco, 261
Cecil, Sir Robert, 100, 110
Central America, 300–3
Channel Islands, 47–8
Charles Edward, Prince, 173–5
cheroots, 59–60, 226, 246, 306
chewing, 68, 273
China, 122–3, 303–5
Chute, Anthony, *Tabaco*, 90
cigarette cards, 276–7
cigarette lighters, 287–8
cigarette smoking: 33, 264–6, 336–7; the United States, 36–7, 266, 272; Britain, 265–6, 275–81, 287, 289, attacks on, 273, 279–80
cigarettes: 69, 225, 333; Russian, 265–6, 274; Virginia, 27, 38, 267–74, 281–2, 337; Turkish, 275, 281; machine manufacture, 271–2, 278–9, 300; brands, 275–6, 278–80;

Wild Woodbine, 280; Camel, 18, 282
cigars: 5–6, 225–33, 240–8, 251, 333, 340–1; brands, 226, 229, 242–6; lighting, 233–8; prices, 247
Clay, Henry, 242–3
cohoba, 64, 69, 163
Colet Court, 4
Columbus, Christopher, 63–4, 68, 71
Cowell, Joseph, 8
Craven Mixture, 26, 285–6
Cromwell, Oliver, 138–40
Crowquill, Alfred, 343–4
Cuba: 63, 70, 75; cigar tobacco, 241–6
cuspadorians, 35–6
Customs incidents, 45–6, 61

Degoute, Captain J-M-J, 21
de Jerez, Rodrigo, 63–4, 70–1
de Léry, Jean, 74
de Medici, Catherine, 73–4
de l'Obel, Matthias, 76–7
de Torres, Luis, 63–4, 70–1
Dickens, Charles, 231–2
dogs' dislike of tobacco, 58
Douglas, Lord Alfred, 19
Douglas, Norman, 39–40
Drake, Sir Francis, 77, 80
Duke, James B., 272, 283–5
Duke, Washington, 270–2
Dunhill, Alfred, 253, 255, 258
Durante, Castore, 75

Elizabeth I, Queen, 84, 94, 99
Elizabeth, Queen Mother, 238
England : introduction of tobacco, 76–83; tobacco-growing, 84, 129–47, 217; medicinal claims, 88–91, 101; tobacco duties, 99, 109, 112, 143, 219–24, 229, 290–2, 295–8; tobacco imports, 99, 111; attacks on smoking, 100, 114, 132, 279–80, 323–31; pipe manufacture, 129; Great Plague, 157–8; Russian trade, 158–60; snuffing, 115, 165–72, 200–5, 218; excise, 179–81, 219–24; smuggling, 220–3; cigar-smoking, 229–33; cigarette-smoking, 265–6, 275–81, 287, 289; cigarette manufacture, 275–6, 278–86; railway carriages, 325–6; prisons, 340

Fairholt, F. W., 225–6, 229
Fielding, Henry, 177
Florida, 73, 78–9
Florio, John, 69–70
France: 73–4, 152; royal monopoly, 154–5; tobacco-growing, 207; Virginia tobacco, 213–15, 218; pipe manufacture, 254–5
Fribourg and Treyer, 200–3, 229, 259–60, 266

Gallacher, Willie, 49–50
George IV, King, 201–3
Germany: 148–9; snuffing, 193; cigars, 227–8
Glasgow: 151; tobacco trade, 210–18; tobacco lords, 215–16
Gold Flake cigarettes, 279

Gordon of Auchterleuchries, General Patrick, 158–9
Graham, Cunninghame, 30
Greece, 42–5
Guiana, 111–12

Hamilton, Sir Ian, 30
Harcourt, Robert, 111
Hardham, John, 204
Hariot, Thomas, 80–2
Havana cigars, 32, 204, 226, 240–4
Hawkins, Sir John, 78–9, 83
henbane, 72, 132
Herrick, Robert, 329–31
Highlander signs, 190–2
Hitler, Adolf, 332
Hogarth, 181
Holland, 136, 148–9, 206
hornworm, 66–7

Imperial Tobacco Company: 182; formation, 283–5
India: 207, 291, 308–11; author's tour, 57–8; introduction of tobacco, 121–2, 126–8; tobacco legends, 311–14
Ireland: 83; tobacco-growing, 145–7, 217; snuffing, 161–2, 172
Italy: 38–40, 75, 152; cigar-smoking, 228–9

Jamaica, 242, 245–6
James I, King: 79, 83, 109, 113–14, 129, 133–4, 327; Sir Walter Ralegh, 85, 100, 102; *Counterblaste to Tobacco*, 102–8, 132; royal monopoly, 112–13
Japan, 122–3, 207
Java, 305–6
Jefferson, Thomas, 208, 218
Jenner, Thomas, 117
John Cotton Mixture, 26, 31, 42, 47
Johnson, Dr, 57, 197
Jonson, Ben, 92–8

King, Humphrey, 91
Kipling, Rudyard, 244–5

Lambert and Butler, 240
latakia, 49, 67, 260
lighting devices, 233–9
London: 129, 211, 214; monopoly, 134, 136–8; clubs, 51, 231; divans, 247
Lovat pipes: 26–7; sent to author in Athens, 42–3
Lowe, Robert, 238–9
lucifers, 235–6
Lyly, John, 89

Macaulay, Lord, 231
Macedonia cigarettes, 38–9
Magellan, Ferdinand, 122
Makhorka, 67
Manilla cheroots, 32–3, 226
Marbecke, Roger, 101
matches: 235–9; tax proposal, 238–9
Meerschaum pipes, 25, 252–3
Mexico, 75, 299
Monardes, Dr Nicholas, 74–5, 81

Murad IV, 124–5
Myddelton, William, 78

Napolitano cigars, 39–40
Nash, Thomas, 91
Negrohead tobacco, 261
New Zealand, 320–2
Nicot, Jean, 73–4
Nicotiana, genus of, 65–8, 73
Nicotiana rustica, 66–8, 71–2,
    74–5, 76–81, 83, 118–19,
    132, 315, 319
Nicotiana tabacum, 66–8, 74–5,
    76–81, 84, 120, 292
North Carolina, 268–72

Oviedo, 64
Oxford, 21, 23–9, 31–4, 113–
    14, 176–7, 198–9, 257

Parr, Dr Samuel, 197–8, 201
Pena, Pierre, 76–7
Pepys, Samuel, 156–7
Perique, 262–3
Persia: 66; introduction of
    tobacco, 125–6
Petersen pipes, 7
petun, 72–4, 96
Philips, Ambrose, 196
pipe-smoking: 33; the United
    States, 36–7; Britain, 78–83,
    121, 198; lighting, 233–5;
    tobacco, 259–63
pipes: 32, 69, 76, 78–81, 184,
    250, 333–4; Sir Walter
    Ralegh, 83–7; silver, 90;
    churchwarden, 27, 219,
    258; clay, 90, 255, 257–8;
    Winchester, 98, 129;
    English manufacture, 129;

brier, 253–9; French manu-
    facture, 254–5; corncob,
    256; bamboo, 304; hookahs,
    309–10; calumet, 324
Pitt's Tobacco Act (1789),
    219–22
Player and Sons Ltd, John,
    279
Porson, Richard, 198
Portugal: 73–5, 207, 301;
    spreading the use of tobacco,
    121–3
Priestley, J. B., 340–2

Ralegh, Sir Walter: 79–87,
    100, 111; pipe-case, 86–7;
    James I, 85, 100, 102
rappee, 164, 170
Rich, Barnaby, 92
Rolfe, John, 109–110, 113,
    266
Rowlands, Samuel, 115
Ruskin, John, 326–7
Russia: 148, 158–60, 265;
    Soviet Union, 67

Scotland: 115, 118–20, 261;
    tobacco-growing, 145–7,
    217; imports, 151; snuffing,
    164, 172–5; tobacco trade,
    210–18; manufacturers,
    286–7
Scott, Sir Walter, 230–1
Seychelles, 61
Shakespeare, 327–9
Siébault, Jean, 74
Slade Brothers, 267–8
Smart, Christopher, 194–5
snuff: 163–5, 207, 251; Span-
    ish, 165, 167, 203; scented,
    166, 168, 204; varieties, 170,

201–5; toasted, 171–2; French, 202–4

snuff boxes, 168

snuffing: 69, 74, 149, 193; in England, 115, 165–72, 176–8, 197–205, 218

snuff manufacture, 205

snuff mills, 172

Spain: 32, 75, 152, 264–5, 301–2; snuffing, 164–6

Spenser, Edmund, 89

spitting, 35–6, 96

spittoons, 35–6, 96

St Claude, 254–5

St Paul's School, 10–12, 14–18

Stukeley, Sir Lewis, 85

Sussex, Duke of, collection, 250–2

Swinburne, A. C., 324–5

Switzerland, 149, 161–2

tabaco, 64, 71

taboca, 64–5

Tavernier, Jean, 126–7

Thackeray, W. M., 248

Thevet, André, *The New Found Worlde*, 72–4

tobacco: 249, 294; cultivation, 292–3; origin of word, 64–5; Spanish, 98, 99–100, 110, 129, 133–6; Turkish, 125, 185, 275; virility, 127–8; fire-raising, 153, 161; prophylactic qualities, 155–8; adulteration, 171, 221–4; brands, 181–90; medicinal claims, 88–91, 101; shag, 259; returns, 259–60; Cavendish, 261; Negrohead, 261; flue-curing, 267–9, 290–1; Rhodesian, 290–1,

294; beneficent effects, 332–44

tobacco jars, 24

tobacconists: 92; retailers' licences, 135–6; labels, 181–90

tobacco pouches, 30–1

Trinidado, 110

Turkey, 123–5, 185, 275

United States: 217–18, 242, 267–74; author's family, 7–9; smoking habits, 36–8; New England, 150; cigar-smoking, 226–7; Civil War, 270–1; Tobacco Trust, 282; British cigarette market, 282–5

Varinas, 260, 302

Veneziano (Virginia) cigar, 39, 246

Vespucci Amerigo, 68

Virginia: 79–82, 109–13, 129, 131–4, 140, 142–3, 181, 206–10, 328; Dutch trade, 136–7, 148; Navigation Acts, 150–1; Russian trade, 158–60; Jacobite prisoners, 175; eighteenth-century trade, 206, 208–18; cigarettes, 266–71, 281–2, 337

Walker, 'Dicky', 15–17

Walker, Frederick William, 14–15, 17

Walpole, Sir Robert, 179–81

whiffs, 56–7

Wilde, Oscar, 333

Wilhelm II, Kaiser, author's visits to, 51–5
Wills, W. D. and H. O., 275–6, 278, 280
Winchcombe, 139–42, 144
Wither, George, 115–17

Women: 195–6, 199, 342–3; cigar-smoking, 57, 225–6; pipe-smoking, 84, 258, 309; snuffing, 169, 200, 203; cigarette-smoking, 37, 266
Woodbine cigarettes, 280